OH, SURE! BLAME IT ON THE DOG!

A Pickles Collection by Brian Crane

Also by Brian Crane

Pickles

Pickles, Too

Still Pickled After All These Years

Let's Get Pickled

How Come I Always Get Blamed For
The Things I Do?

OH, SURE! BLAME IT ON THE DOG!

A Pickles Collection by Brian Crane

BAOBAB PRESS • NEVADA

Published in 2013 by Baobab Press
The publishing imprint of Baobab Books, Inc.
Reno, Nevada
www.baobabpress.com

PICKLES is syndicated by the Washington Post Writers Group.

Library of Congress Control Number: 2013912317

First Edition

13 14 15 10 9 8 7 6 5 4 3 2 1
ISBN-13: 978-1-936097-04-3
ISBN-10: 1-936097-04-4

Printed and bound in the United States of America

MIX
Paper from responsible sources
FSC® C011935

Acknowledgements

I'd like to thank three people and one group of people for making this book possible. The first is my wife, best friend and chief cheerleader, Diana. Without her believing in me and my work when I didn't, PICKLES would never have become a reality. And she often inspires ideas for this comic strip, occasionally even on purpose.

Next I must thank Alan Shearer and Amy Lago at the Washington Post Writers Group, my syndicator. Without them PICKLES would not have made it into the 800 or so newspapers that carry it. And I would have to find a real job and actually work for a living.

And finally, I want to thank Christine Kelly and Casey Berger of Baobab Press and Sundance Books and Music for their unfailing support over many years and for making this collection possible.

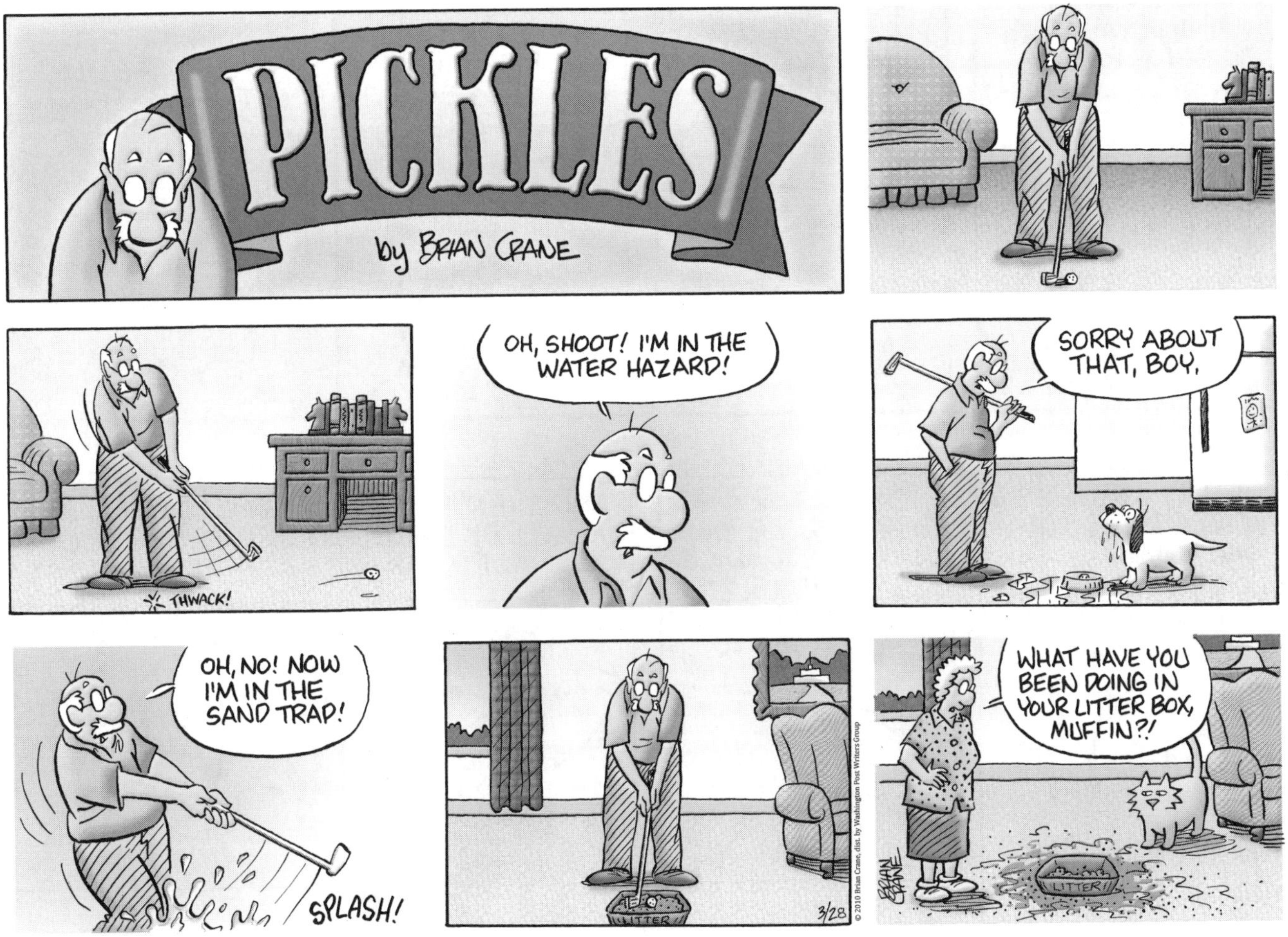
PICKLES
by BRIAN CRANE
THWACK!
OH, SHOOT! I'M IN THE WATER HAZARD!
SORRY ABOUT THAT, BOY.
OH, NO! NOW I'M IN THE SAND TRAP!
SPLASH!
LITTER
3/28
© 2010 Brian Crane, dist. by Washington Post Writers Group
WHAT HAVE YOU BEEN DOING IN YOUR LITTER BOX, MUFFIN?!
LITTER

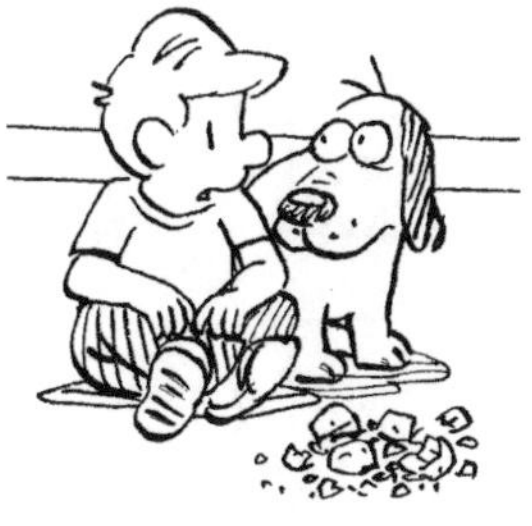

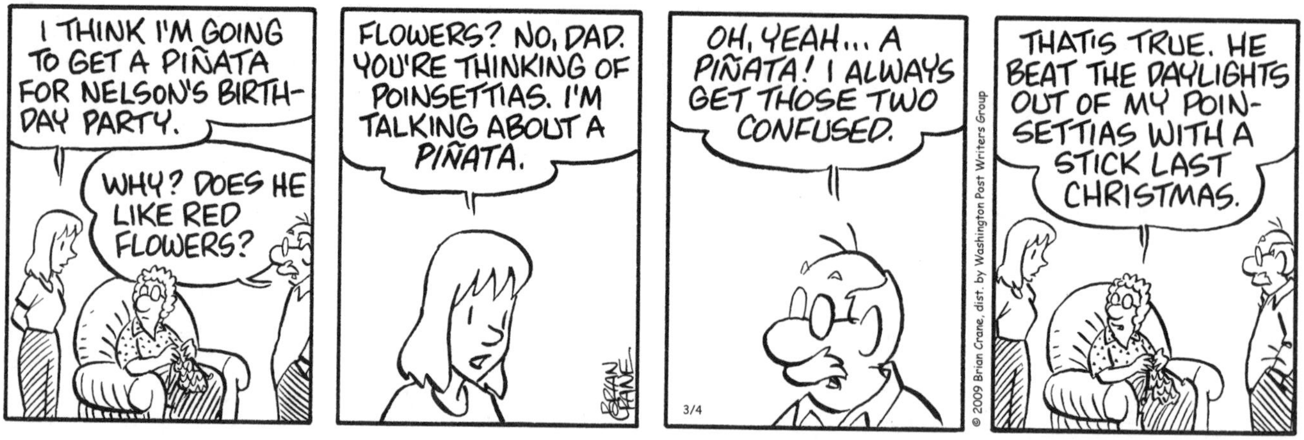
I THINK I'M GOING TO GET A PIÑATA FOR NELSON'S BIRTHDAY PARTY.
WHY? DOES HE LIKE RED FLOWERS?
FLOWERS? NO, DAD. YOU'RE THINKING OF POINSETTIAS. I'M TALKING ABOUT A PIÑATA.
BRIAN CRANE
3/4
OH, YEAH... A PIÑATA! I ALWAYS GET THOSE TWO CONFUSED.
© 2009 Brian Crane, dist. by Washington Post Writers Group
THAT'S TRUE. HE BEAT THE DAYLIGHTS OUT OF MY POINSETTIAS WITH A STICK LAST CHRISTMAS.

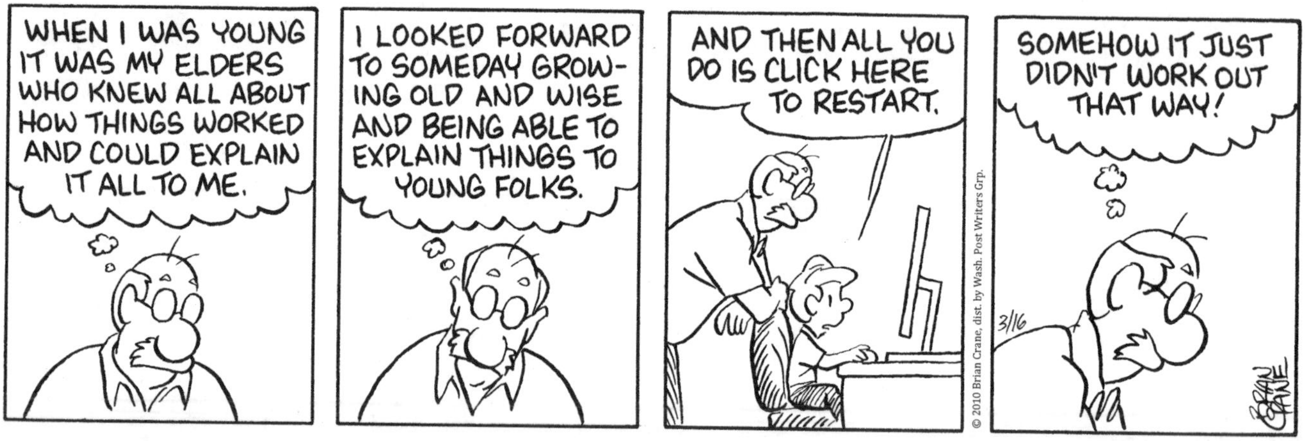
WHEN I WAS YOUNG IT WAS MY ELDERS WHO KNEW ALL ABOUT HOW THINGS WORKED AND COULD EXPLAIN IT ALL TO ME.
I LOOKED FORWARD TO SOMEDAY GROWING OLD AND WISE AND BEING ABLE TO EXPLAIN THINGS TO YOUNG FOLKS.
AND THEN ALL YOU DO IS CLICK HERE TO RESTART.
© 2010 Brian Crane, dist. by Wash. Post Writers Grp.
SOMEHOW IT JUST DIDN'T WORK OUT THAT WAY!
3/16
BRIAN CRANE

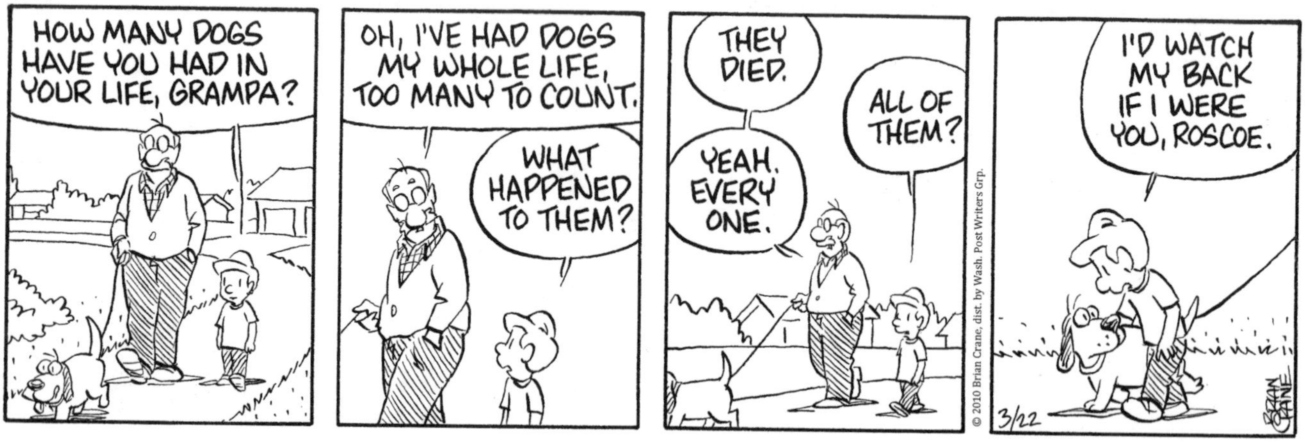
HOW MANY DOGS HAVE YOU HAD IN YOUR LIFE, GRAMPA?
OH, I'VE HAD DOGS MY WHOLE LIFE, TOO MANY TO COUNT.
WHAT HAPPENED TO THEM?
THEY DIED.
ALL OF THEM?
YEAH. EVERY ONE.
© 2010 Brian Crane, dist. by Wash. Post Writers Grp.
I'D WATCH MY BACK IF I WERE YOU, ROSCOE.
3/22
BRIAN CRANE

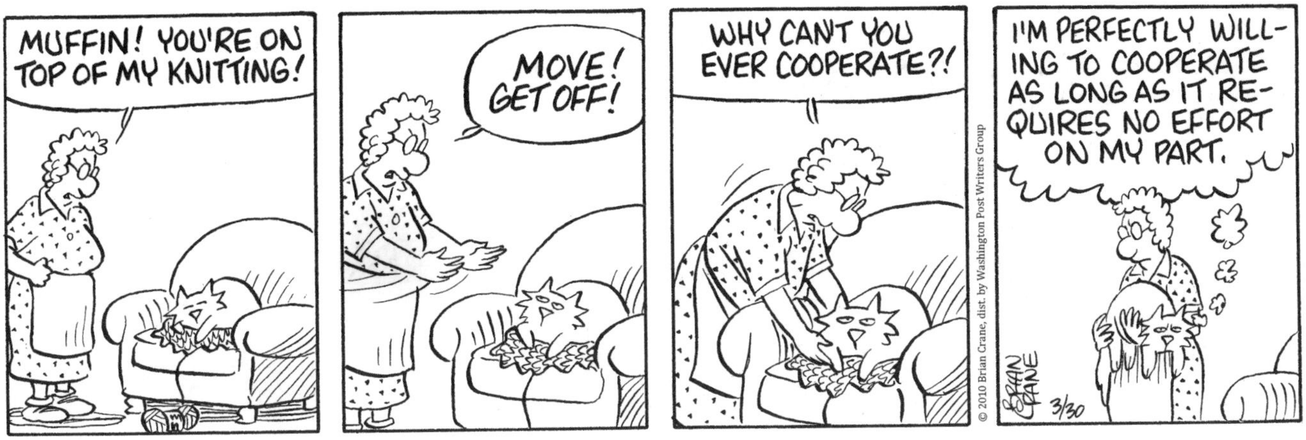
MUFFIN! YOU'RE ON TOP OF MY KNITTING!
MOVE! GET OFF!
WHY CAN'T YOU EVER COOPERATE?!
I'M PERFECTLY WILLING TO COOPERATE AS LONG AS IT REQUIRES NO EFFORT ON MY PART.
© 2010 Brian Crane, dist. by Washington Post Writers Group
BRIAN CRANE 3/30

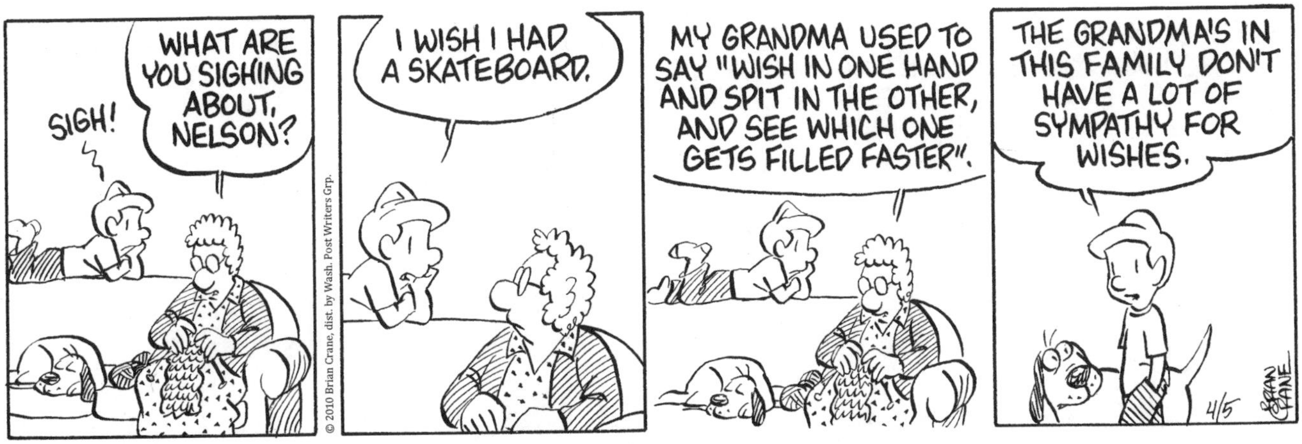
SIGH!
WHAT ARE YOU SIGHING ABOUT, NELSON?
© 2010 Brian Crane, dist. by Wash. Post Writers Grp.
I WISH I HAD A SKATEBOARD.
MY GRANDMA USED TO SAY "WISH IN ONE HAND AND SPIT IN THE OTHER, AND SEE WHICH ONE GETS FILLED FASTER".
THE GRANDMA'S IN THIS FAMILY DON'T HAVE A LOT OF SYMPATHY FOR WISHES.
BRIAN CRANE 4/5

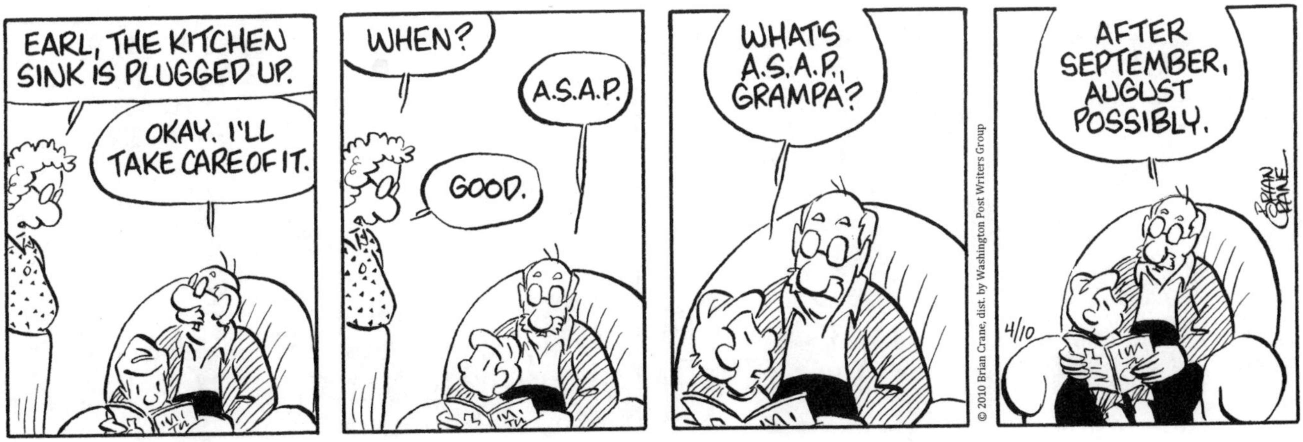
EARL, THE KITCHEN SINK IS PLUGGED UP.
OKAY. I'LL TAKE CARE OF IT.
WHEN?
A.S.A.P.
GOOD.
WHAT'S A.S.A.P., GRAMPA?
AFTER SEPTEMBER, AUGUST POSSIBLY.
© 2010 Brian Crane, dist. by Washington Post Writers Group
BRIAN CRANE 4/10

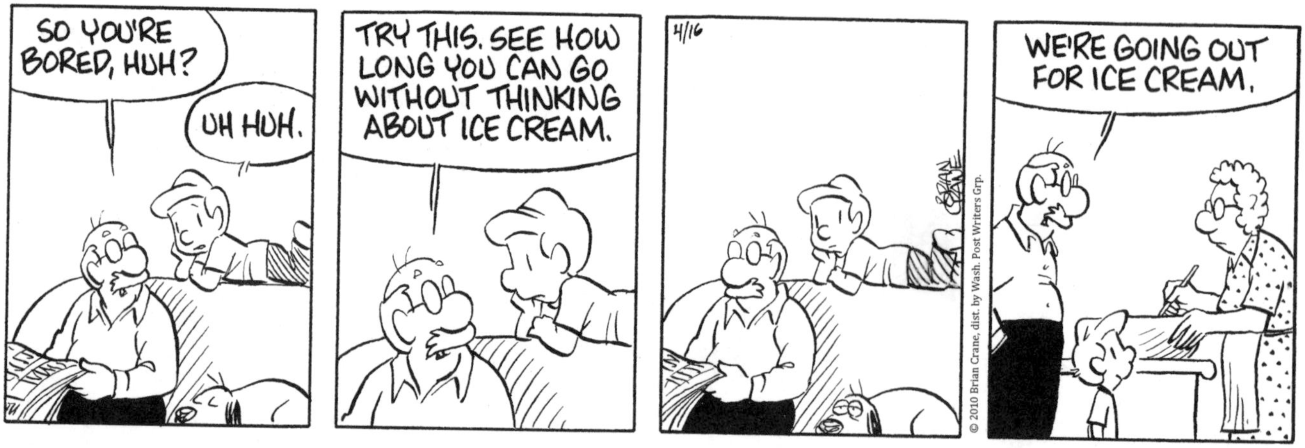
SO YOU'RE BORED, HUH?
UH HUH.
TRY THIS. SEE HOW LONG YOU CAN GO WITHOUT THINKING ABOUT ICE CREAM.
4/16
WE'RE GOING OUT FOR ICE CREAM.

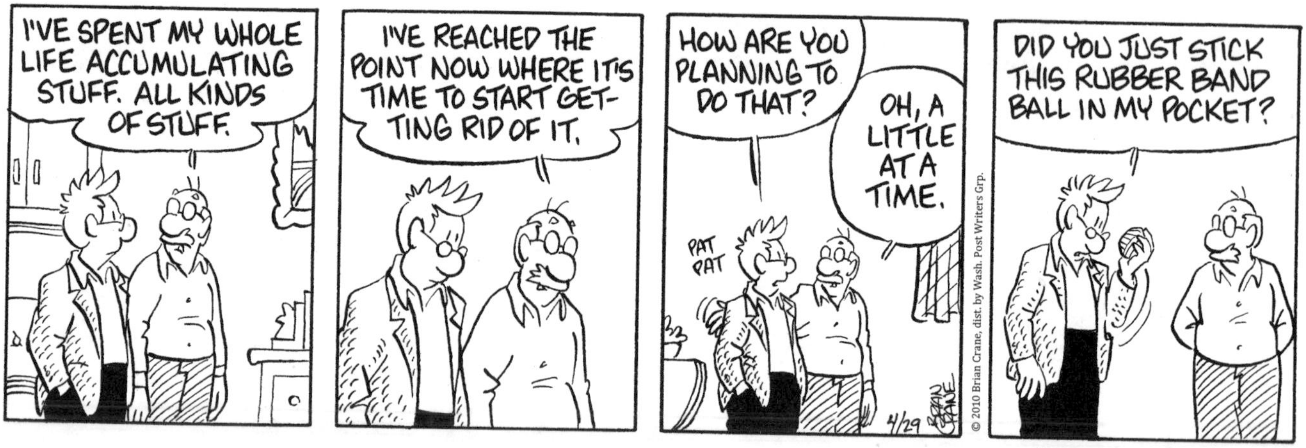
I'VE SPENT MY WHOLE LIFE ACCUMULATING STUFF. ALL KINDS OF STUFF.
I'VE REACHED THE POINT NOW WHERE IT'S TIME TO START GET-TING RID OF IT.
HOW ARE YOU PLANNING TO DO THAT?
OH, A LITTLE AT A TIME.
PAT PAT
4/29
DID YOU JUST STICK THIS RUBBER BAND BALL IN MY POCKET?

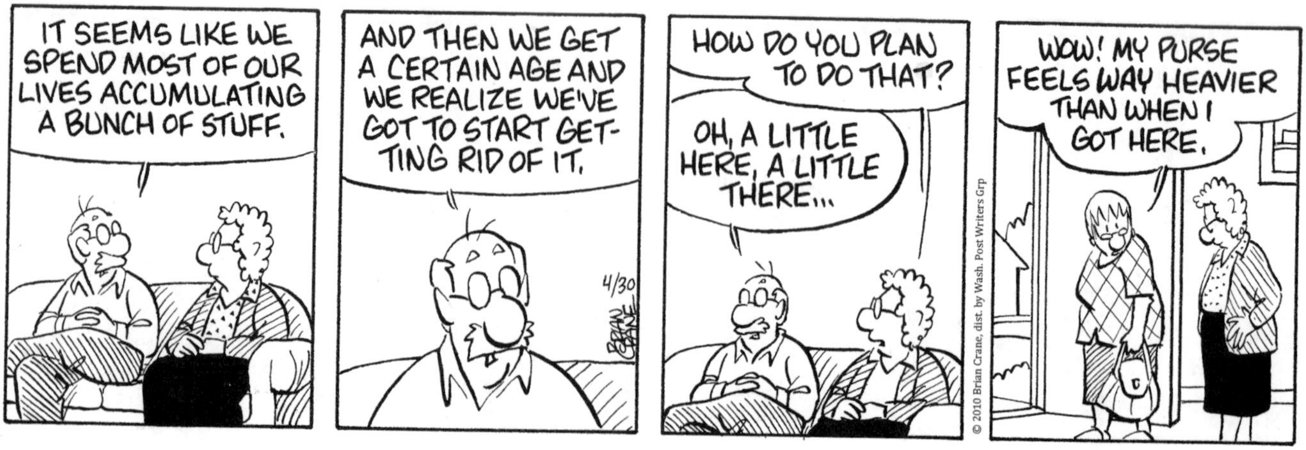
IT SEEMS LIKE WE SPEND MOST OF OUR LIVES ACCUMULATING A BUNCH OF STUFF.
AND THEN WE GET A CERTAIN AGE AND WE REALIZE WE'VE GOT TO START GET-TING RID OF IT.
4/30
HOW DO YOU PLAN TO DO THAT?
OH, A LITTLE HERE, A LITTLE THERE...
WOW! MY PURSE FEELS WAY HEAVIER THAN WHEN I GOT HERE.

Panel 1: DAD, WHAT'S GOING ON HERE? EVERY TIME I GO HOME FROM VISITING YOU I FIND A LOT OF JUNK STUFFED INTO MY PURSE AND POCKETS.

JUNK?

Panel 2: YES. OLD 8-TRACK TAPES, SOUVENIR MAGNETS, KEY FOBS, RUSTY FINGERNAIL CLIPPERS, BROKEN FOUNTAIN PENS... YOU NAME IT.

5/1

Panel 3: OH, THAT. WELL, I'VE BEEN GETTING RID OF SOME STUFF WE DON'T USE ANYMORE. I CAN'T BEAR TO THROW IT AWAY.

Panel 4: REALLY? SO YOU SURREPTITIOUSLY STASH IT IN THE BELONGINGS OF VISITORS?

THINK OF IT AS DOOR PRIZES.

© 2010 Brian Crane, dist. by Wash. Post Writers Grp.

Panel 5: WHAT'S FOR BREAKFAST?

Panel 6: EGGS.

OH, GOOD.

Panel 7: HOW WOULD YOU LIKE YOURS COOKED?

5/17

Panel 8: YES, PLEASE. I WOULD LIKE THAT VERY MUCH.

© 2010 Brian Crane, dist. by Wash. Post Writers Grp.

Panel 9: (no dialogue)

Panel 10: WHY ARE YOU STARING AT ME, NELSON?

Panel 11: I WAS JUST WONDERING...

5/24

Panel 12: ARE YOU VINTAGE OR ANTIQUE?

© 2010 Brian Crane, dist. by Wash. Post Writers Grp.

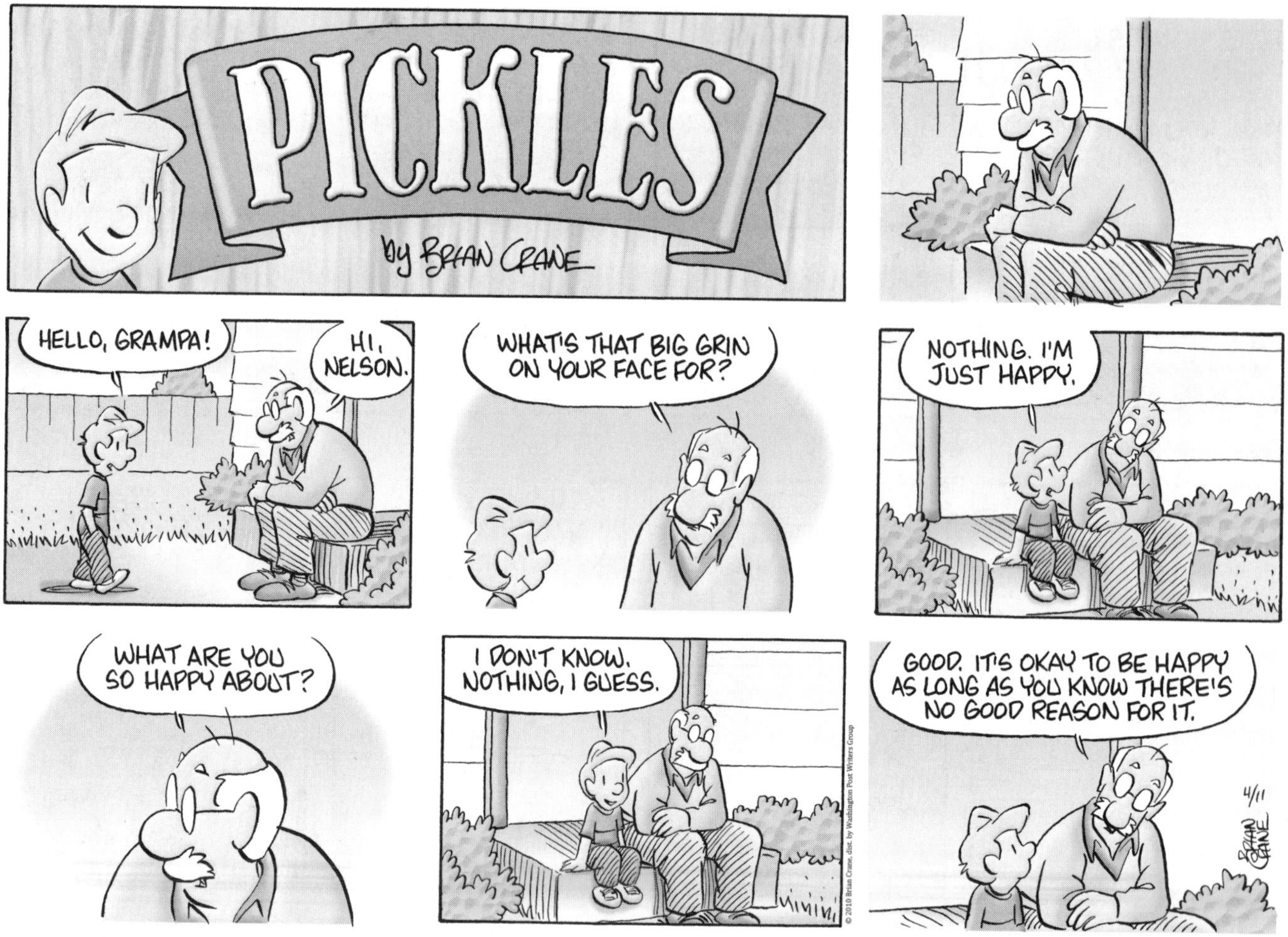
PICKLES
by Brian Crane
HELLO, GRAMPA!
HI, NELSON.
WHAT'S THAT BIG GRIN ON YOUR FACE FOR?
NOTHING. I'M JUST HAPPY.
WHAT ARE YOU SO HAPPY ABOUT?
I DON'T KNOW. NOTHING, I GUESS.
GOOD. IT'S OKAY TO BE HAPPY AS LONG AS YOU KNOW THERE'S NO GOOD REASON FOR IT.
4/11
BRIAN CRANE
© 2010 Brian Crane, dist. by Washington Post Writers Group

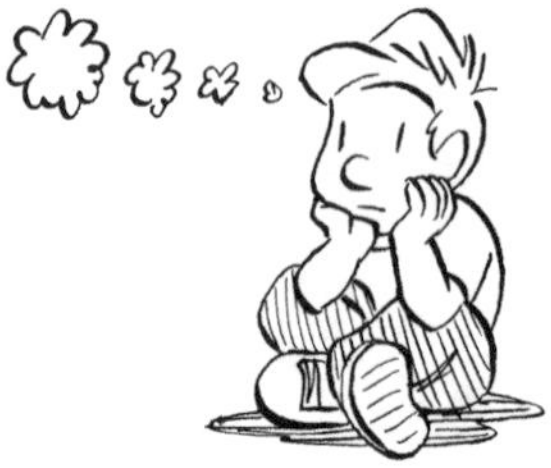

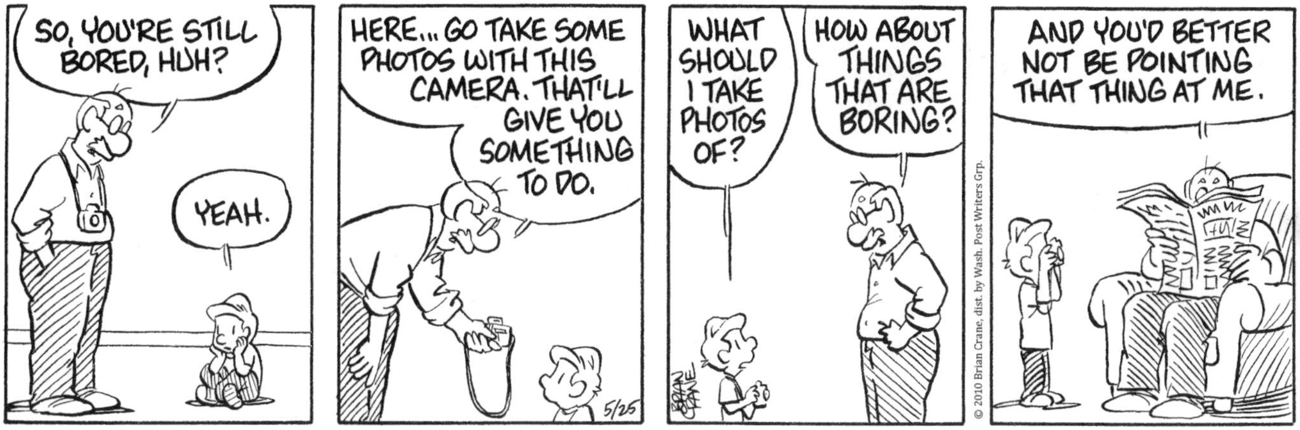
SO, YOU'RE STILL BORED, HUH?
YEAH.
HERE... GO TAKE SOME PHOTOS WITH THIS CAMERA. THAT'LL GIVE YOU SOMETHING TO DO.
5/25
WHAT SHOULD I TAKE PHOTOS OF?
HOW ABOUT THINGS THAT ARE BORING?
AND YOU'D BETTER NOT BE POINTING THAT THING AT ME.

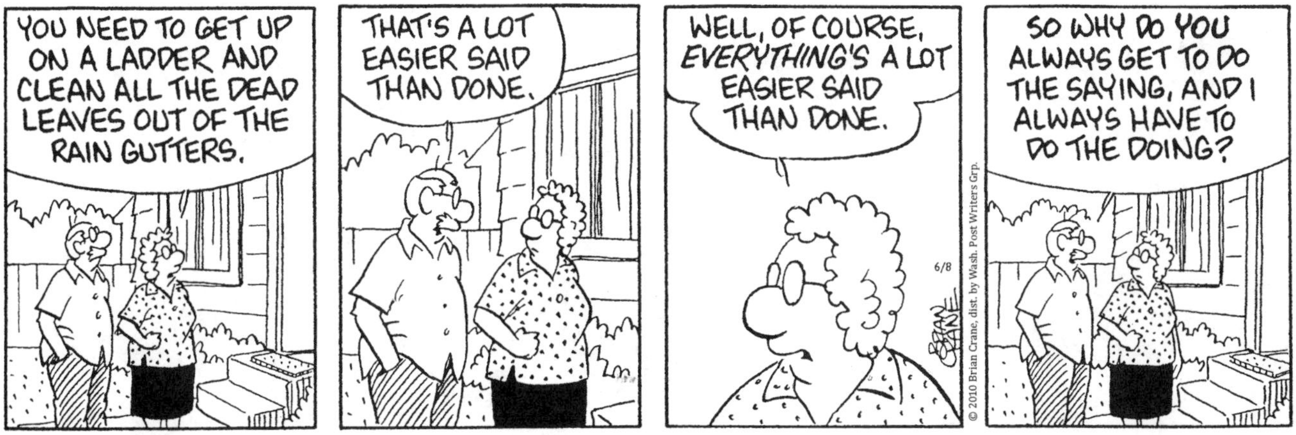
YOU NEED TO GET UP ON A LADDER AND CLEAN ALL THE DEAD LEAVES OUT OF THE RAIN GUTTERS.
THAT'S A LOT EASIER SAID THAN DONE.
WELL, OF COURSE, *EVERYTHING'S* A LOT EASIER SAID THAN DONE.
6/8
SO WHY DO *YOU* ALWAYS GET TO DO THE SAYING, AND I ALWAYS HAVE TO DO THE DOING?

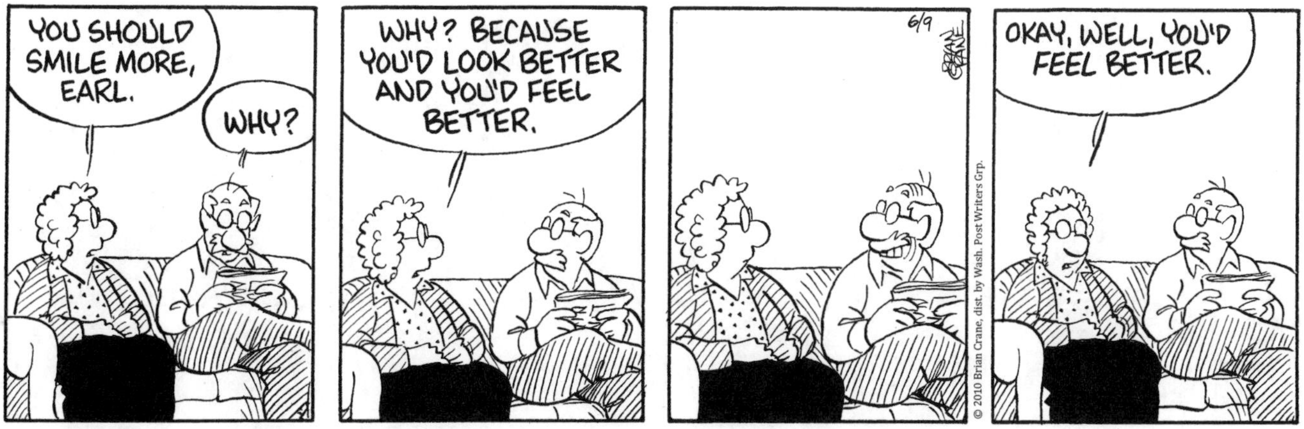
YOU SHOULD SMILE MORE, EARL.
WHY?
WHY? BECAUSE YOU'D LOOK BETTER AND YOU'D FEEL BETTER.
6/9
OKAY, WELL, YOU'D FEEL BETTER.

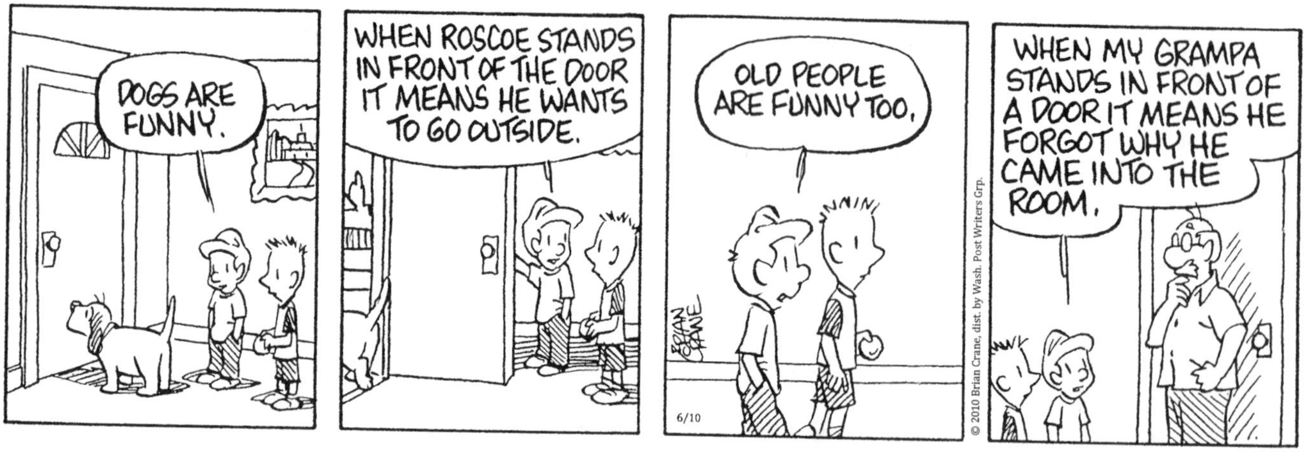
DOGS ARE FUNNY.
WHEN ROSCOE STANDS IN FRONT OF THE DOOR IT MEANS HE WANTS TO GO OUTSIDE.
OLD PEOPLE ARE FUNNY TOO,
WHEN MY GRAMPA STANDS IN FRONT OF A DOOR IT MEANS HE FORGOT WHY HE CAME INTO THE ROOM.

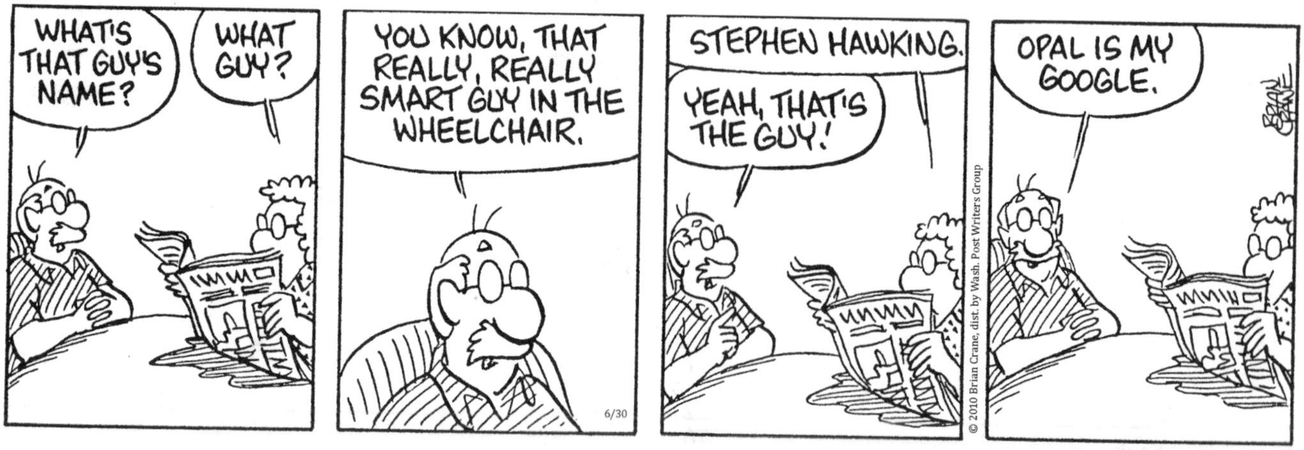
WHAT'S THAT GUY'S NAME?
WHAT GUY?
YOU KNOW, THAT REALLY, REALLY SMART GUY IN THE WHEELCHAIR.
STEPHEN HAWKING.
YEAH, THAT'S THE GUY!
OPAL IS MY GOOGLE.

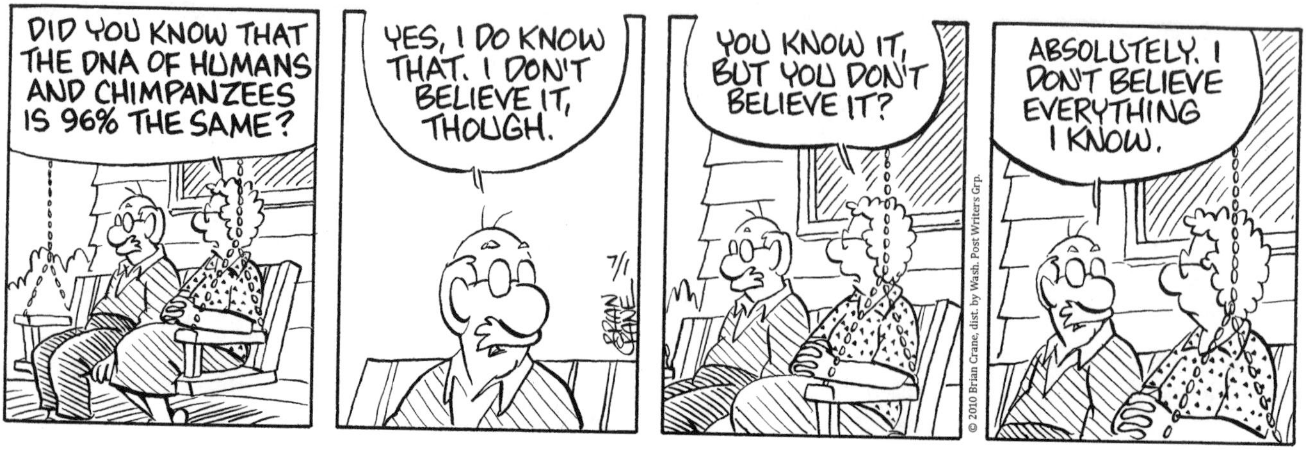
DID YOU KNOW THAT THE DNA OF HUMANS AND CHIMPANZEES IS 96% THE SAME?
YES, I DO KNOW THAT. I DON'T BELIEVE IT, THOUGH.
YOU KNOW IT, BUT YOU DON'T BELIEVE IT?
ABSOLUTELY. I DON'T BELIEVE EVERYTHING I KNOW.

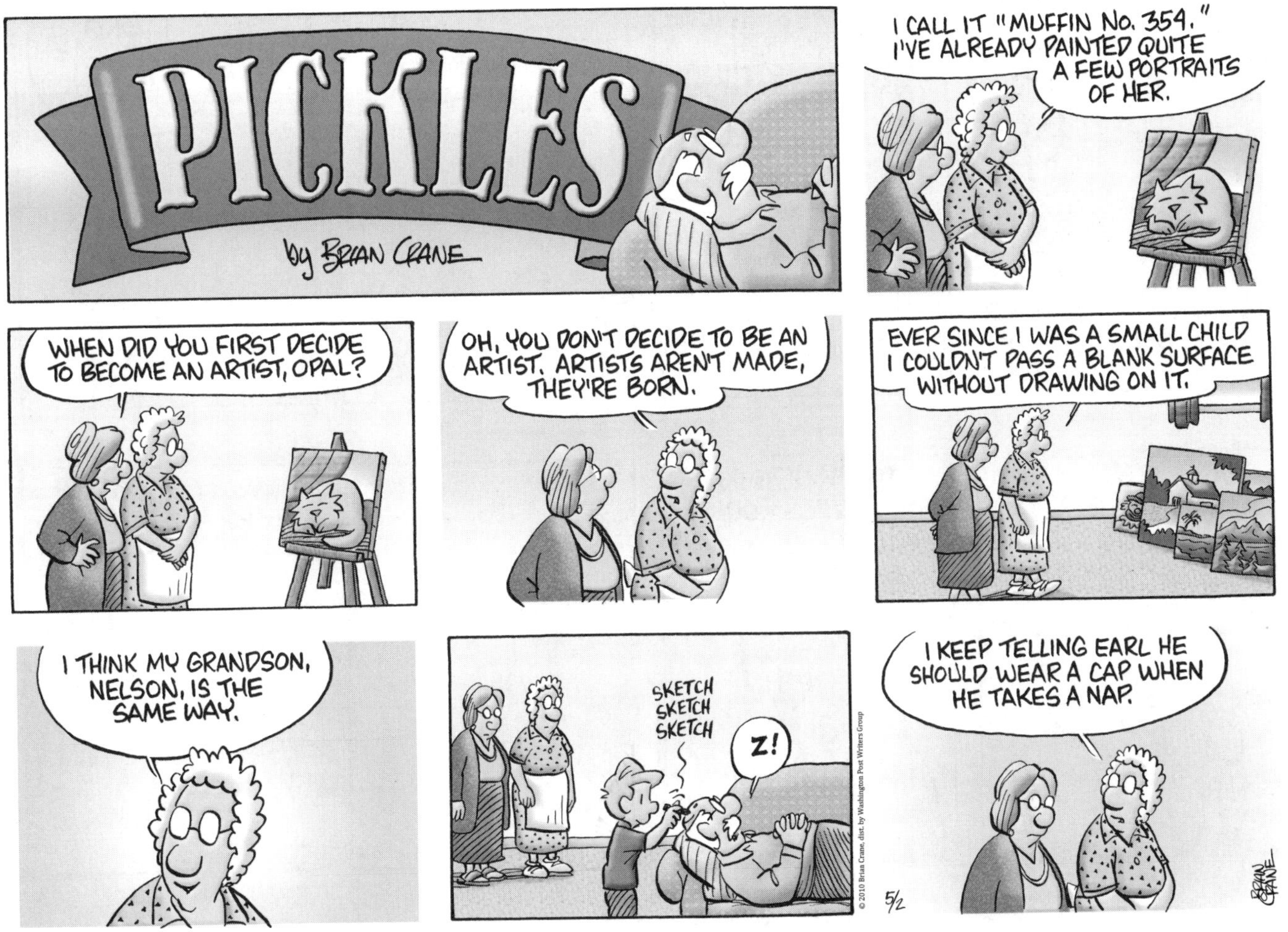
PICKLES
by BRIAN CRANE
I CALL IT "MUFFIN NO. 354." I'VE ALREADY PAINTED QUITE A FEW PORTRAITS OF HER.
WHEN DID YOU FIRST DECIDE TO BECOME AN ARTIST, OPAL?
OH, YOU DON'T DECIDE TO BE AN ARTIST. ARTISTS AREN'T MADE, THEY'RE BORN.
EVER SINCE I WAS A SMALL CHILD I COULDN'T PASS A BLANK SURFACE WITHOUT DRAWING ON IT.
I THINK MY GRANDSON, NELSON, IS THE SAME WAY.
SKETCH SKETCH SKETCH
Z!
© 2010 Brian Crane, dist. by Washington Post Writers Group
5/2
I KEEP TELLING EARL HE SHOULD WEAR A CAP WHEN HE TAKES A NAP.
BRIAN CRANE

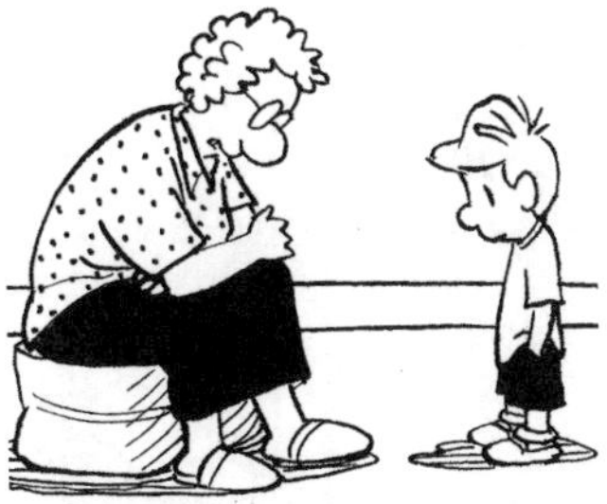

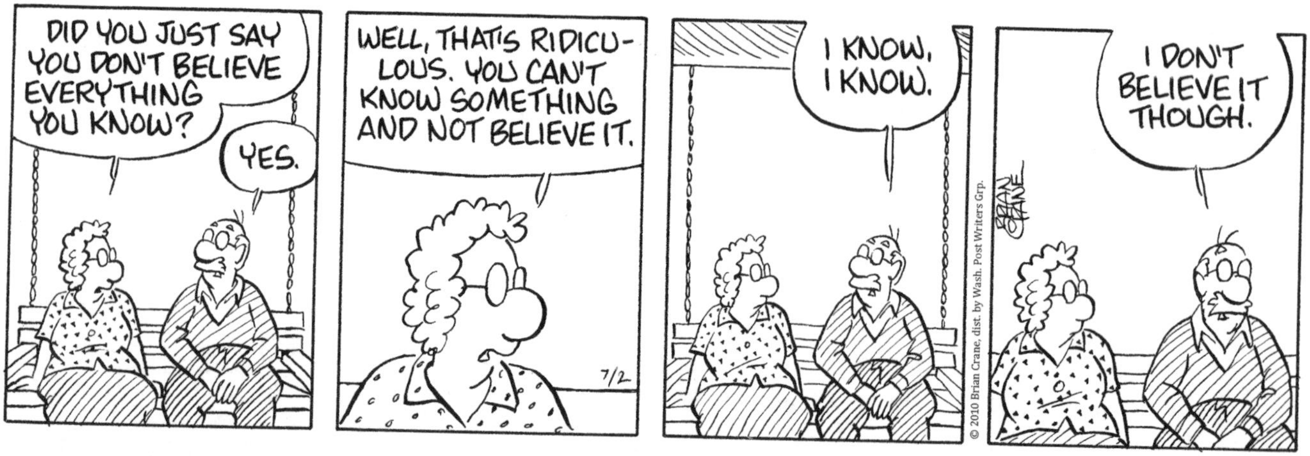
DID YOU JUST SAY YOU DON'T BELIEVE EVERYTHING YOU KNOW?
YES.
WELL, THAT'S RIDICU-LOUS. YOU CAN'T KNOW SOMETHING AND NOT BELIEVE IT.
7/2
I KNOW, I KNOW.
I DON'T BELIEVE IT THOUGH.
BRIAN CRANE
© 2010 Brian Crane, dist. by Wash. Post Writers Grp.

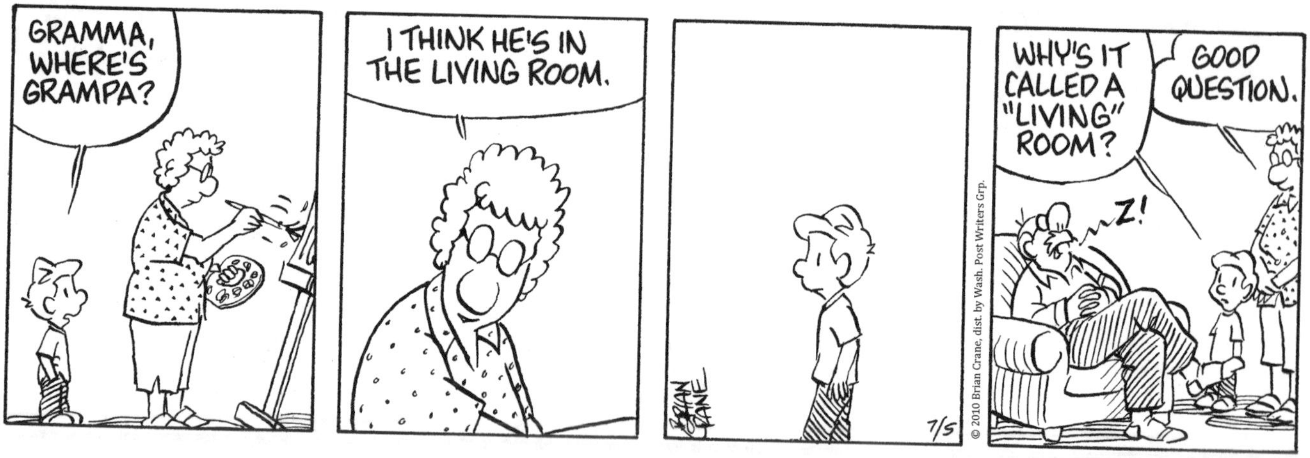
GRAMMA, WHERE'S GRAMPA?
I THINK HE'S IN THE LIVING ROOM.
BRIAN CRANE
7/5
© 2010 Brian Crane, dist. by Wash. Post Writers Grp.
WHY'S IT CALLED A "LIVING" ROOM?
GOOD QUESTION.
Z!

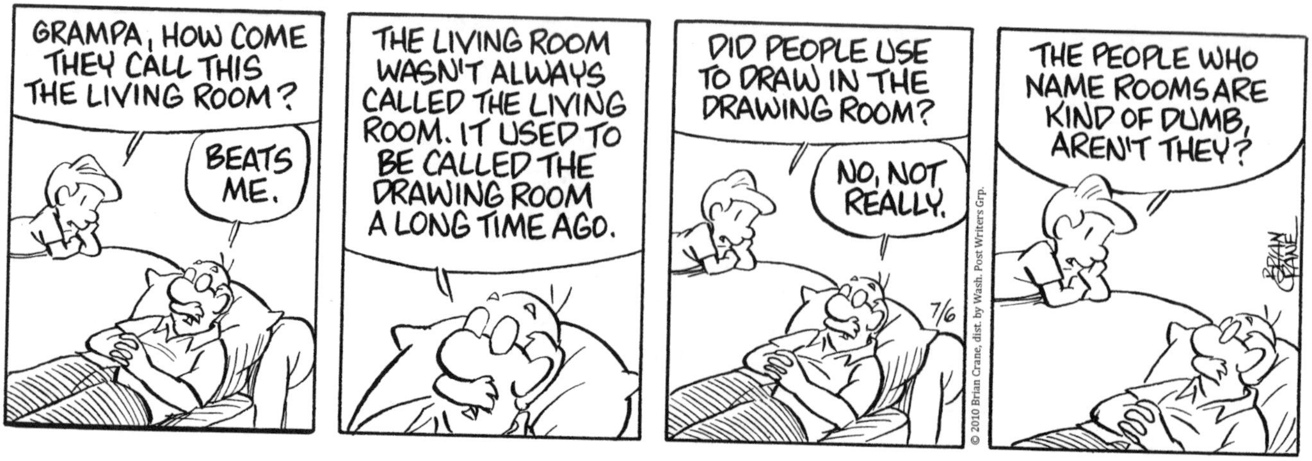
GRAMPA, HOW COME THEY CALL THIS THE LIVING ROOM?
BEATS ME.
THE LIVING ROOM WASN'T ALWAYS CALLED THE LIVING ROOM. IT USED TO BE CALLED THE DRAWING ROOM A LONG TIME AGO.
DID PEOPLE USE TO DRAW IN THE DRAWING ROOM?
NO, NOT REALLY.
7/6
© 2010 Brian Crane, dist. by Wash. Post Writers Grp.
THE PEOPLE WHO NAME ROOMS ARE KIND OF DUMB, AREN'T THEY?
BRIAN CRANE

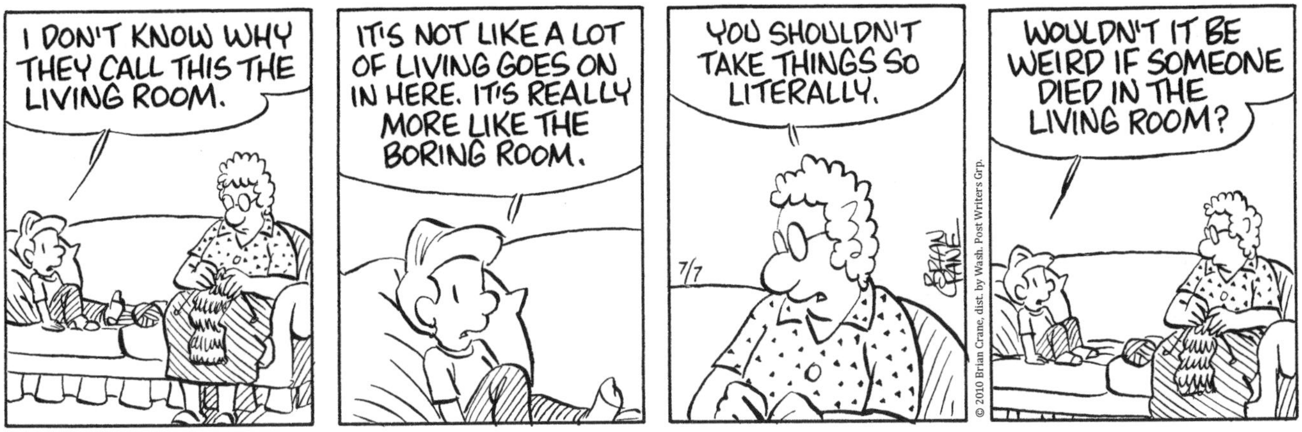
I DON'T KNOW WHY THEY CALL THIS THE LIVING ROOM.
IT'S NOT LIKE A LOT OF LIVING GOES ON IN HERE. IT'S REALLY MORE LIKE THE BORING ROOM.
YOU SHOULDN'T TAKE THINGS SO LITERALLY.
7/7
BRIAN CRANE
WOULDN'T IT BE WEIRD IF SOMEONE DIED IN THE LIVING ROOM?

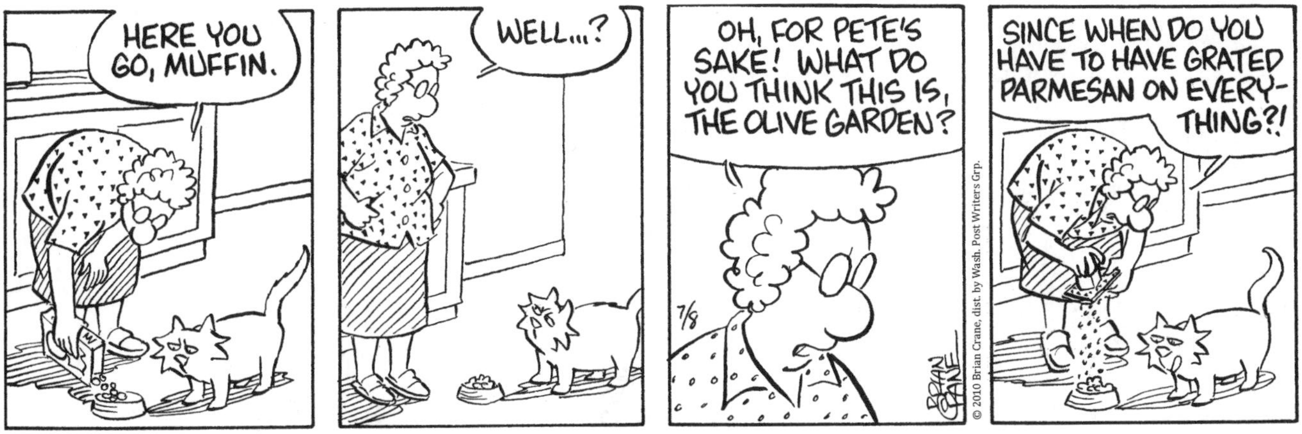
HERE YOU GO, MUFFIN.
WELL...?
OH, FOR PETE'S SAKE! WHAT DO YOU THINK THIS IS, THE OLIVE GARDEN?
7/8
BRIAN CRANE
SINCE WHEN DO YOU HAVE TO HAVE GRATED PARMESAN ON EVERY-THING?!

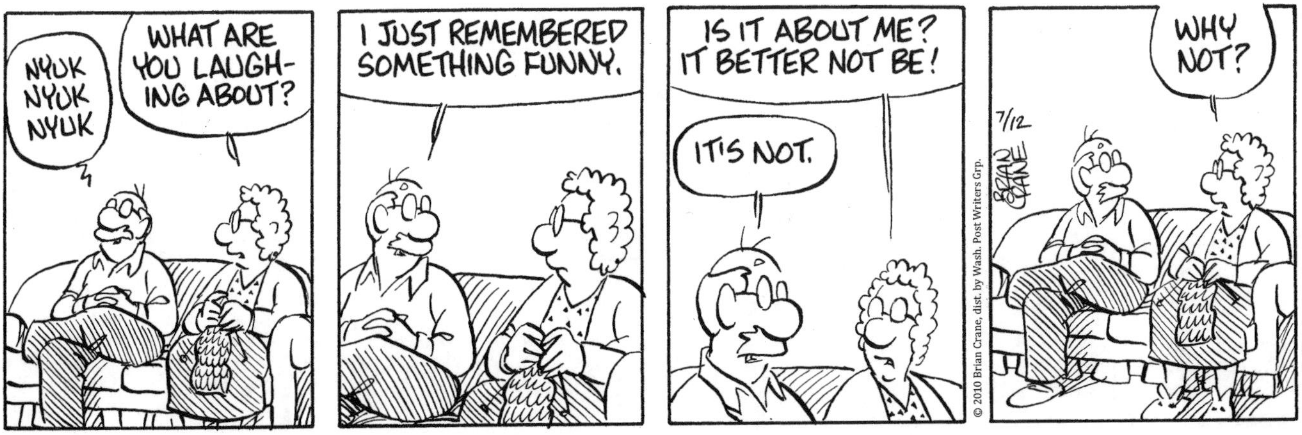
NYUK NYUK NYUK
WHAT ARE YOU LAUGH-ING ABOUT?
I JUST REMEMBERED SOMETHING FUNNY.
IS IT ABOUT ME? IT BETTER NOT BE!
IT'S NOT.
7/12
BRIAN CRANE
WHY NOT?

PICKLES
by BRIAN CRANE
YOU'RE COOKING BREAKFAST, DAD?
YEAH, I DO THAT ONCE EVERY BLUE MOON.
SO, WHAT ARE YOU MAKING?
CREEPIES. WOULD YOU LIKE SOME?
CREEPIES? UM... I THINK THEY'RE PRONOUNCED "CREPES," DAD.
5/16
BRIAN CRANE
© 2010 Brian Crane, dist. by Washington Post Writers Group
YOU HAVEN'T TASTED THEM, HAVE YOU?

EGGS

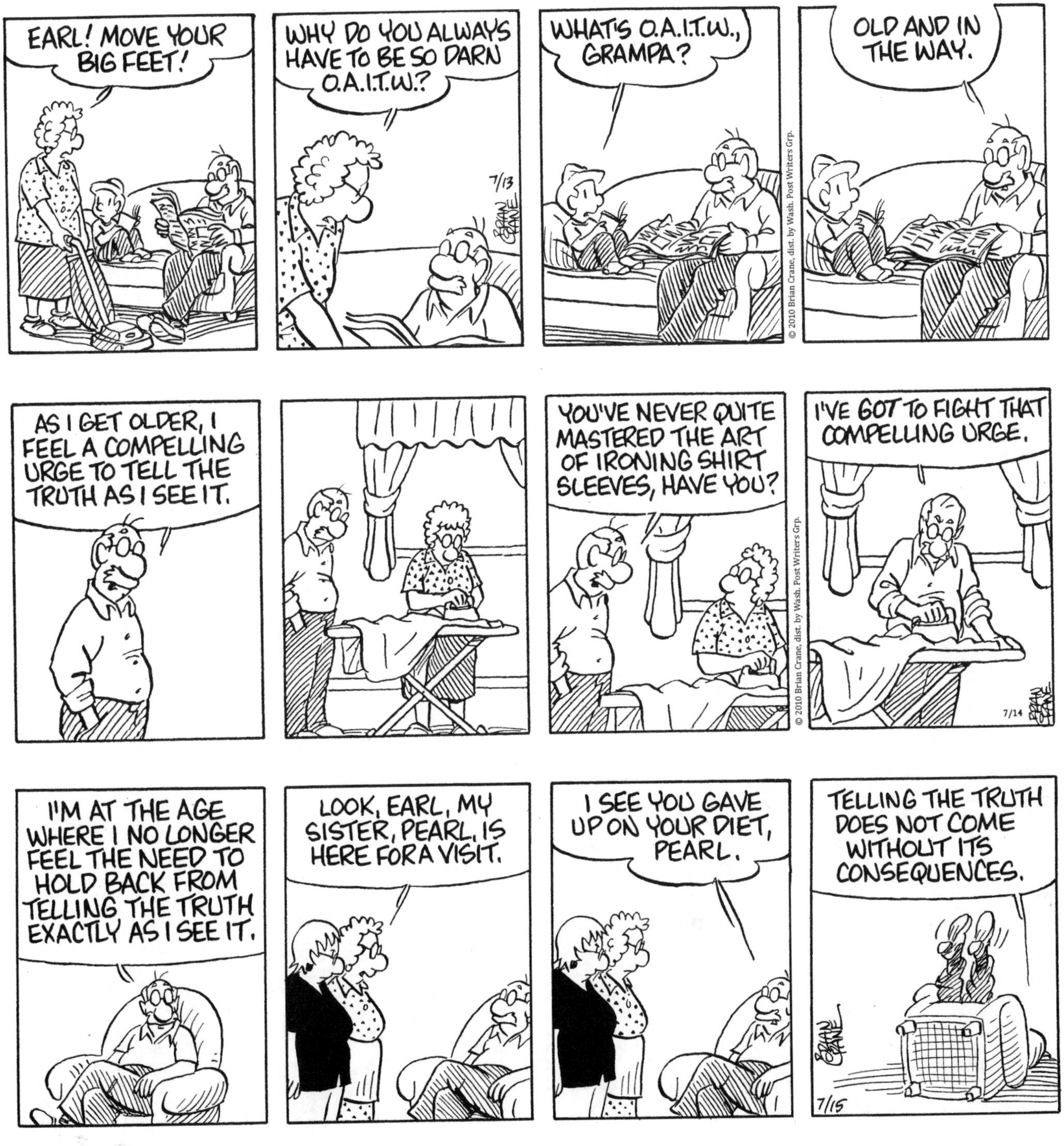
EARL! MOVE YOUR BIG FEET!
WHY DO YOU ALWAYS HAVE TO BE SO DARN O.A.I.T.W.?
7/13
BRIAN CRANE
WHAT'S O.A.I.T.W., GRAMPA?
© 2010 Brian Crane, dist. by Wash. Post Writers Grp.
OLD AND IN THE WAY.
AS I GET OLDER, I FEEL A COMPELLING URGE TO TELL THE TRUTH AS I SEE IT.
YOU'VE NEVER QUITE MASTERED THE ART OF IRONING SHIRT SLEEVES, HAVE YOU?
© 2010 Brian Crane, dist. by Wash. Post Writers Grp.
I'VE GOT TO FIGHT THAT COMPELLING URGE.
7/14
I'M AT THE AGE WHERE I NO LONGER FEEL THE NEED TO HOLD BACK FROM TELLING THE TRUTH EXACTLY AS I SEE IT.
LOOK, EARL, MY SISTER, PEARL, IS HERE FOR A VISIT.
I SEE YOU GAVE UP ON YOUR DIET, PEARL.
© 2010 Brian Crane, dist. by Wash. Post Writers Grp.
TELLING THE TRUTH DOES NOT COME WITHOUT ITS CONSEQUENCES.
BRIAN CRANE
7/15

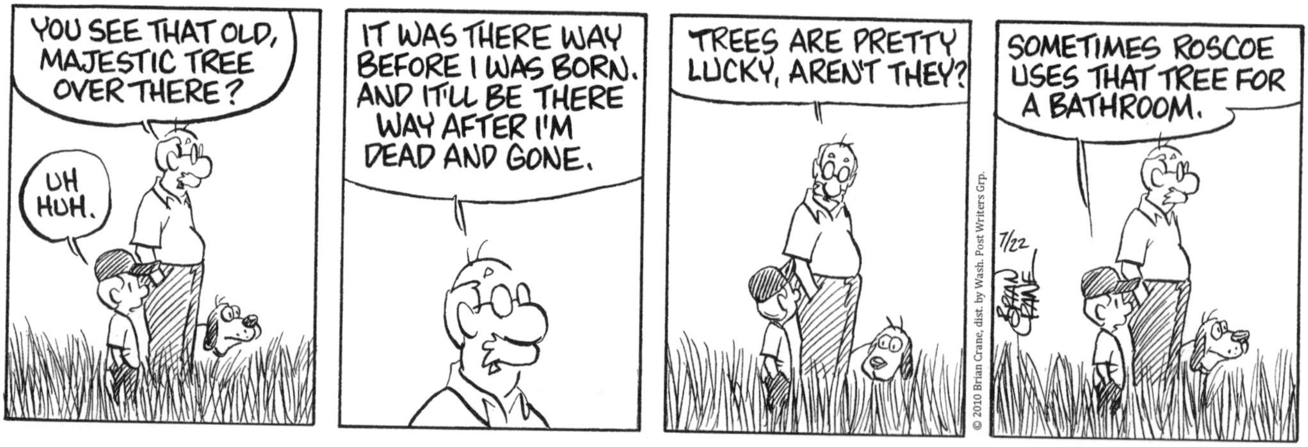
YOU SEE THAT OLD, MAJESTIC TREE OVER THERE?
UH HUH.
IT WAS THERE WAY BEFORE I WAS BORN. AND IT'LL BE THERE WAY AFTER I'M DEAD AND GONE.
TREES ARE PRETTY LUCKY, AREN'T THEY?
SOMETIMES ROSCOE USES THAT TREE FOR A BATHROOM.
7/22
© 2010 Brian Crane, dist. by Wash. Post Writers Grp.

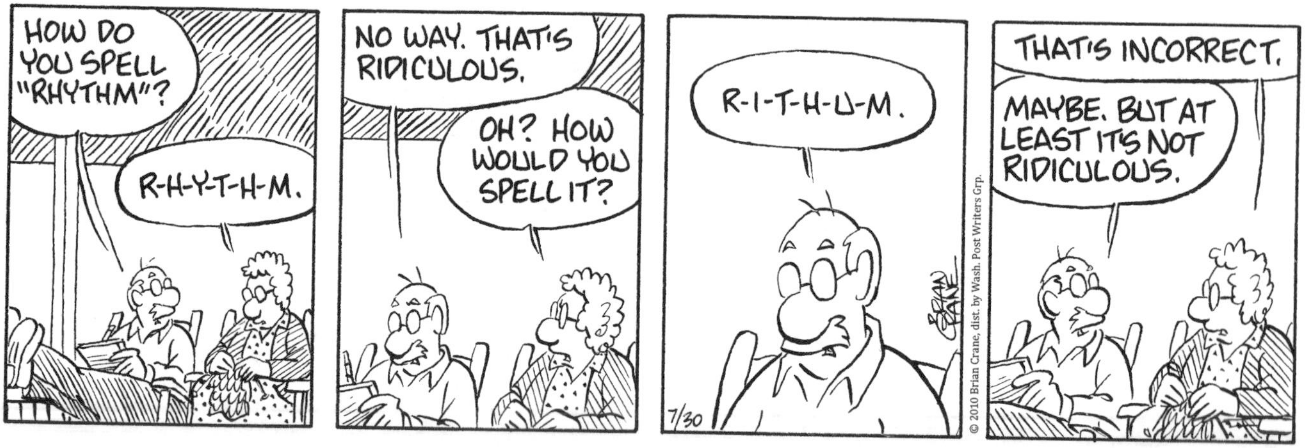
HOW DO YOU SPELL "RHYTHM"?
R-H-Y-T-H-M.
NO WAY. THAT'S RIDICULOUS.
OH? HOW WOULD YOU SPELL IT?
R-I-T-H-U-M.
7/30
THAT'S INCORRECT.
MAYBE. BUT AT LEAST IT'S NOT RIDICULOUS.
© 2010 Brian Crane, dist. by Wash. Post Writers Grp.

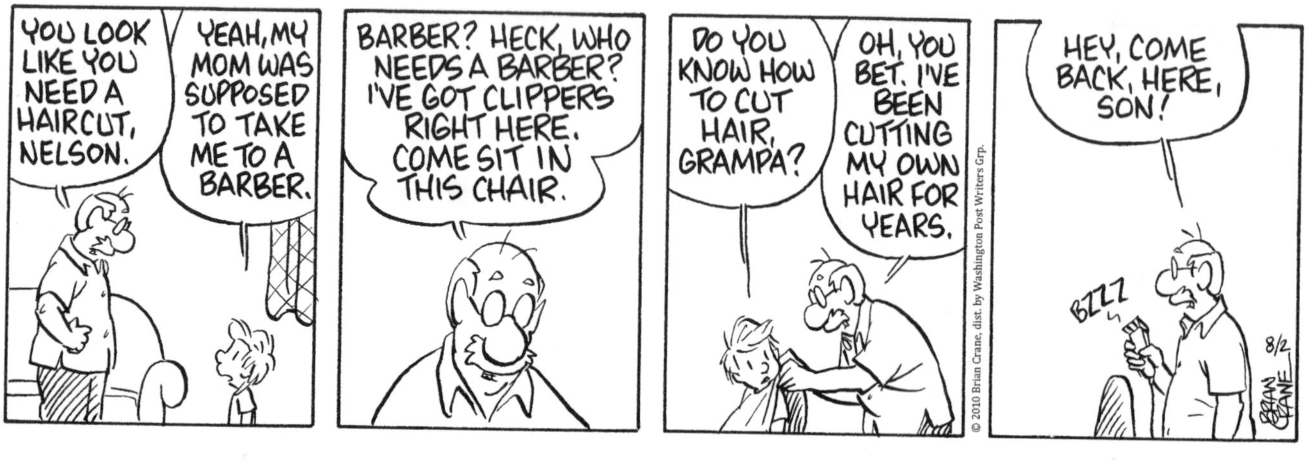
YOU LOOK LIKE YOU NEED A HAIRCUT, NELSON.
YEAH, MY MOM WAS SUPPOSED TO TAKE ME TO A BARBER.
BARBER? HECK, WHO NEEDS A BARBER? I'VE GOT CLIPPERS RIGHT HERE. COME SIT IN THIS CHAIR.
DO YOU KNOW HOW TO CUT HAIR, GRAMPA?
OH, YOU BET. I'VE BEEN CUTTING MY OWN HAIR FOR YEARS.
HEY, COME BACK, HERE, SON!
BZZZ
8/2
© 2010 Brian Crane, dist. by Washington Post Writers Grp.

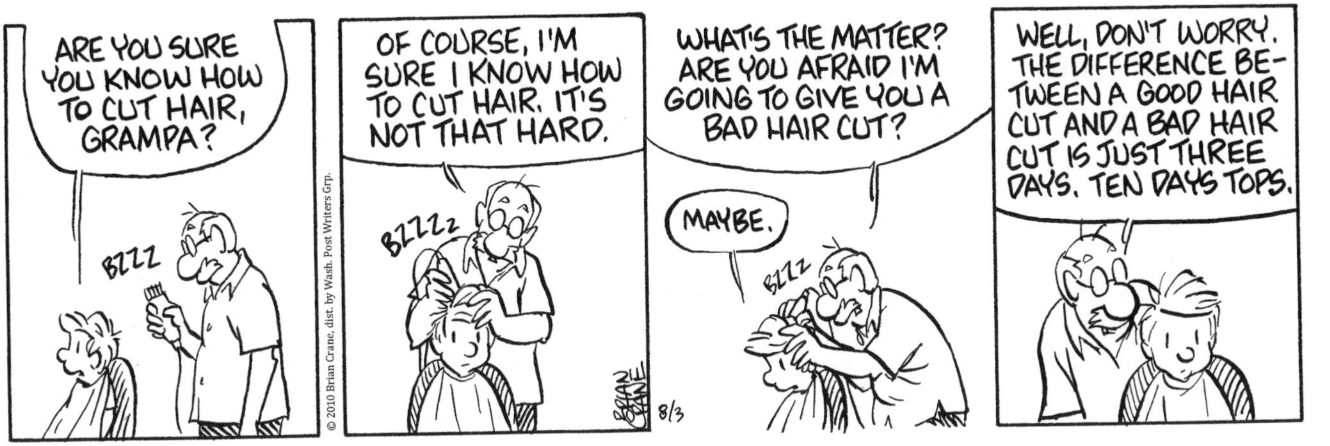
ARE YOU SURE YOU KNOW HOW TO CUT HAIR, GRAMPA?
BZZZ
© 2010 Brian Crane, dist. by Wash. Post Writers Grp.
OF COURSE, I'M SURE I KNOW HOW TO CUT HAIR. IT'S NOT THAT HARD.
BZZZZ
BRIAN CRANE 8/3
WHAT'S THE MATTER? ARE YOU AFRAID I'M GOING TO GIVE YOU A BAD HAIR CUT?
MAYBE.
BZZZ
WELL, DON'T WORRY. THE DIFFERENCE BETWEEN A GOOD HAIR CUT AND A BAD HAIR CUT IS JUST THREE DAYS. TEN DAYS TOPS.

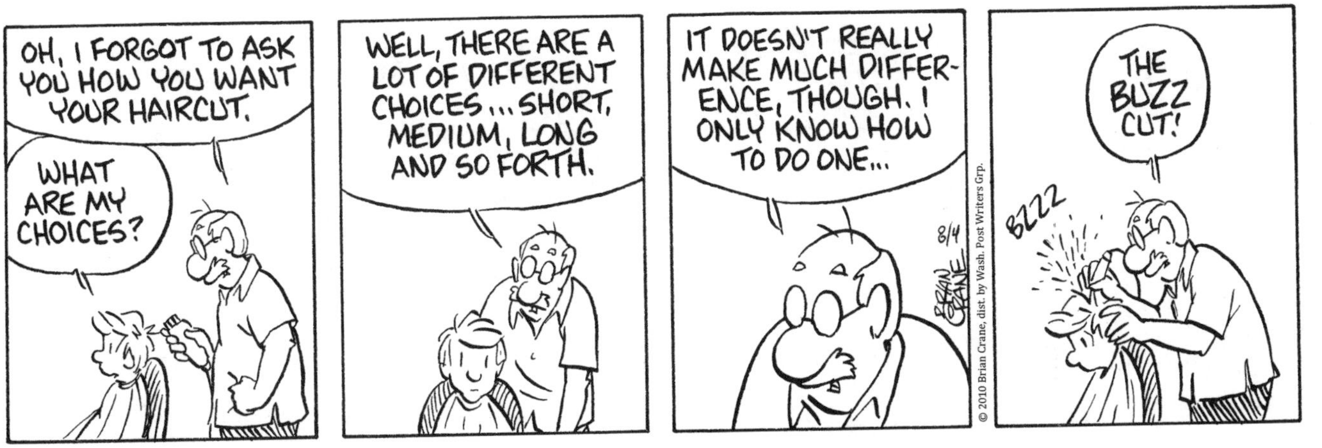
OH, I FORGOT TO ASK YOU HOW YOU WANT YOUR HAIRCUT.
WHAT ARE MY CHOICES?
WELL, THERE ARE A LOT OF DIFFERENT CHOICES... SHORT, MEDIUM, LONG AND SO FORTH.
IT DOESN'T REALLY MAKE MUCH DIFFERENCE, THOUGH. I ONLY KNOW HOW TO DO ONE...
8/4 BRIAN CRANE
© 2010 Brian Crane, dist. by Wash. Post Writers Grp.
THE BUZZ CUT!
BZZZ

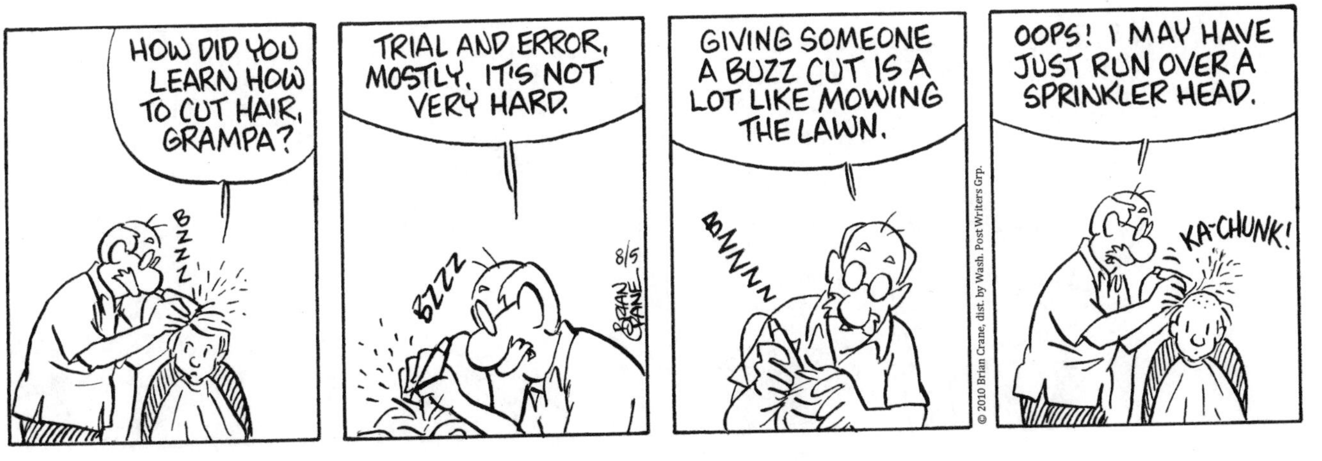
HOW DID YOU LEARN HOW TO CUT HAIR, GRAMPA?
BZZZ
TRIAL AND ERROR, MOSTLY. IT'S NOT VERY HARD.
BZZZ
8/5 BRIAN CRANE
GIVING SOMEONE A BUZZ CUT IS A LOT LIKE MOWING THE LAWN.
BNNNNN
© 2010 Brian Crane, dist. by Wash. Post Writers Grp.
OOPS! I MAY HAVE JUST RUN OVER A SPRINKLER HEAD.
KA-CHUNK!

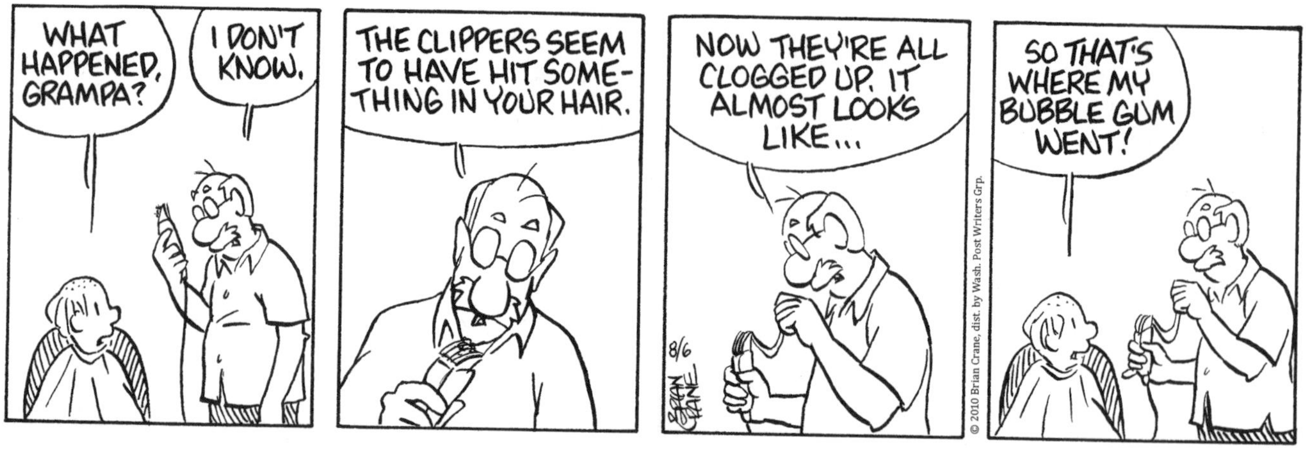
WHAT HAPPENED, GRAMPA?
I DON'T KNOW.
THE CLIPPERS SEEM TO HAVE HIT SOMETHING IN YOUR HAIR.
NOW THEY'RE ALL CLOGGED UP. IT ALMOST LOOKS LIKE...
8/6
BRIAN CRANE
SO THAT'S WHERE MY BUBBLE GUM WENT!
© 2010 Brian Crane, dist. by Wash. Post Writers Grp.

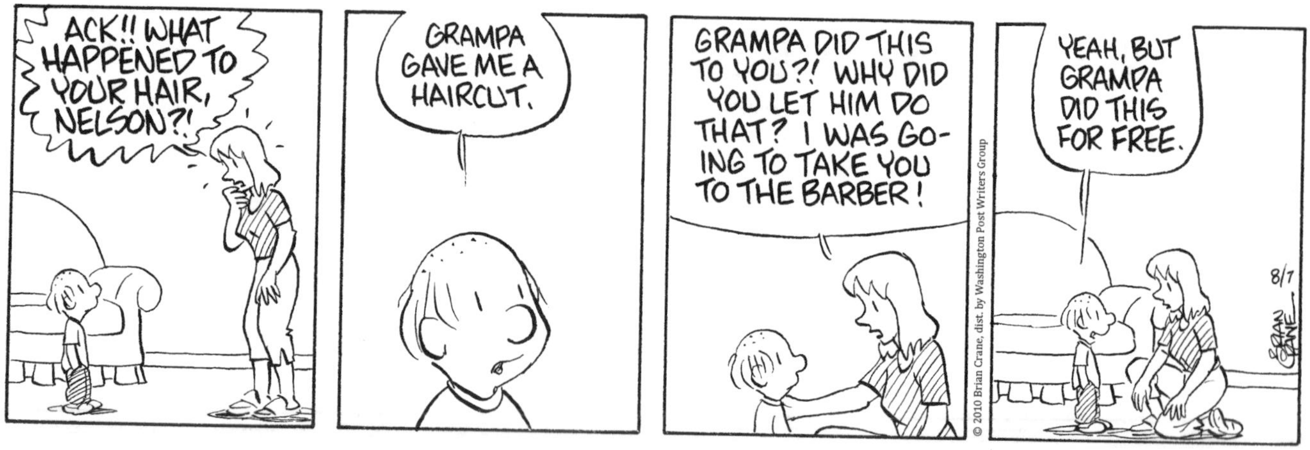
ACK!! WHAT HAPPENED TO YOUR HAIR, NELSON?!
GRAMPA GAVE ME A HAIRCUT.
GRAMPA DID THIS TO YOU?! WHY DID YOU LET HIM DO THAT? I WAS GOING TO TAKE YOU TO THE BARBER!
© 2010 Brian Crane, dist. by Washington Post Writers Group
YEAH, BUT GRAMPA DID THIS FOR FREE.
8/7
BRIAN CRANE

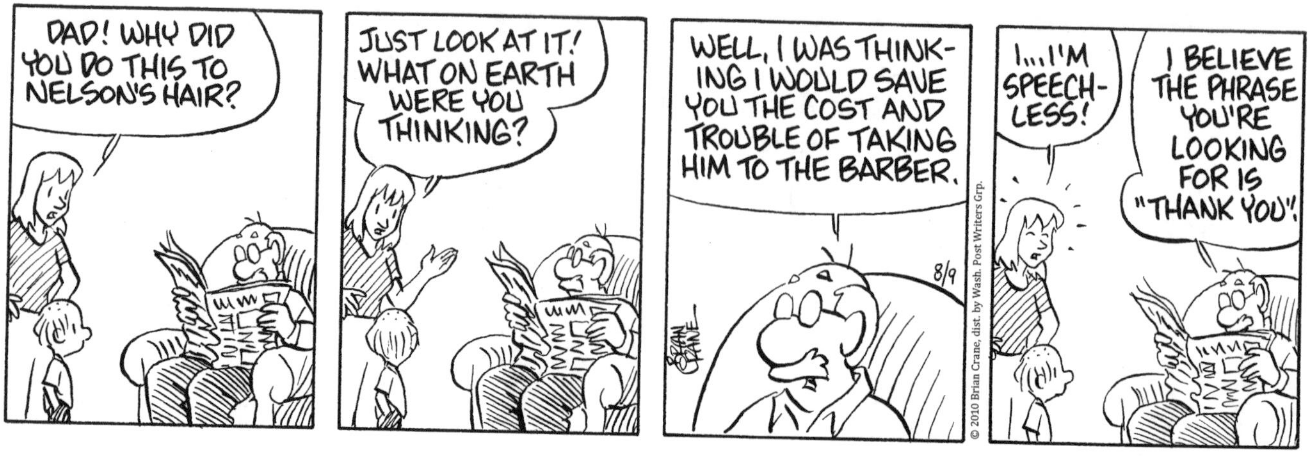
DAD! WHY DID YOU DO THIS TO NELSON'S HAIR?
JUST LOOK AT IT! WHAT ON EARTH WERE YOU THINKING?
WELL, I WAS THINKING I WOULD SAVE YOU THE COST AND TROUBLE OF TAKING HIM TO THE BARBER.
BRIAN CRANE
8/9
© 2010 Brian Crane, dist. by Wash. Post Writers Grp.
I...I'M SPEECHLESS!
I BELIEVE THE PHRASE YOU'RE LOOKING FOR IS "THANK YOU".

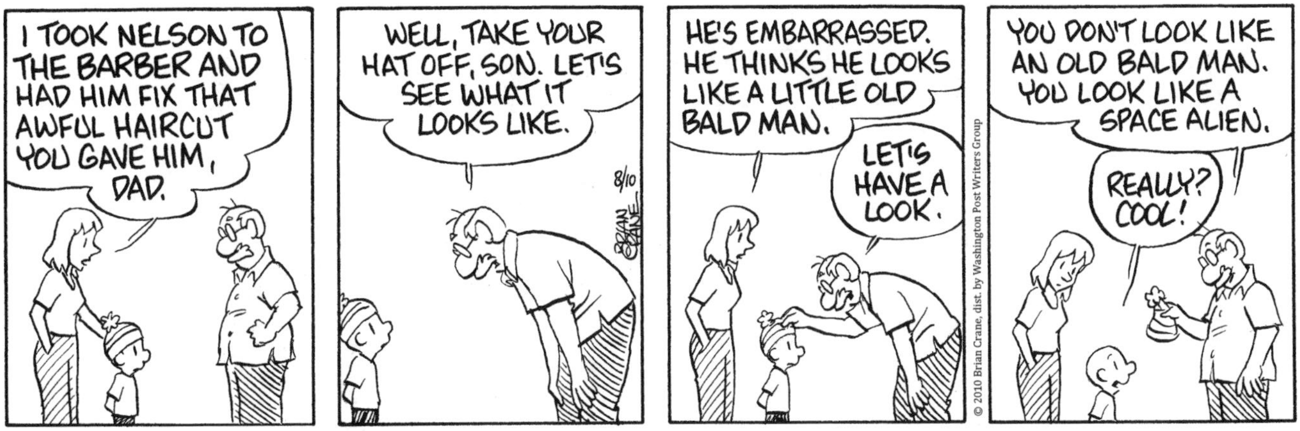
I TOOK NELSON TO THE BARBER AND HAD HIM FIX THAT AWFUL HAIRCUT YOU GAVE HIM, DAD.
WELL, TAKE YOUR HAT OFF, SON. LET'S SEE WHAT IT LOOKS LIKE.
8/10
BRIAN CRANE
HE'S EMBARRASSED. HE THINKS HE LOOKS LIKE A LITTLE OLD BALD MAN.
LET'S HAVE A LOOK.
YOU DON'T LOOK LIKE AN OLD BALD MAN. YOU LOOK LIKE A SPACE ALIEN.
REALLY? COOL!

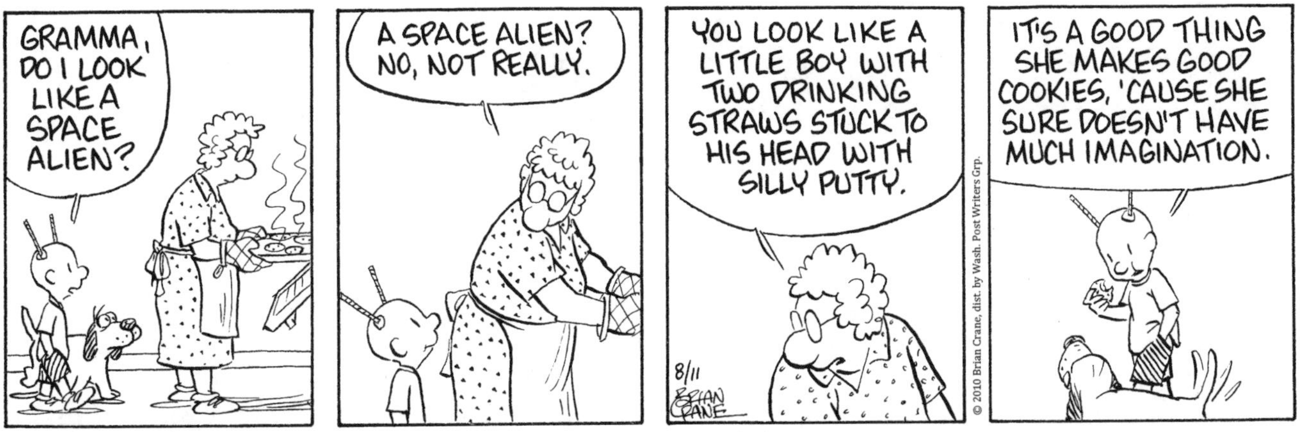
GRAMMA, DO I LOOK LIKE A SPACE ALIEN?
A SPACE ALIEN? NO, NOT REALLY.
YOU LOOK LIKE A LITTLE BOY WITH TWO DRINKING STRAWS STUCK TO HIS HEAD WITH SILLY PUTTY.
8/11
BRIAN CRANE
IT'S A GOOD THING SHE MAKES GOOD COOKIES, 'CAUSE SHE SURE DOESN'T HAVE MUCH IMAGINATION.

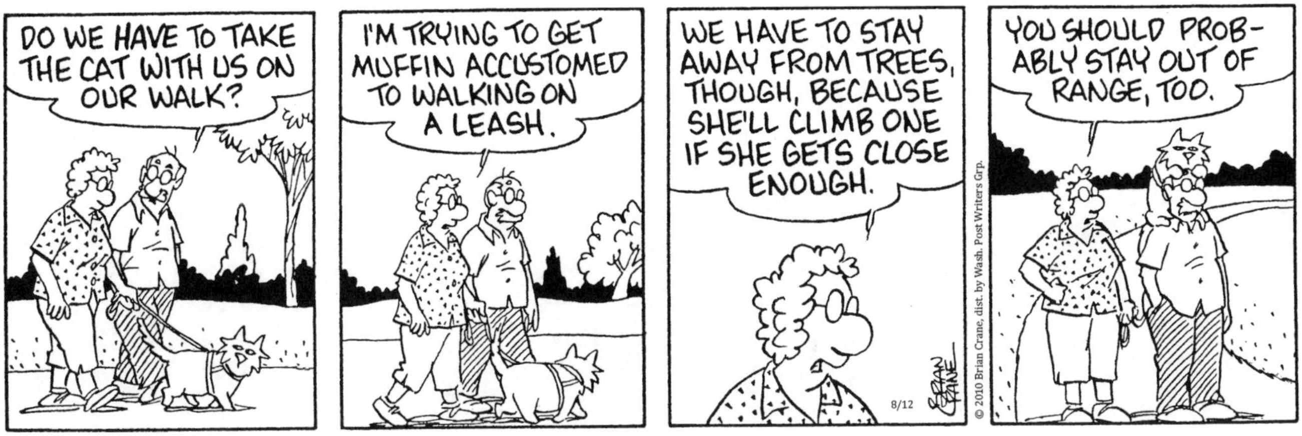
DO WE HAVE TO TAKE THE CAT WITH US ON OUR WALK?
I'M TRYING TO GET MUFFIN ACCUSTOMED TO WALKING ON A LEASH.
WE HAVE TO STAY AWAY FROM TREES, THOUGH, BECAUSE SHE'LL CLIMB ONE IF SHE GETS CLOSE ENOUGH.
BRIAN CRANE
8/12
YOU SHOULD PROBABLY STAY OUT OF RANGE, TOO.

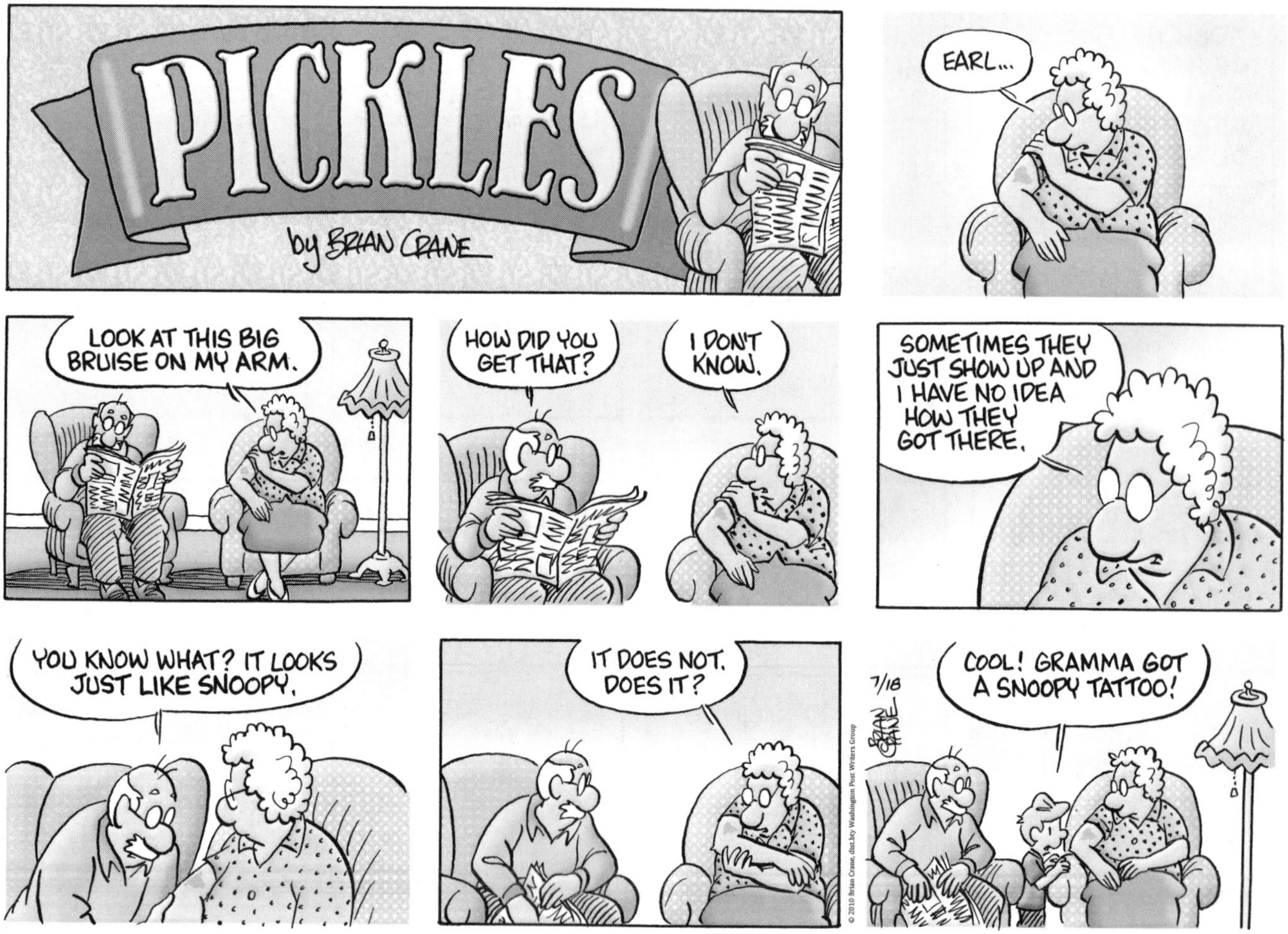
PICKLES
by BRIAN CRANE
EARL...
LOOK AT THIS BIG BRUISE ON MY ARM.
HOW DID YOU GET THAT?
I DON'T KNOW.
SOMETIMES THEY JUST SHOW UP AND I HAVE NO IDEA HOW THEY GOT THERE.
YOU KNOW WHAT? IT LOOKS JUST LIKE SNOOPY.
IT DOES NOT. DOES IT?
7/18
© 2010 Brian Crane, dist. by Washington Post Writers Group
COOL! GRAMMA GOT A SNOOPY TATTOO!

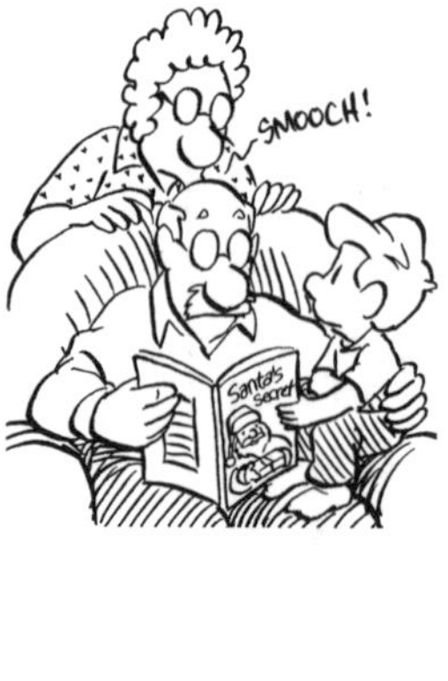
SMOOCH!
Santa's Secret

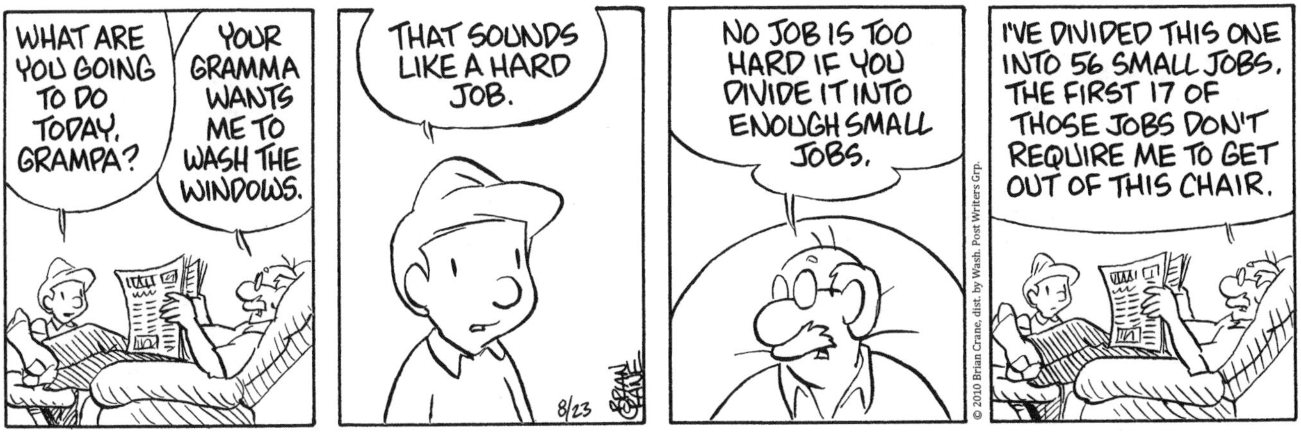
WHAT ARE YOU GOING TO DO TODAY, GRAMPA?
YOUR GRAMMA WANTS ME TO WASH THE WINDOWS.
THAT SOUNDS LIKE A HARD JOB.
8/23
NO JOB IS TOO HARD IF YOU DIVIDE IT INTO ENOUGH SMALL JOBS.
© 2010 Brian Crane, dist. by Wash. Post Writers Grp.
I'VE DIVIDED THIS ONE INTO 56 SMALL JOBS. THE FIRST 17 OF THOSE JOBS DON'T REQUIRE ME TO GET OUT OF THIS CHAIR.

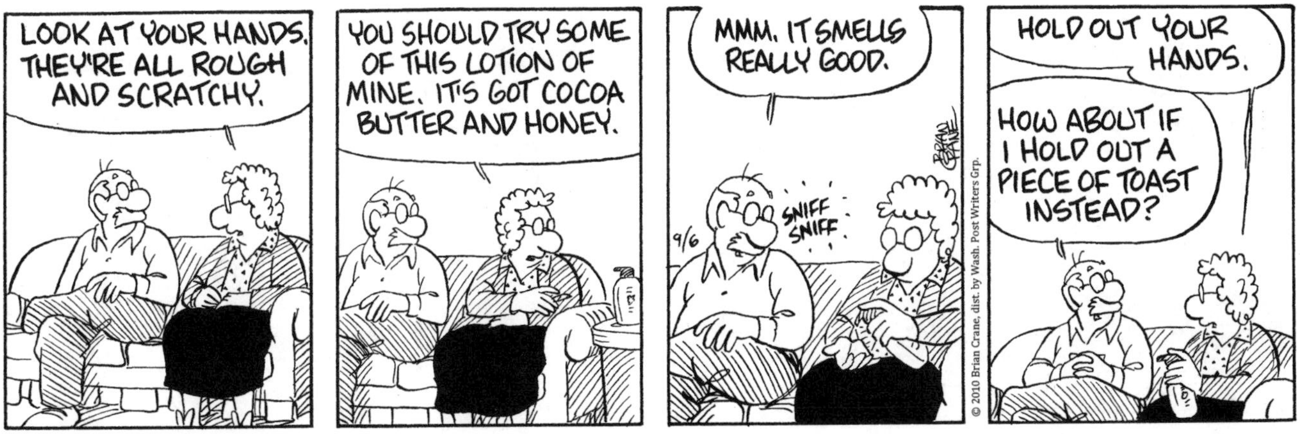
LOOK AT YOUR HANDS. THEY'RE ALL ROUGH AND SCRATCHY.
YOU SHOULD TRY SOME OF THIS LOTION OF MINE. IT'S GOT COCOA BUTTER AND HONEY.
MMM. IT SMELLS REALLY GOOD.
SNIFF SNIFF
9/6
© 2010 Brian Crane, dist. by Wash. Post Writers Grp.
HOLD OUT YOUR HANDS.
HOW ABOUT IF I HOLD OUT A PIECE OF TOAST INSTEAD?

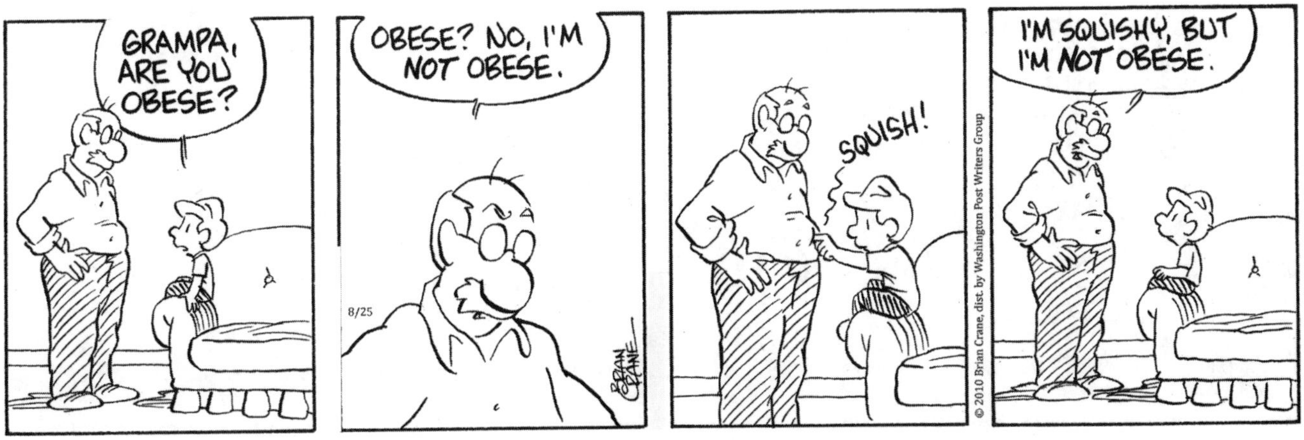
GRAMPA, ARE YOU OBESE?
OBESE? NO, I'M NOT OBESE.
8/25
SQUISH!
© 2010 Brian Crane, dist. by Washington Post Writers Group
I'M SQUISHY, BUT I'M ***NOT*** OBESE.

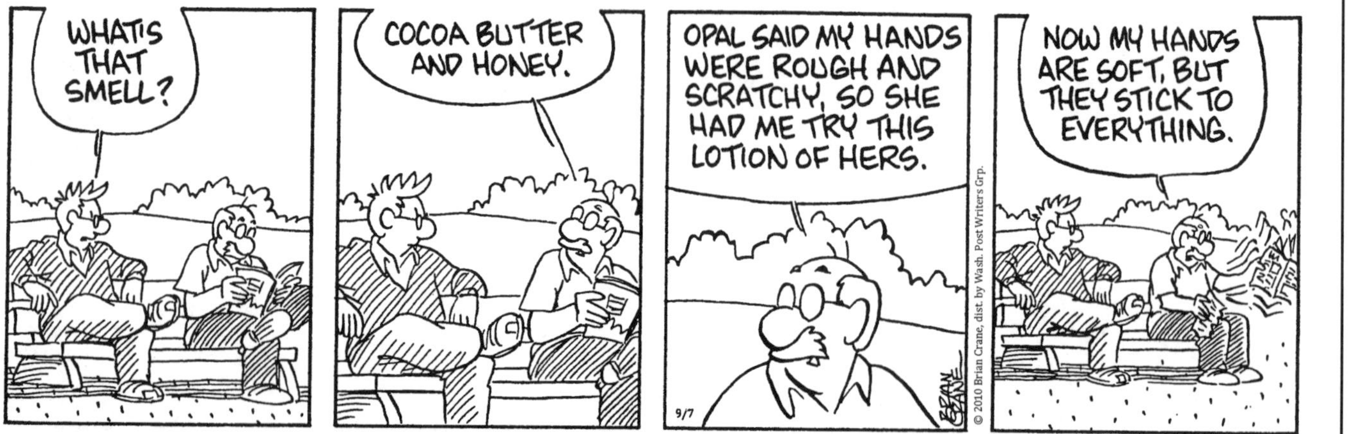
WHAT'S THAT SMELL?
COCOA BUTTER AND HONEY.
OPAL SAID MY HANDS WERE ROUGH AND SCRATCHY, SO SHE HAD ME TRY THIS LOTION OF HERS.
9/7
BRIAN CRANE
© 2010 Brian Crane, dist. by Wash. Post Writers Grp.
NOW MY HANDS ARE SOFT, BUT THEY STICK TO EVERYTHING.

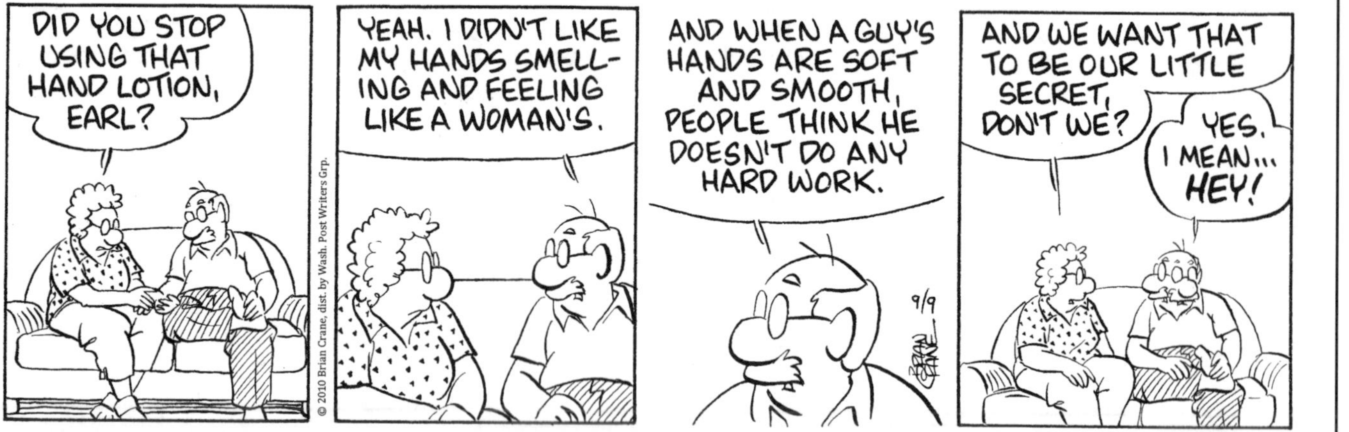
DID YOU STOP USING THAT HAND LOTION, EARL?
© 2010 Brian Crane, dist. by Wash. Post Writers Grp.
YEAH. I DIDN'T LIKE MY HANDS SMELLING AND FEELING LIKE A WOMAN'S.
AND WHEN A GUY'S HANDS ARE SOFT AND SMOOTH, PEOPLE THINK HE DOESN'T DO ANY HARD WORK.
9/9
BRIAN CRANE
AND WE WANT THAT TO BE OUR LITTLE SECRET, DON'T WE?
YES. I MEAN... HEY!

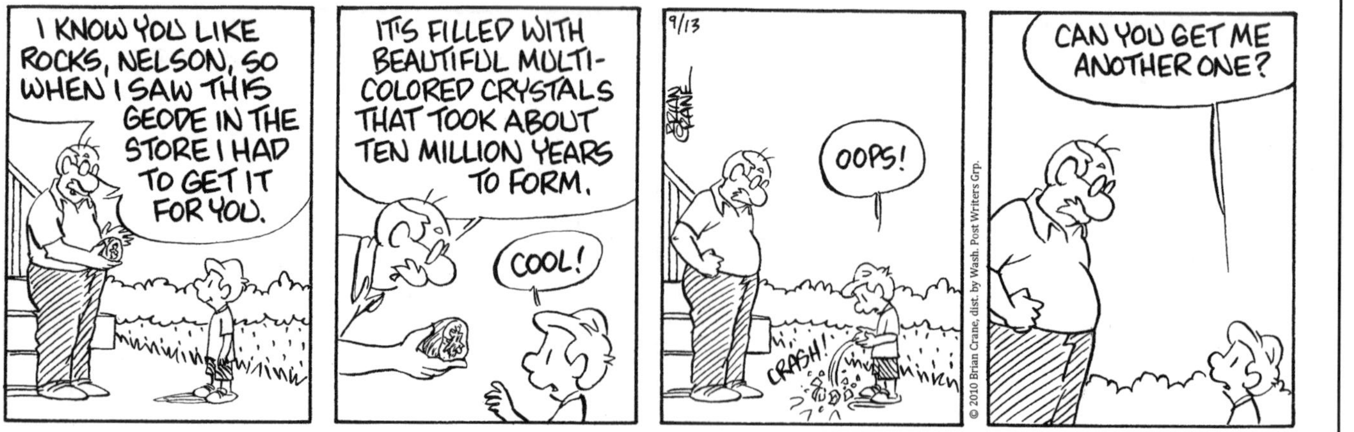
I KNOW YOU LIKE ROCKS, NELSON, SO WHEN I SAW THIS GEODE IN THE STORE I HAD TO GET IT FOR YOU.
IT'S FILLED WITH BEAUTIFUL MULTI-COLORED CRYSTALS THAT TOOK ABOUT TEN MILLION YEARS TO FORM.
COOL!
9/13
BRIAN CRANE
OOPS!
CRASH!
© 2010 Brian Crane, dist. by Wash. Post Writers Grp.
CAN YOU GET ME ANOTHER ONE?

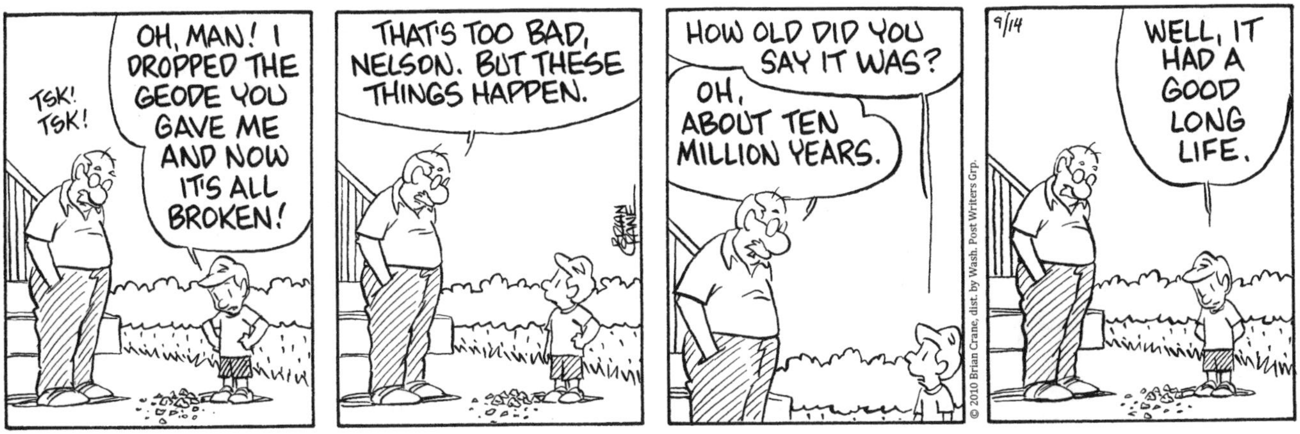
TSK! TSK!
OH, MAN! I DROPPED THE GEODE YOU GAVE ME AND NOW IT'S ALL BROKEN!
THAT'S TOO BAD, NELSON. BUT THESE THINGS HAPPEN.
BRIAN CRANE
HOW OLD DID YOU SAY IT WAS?
OH, ABOUT TEN MILLION YEARS.
9/14
WELL, IT HAD A GOOD LONG LIFE.
© 2010 Brian Crane, dist. by Wash. Post Writers Grp.

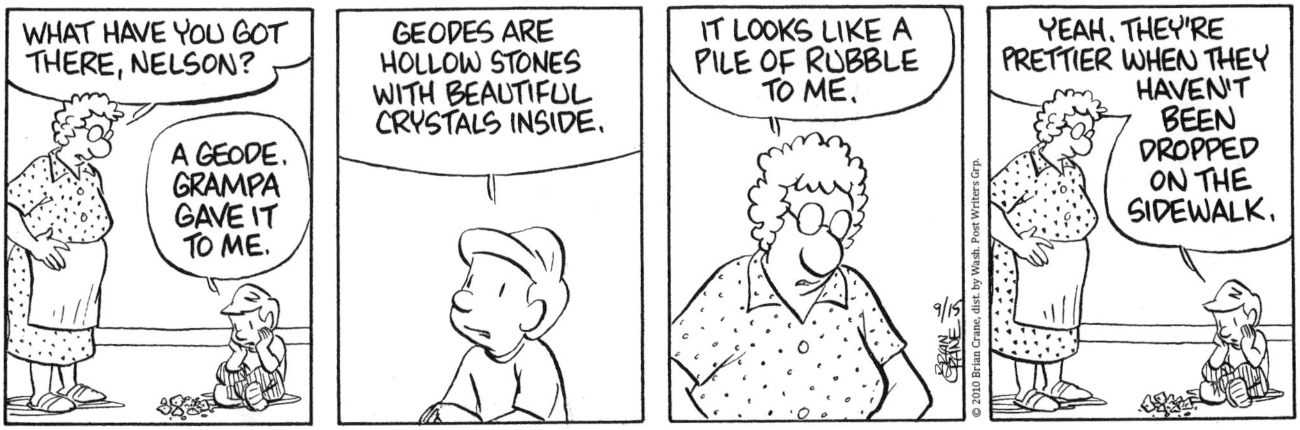
WHAT HAVE YOU GOT THERE, NELSON?
A GEODE. GRAMPA GAVE IT TO ME.
GEODES ARE HOLLOW STONES WITH BEAUTIFUL CRYSTALS INSIDE.
IT LOOKS LIKE A PILE OF RUBBLE TO ME.
9/15
BRIAN CRANE
YEAH. THEY'RE PRETTIER WHEN THEY HAVEN'T BEEN DROPPED ON THE SIDEWALK.
© 2010 Brian Crane, dist. by Wash. Post Writers Grp.

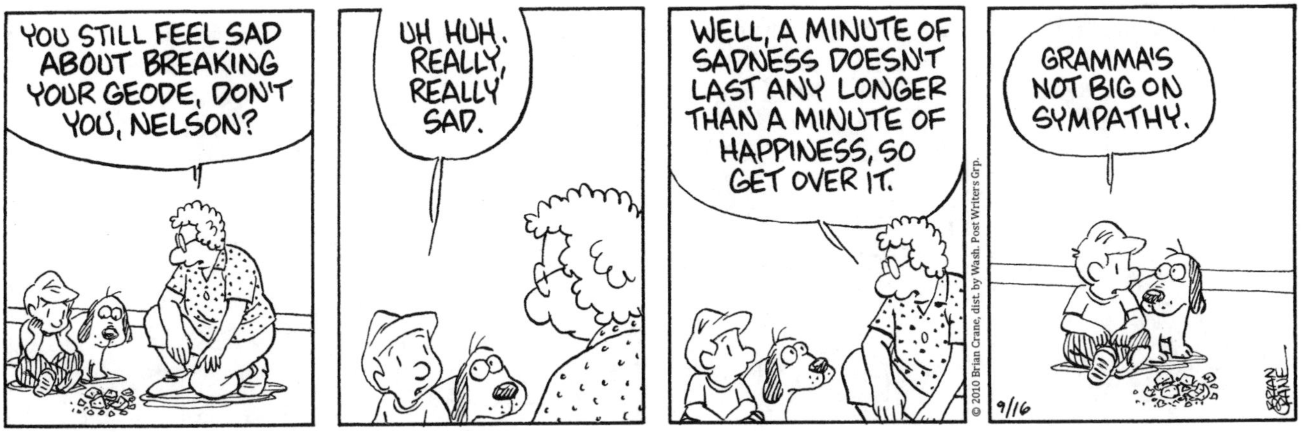
YOU STILL FEEL SAD ABOUT BREAKING YOUR GEODE, DON'T YOU, NELSON?
UH HUH. REALLY, REALLY SAD.
WELL, A MINUTE OF SADNESS DOESN'T LAST ANY LONGER THAN A MINUTE OF HAPPINESS, SO GET OVER IT.
GRAMMA'S NOT BIG ON SYMPATHY.
9/16
BRIAN CRANE
© 2010 Brian Crane, dist. by Wash. Post Writers Grp.

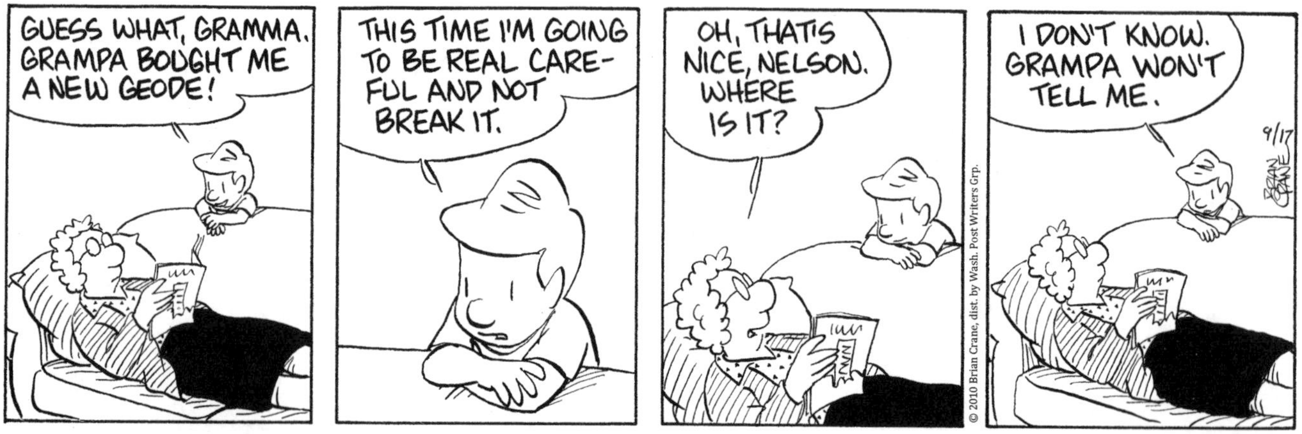
GUESS WHAT, GRAMMA. GRAMPA BOUGHT ME A NEW GEODE!
THIS TIME I'M GOING TO BE REAL CAREFUL AND NOT BREAK IT.
OH, THAT'S NICE, NELSON. WHERE IS IT?
I DON'T KNOW. GRAMPA WON'T TELL ME.

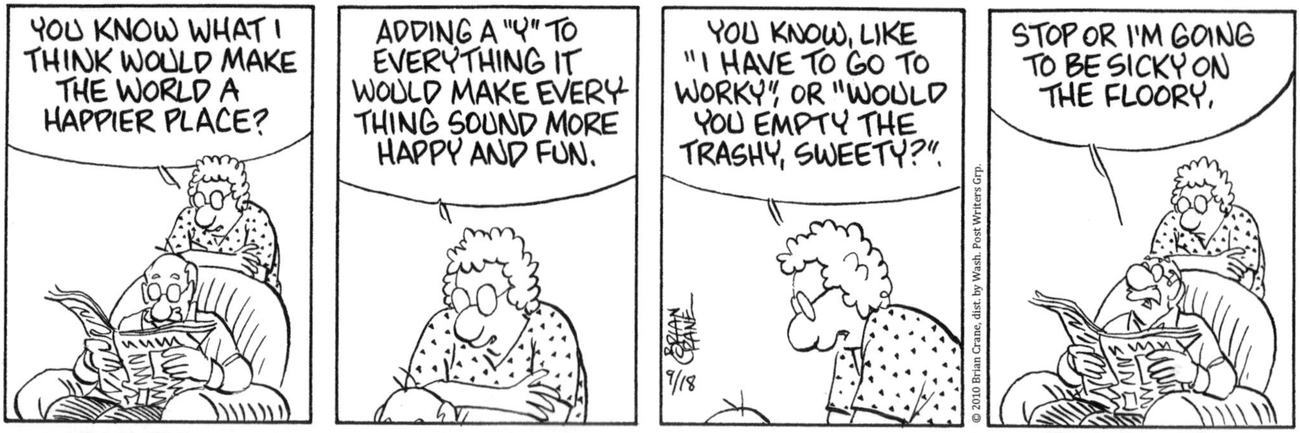
YOU KNOW WHAT I THINK WOULD MAKE THE WORLD A HAPPIER PLACE?
ADDING A "Y" TO EVERYTHING IT WOULD MAKE EVERYTHING SOUND MORE HAPPY AND FUN.
YOU KNOW, LIKE "I HAVE TO GO TO WORKY", OR "WOULD YOU EMPTY THE TRASHY, SWEETY?".
STOP OR I'M GOING TO BE SICKY ON THE FLOORY.

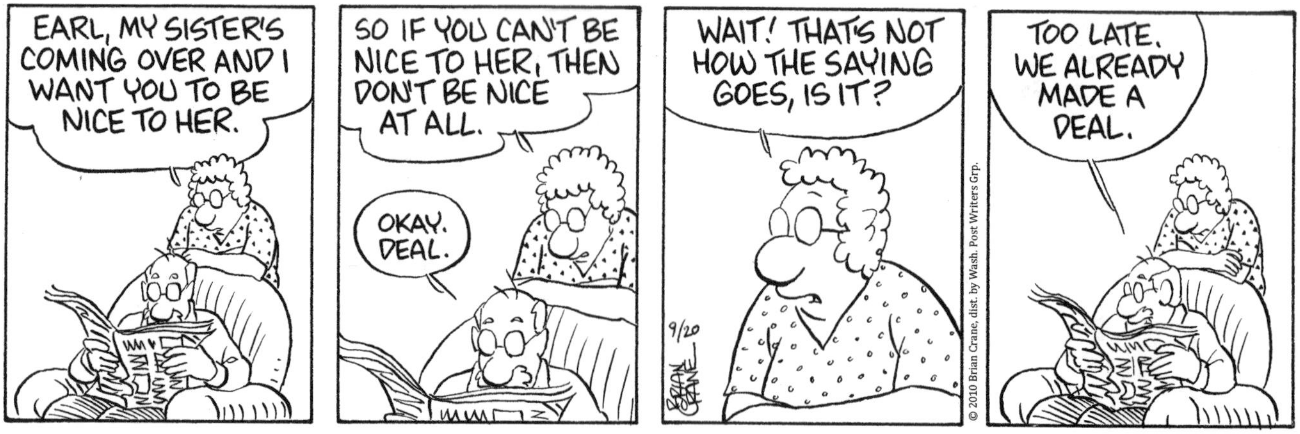
EARL, MY SISTER'S COMING OVER AND I WANT YOU TO BE NICE TO HER.
SO IF YOU CAN'T BE NICE TO HER, THEN DON'T BE NICE AT ALL.
OKAY. DEAL.
WAIT! THAT'S NOT HOW THE SAYING GOES, IS IT?
TOO LATE. WE ALREADY MADE A DEAL.

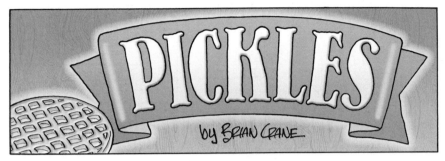

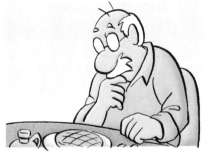

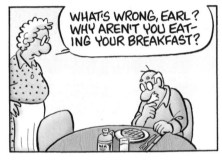

PICKLES
by Brian Crane
WHAT'S WRONG, EARL? WHY AREN'T YOU EAT-ING YOUR BREAKFAST?
I'M ON THE HORNS OF A DILEMMA.
I'VE GOT THIS LITTLE JUG OF PURE MAPLE SYRUP. YOU KNOW, THE GOOD STUFF.
IT TAKES FOUR MAPLE TREES, EACH OF THEM AT LEAST FORTY YEARS OLD, TO MAKE ENOUGH SAP TO YIELD JUST ONE GALLON OF THIS SYRUP.
SO?
SO, I'M PONDERING THE MORAL AND ETHICAL IMPLICATIONS OF POUR-ING IT ON EGGOS WAFFLES.
© 2010 Brian Crane, dist. by Washington Post Writers Group
7/25
BRIAN CRANE

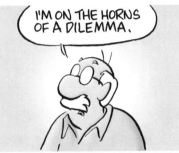

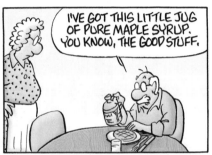

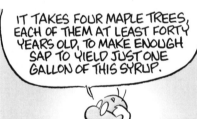

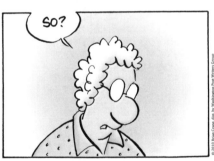

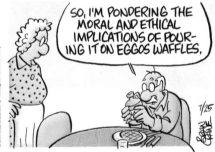

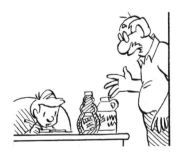

PICKLES
by BRIAN CRANE
WHAT'S IT LIKE TO HAVE A DOG?
DOGS ARE KIND OF LIKE BABIES.
YOU HAVE TO DO EVERY-THING FOR THEM.
YOU HAVE TO FEED THEM AND CLEAN UP AFTER THEM...
WHEN'S DINNER GOING TO BE READY, OPAL?
WHO KNOWS? I'VE BEEN TOO BUSY CLEANING UP THAT MESS YOU LEFT IN THE BEDROOM TO THINK ABOUT MAKING DINNER!
BRIAN CRANE
8/8
© 2010 Brian Crane, dist. by Washington Post Writers Group
ACTUALLY, DOGS ARE KIND OF LIKE OLD MEN.

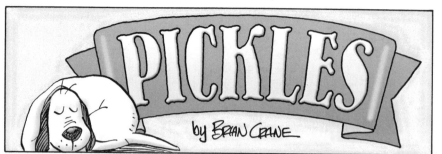

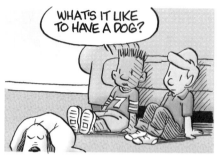

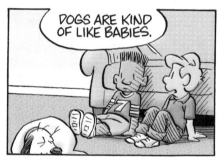

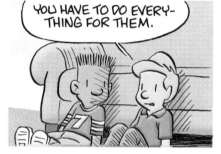

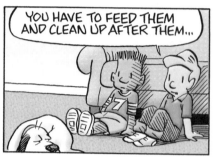

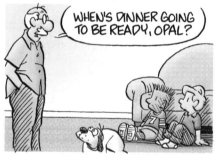

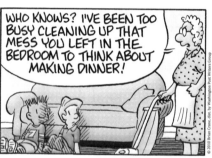

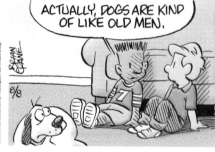

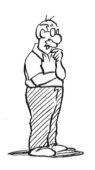

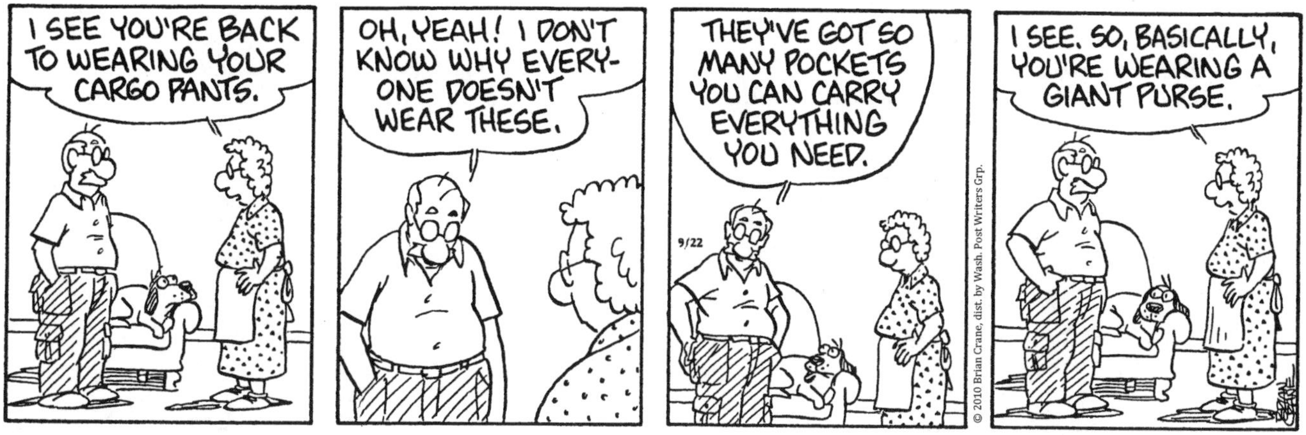
I SEE YOU'RE BACK TO WEARING YOUR CARGO PANTS.
OH, YEAH! I DON'T KNOW WHY EVERY-ONE DOESN'T WEAR THESE.
THEY'VE GOT SO MANY POCKETS YOU CAN CARRY EVERYTHING YOU NEED.
9/22
I SEE. SO, BASICALLY, YOU'RE WEARING A GIANT PURSE.

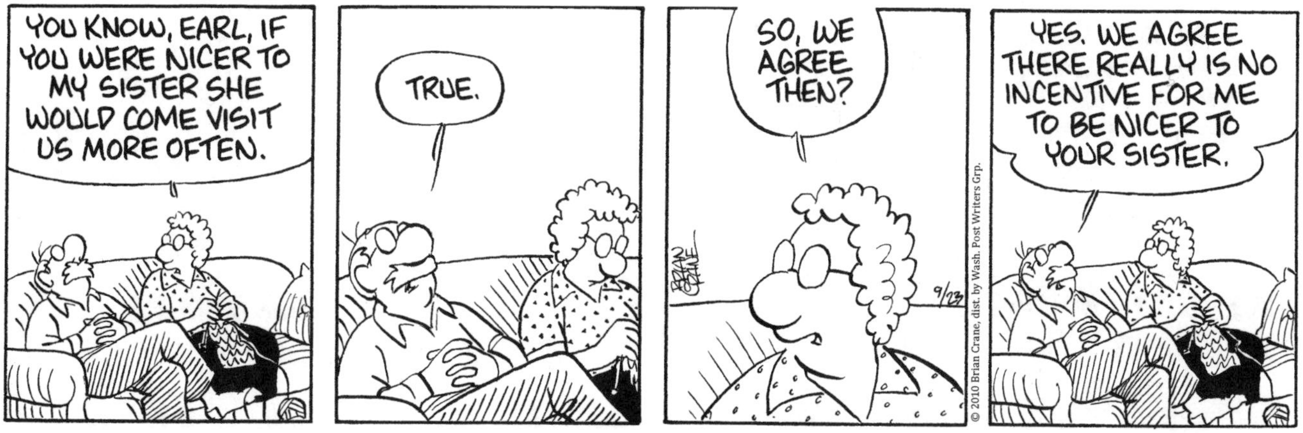
YOU KNOW, EARL, IF YOU WERE NICER TO MY SISTER SHE WOULD COME VISIT US MORE OFTEN.
TRUE.
SO, WE AGREE THEN?
9/23
YES. WE AGREE THERE REALLY IS NO INCENTIVE FOR ME TO BE NICER TO YOUR SISTER.

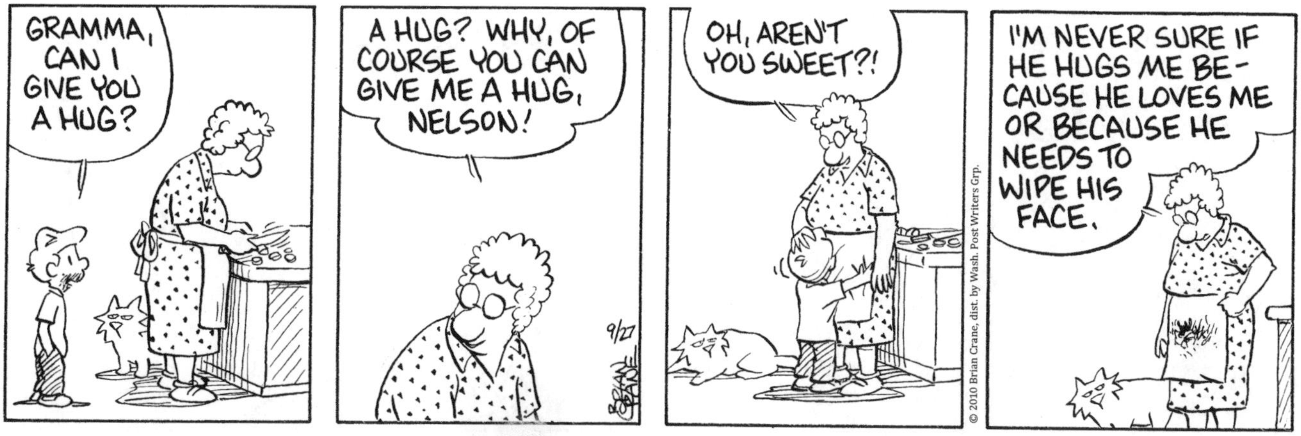
GRAMMA, CAN I GIVE YOU A HUG?
A HUG? WHY, OF COURSE YOU CAN GIVE ME A HUG, NELSON!
9/27
OH, AREN'T YOU SWEET?!
I'M NEVER SURE IF HE HUGS ME BE-CAUSE HE LOVES ME OR BECAUSE HE NEEDS TO WIPE HIS FACE.

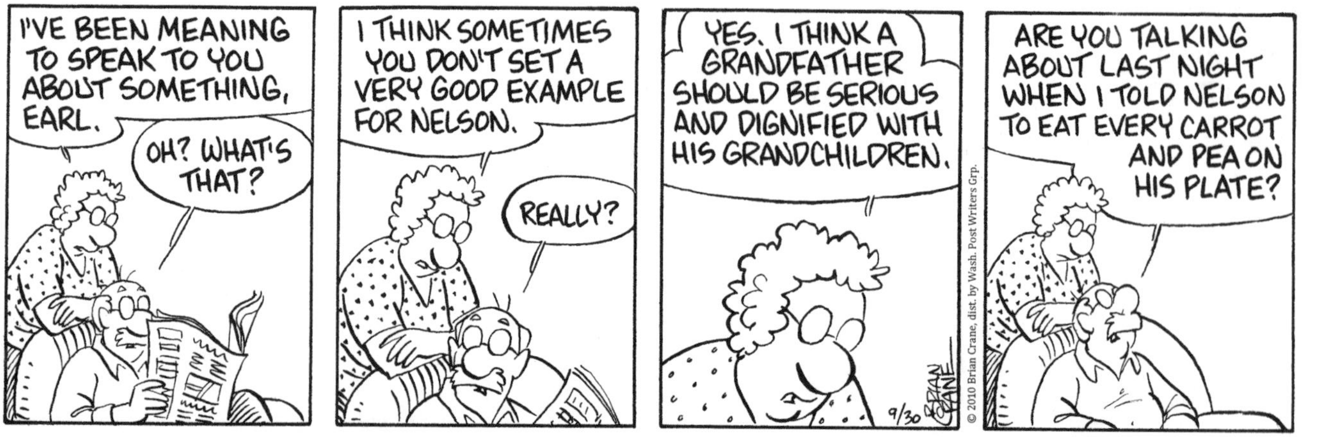
I'VE BEEN MEANING TO SPEAK TO YOU ABOUT SOMETHING, EARL.
OH? WHAT'S THAT?
I THINK SOMETIMES YOU DON'T SET A VERY GOOD EXAMPLE FOR NELSON.
REALLY?
YES. I THINK A GRANDFATHER SHOULD BE SERIOUS AND DIGNIFIED WITH HIS GRANDCHILDREN.
9/30
© 2010 Brian Crane, dist. by Wash. Post Writers Grp.
ARE YOU TALKING ABOUT LAST NIGHT WHEN I TOLD NELSON TO EAT EVERY CARROT AND PEA ON HIS PLATE?

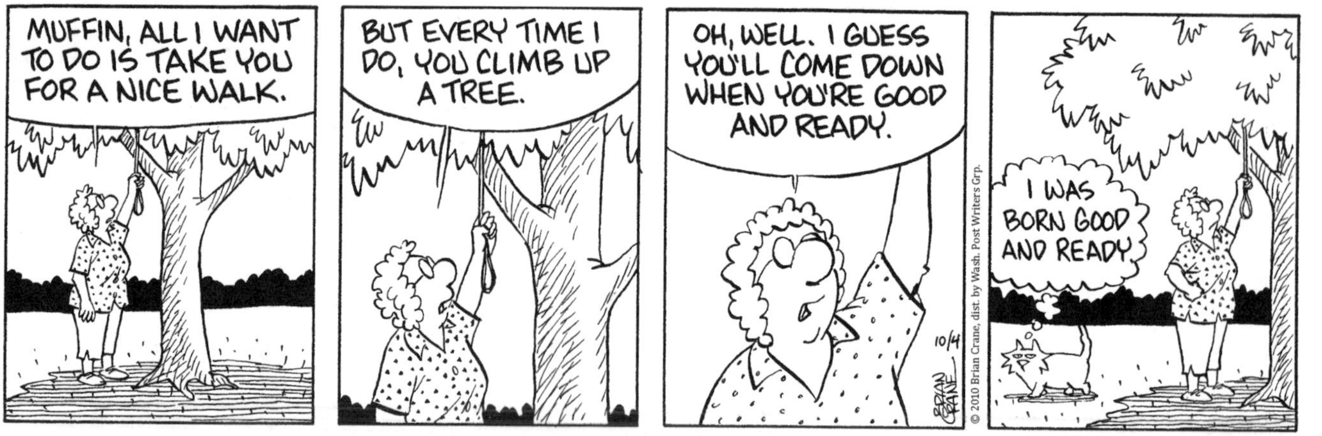
MUFFIN, ALL I WANT TO DO IS TAKE YOU FOR A NICE WALK.
BUT EVERY TIME I DO, YOU CLIMB UP A TREE.
OH, WELL. I GUESS YOU'LL COME DOWN WHEN YOU'RE GOOD AND READY.
10/4
© 2010 Brian Crane, dist. by Wash. Post Writers Grp.
I WAS BORN GOOD AND READY.

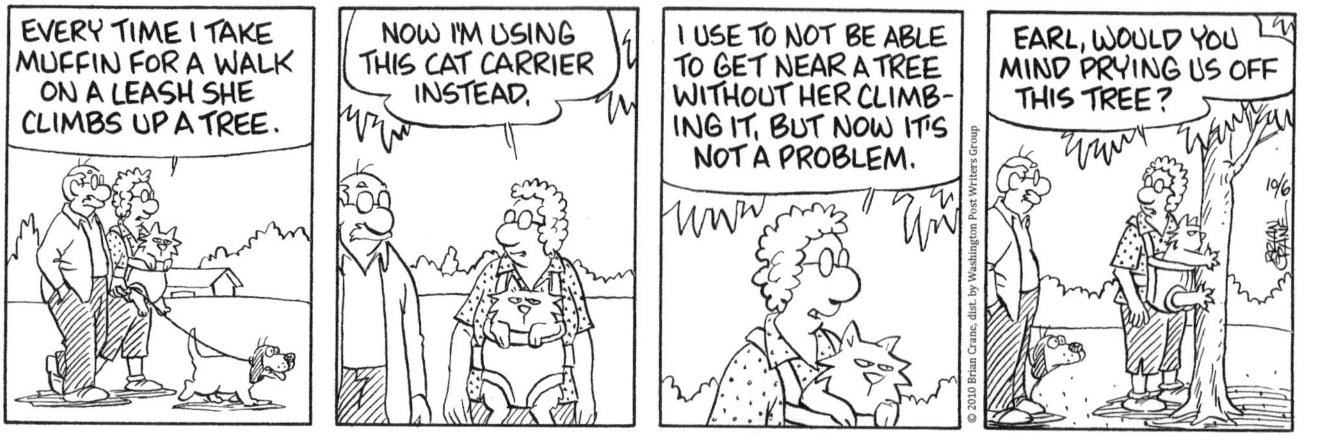
EVERY TIME I TAKE MUFFIN FOR A WALK ON A LEASH SHE CLIMBS UP A TREE.
NOW I'M USING THIS CAT CARRIER INSTEAD.
I USE TO NOT BE ABLE TO GET NEAR A TREE WITHOUT HER CLIMBING IT, BUT NOW IT'S NOT A PROBLEM.
© 2010 Brian Crane, dist. by Washington Post Writers Group
EARL, WOULD YOU MIND PRYING US OFF THIS TREE?
10/6

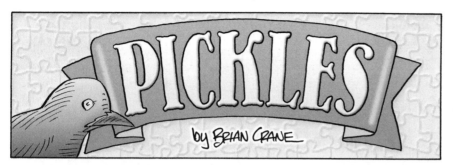

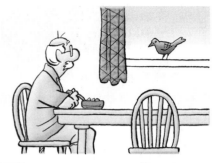

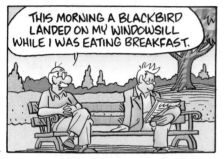

PICKLES
by BRIAN CRANE
THIS MORNING A BLACKBIRD LANDED ON MY WINDOWSILL WHILE I WAS EATING BREAKFAST.
I LOOKED AT HIM AND THEN I THINK HE WINKED AT ME.
ISN'T THAT A BAD OMEN OR SOMETHING?
A BAD OMEN?
YOU KNOW, A FORESHADOWING OF BAD FORTUNE TO COME.
I DON'T KNOW. MAYBE.
MY CORN FLAKES DID SEEM TO GET SOGGY UNUSUALLY FAST.
© 2010 Brian Crane, dist. by Washington Post Writers Group
8/15

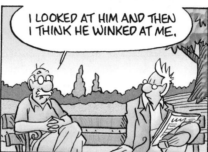

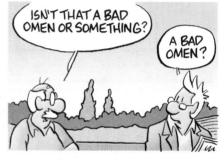

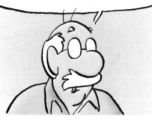

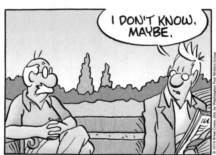

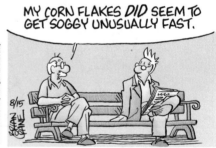

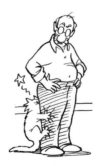

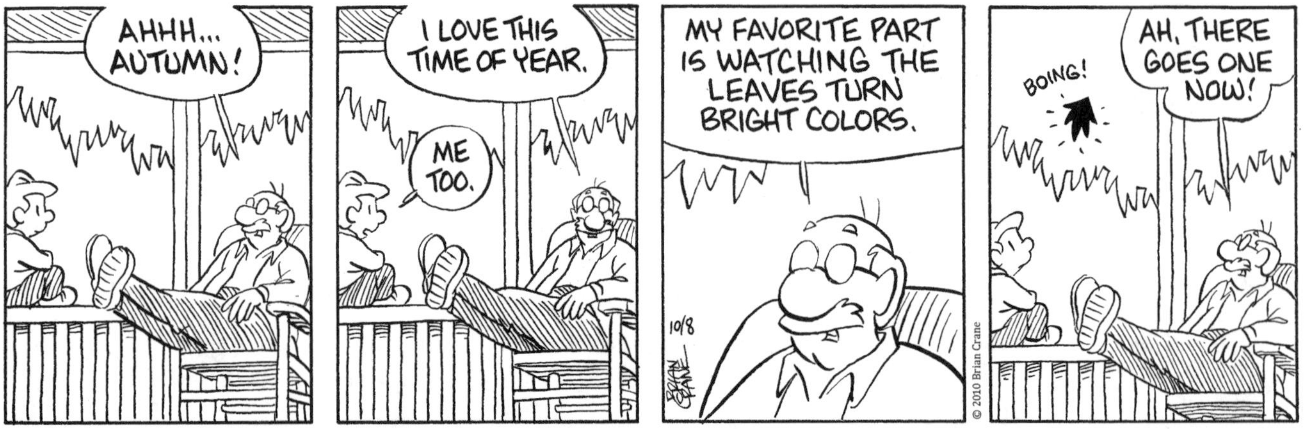
AHHH... AUTUMN!
I LOVE THIS TIME OF YEAR.
ME TOO.
MY FAVORITE PART IS WATCHING THE LEAVES TURN BRIGHT COLORS.
BOING!
AH, THERE GOES ONE NOW!

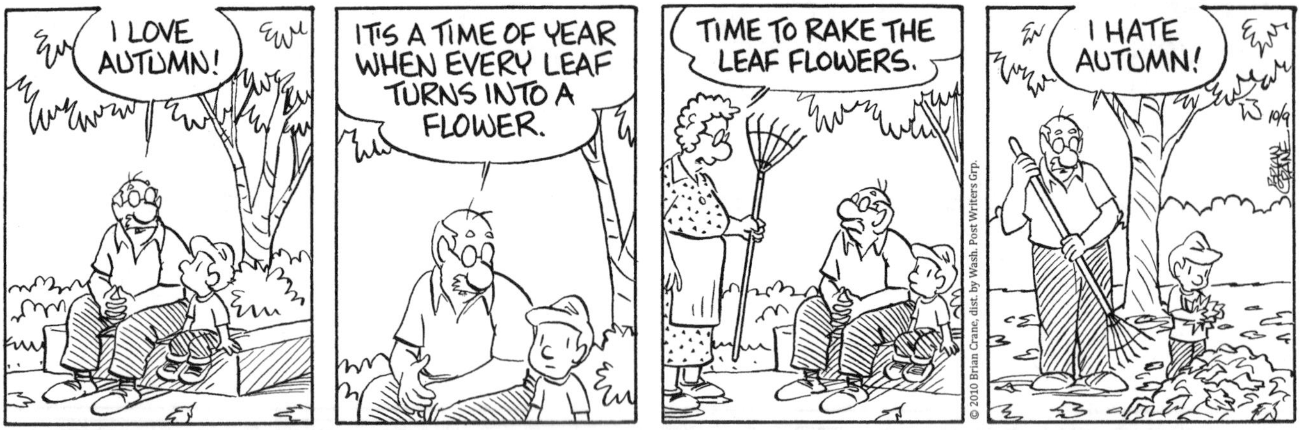
I LOVE AUTUMN!
IT'S A TIME OF YEAR WHEN EVERY LEAF TURNS INTO A FLOWER.
TIME TO RAKE THE LEAF FLOWERS.
I HATE AUTUMN!

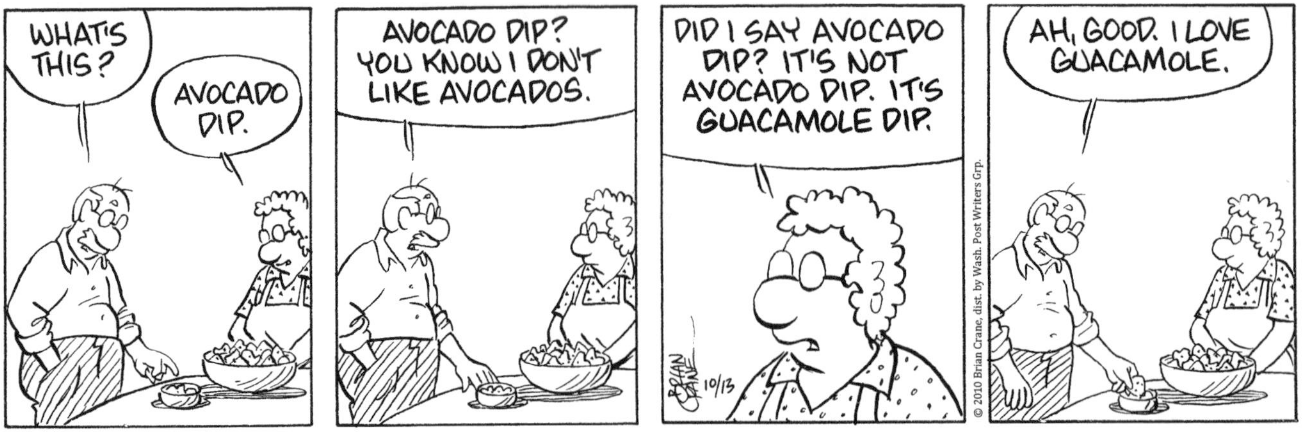
WHAT'S THIS?
AVOCADO DIP.
AVOCADO DIP? YOU KNOW I DON'T LIKE AVOCADOS.
DID I SAY AVOCADO DIP? IT'S NOT AVOCADO DIP. IT'S GUACAMOLE DIP.
AH, GOOD. I LOVE GUACAMOLE.

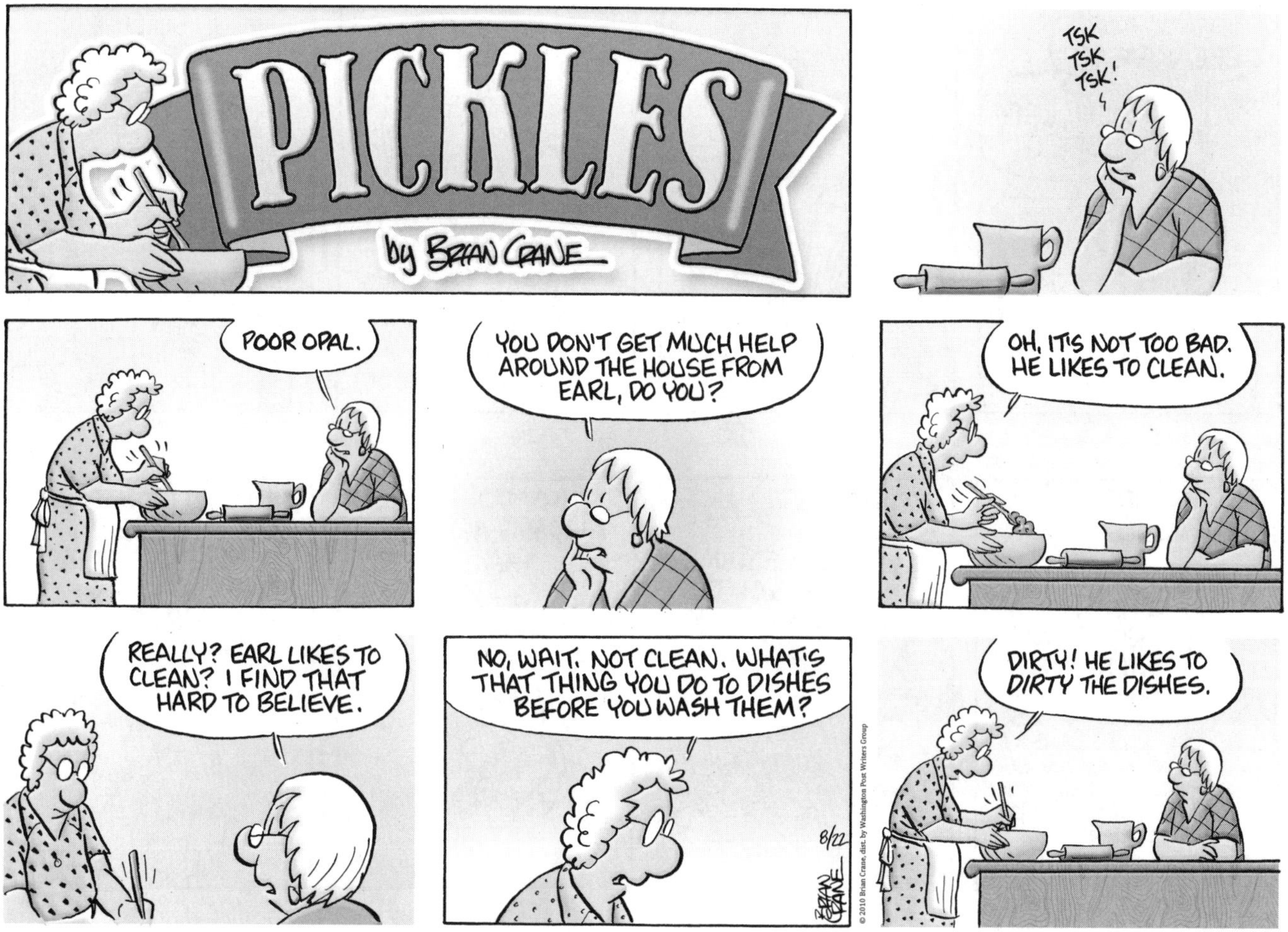
PICKLES
by BRIAN CRANE
TSK TSK TSK!
POOR OPAL.
YOU DON'T GET MUCH HELP AROUND THE HOUSE FROM EARL, DO YOU?
OH, IT'S NOT TOO BAD. HE LIKES TO CLEAN.
REALLY? EARL LIKES TO CLEAN? I FIND THAT HARD TO BELIEVE.
NO, WAIT. NOT CLEAN. WHAT'S THAT THING YOU DO TO DISHES BEFORE YOU WASH THEM?
8/22
BRIAN CRANE
© 2010 Brian Crane, dist. by Washington Post Writers Group
DIRTY! HE LIKES TO *DIRTY* THE DISHES.

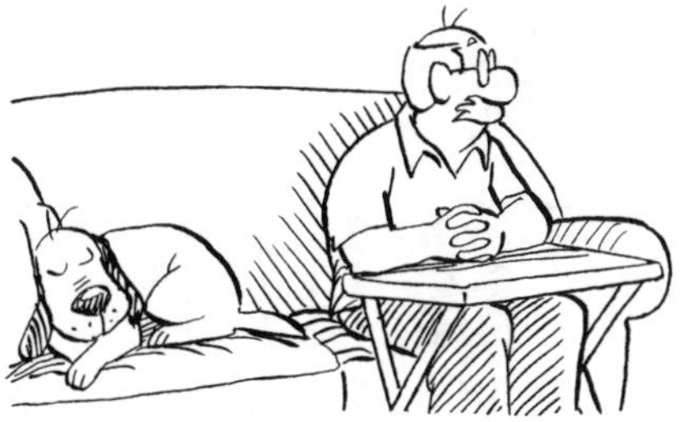

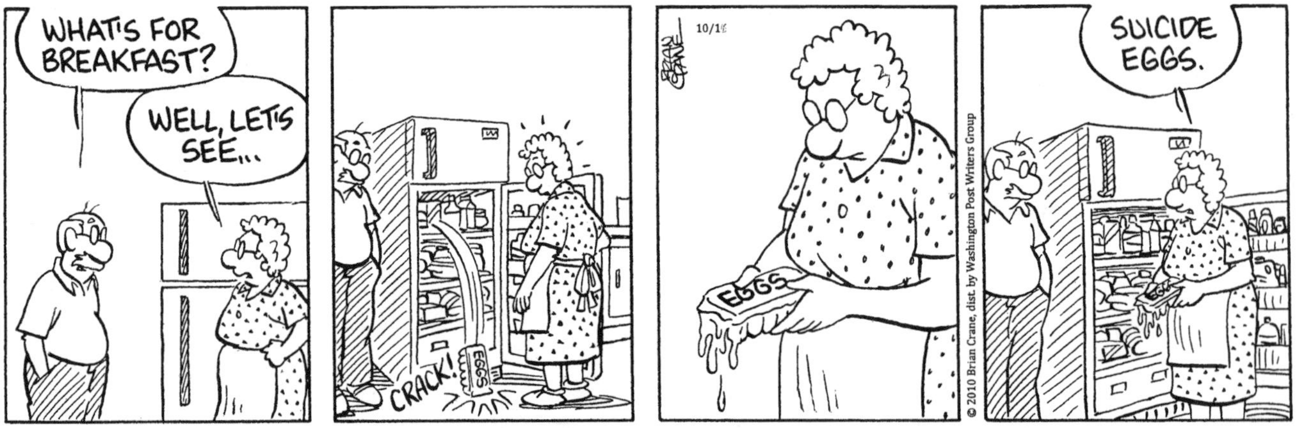
WHAT'S FOR BREAKFAST?
WELL, LET'S SEE...
CRACK!
EGGS
EGGS
SUICIDE EGGS.
© 2010 Brian Crane, dist. by Washington Post Writers Group

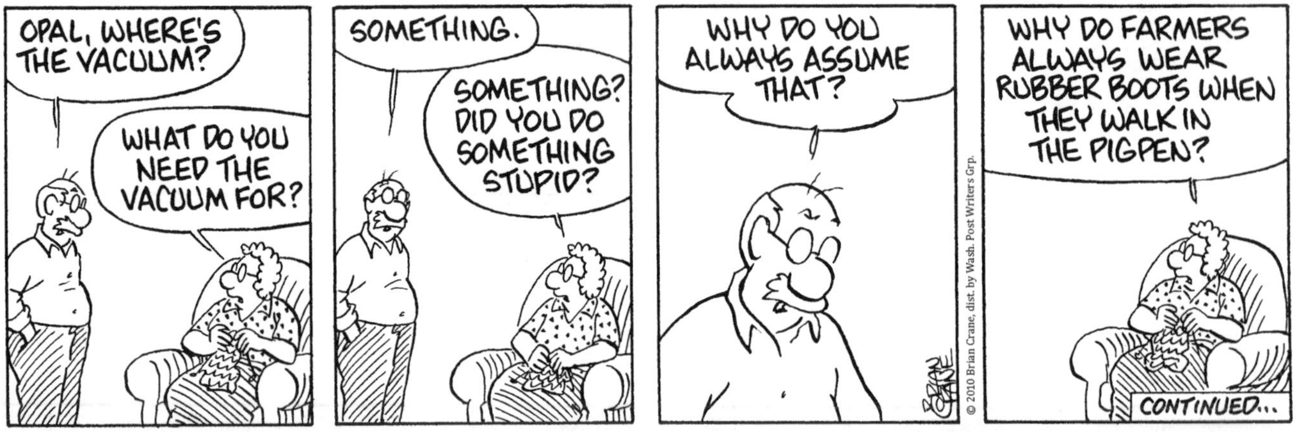
OPAL, WHERE'S THE VACUUM?
WHAT DO YOU NEED THE VACUUM FOR?
SOMETHING.
SOMETHING? DID YOU DO SOMETHING STUPID?
WHY DO YOU ALWAYS ASSUME THAT?
© 2010 Brian Crane, dist. by Wash. Post Writers Grp.
WHY DO FARMERS ALWAYS WEAR RUBBER BOOTS WHEN THEY WALK IN THE PIGPEN?
CONTINUED...

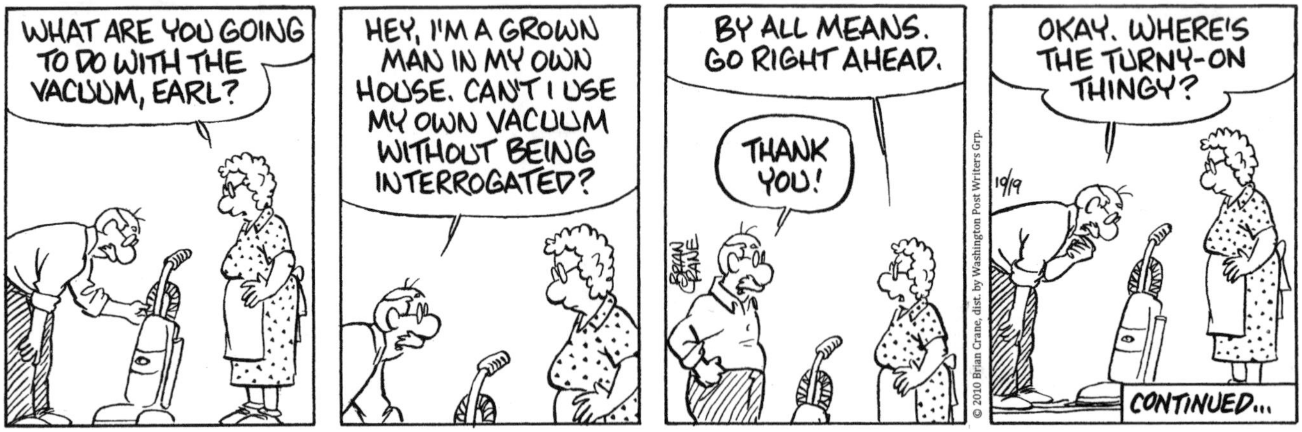
WHAT ARE YOU GOING TO DO WITH THE VACUUM, EARL?
HEY, I'M A GROWN MAN IN MY OWN HOUSE. CAN'T I USE MY OWN VACUUM WITHOUT BEING INTERROGATED?
BY ALL MEANS. GO RIGHT AHEAD.
THANK YOU!
© 2010 Brian Crane, dist. by Washington Post Writers Grp.
OKAY. WHERE'S THE TURNY-ON THINGY?
CONTINUED...

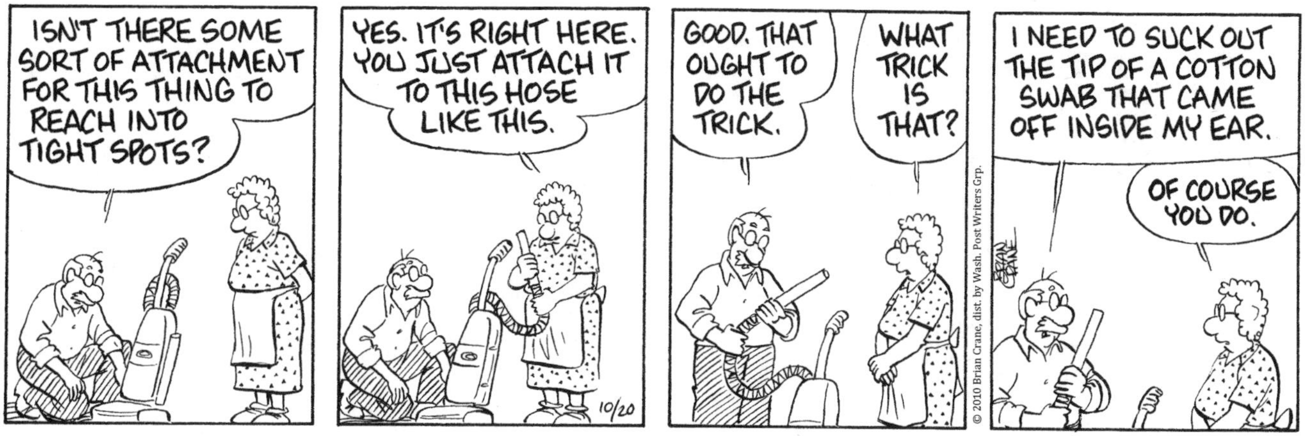
ISN'T THERE SOME SORT OF ATTACHMENT FOR THIS THING TO REACH INTO TIGHT SPOTS?
YES. IT'S RIGHT HERE. YOU JUST ATTACH IT TO THIS HOSE LIKE THIS.
10/20
GOOD. THAT OUGHT TO DO THE TRICK.
WHAT TRICK IS THAT?
© 2010 Brian Crane, dist. by Wash. Post Writers Grp.
I NEED TO SUCK OUT THE TIP OF A COTTON SWAB THAT CAME OFF INSIDE MY EAR.
OF COURSE YOU DO.
BRIAN CRANE

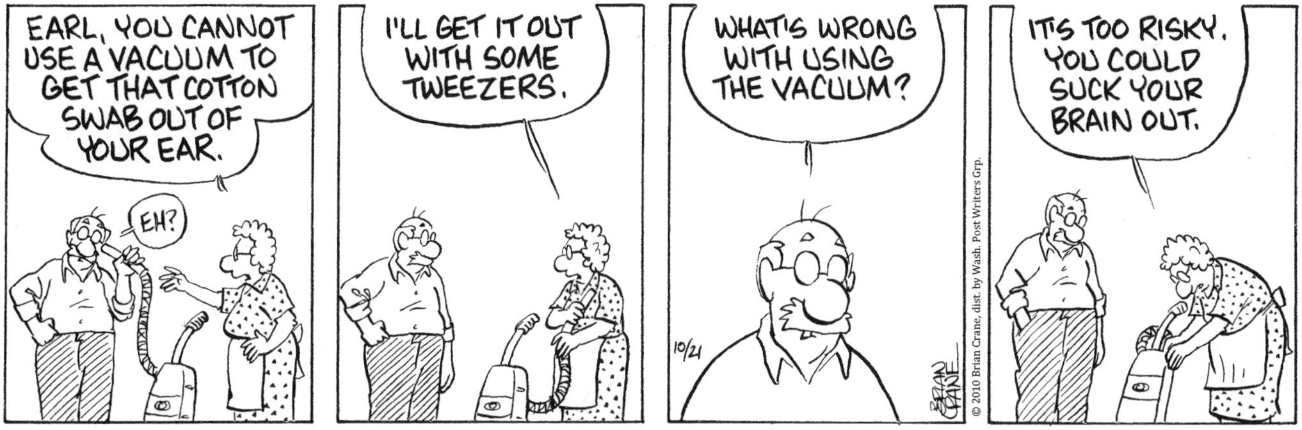
EARL, YOU CANNOT USE A VACUUM TO GET THAT COTTON SWAB OUT OF YOUR EAR.
EH?
I'LL GET IT OUT WITH SOME TWEEZERS.
WHAT'S WRONG WITH USING THE VACUUM?
10/21
BRIAN CRANE
© 2010 Brian Crane, dist. by Wash. Post Writers Grp.
IT'S TOO RISKY. YOU COULD SUCK YOUR BRAIN OUT.

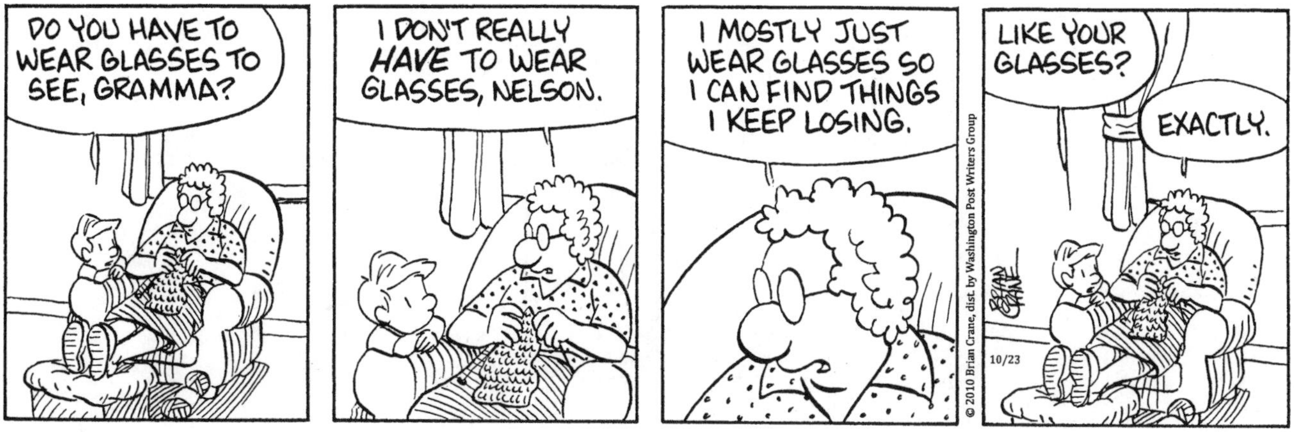
DO YOU HAVE TO WEAR GLASSES TO SEE, GRAMMA?
I DON'T REALLY *HAVE* TO WEAR GLASSES, NELSON.
I MOSTLY JUST WEAR GLASSES SO I CAN FIND THINGS I KEEP LOSING.
© 2010 Brian Crane, dist. by Washington Post Writers Group
LIKE YOUR GLASSES?
EXACTLY.
BRIAN CRANE
10/23

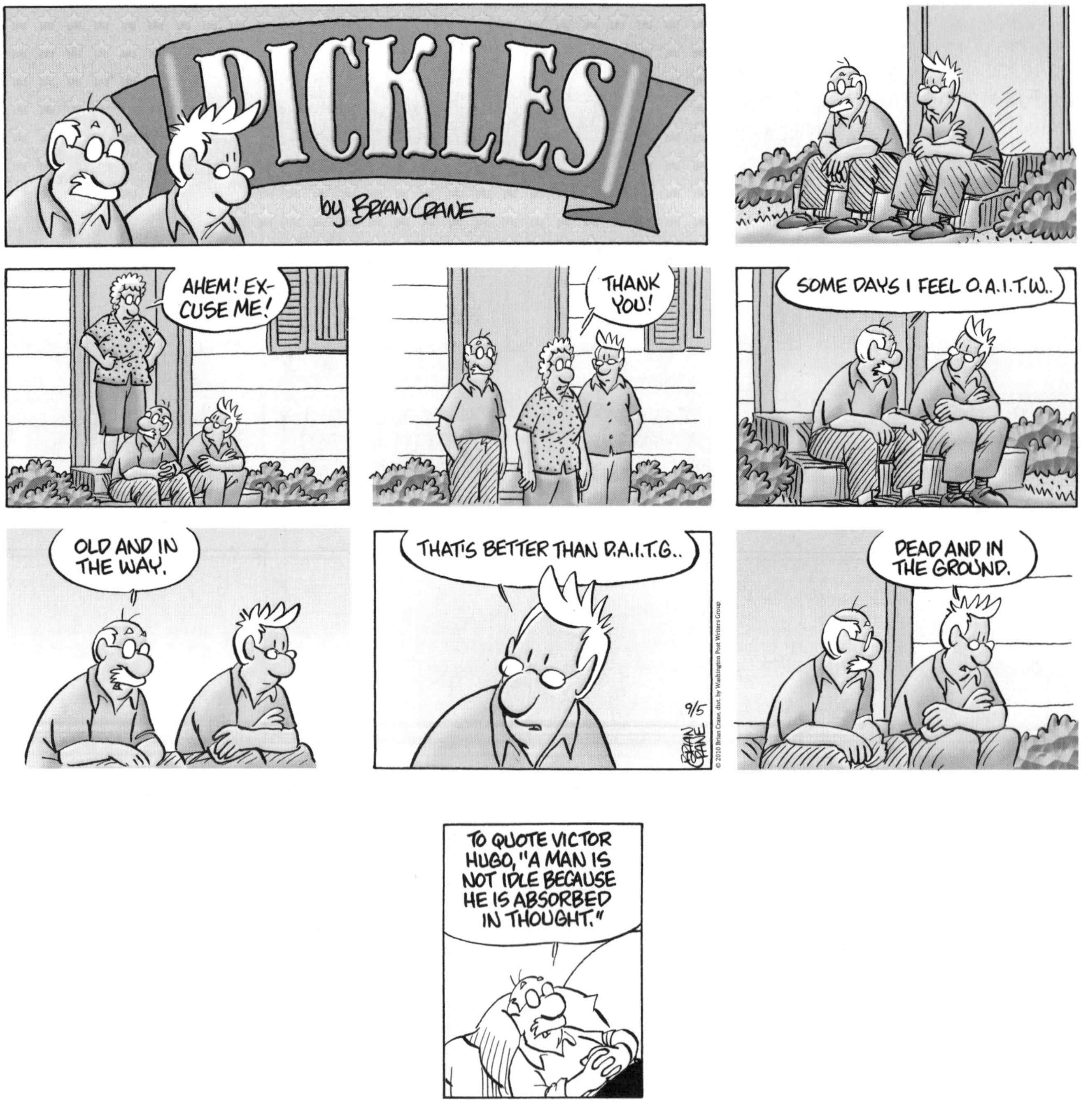
PICKLES
by BRIAN CRANE
AHEM! EX-CUSE ME!
THANK YOU!
SOME DAYS I FEEL O.A.I.T.W..
OLD AND IN THE WAY.
THAT'S BETTER THAN D.A.I.T.G..
9/5
BRIAN CRANE
© 2010 Brian Crane, dist. by Washington Post Writers Group
DEAD AND IN THE GROUND.
TO QUOTE VICTOR HUGO, "A MAN IS NOT IDLE BECAUSE HE IS ABSORBED IN THOUGHT."

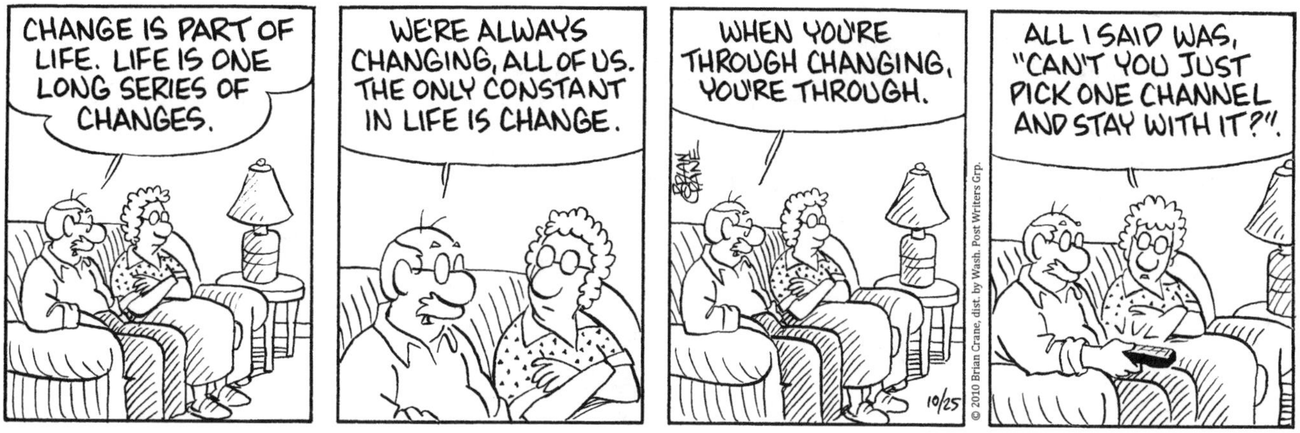
CHANGE IS PART OF LIFE. LIFE IS ONE LONG SERIES OF CHANGES.
WE'RE ALWAYS CHANGING, ALL OF US. THE ONLY CONSTANT IN LIFE IS CHANGE.
WHEN YOU'RE THROUGH CHANGING, YOU'RE THROUGH.
ALL I SAID WAS, "CAN'T YOU JUST PICK ONE CHANNEL AND STAY WITH IT?".
BRIAN CRANE
10/25
© 2010 Brian Crane, dist. by Wash. Post Writers Grp.

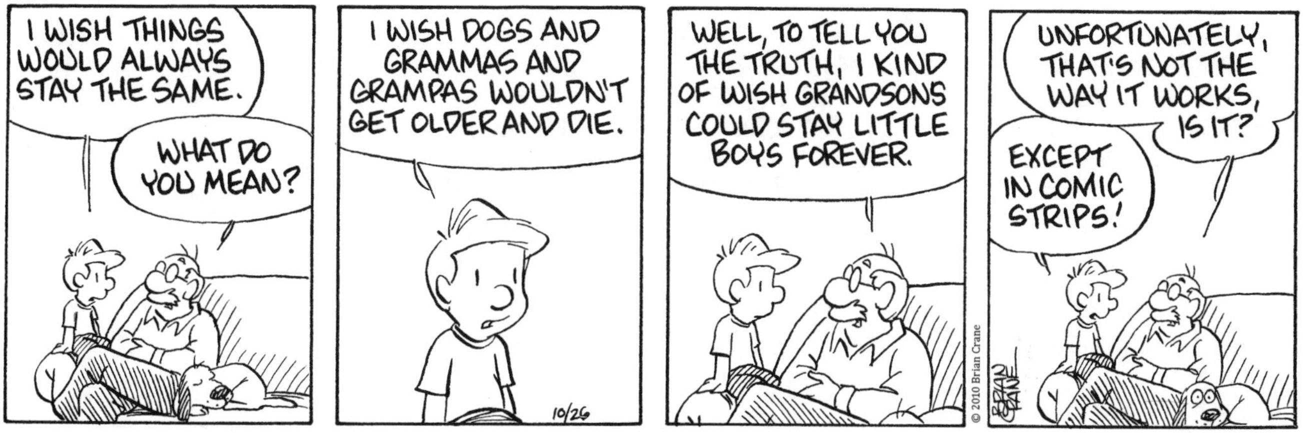
I WISH THINGS WOULD ALWAYS STAY THE SAME.
WHAT DO YOU MEAN?
I WISH DOGS AND GRAMMAS AND GRAMPAS WOULDN'T GET OLDER AND DIE.
10/26
WELL, TO TELL YOU THE TRUTH, I KIND OF WISH GRANDSONS COULD STAY LITTLE BOYS FOREVER.
© 2010 Brian Crane
UNFORTUNATELY, THAT'S NOT THE WAY IT WORKS, IS IT?
EXCEPT IN COMIC STRIPS!
BRIAN CRANE

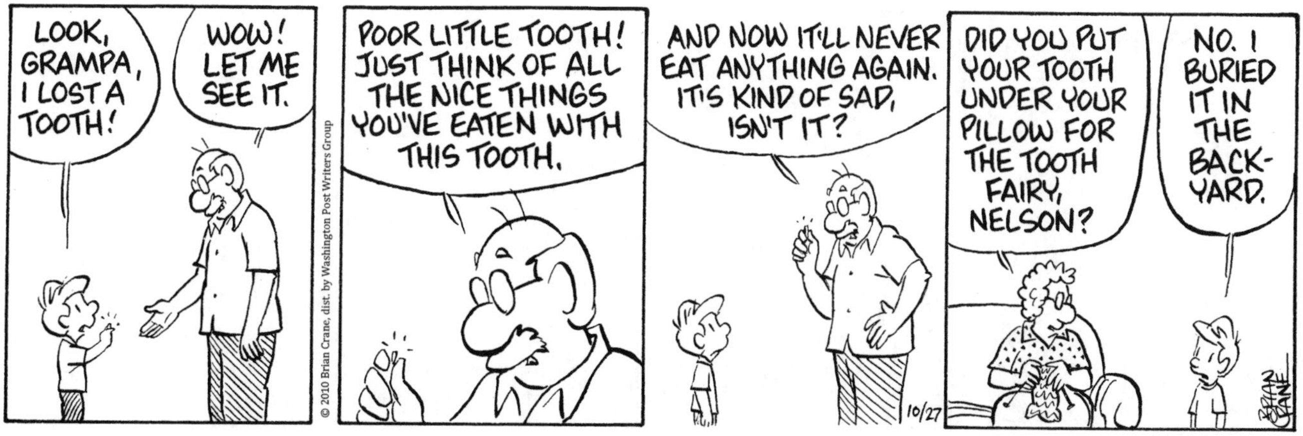
LOOK, GRAMPA, I LOST A TOOTH!
WOW! LET ME SEE IT.
© 2010 Brian Crane, dist. by Washington Post Writers Group
POOR LITTLE TOOTH! JUST THINK OF ALL THE NICE THINGS YOU'VE EATEN WITH THIS TOOTH.
AND NOW IT'LL NEVER EAT ANYTHING AGAIN. IT'S KIND OF SAD, ISN'T IT?
10/27
DID YOU PUT YOUR TOOTH UNDER YOUR PILLOW FOR THE TOOTH FAIRY, NELSON?
NO. I BURIED IT IN THE BACK-YARD.
BRIAN CRANE

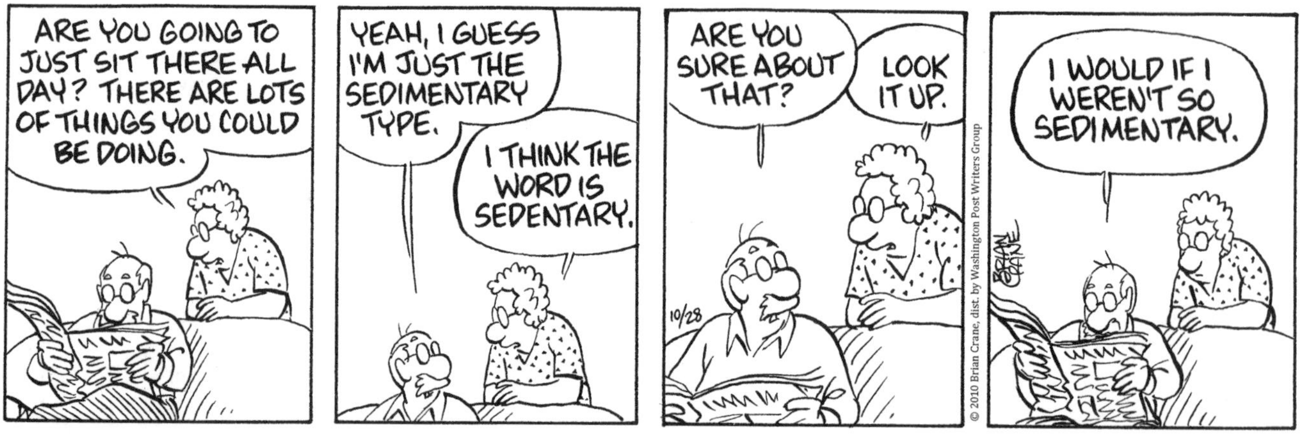
ARE YOU GOING TO JUST SIT THERE ALL DAY? THERE ARE LOTS OF THINGS YOU COULD BE DOING.
YEAH, I GUESS I'M JUST THE SEDIMENTARY TYPE.
I THINK THE WORD IS SEDENTARY.
ARE YOU SURE ABOUT THAT?
LOOK IT UP.
10/28
I WOULD IF I WEREN'T SO SEDIMENTARY.
BRIAN CRANE

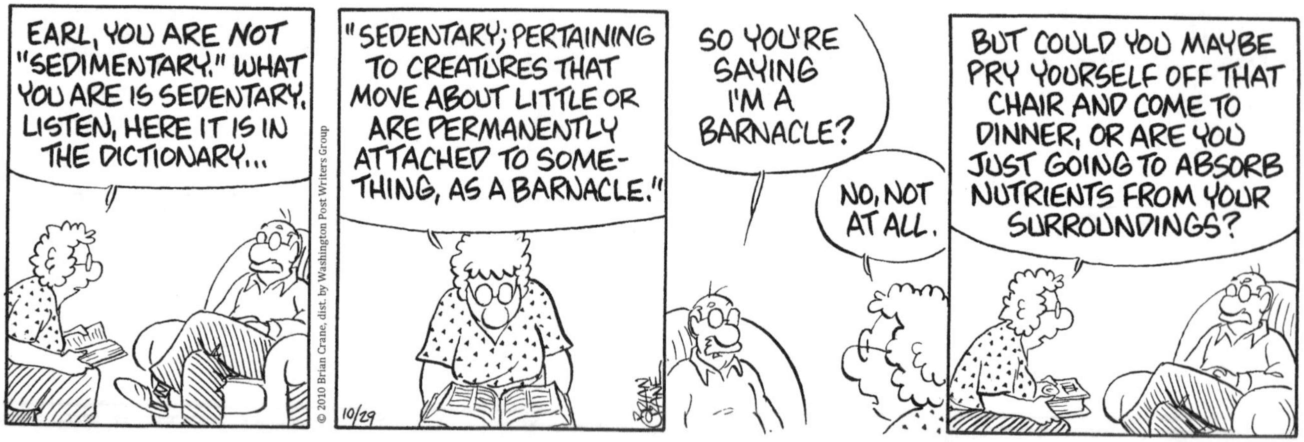
EARL, YOU ARE *NOT* "SEDIMENTARY." WHAT YOU ARE IS SEDENTARY. LISTEN, HERE IT IS IN THE DICTIONARY...
"SEDENTARY; PERTAINING TO CREATURES THAT MOVE ABOUT LITTLE OR ARE PERMANENTLY ATTACHED TO SOMETHING, AS A BARNACLE."
10/29
BRIAN CRANE
SO YOU'RE SAYING I'M A BARNACLE?
NO, NOT AT ALL.
BUT COULD YOU MAYBE PRY YOURSELF OFF THAT CHAIR AND COME TO DINNER, OR ARE YOU JUST GOING TO ABSORB NUTRIENTS FROM YOUR SURROUNDINGS?

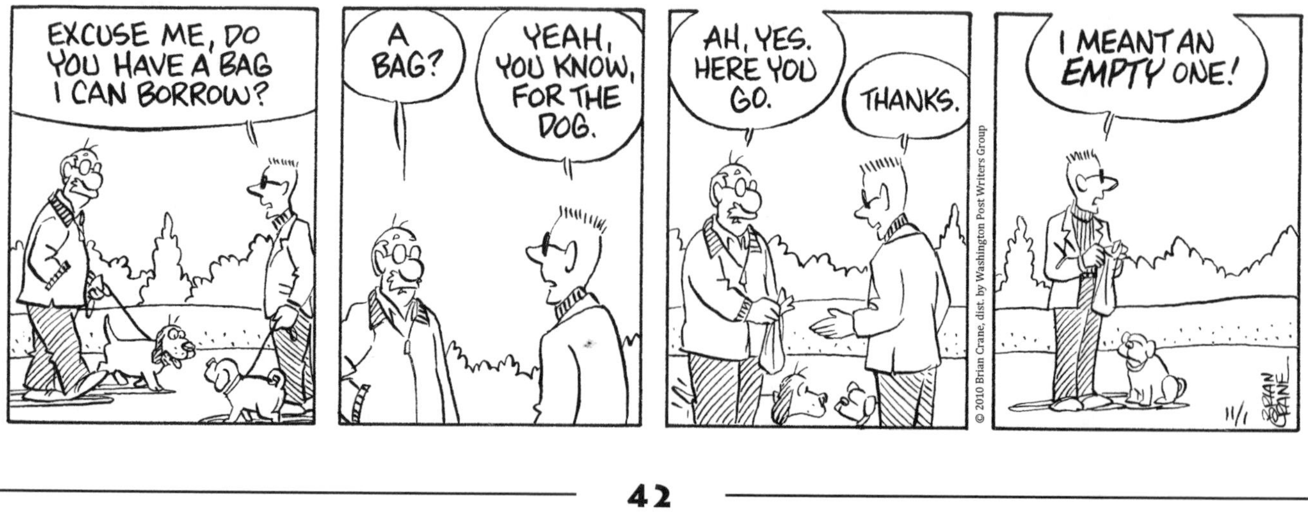
EXCUSE ME, DO YOU HAVE A BAG I CAN BORROW?
A BAG?
YEAH, YOU KNOW, FOR THE DOG.
AH, YES. HERE YOU GO.
THANKS.
I MEANT AN *EMPTY* ONE!
11/1
BRIAN CRANE

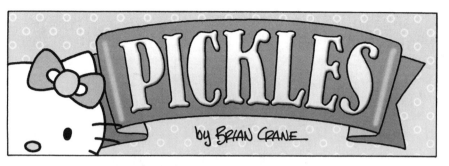

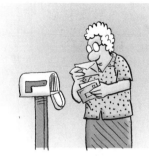

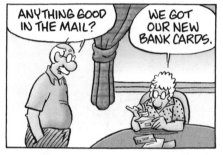

PICKLES
by BRIAN CRANE
ANYTHING GOOD IN THE MAIL?
WE GOT OUR NEW BANK CARDS.
GREAT. MY OLD CARD'S JUST ABOUT EXPIRED.
WELL, HERE'S A BRAND NEW ONE FOR YOU.
THANKS.
WHAT THE...?!
EARL PICKLES
WHY DOES MY CARD HAVE A "HELLO KITTY" DESIGN ON IT?!
© 2010 Brian Crane, dist. by Washington Post Writers Group
I THOUGHT THAT MIGHT KEEP YOU FROM USING IT SO MUCH.
9/12
BRIAN CRANE

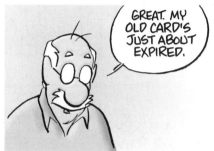

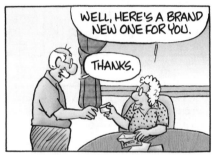

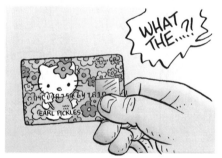

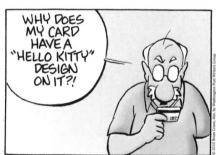

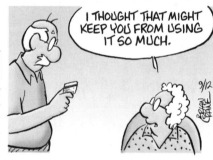

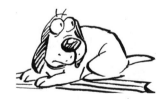

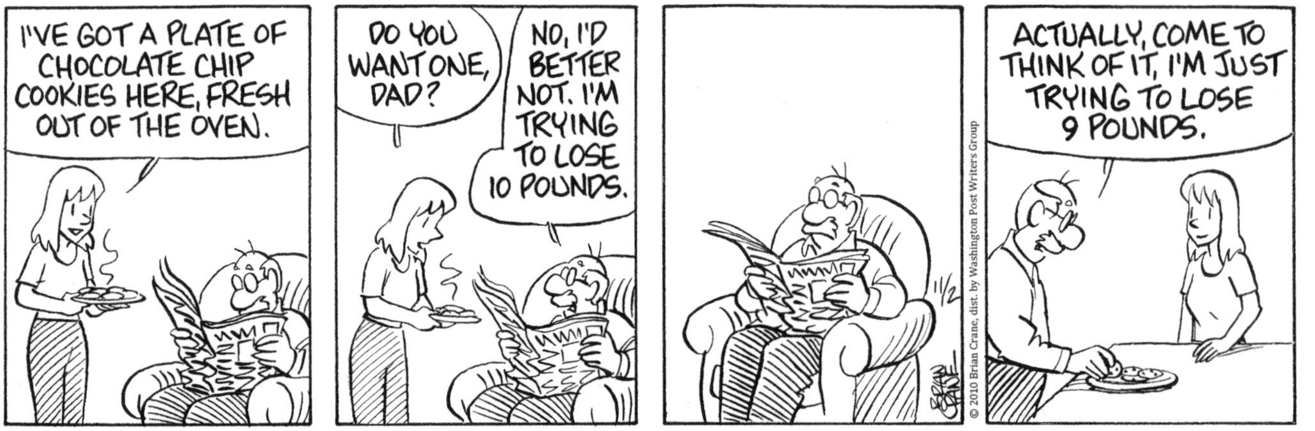
I'VE GOT A PLATE OF CHOCOLATE CHIP COOKIES HERE, FRESH OUT OF THE OVEN.
DO YOU WANT ONE, DAD?
NO, I'D BETTER NOT. I'M TRYING TO LOSE 10 POUNDS.
11/2
ACTUALLY, COME TO THINK OF IT, I'M JUST TRYING TO LOSE 9 POUNDS.
© 2010 Brian Crane, dist. by Washington Post Writers Group

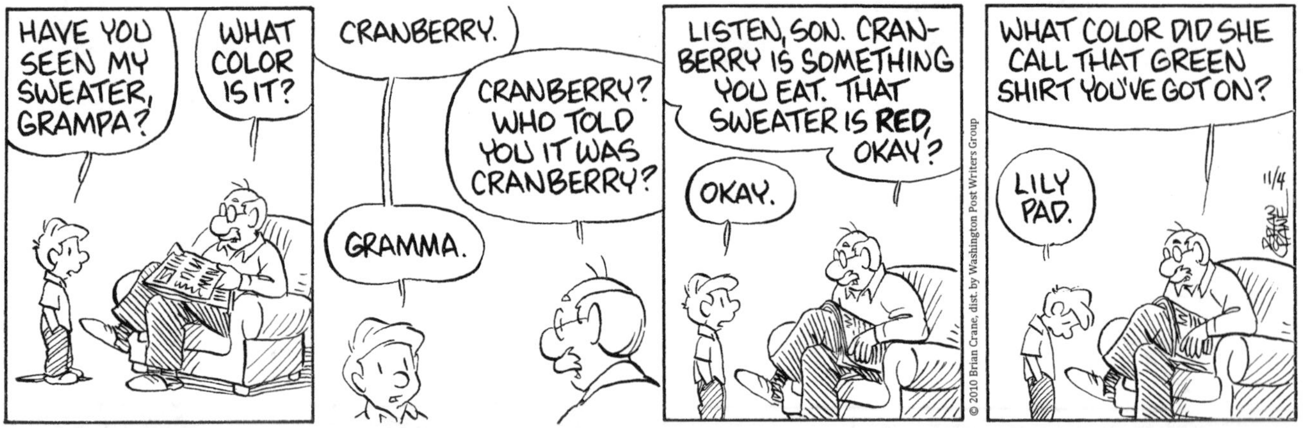
HAVE YOU SEEN MY SWEATER, GRAMPA?
WHAT COLOR IS IT?
CRANBERRY.
CRANBERRY? WHO TOLD YOU IT WAS CRANBERRY?
GRAMMA.
LISTEN, SON. CRANBERRY IS SOMETHING YOU EAT. THAT SWEATER IS **RED**, OKAY?
OKAY.
WHAT COLOR DID SHE CALL THAT GREEN SHIRT YOU'VE GOT ON?
LILY PAD.
11/4
© 2010 Brian Crane, dist. by Washington Post Writers Group

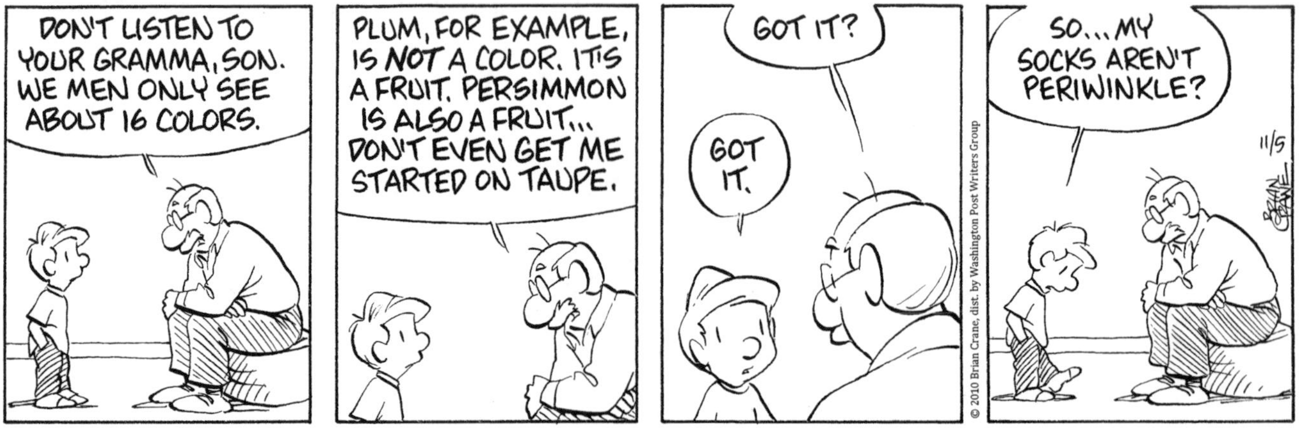
DON'T LISTEN TO YOUR GRAMMA, SON. WE MEN ONLY SEE ABOUT 16 COLORS.
PLUM, FOR EXAMPLE, IS **NOT** A COLOR. IT'S A FRUIT. PERSIMMON IS ALSO A FRUIT... DON'T EVEN GET ME STARTED ON TAUPE.
GOT IT?
GOT IT.
SO... MY SOCKS AREN'T PERIWINKLE?
11/5
© 2010 Brian Crane, dist. by Washington Post Writers Group

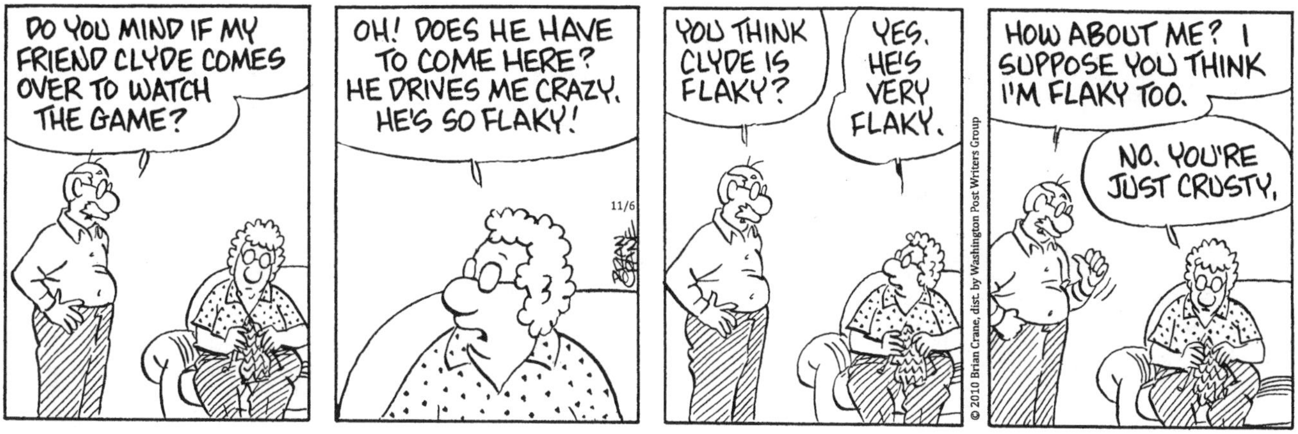
DO YOU MIND IF MY FRIEND CLYDE COMES OVER TO WATCH THE GAME?
OH! DOES HE HAVE TO COME HERE? HE DRIVES ME CRAZY. HE'S SO FLAKY!
11/6
YOU THINK CLYDE IS FLAKY?
YES. HE'S VERY FLAKY.
HOW ABOUT ME? I SUPPOSE YOU THINK I'M FLAKY TOO.
NO. YOU'RE JUST CRUSTY.

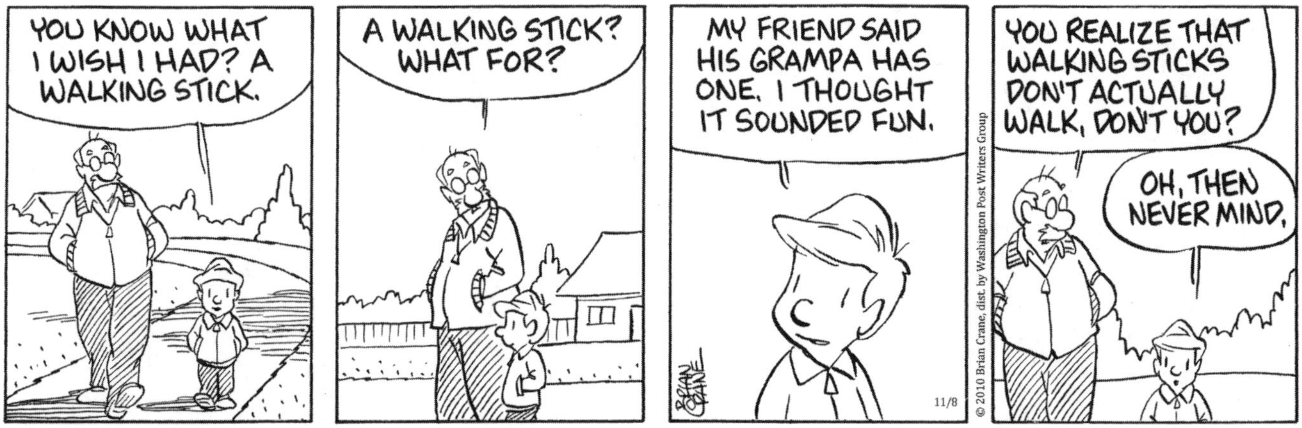
YOU KNOW WHAT I WISH I HAD? A WALKING STICK.
A WALKING STICK? WHAT FOR?
MY FRIEND SAID HIS GRAMPA HAS ONE. I THOUGHT IT SOUNDED FUN.
11/8
YOU REALIZE THAT WALKING STICKS DON'T ACTUALLY WALK, DON'T YOU?
OH, THEN NEVER MIND.

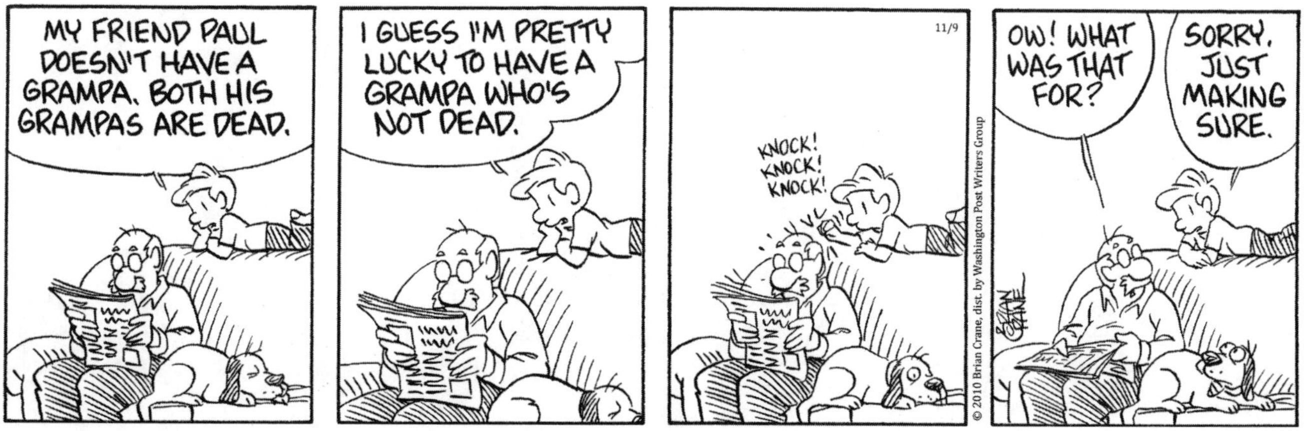
MY FRIEND PAUL DOESN'T HAVE A GRAMPA. BOTH HIS GRAMPAS ARE DEAD.
I GUESS I'M PRETTY LUCKY TO HAVE A GRAMPA WHO'S NOT DEAD.
11/9
KNOCK! KNOCK! KNOCK!
OW! WHAT WAS THAT FOR?
SORRY. JUST MAKING SURE.

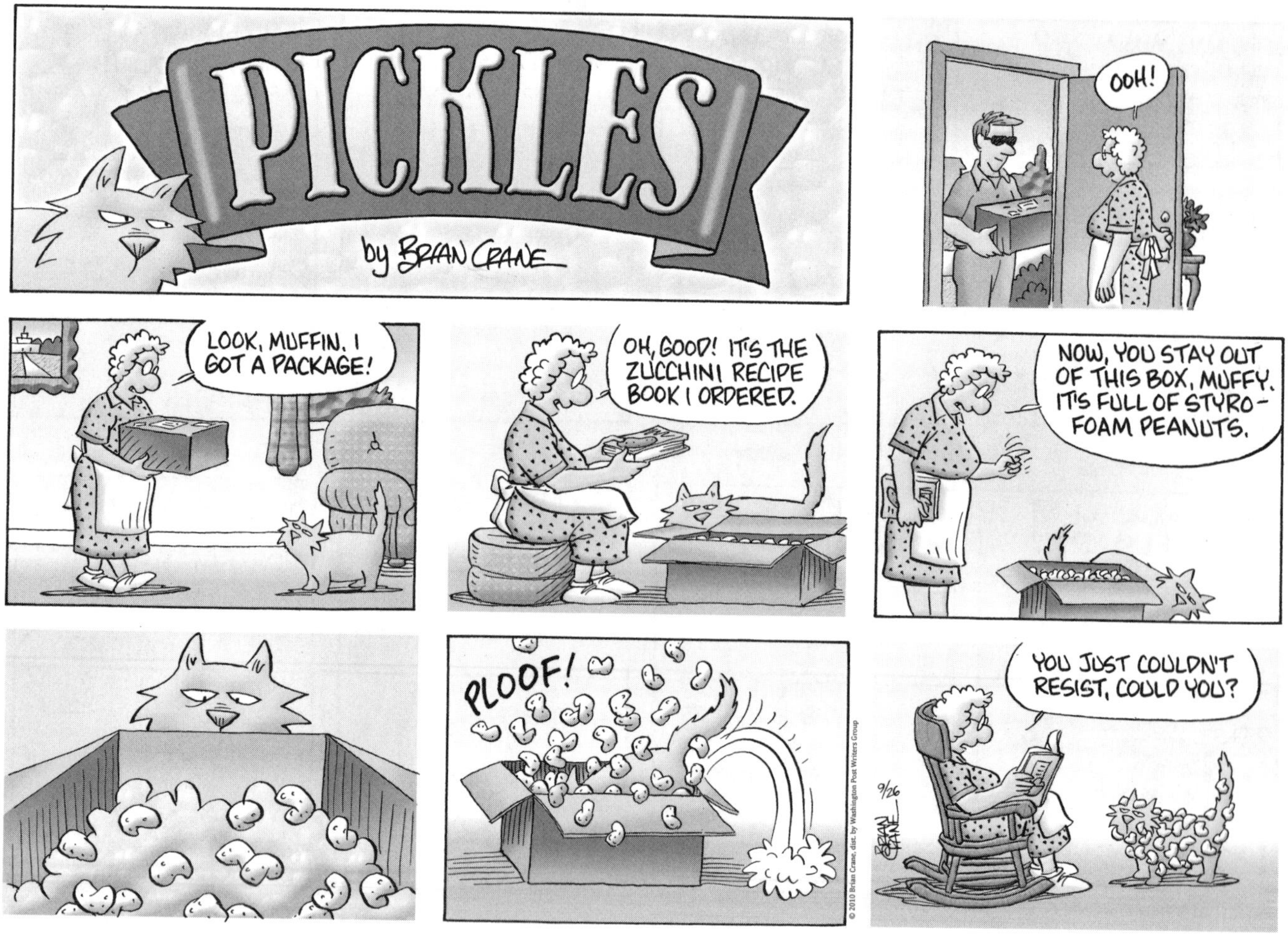
PICKLES
by BRIAN CRANE
OOH!
LOOK, MUFFIN. I GOT A PACKAGE!
OH, GOOD! IT'S THE ZUCCHINI RECIPE BOOK I ORDERED.
NOW, YOU STAY OUT OF THIS BOX, MUFFY. IT'S FULL OF STYRO-FOAM PEANUTS.
PLOOF!
© 2010 Brian Crane, dist. by Washington Post Writers Group
YOU JUST COULDN'T RESIST, COULD YOU?
9/26
BRIAN CRANE

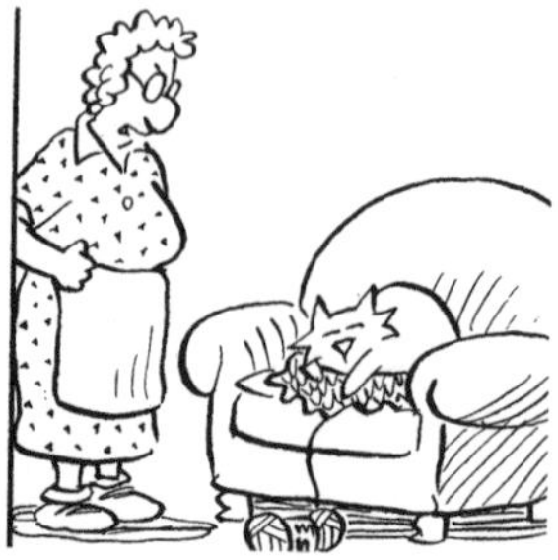

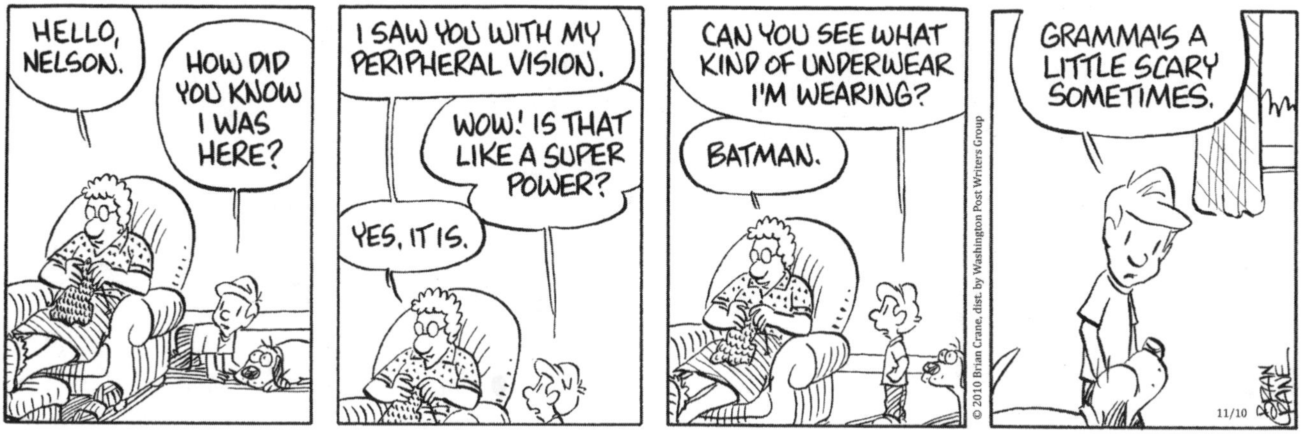
HELLO, NELSON.
HOW DID YOU KNOW I WAS HERE?
I SAW YOU WITH MY PERIPHERAL VISION.
WOW! IS THAT LIKE A SUPER POWER?
YES, IT IS.
CAN YOU SEE WHAT KIND OF UNDERWEAR I'M WEARING?
BATMAN.
GRAMMA'S A LITTLE SCARY SOMETIMES.
© 2010 Brian Crane, dist. by Washington Post Writers Group
11/10

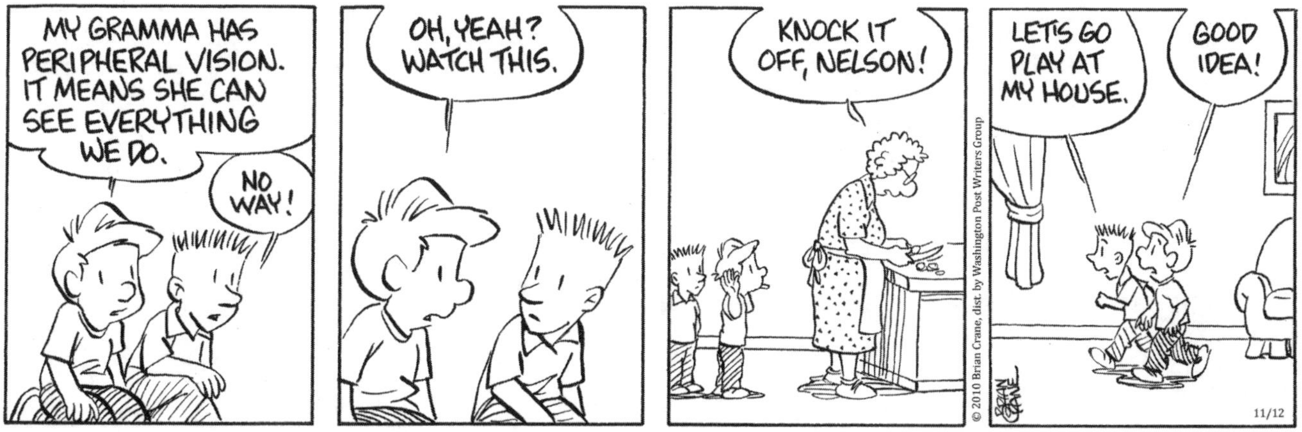
MY GRAMMA HAS PERIPHERAL VISION. IT MEANS SHE CAN SEE EVERYTHING WE DO.
NO WAY!
OH, YEAH? WATCH THIS.
KNOCK IT OFF, NELSON!
LET'S GO PLAY AT MY HOUSE.
GOOD IDEA!
© 2010 Brian Crane, dist. by Washington Post Writers Group
11/12

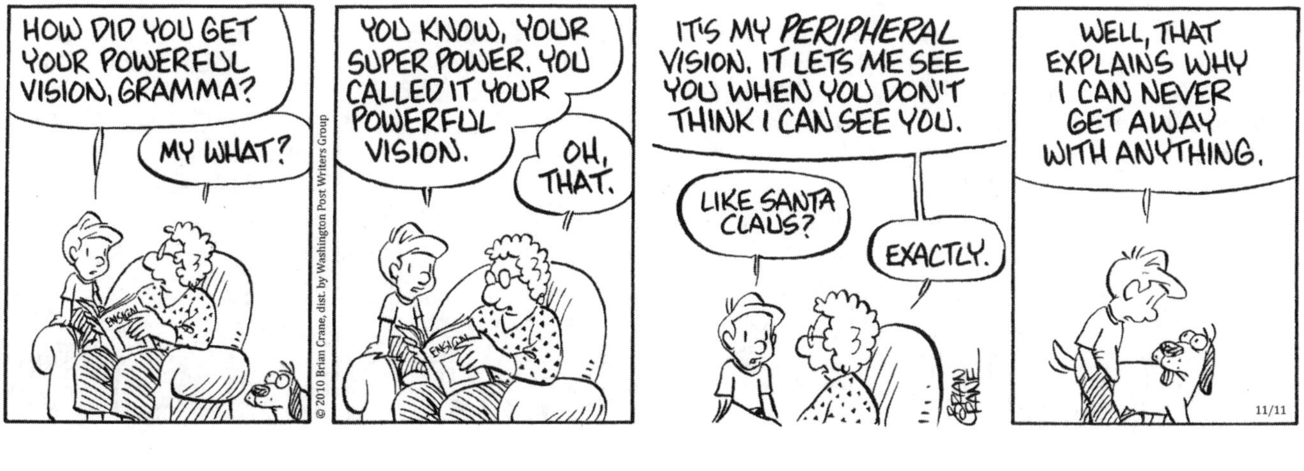
HOW DID YOU GET YOUR POWERFUL VISION, GRAMMA?
MY WHAT?
YOU KNOW, YOUR SUPER POWER. YOU CALLED IT YOUR POWERFUL VISION.
OH, THAT.
IT'S MY PERIPHERAL VISION. IT LETS ME SEE YOU WHEN YOU DON'T THINK I CAN SEE YOU.
LIKE SANTA CLAUS?
EXACTLY.
WELL, THAT EXPLAINS WHY I CAN NEVER GET AWAY WITH ANYTHING.
© 2010 Brian Crane, dist. by Washington Post Writers Group
11/11

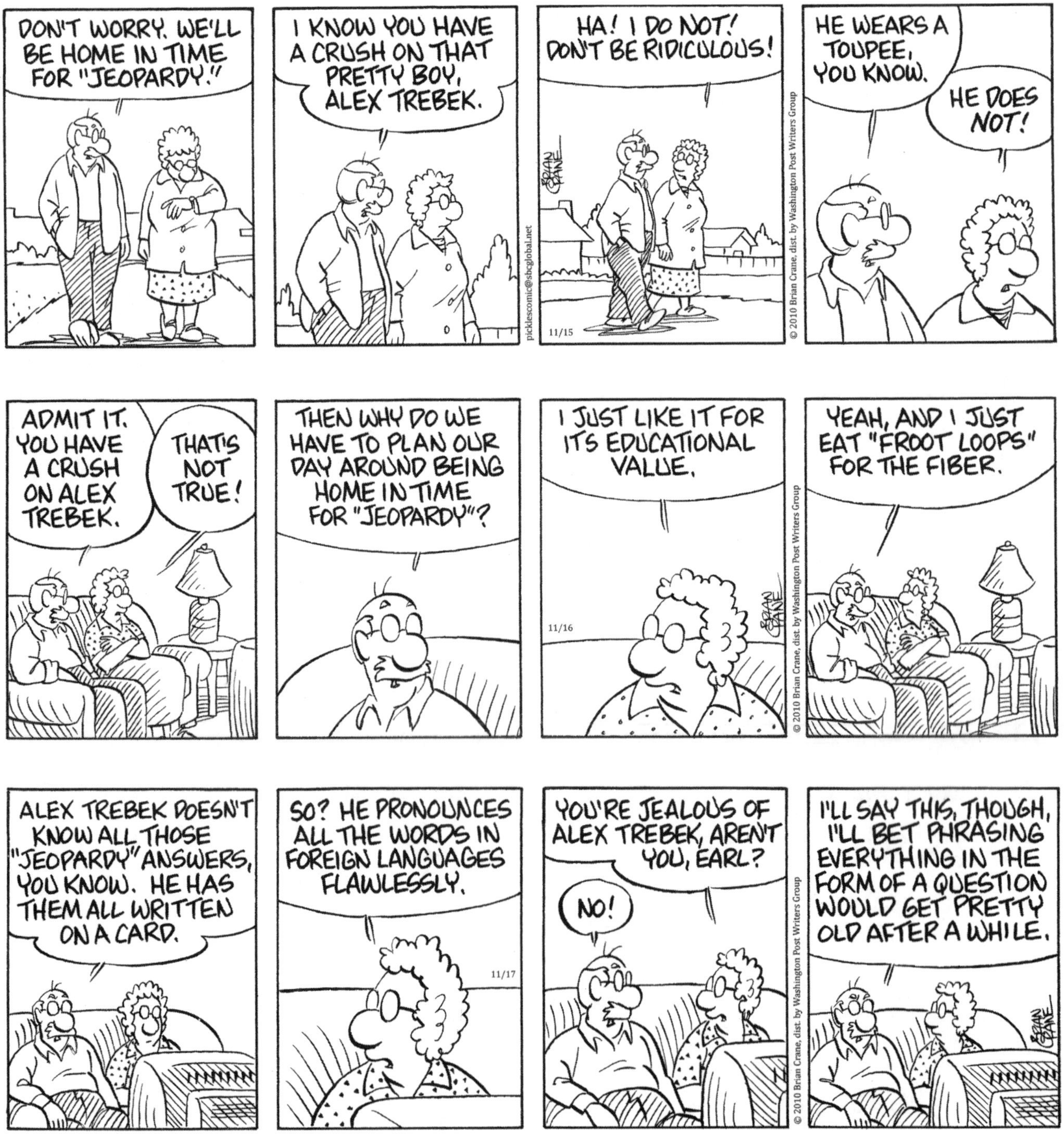
DON'T WORRY. WE'LL BE HOME IN TIME FOR "JEOPARDY."
I KNOW YOU HAVE A CRUSH ON THAT PRETTY BOY, ALEX TREBEK.
HA! I DO NOT! DON'T BE RIDICULOUS!
HE WEARS A TOUPEE, YOU KNOW.
HE DOES NOT!
picklescomic@sbcglobal.net
11/15
© 2010 Brian Crane, dist. by Washington Post Writers Group
ADMIT IT. YOU HAVE A CRUSH ON ALEX TREBEK.
THAT'S NOT TRUE!
THEN WHY DO WE HAVE TO PLAN OUR DAY AROUND BEING HOME IN TIME FOR "JEOPARDY"?
I JUST LIKE IT FOR ITS EDUCATIONAL VALUE.
11/16
YEAH, AND I JUST EAT "FROOT LOOPS" FOR THE FIBER.
© 2010 Brian Crane, dist. by Washington Post Writers Group
ALEX TREBEK DOESN'T KNOW ALL THOSE "JEOPARDY" ANSWERS, YOU KNOW. HE HAS THEM ALL WRITTEN ON A CARD.
SO? HE PRONOUNCES ALL THE WORDS IN FOREIGN LANGUAGES FLAWLESSLY.
11/17
YOU'RE JEALOUS OF ALEX TREBEK, AREN'T YOU, EARL?
NO!
I'LL SAY THIS, THOUGH, I'LL BET PHRASING EVERYTHING IN THE FORM OF A QUESTION WOULD GET PRETTY OLD AFTER A WHILE.
© 2010 Brian Crane, dist. by Washington Post Writers Group

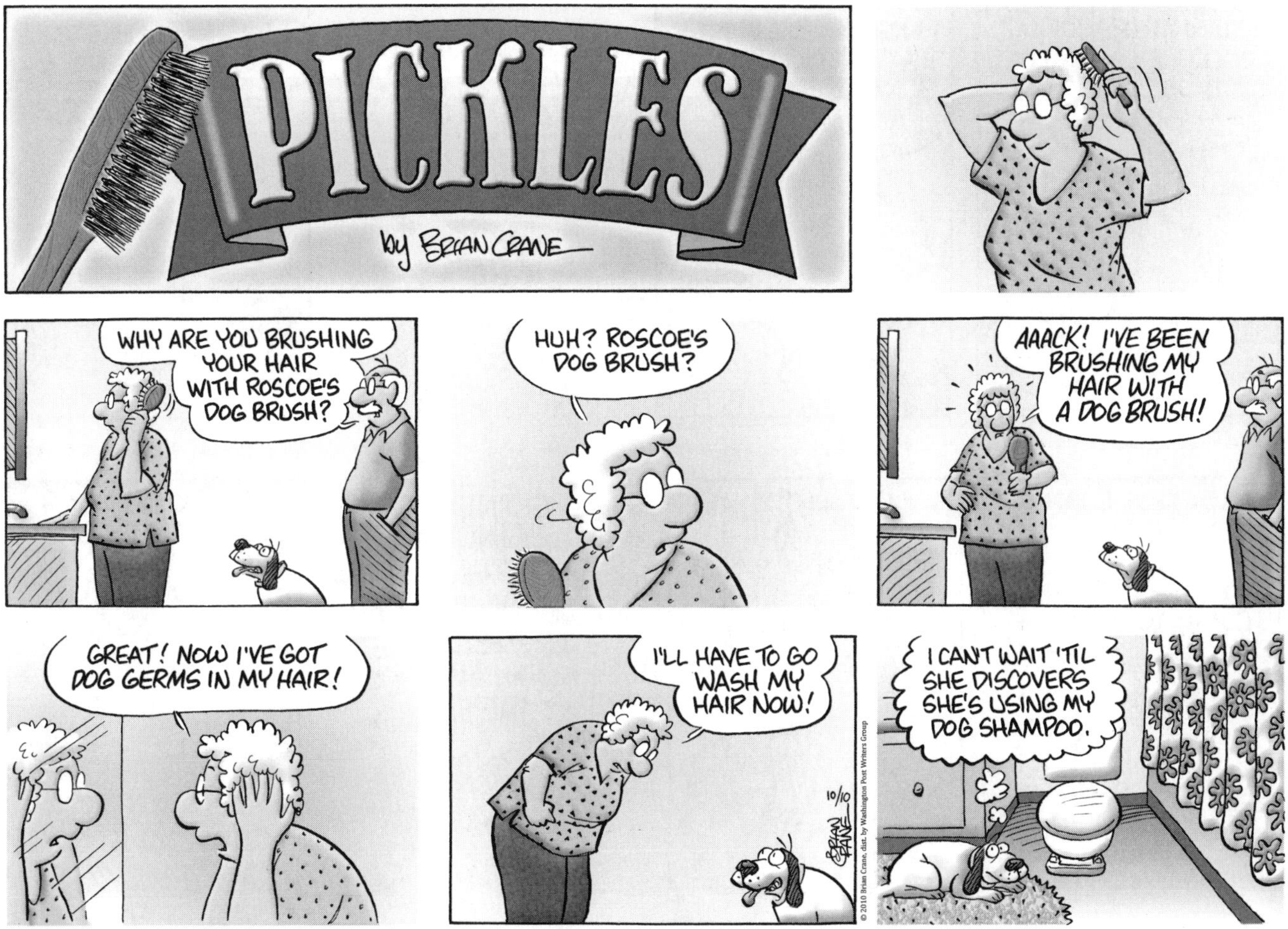
PICKLES
by Brian Crane
WHY ARE YOU BRUSHING YOUR HAIR WITH ROSCOE'S DOG BRUSH?
HUH? ROSCOE'S DOG BRUSH?
AAACK! I'VE BEEN BRUSHING MY HAIR WITH A DOG BRUSH!
GREAT! NOW I'VE GOT DOG GERMS IN MY HAIR!
I'LL HAVE TO GO WASH MY HAIR NOW!
10/10
BRIAN CRANE
© 2010 Brian Crane, dist. by Washington Post Writers Group
I CAN'T WAIT 'TIL SHE DISCOVERS SHE'S USING MY DOG SHAMPOO.

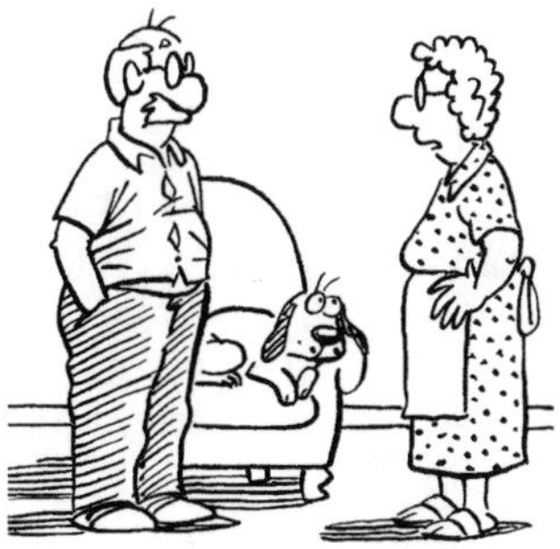

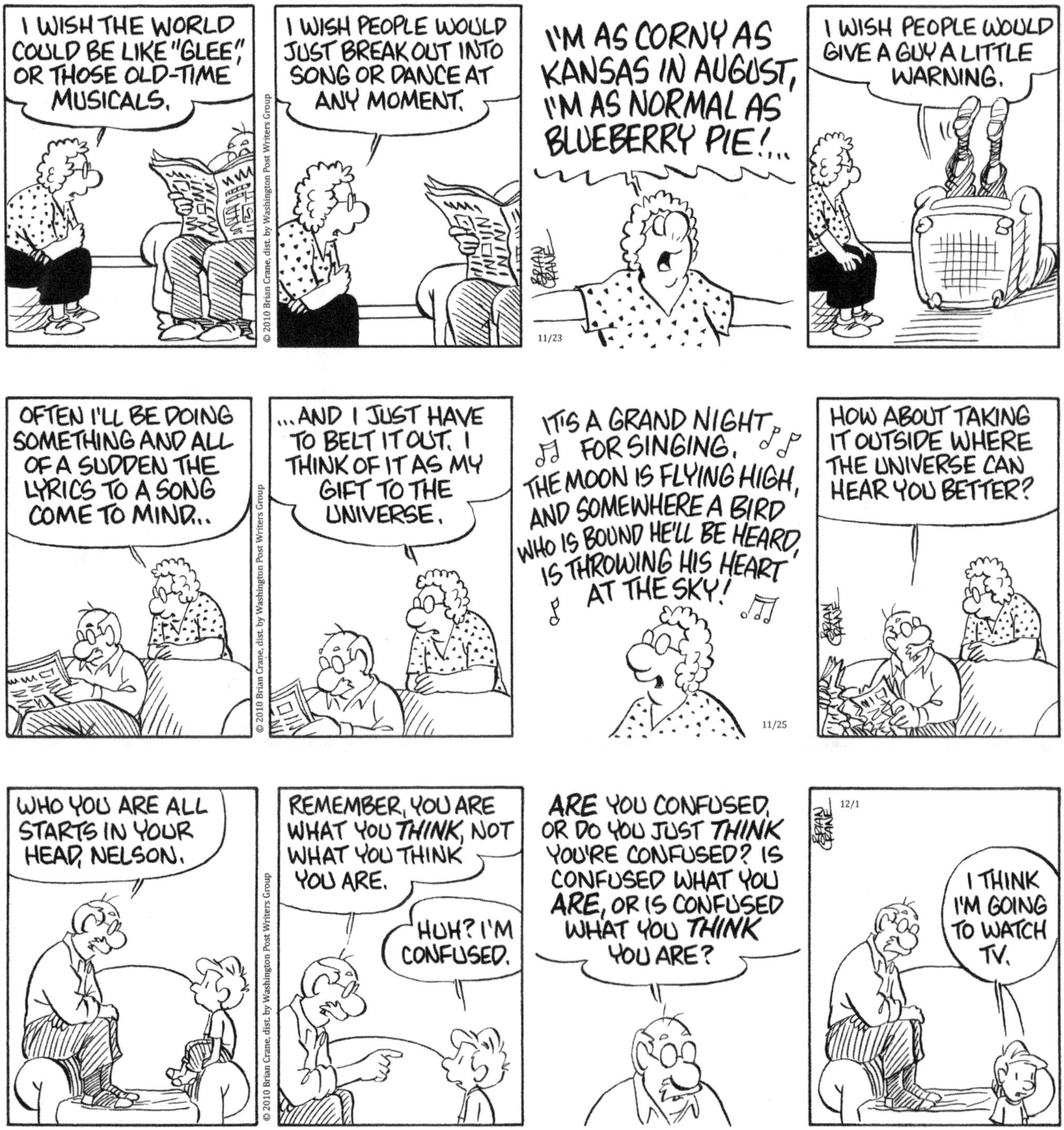
I WISH THE WORLD COULD BE LIKE "GLEE," OR THOSE OLD-TIME MUSICALS.
I WISH PEOPLE WOULD JUST BREAK OUT INTO SONG OR DANCE AT ANY MOMENT.
I'M AS CORNY AS KANSAS IN AUGUST, I'M AS NORMAL AS BLUEBERRY PIE!...
I WISH PEOPLE WOULD GIVE A GUY A LITTLE WARNING.
© 2010 Brian Crane, dist. by Washington Post Writers Group
11/23
OFTEN I'LL BE DOING SOMETHING AND ALL OF A SUDDEN THE LYRICS TO A SONG COME TO MIND...
...AND I JUST HAVE TO BELT IT OUT. I THINK OF IT AS MY GIFT TO THE UNIVERSE.
IT'S A GRAND NIGHT FOR SINGING. THE MOON IS FLYING HIGH, AND SOMEWHERE A BIRD WHO IS BOUND HE'LL BE HEARD, IS THROWING HIS HEART AT THE SKY!
HOW ABOUT TAKING IT OUTSIDE WHERE THE UNIVERSE CAN HEAR YOU BETTER?
© 2010 Brian Crane, dist. by Washington Post Writers Group
11/25
WHO YOU ARE ALL STARTS IN YOUR HEAD, NELSON.
REMEMBER, YOU ARE WHAT YOU THINK, NOT WHAT YOU THINK YOU ARE.
HUH? I'M CONFUSED.
ARE YOU CONFUSED, OR DO YOU JUST THINK YOU'RE CONFUSED? IS CONFUSED WHAT YOU ARE, OR IS CONFUSED WHAT YOU THINK YOU ARE?
I THINK I'M GOING TO WATCH TV.
© 2010 Brian Crane, dist. by Washington Post Writers Group
12/1

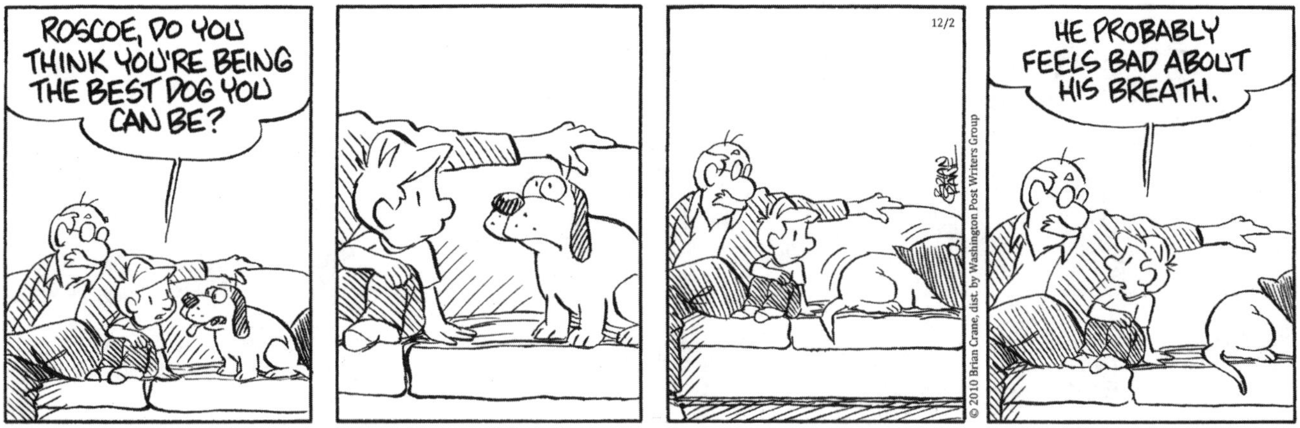
ROSCOE, DO YOU THINK YOU'RE BEING THE BEST DOG YOU CAN BE?
12/2
© 2010 Brian Crane, dist. by Washington Post Writers Group
HE PROBABLY FEELS BAD ABOUT HIS BREATH.

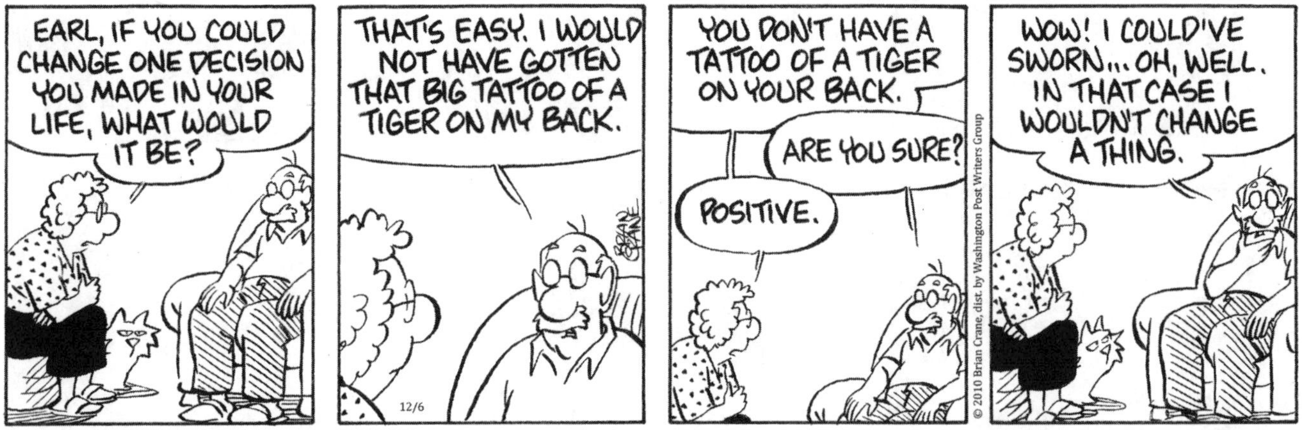
EARL, IF YOU COULD CHANGE ONE DECISION YOU MADE IN YOUR LIFE, WHAT WOULD IT BE?
THAT'S EASY. I WOULD NOT HAVE GOTTEN THAT BIG TATTOO OF A TIGER ON MY BACK.
12/6
YOU DON'T HAVE A TATTOO OF A TIGER ON YOUR BACK.
ARE YOU SURE?
POSITIVE.
© 2010 Brian Crane, dist. by Washington Post Writers Group
WOW! I COULD'VE SWORN... OH, WELL. IN THAT CASE I WOULDN'T CHANGE A THING.

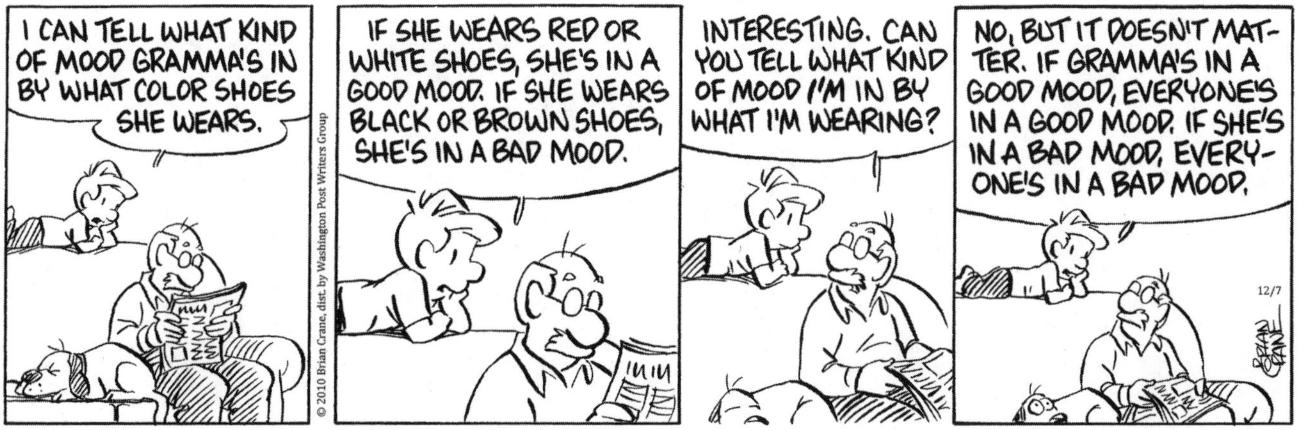
I CAN TELL WHAT KIND OF MOOD GRAMMA'S IN BY WHAT COLOR SHOES SHE WEARS.
© 2010 Brian Crane, dist. by Washington Post Writers Group
IF SHE WEARS RED OR WHITE SHOES, SHE'S IN A GOOD MOOD. IF SHE WEARS BLACK OR BROWN SHOES, SHE'S IN A BAD MOOD.
INTERESTING. CAN YOU TELL WHAT KIND OF MOOD I'M IN BY WHAT I'M WEARING?
NO, BUT IT DOESN'T MATTER. IF GRAMMA'S IN A GOOD MOOD, EVERYONE'S IN A GOOD MOOD. IF SHE'S IN A BAD MOOD, EVERYONE'S IN A BAD MOOD.
12/7

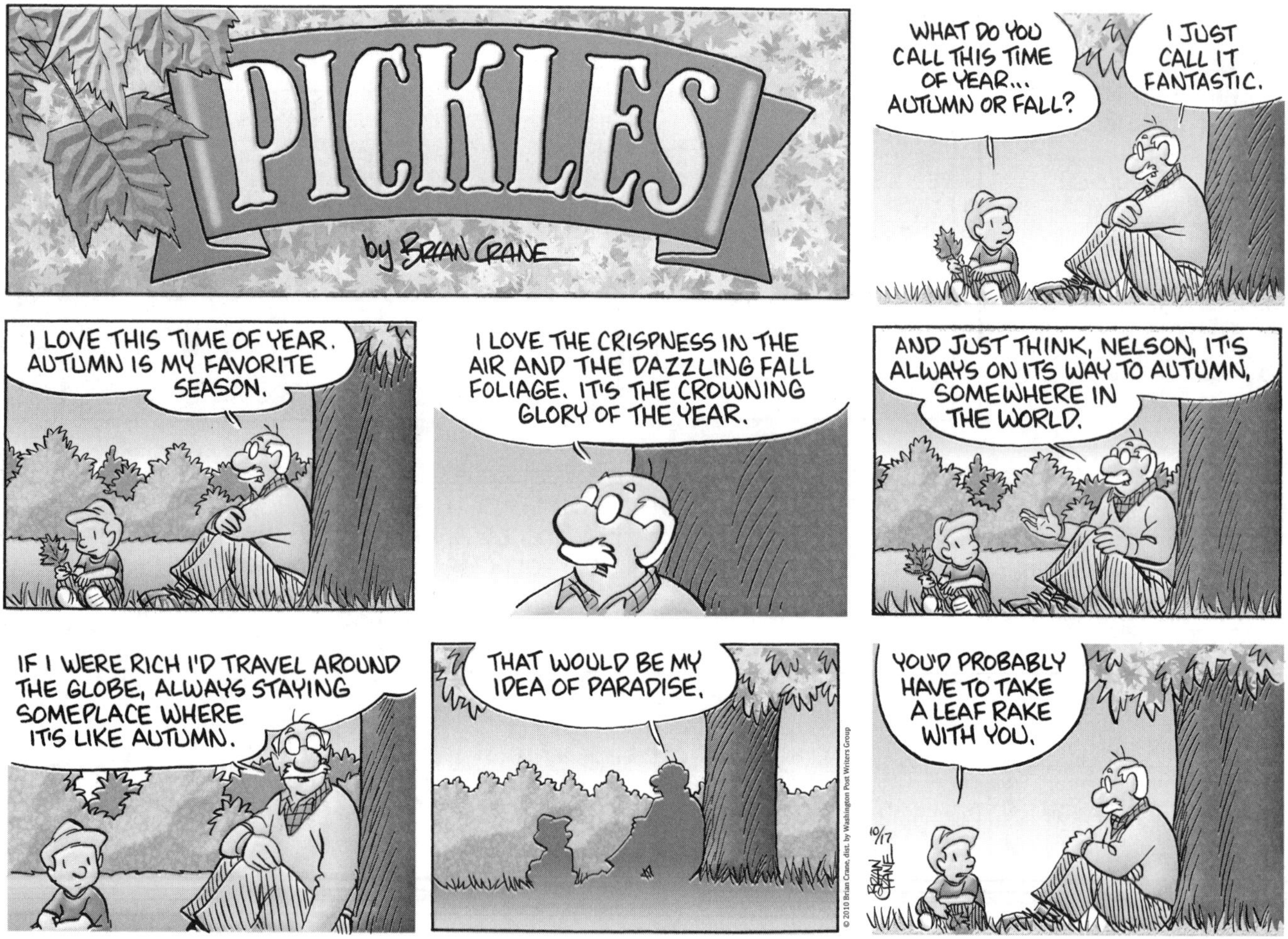
PICKLES
by BRIAN CRANE
WHAT DO YOU CALL THIS TIME OF YEAR... AUTUMN OR FALL?
I JUST CALL IT FANTASTIC.
I LOVE THIS TIME OF YEAR. AUTUMN IS MY FAVORITE SEASON.
I LOVE THE CRISPNESS IN THE AIR AND THE DAZZLING FALL FOLIAGE. IT'S THE CROWNING GLORY OF THE YEAR.
AND JUST THINK, NELSON, IT'S ALWAYS ON ITS WAY TO AUTUMN, SOMEWHERE IN THE WORLD.
IF I WERE RICH I'D TRAVEL AROUND THE GLOBE, ALWAYS STAYING SOMEPLACE WHERE IT'S LIKE AUTUMN.
THAT WOULD BE MY IDEA OF PARADISE.
YOU'D PROBABLY HAVE TO TAKE A LEAF RAKE WITH YOU.
© 2010 Brian Crane, dist. by Washington Post Writers Group
10/17
BRIAN CRANE

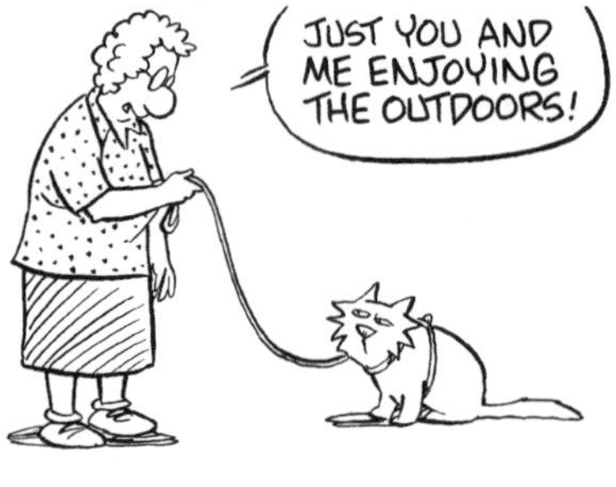
JUST YOU AND ME ENJOYING THE OUTDOORS!

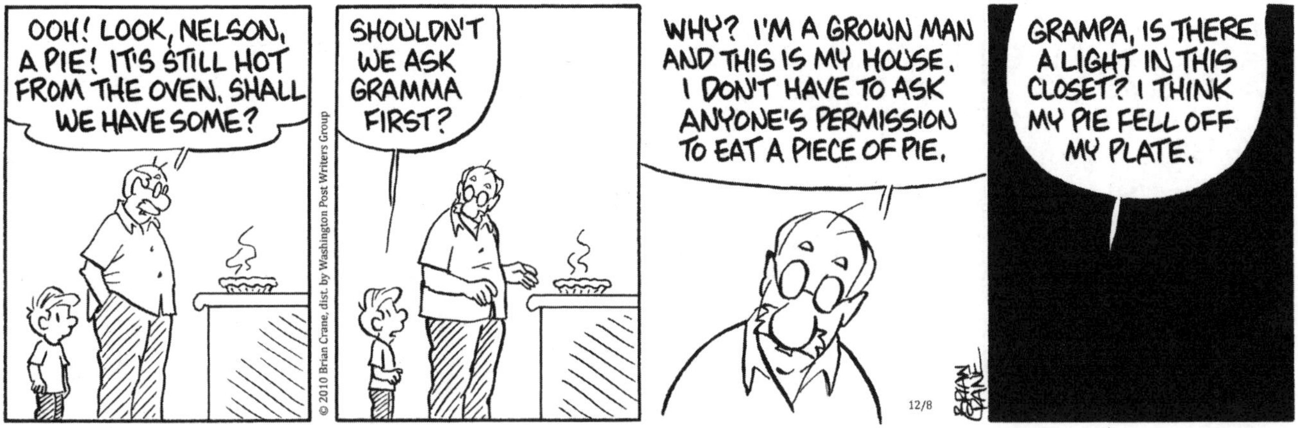
OOH! LOOK, NELSON, A PIE! IT'S STILL HOT FROM THE OVEN. SHALL WE HAVE SOME?
SHOULDN'T WE ASK GRAMMA FIRST?
WHY? I'M A GROWN MAN AND THIS IS MY HOUSE. I DON'T HAVE TO ASK ANYONE'S PERMISSION TO EAT A PIECE OF PIE.
GRAMPA, IS THERE A LIGHT IN THIS CLOSET? I THINK MY PIE FELL OFF MY PLATE.
© 2010 Brian Crane, dist. by Washington Post Writers Group
12/8
BRIAN CRANE

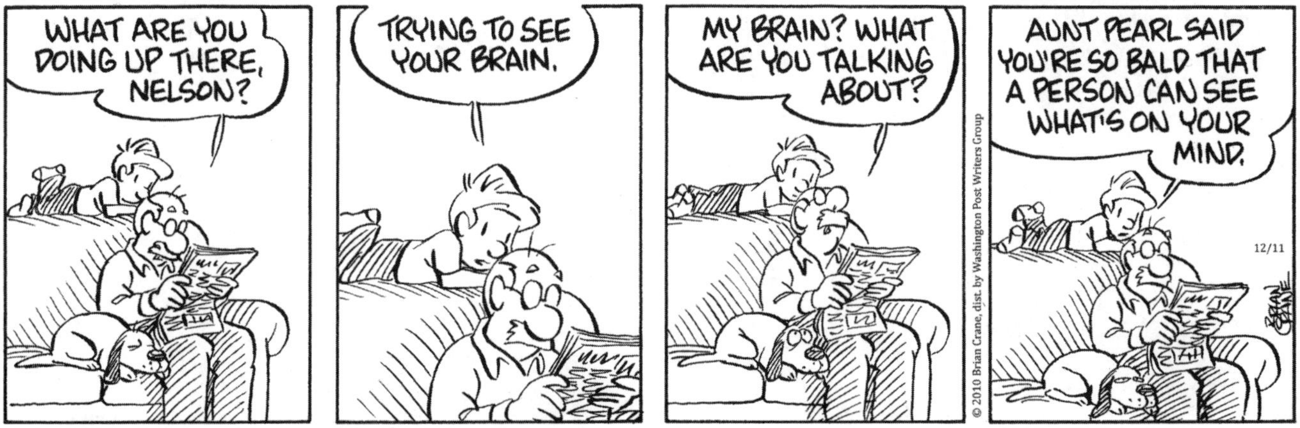
WHAT ARE YOU DOING UP THERE, NELSON?
TRYING TO SEE YOUR BRAIN.
MY BRAIN? WHAT ARE YOU TALKING ABOUT?
AUNT PEARL SAID YOU'RE SO BALD THAT A PERSON CAN SEE WHAT'S ON YOUR MIND.
© 2010 Brian Crane, dist. by Washington Post Writers Group
12/11
BRIAN CRANE

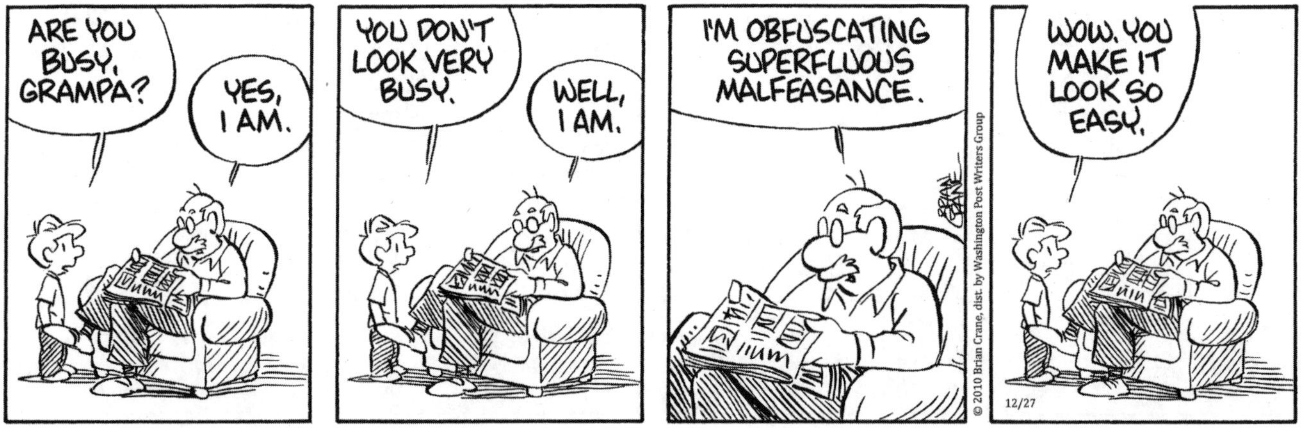
ARE YOU BUSY, GRAMPA?
YES, I AM.
YOU DON'T LOOK VERY BUSY.
WELL, I AM.
I'M OBFUSCATING SUPERFLUOUS MALFEASANCE.
WOW. YOU MAKE IT LOOK SO EASY.
BRIAN CRANE
© 2010 Brian Crane, dist. by Washington Post Writers Group
12/27

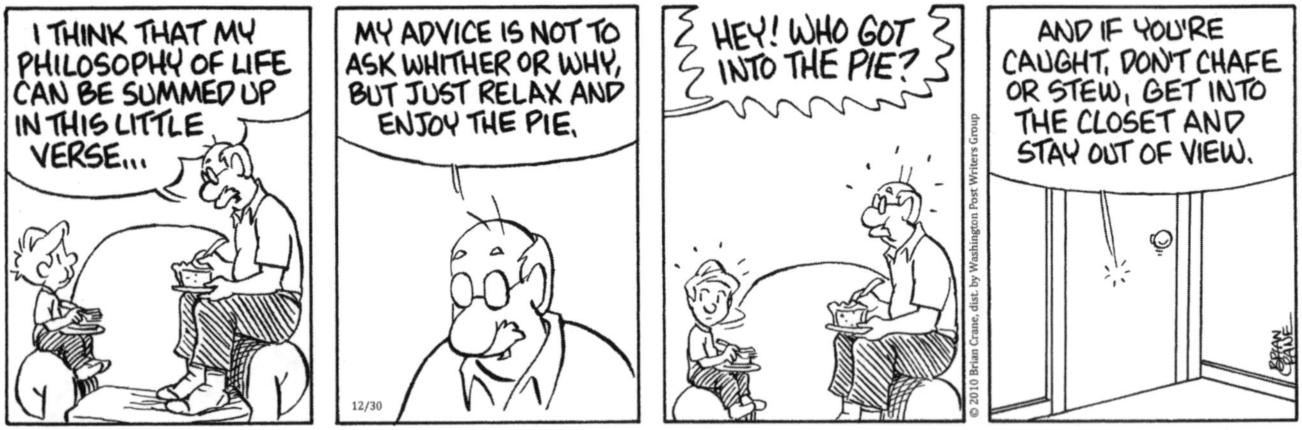
I THINK THAT MY PHILOSOPHY OF LIFE CAN BE SUMMED UP IN THIS LITTLE VERSE...
MY ADVICE IS NOT TO ASK WHITHER OR WHY, BUT JUST RELAX AND ENJOY THE PIE.
12/30
HEY! WHO GOT INTO THE PIE?
AND IF YOU'RE CAUGHT, DON'T CHAFE OR STEW, GET INTO THE CLOSET AND STAY OUT OF VIEW.
BRIAN CRANE

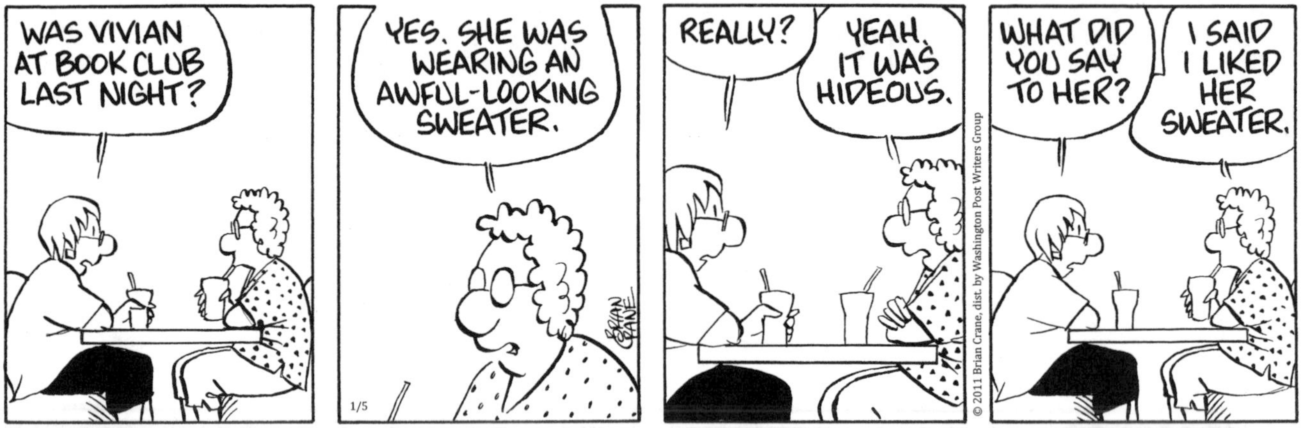
WAS VIVIAN AT BOOK CLUB LAST NIGHT?
YES. SHE WAS WEARING AN AWFUL-LOOKING SWEATER.
BRIAN CRANE
1/5
REALLY?
YEAH, IT WAS HIDEOUS.
WHAT DID YOU SAY TO HER?
I SAID I LIKED HER SWEATER.

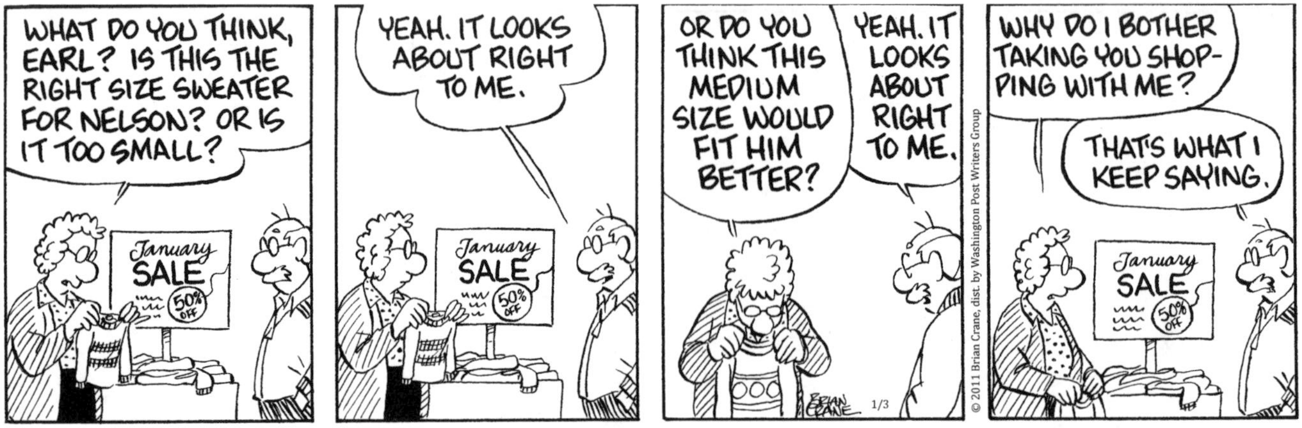
WHAT DO YOU THINK, EARL? IS THIS THE RIGHT SIZE SWEATER FOR NELSON? OR IS IT TOO SMALL?
January SALE 50% OFF
YEAH. IT LOOKS ABOUT RIGHT TO ME.
OR DO YOU THINK THIS MEDIUM SIZE WOULD FIT HIM BETTER?
YEAH. IT LOOKS ABOUT RIGHT TO ME.
BRIAN CRANE
1/3
WHY DO I BOTHER TAKING YOU SHOPPING WITH ME?
THAT'S WHAT I KEEP SAYING.

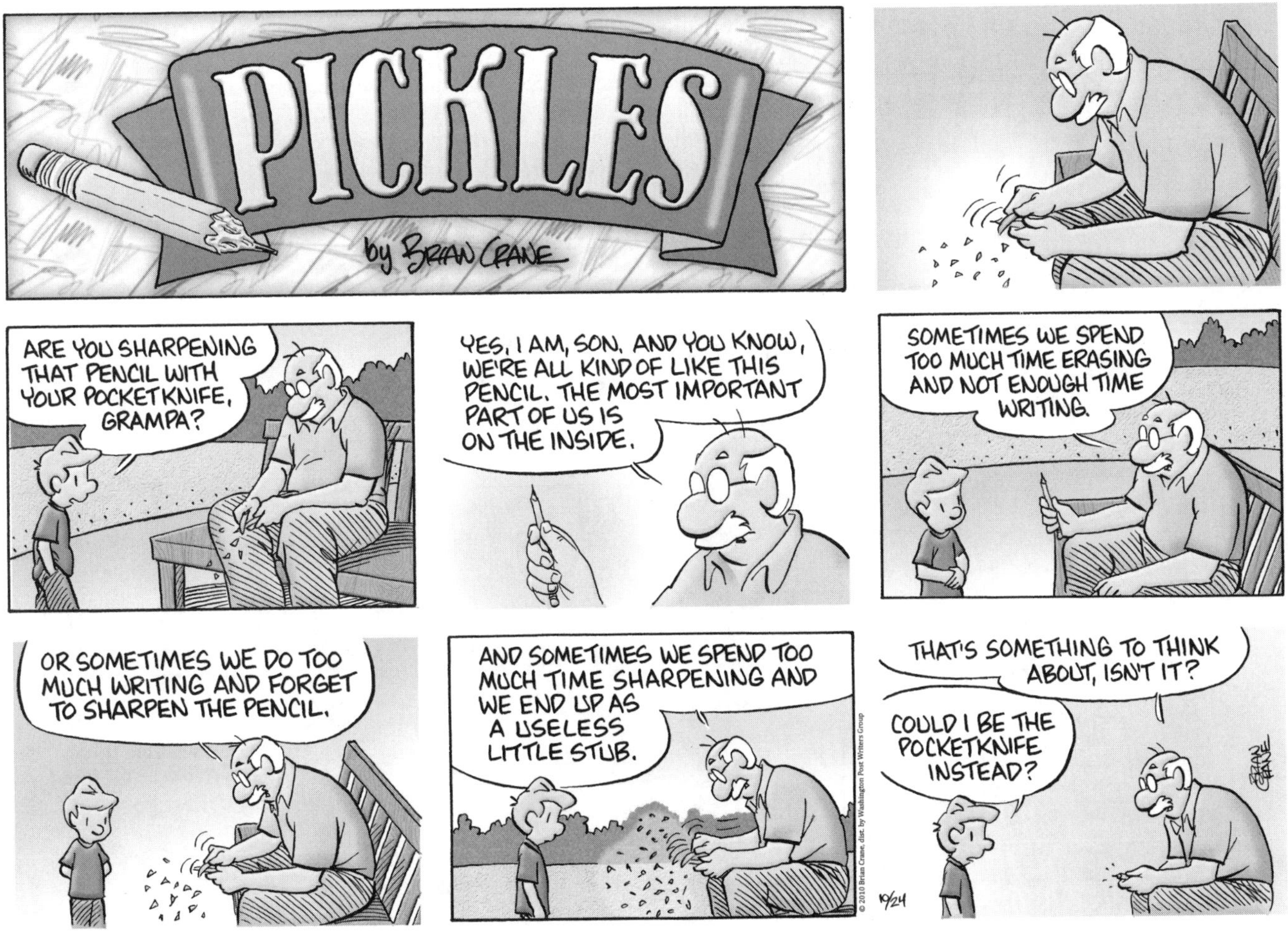
PICKLES
by BRIAN CRANE
ARE YOU SHARPENING THAT PENCIL WITH YOUR POCKETKNIFE, GRAMPA?
YES, I AM, SON. AND YOU KNOW, WE'RE ALL KIND OF LIKE THIS PENCIL. THE MOST IMPORTANT PART OF US IS ON THE INSIDE.
SOMETIMES WE SPEND TOO MUCH TIME ERASING AND NOT ENOUGH TIME WRITING.
OR SOMETIMES WE DO TOO MUCH WRITING AND FORGET TO SHARPEN THE PENCIL.
AND SOMETIMES WE SPEND TOO MUCH TIME SHARPENING AND WE END UP AS A USELESS LITTLE STUB.
© 2010 Brian Crane, dist. by Washington Post Writers Group
10/24
THAT'S SOMETHING TO THINK ABOUT, ISN'T IT?
COULD I BE THE POCKETKNIFE INSTEAD?
BRIAN CRANE

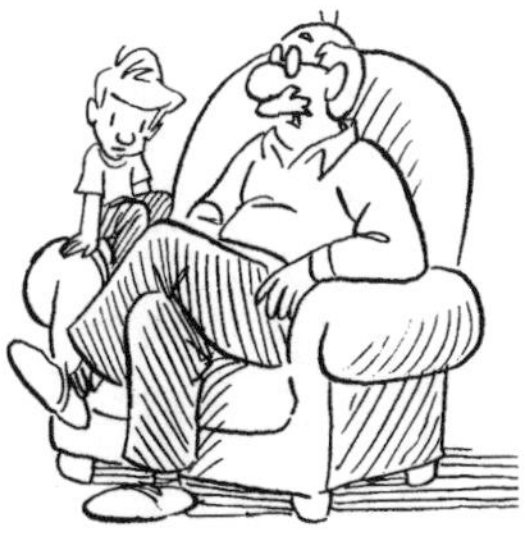

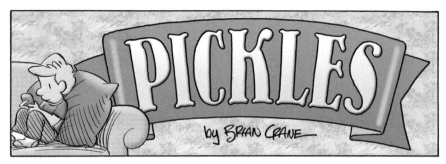

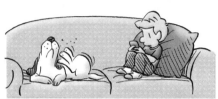

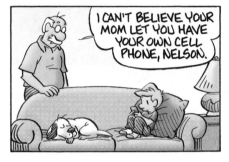

PICKLES
by BRIAN CRANE
I CAN'T BELIEVE YOUR MOM LET YOU HAVE YOUR OWN CELL PHONE, NELSON.
THIS IS HER OLD ONE. SHE GOT A NEW ONE. I JUST USE IT TO PLAY GAMES ON.
TWEEDLE!
HELLO? YES, HE IS. JUST A MINUTE, PLEASE.
IT'S FOR YOU, GRAMPA.
FOR ME?
HELLO?
11/14
BRIAN CRANE
© 2010 Brian Crane, dist. by Washington Post Writers Group
HELLO? HELLO? WHO'S THERE?
THIS IS ONE OF MY FAVORITE GAMES!

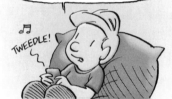

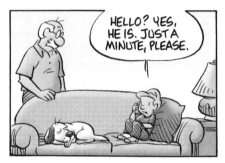

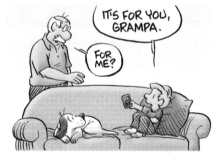

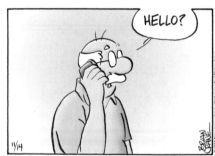

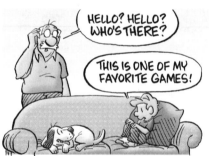

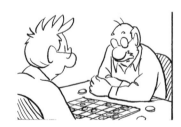

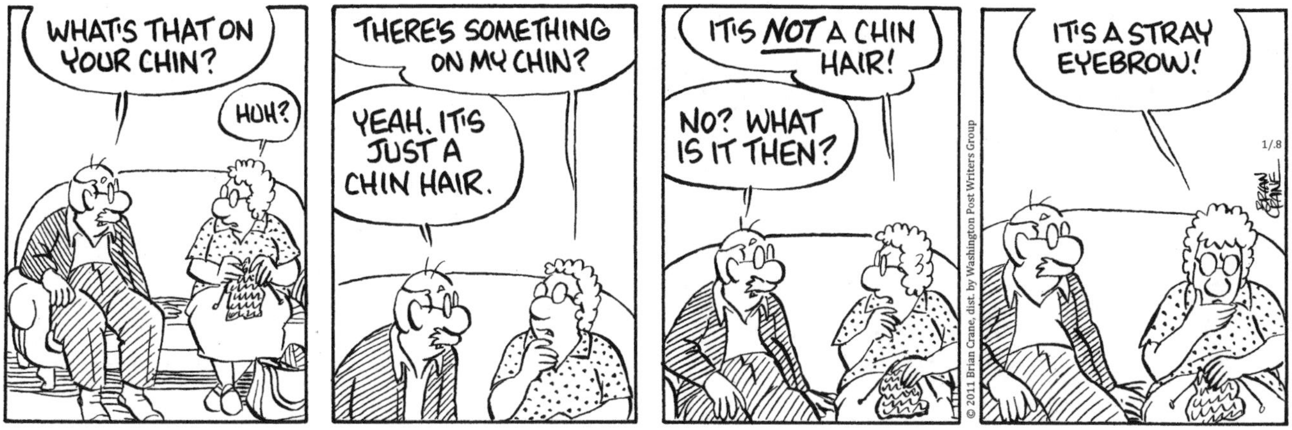
WHAT'S THAT ON YOUR CHIN?
HUH?
THERE'S SOMETHING ON MY CHIN?
YEAH. IT'S JUST A CHIN HAIR.
IT'S NOT A CHIN HAIR!
NO? WHAT IS IT THEN?
IT'S A STRAY EYEBROW!
1/8
BRIAN CRANE
© 2011 Brian Crane, dist. by Washington Post Writers Group

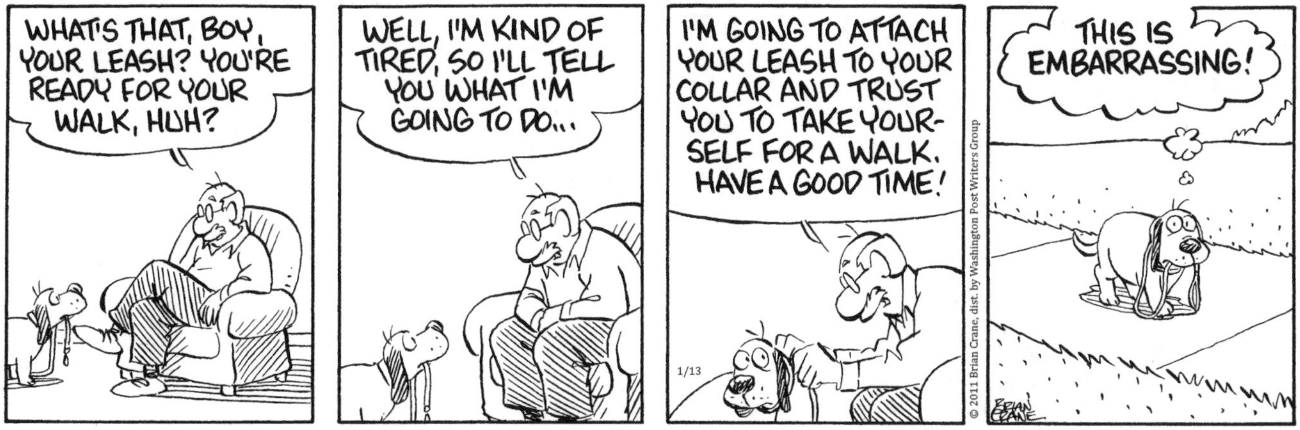
WHAT'S THAT, BOY, YOUR LEASH? YOU'RE READY FOR YOUR WALK, HUH?
WELL, I'M KIND OF TIRED, SO I'LL TELL YOU WHAT I'M GOING TO DO...
I'M GOING TO ATTACH YOUR LEASH TO YOUR COLLAR AND TRUST YOU TO TAKE YOURSELF FOR A WALK. HAVE A GOOD TIME!
1/13
THIS IS EMBARRASSING!
BRIAN CRANE
© 2011 Brian Crane, dist. by Washington Post Writers Group

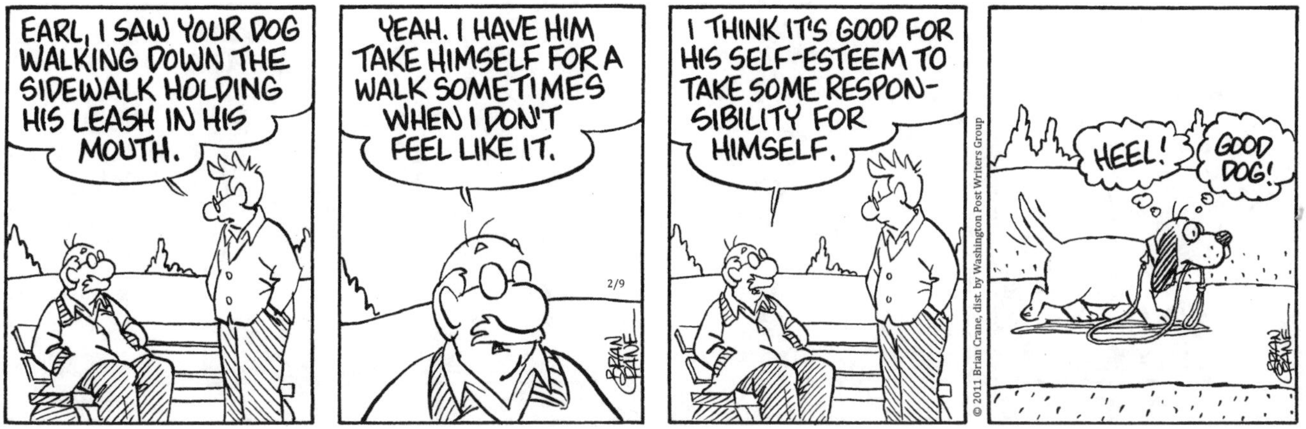
EARL, I SAW YOUR DOG WALKING DOWN THE SIDEWALK HOLDING HIS LEASH IN HIS MOUTH.
YEAH. I HAVE HIM TAKE HIMSELF FOR A WALK SOMETIMES WHEN I DON'T FEEL LIKE IT.
2/9
BRIAN CRANE
I THINK IT'S GOOD FOR HIS SELF-ESTEEM TO TAKE SOME RESPONSIBILITY FOR HIMSELF.
© 2011 Brian Crane, dist. by Washington Post Writers Group
HEEL!
GOOD DOG!
BRIAN CRANE

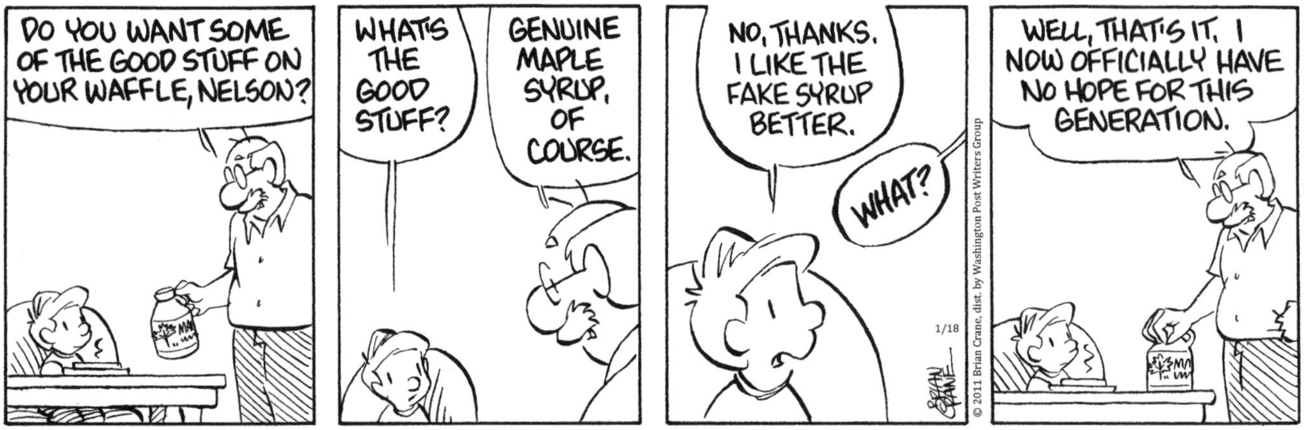
DO YOU WANT SOME OF THE GOOD STUFF ON YOUR WAFFLE, NELSON?
WHAT'S THE GOOD STUFF?
GENUINE MAPLE SYRUP, OF COURSE.
NO, THANKS. I LIKE THE FAKE SYRUP BETTER.
WHAT?
1/18
WELL, THAT'S IT. I NOW OFFICIALLY HAVE NO HOPE FOR THIS GENERATION.

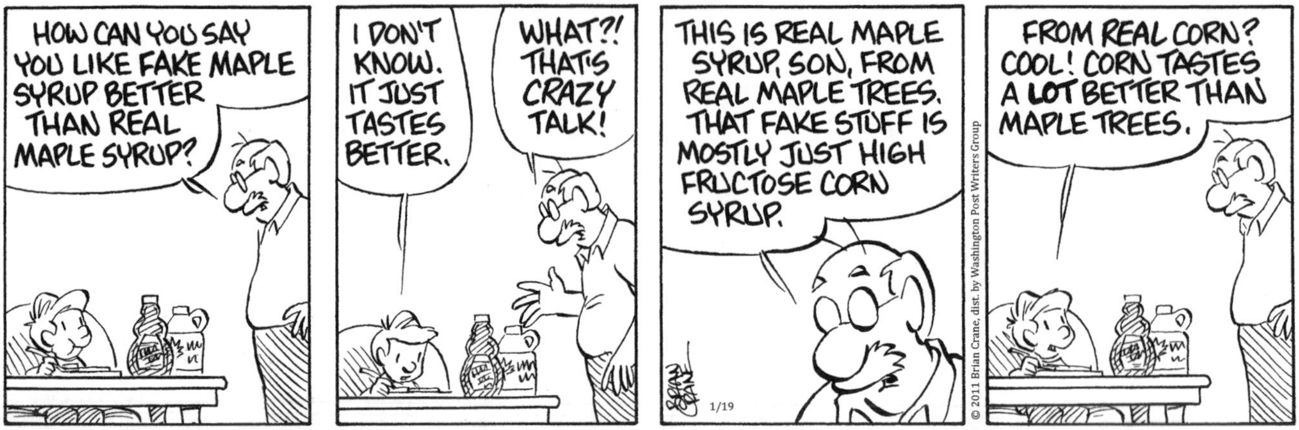
HOW CAN YOU SAY YOU LIKE FAKE MAPLE SYRUP BETTER THAN REAL MAPLE SYRUP?
I DON'T KNOW. IT JUST TASTES BETTER.
WHAT?! THAT'S CRAZY TALK!
THIS IS REAL MAPLE SYRUP, SON, FROM REAL MAPLE TREES. THAT FAKE STUFF IS MOSTLY JUST HIGH FRUCTOSE CORN SYRUP.
1/19
FROM REAL CORN? COOL! CORN TASTES A LOT BETTER THAN MAPLE TREES.

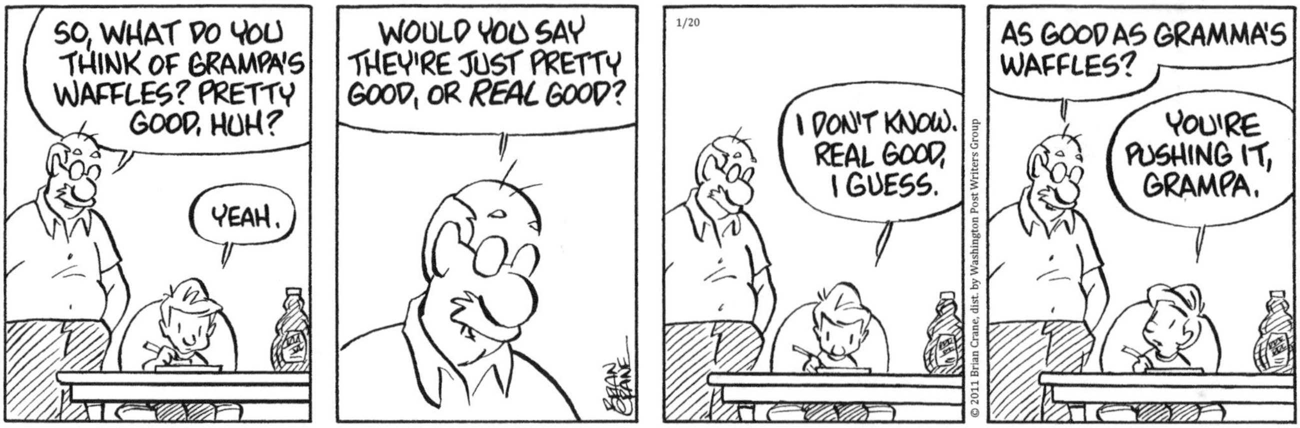
SO, WHAT DO YOU THINK OF GRAMPA'S WAFFLES? PRETTY GOOD, HUH?
YEAH.
WOULD YOU SAY THEY'RE JUST PRETTY GOOD, OR REAL GOOD?
1/20
I DON'T KNOW. REAL GOOD, I GUESS.
AS GOOD AS GRAMMA'S WAFFLES?
YOU'RE PUSHING IT, GRAMPA.

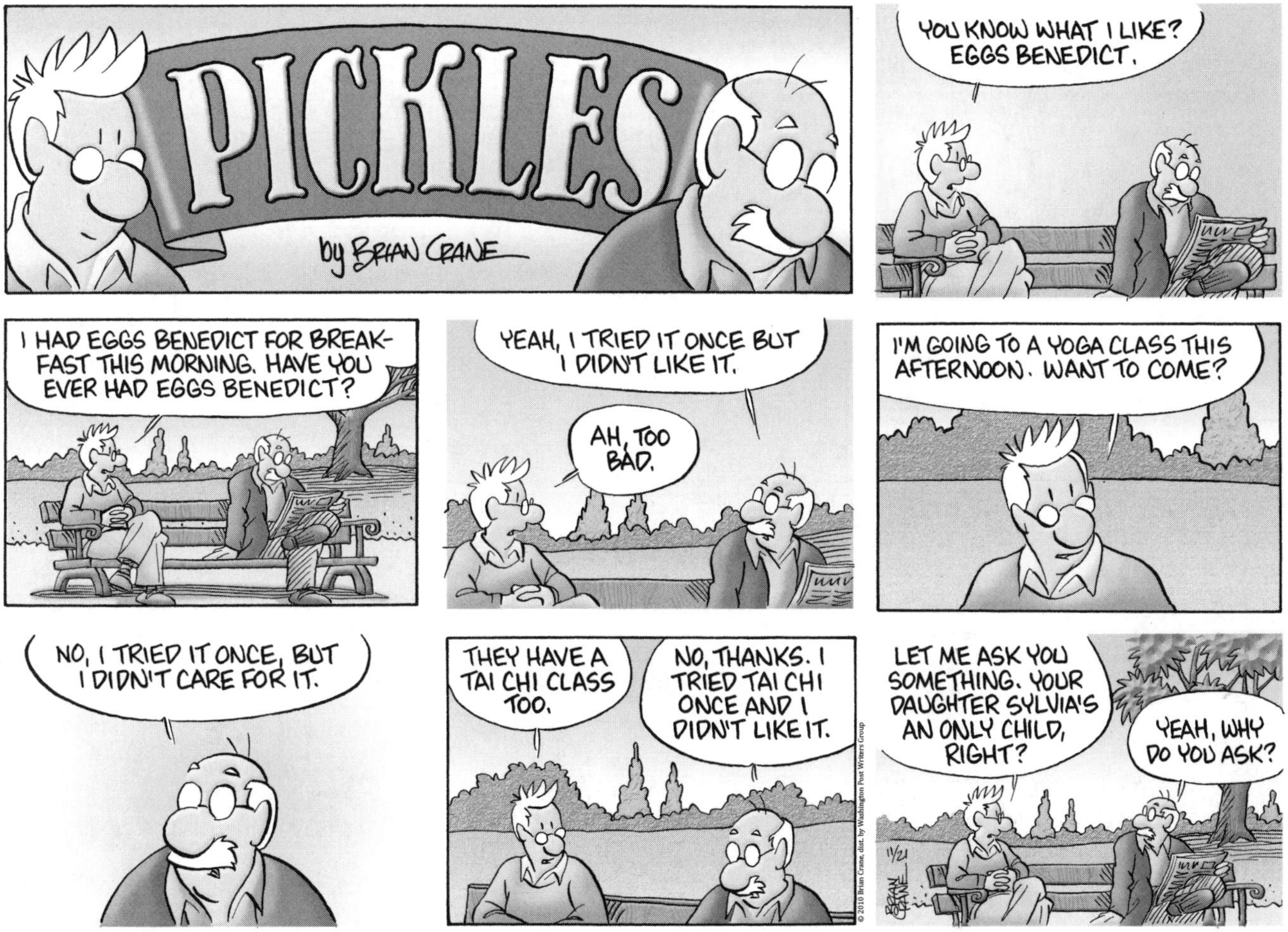
PICKLES
by BRIAN CRANE
YOU KNOW WHAT I LIKE? EGGS BENEDICT.
I HAD EGGS BENEDICT FOR BREAK-FAST THIS MORNING. HAVE YOU EVER HAD EGGS BENEDICT?
YEAH, I TRIED IT ONCE BUT I DIDN'T LIKE IT.
AH, TOO BAD.
I'M GOING TO A YOGA CLASS THIS AFTERNOON. WANT TO COME?
NO, I TRIED IT ONCE, BUT I DIDN'T CARE FOR IT.
THEY HAVE A TAI CHI CLASS TOO.
NO, THANKS. I TRIED TAI CHI ONCE AND I DIDN'T LIKE IT.
© 2010 Brian Crane, dist. by Washington Post Writers Group
LET ME ASK YOU SOMETHING. YOUR DAUGHTER SYLVIA'S AN ONLY CHILD, RIGHT?
YEAH, WHY DO YOU ASK?
11/21
BRIAN CRANE

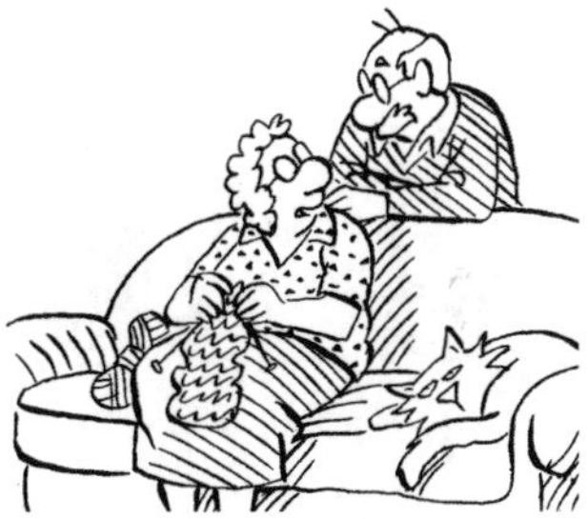

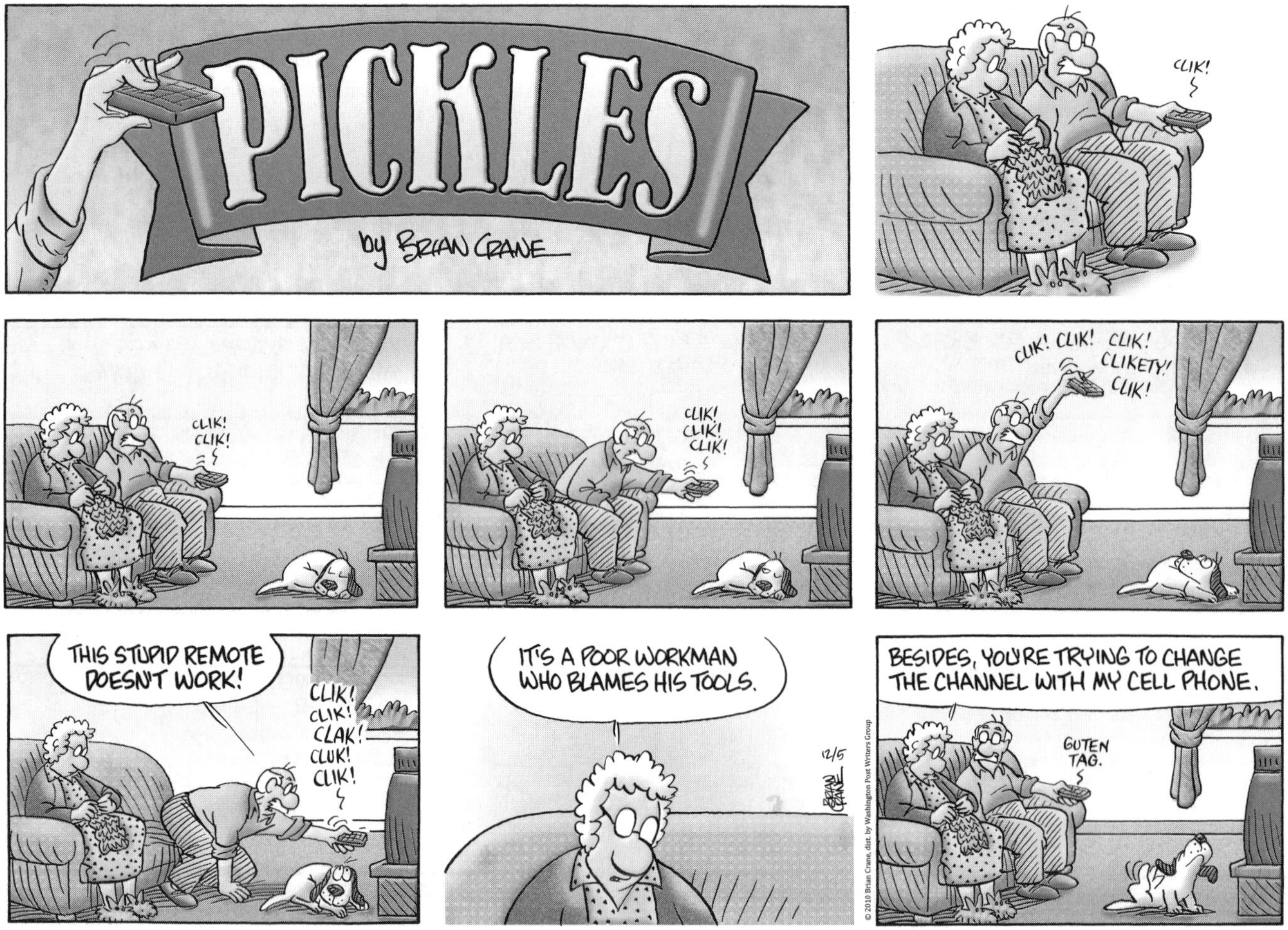
PICKLES
by BRIAN CRANE
CLIK!
CLIK! CLIK!
CLIK! CLIK! CLIK!
CLIK! CLIK! CLIK! CLIKETY! CLIK!
THIS STUPID REMOTE DOESN'T WORK!
CLIK! CLIK! CLAK! CLUK! CLIK!
IT'S A POOR WORKMAN WHO BLAMES HIS TOOLS.
12/5
© 2010 Brian Crane, dist. by Washington Post Writers Group
BESIDES, YOU'RE TRYING TO CHANGE THE CHANNEL WITH MY CELL PHONE.
GUTEN TAG.

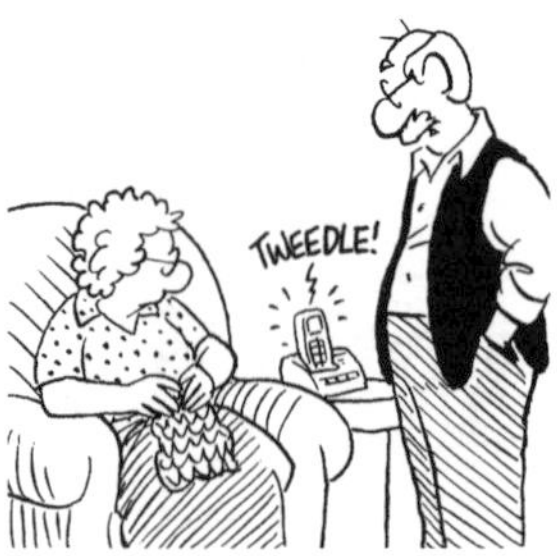
TWEEDLE!

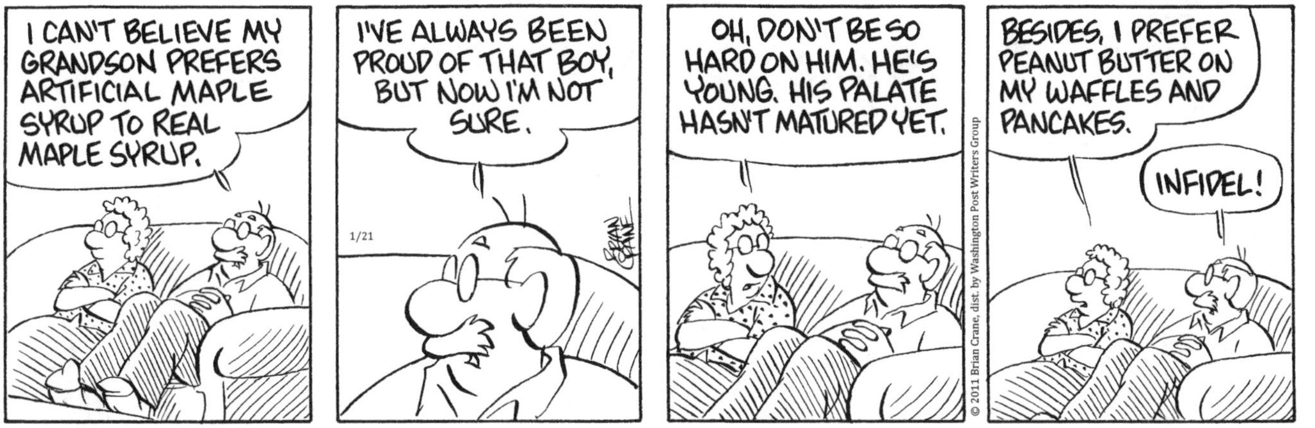
I CAN'T BELIEVE MY GRANDSON PREFERS ARTIFICIAL MAPLE SYRUP TO REAL MAPLE SYRUP.
I'VE ALWAYS BEEN PROUD OF THAT BOY, BUT NOW I'M NOT SURE.
1/21
BRIAN CRANE
OH, DON'T BE SO HARD ON HIM. HE'S YOUNG. HIS PALATE HASN'T MATURED YET.
BESIDES, I PREFER PEANUT BUTTER ON MY WAFFLES AND PANCAKES.
INFIDEL!

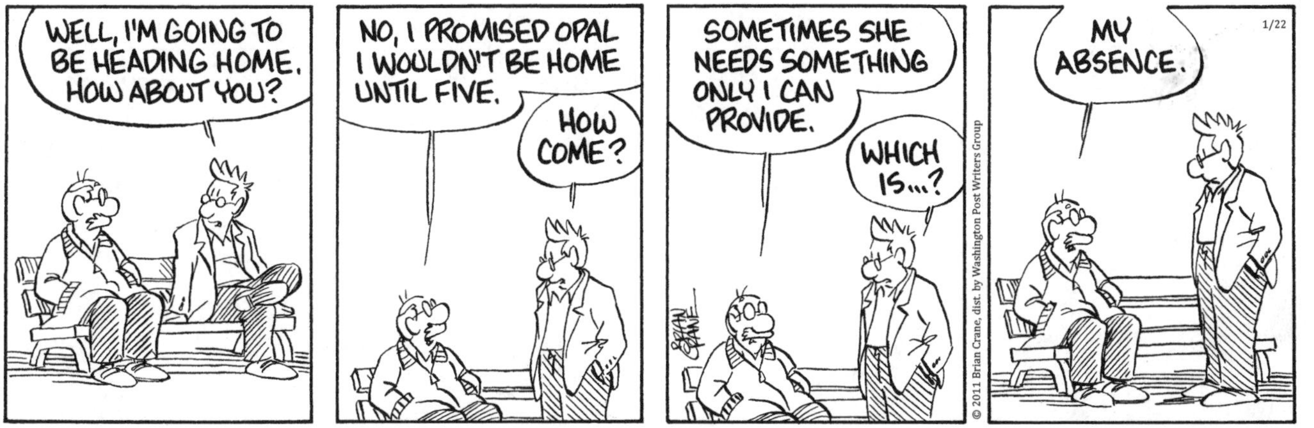
WELL, I'M GOING TO BE HEADING HOME. HOW ABOUT YOU?
NO, I PROMISED OPAL I WOULDN'T BE HOME UNTIL FIVE.
HOW COME?
SOMETIMES SHE NEEDS SOMETHING ONLY I CAN PROVIDE.
WHICH IS...?
BRIAN CRANE
MY ABSENCE.
1/22

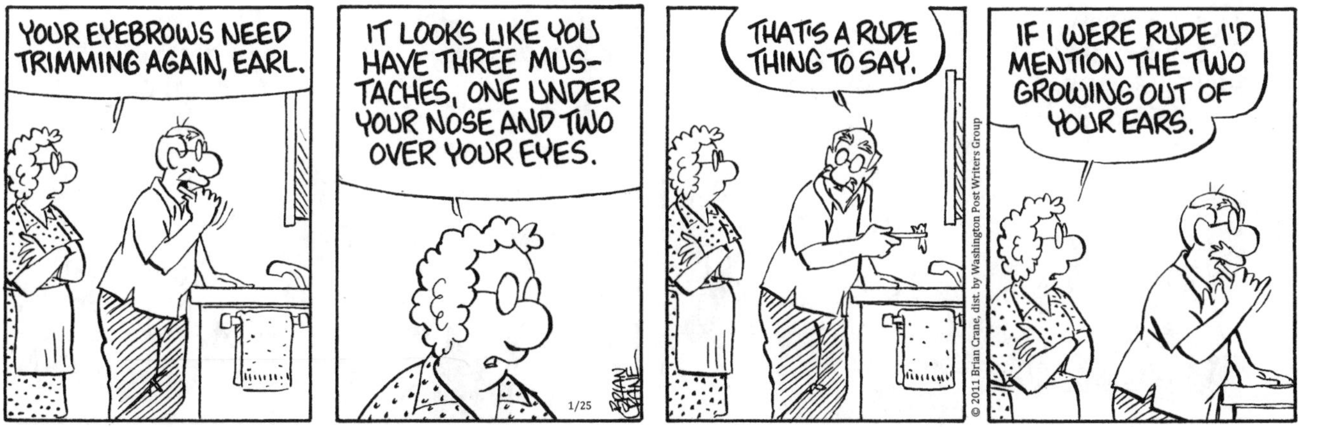
YOUR EYEBROWS NEED TRIMMING AGAIN, EARL.
IT LOOKS LIKE YOU HAVE THREE MUS-TACHES, ONE UNDER YOUR NOSE AND TWO OVER YOUR EYES.
1/25
BRIAN CRANE
THAT'S A RUDE THING TO SAY.
IF I WERE RUDE I'D MENTION THE TWO GROWING OUT OF YOUR EARS.

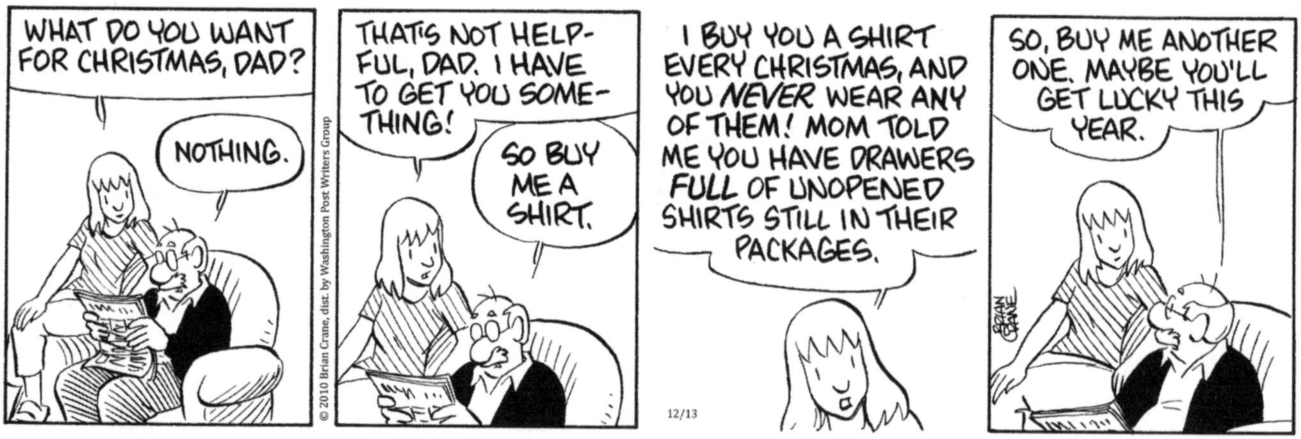
WHAT DO YOU WANT FOR CHRISTMAS, DAD?
NOTHING.
© 2010 Brian Crane, dist. by Washington Post Writers Group
THAT'S NOT HELP-FUL, DAD. I HAVE TO GET YOU SOME-THING!
SO BUY ME A SHIRT.
I BUY YOU A SHIRT EVERY CHRISTMAS, AND YOU *NEVER* WEAR ANY OF THEM! MOM TOLD ME YOU HAVE DRAWERS *FULL* OF UNOPENED SHIRTS STILL IN THEIR PACKAGES.
12/13
SO, BUY ME ANOTHER ONE. MAYBE YOU'LL GET LUCKY THIS YEAR.
BRIAN CRANE

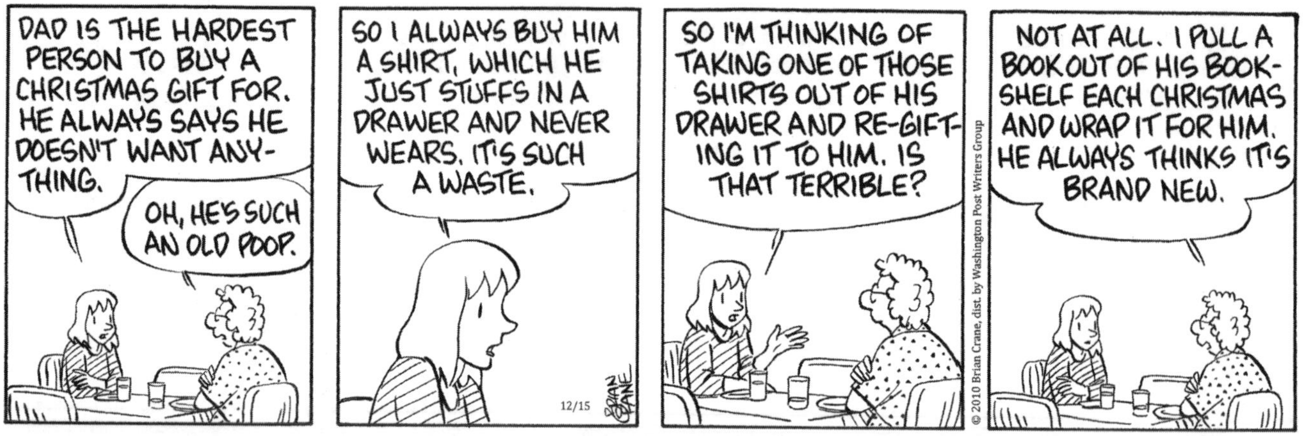
DAD IS THE HARDEST PERSON TO BUY A CHRISTMAS GIFT FOR. HE ALWAYS SAYS HE DOESN'T WANT ANY-THING.
OH, HE'S SUCH AN OLD POOP.
SO I ALWAYS BUY HIM A SHIRT, WHICH HE JUST STUFFS IN A DRAWER AND NEVER WEARS. IT'S SUCH A WASTE.
12/15
BRIAN CRANE
SO I'M THINKING OF TAKING ONE OF THOSE SHIRTS OUT OF HIS DRAWER AND RE-GIFT-ING IT TO HIM. IS THAT TERRIBLE?
© 2010 Brian Crane, dist. by Washington Post Writers Group
NOT AT ALL. I PULL A BOOK OUT OF HIS BOOK-SHELF EACH CHRISTMAS AND WRAP IT FOR HIM. HE ALWAYS THINKS IT'S BRAND NEW.

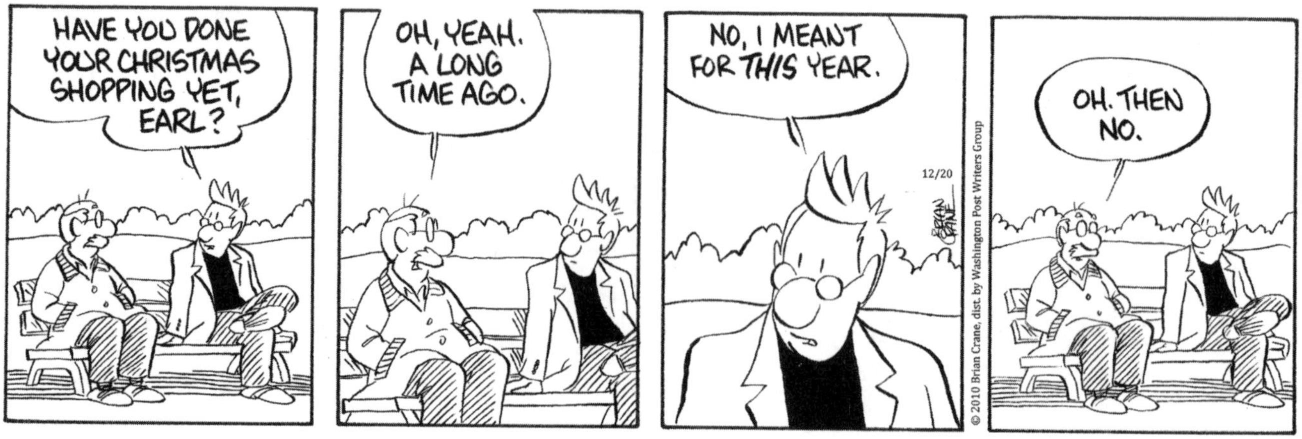
HAVE YOU DONE YOUR CHRISTMAS SHOPPING YET, EARL?
OH, YEAH. A LONG TIME AGO.
NO, I MEANT FOR *THIS* YEAR.
12/20
BRIAN CRANE
© 2010 Brian Crane, dist. by Washington Post Writers Group
OH. THEN NO.

PICKLES
by BRIAN CRANE
HAVE YOU BEEN A GOOD BOY, NELSON?
YUP!
WHAT'S SANTA GOING TO BRING YOU FOR CHRISTMAS THIS YEAR?
A NEW SET OF LEGO BLOCKS, A NINTENDO DSi, AND A SKATEBOARD.
WOW! SANTA MUST BE DOING A LOT BETTER NOW THAN WHEN I WAS A KID. BACK THEN WE NEVER GOT TOYS.
WHAT DID YOU GET?
OH, THINGS WE NEEDED, LIKE UNDERWEAR.
THAT'S ALL YOU GOT FOR CHRISTMAS? NEW UNDERWEAR?
HA! I WOULD'VE *LOVED* TO GET NEW UNDERWEAR. I'M TALKIN' HAND-ME-DOWNS FROM MY OLDER BROTHER.
12/12
© 2010 Brian Crane, dist. by Washington Post Writers Group

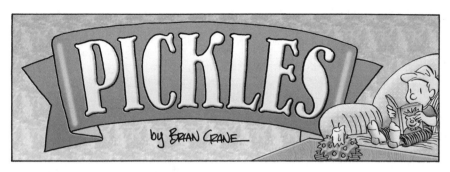

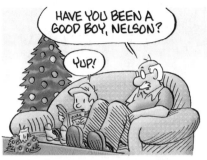

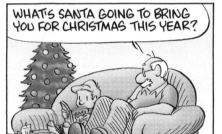

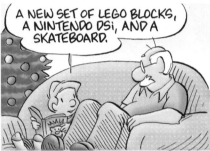

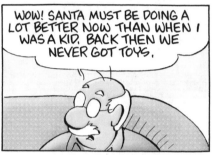

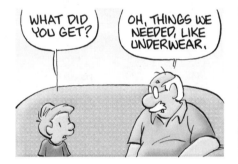

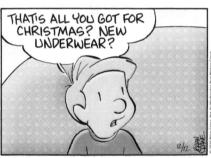

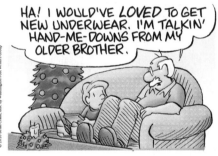

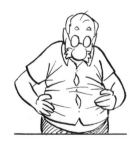

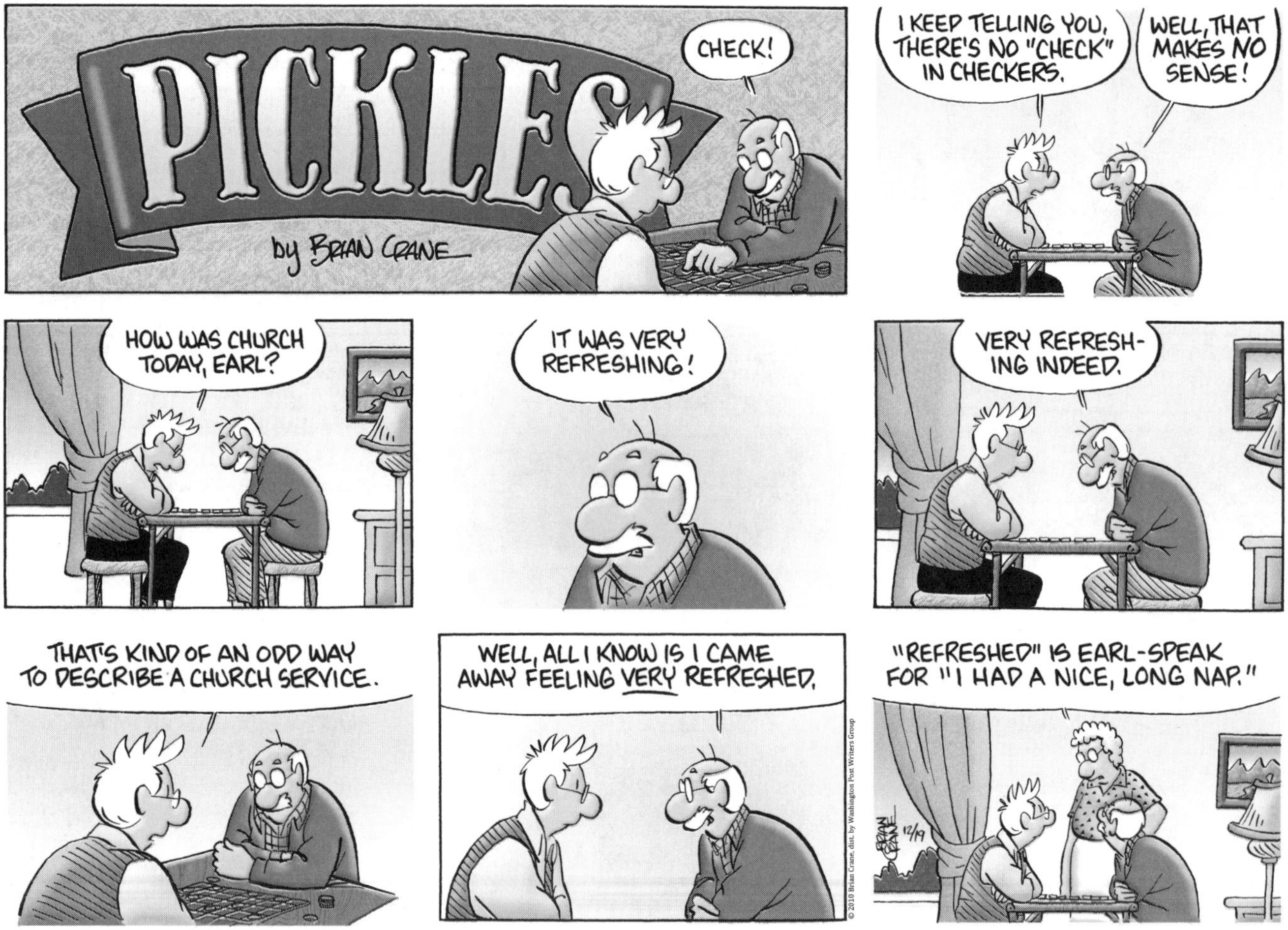
PICKLES
by BRIAN CRANE
CHECK!
I KEEP TELLING YOU, THERE'S NO "CHECK" IN CHECKERS.
WELL, THAT MAKES NO SENSE!
HOW WAS CHURCH TODAY, EARL?
IT WAS VERY REFRESHING!
VERY REFRESHING INDEED.
THAT'S KIND OF AN ODD WAY TO DESCRIBE A CHURCH SERVICE.
WELL, ALL I KNOW IS I CAME AWAY FEELING VERY REFRESHED.
"REFRESHED" IS EARL-SPEAK FOR "I HAD A NICE, LONG NAP."
© 2010 Brian Crane, dist. by Washington Post Writers Group
BRIAN CRANE 12/19

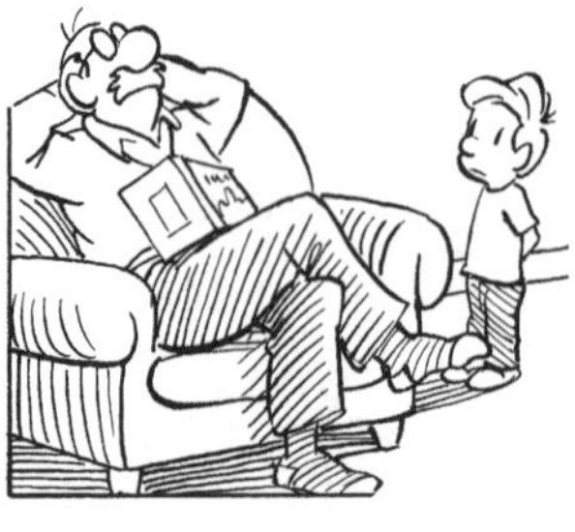

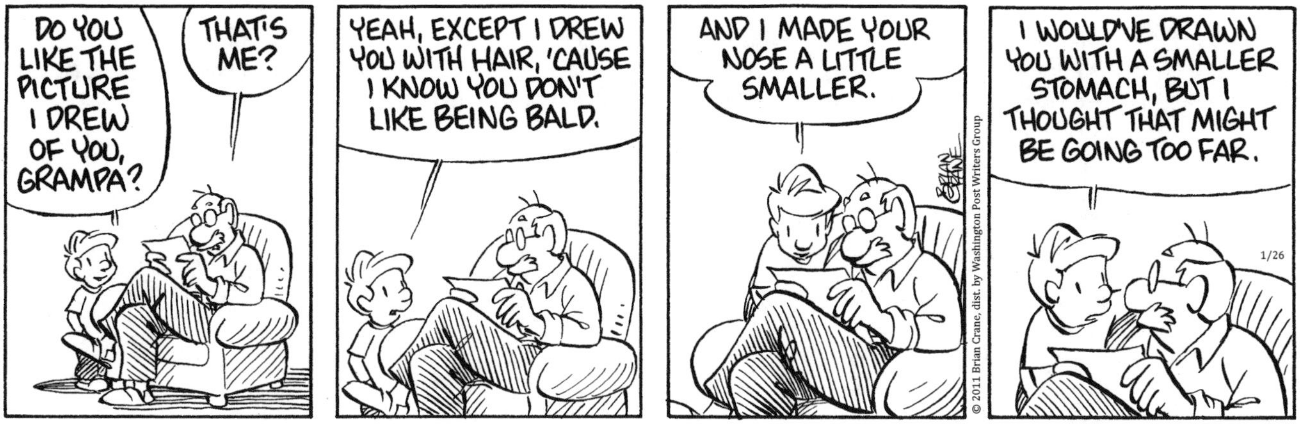
DO YOU LIKE THE PICTURE I DREW OF YOU, GRAMPA?
THAT'S ME?
YEAH, EXCEPT I DREW YOU WITH HAIR, 'CAUSE I KNOW YOU DON'T LIKE BEING BALD.
AND I MADE YOUR NOSE A LITTLE SMALLER.
I WOULD'VE DRAWN YOU WITH A SMALLER STOMACH, BUT I THOUGHT THAT MIGHT BE GOING TOO FAR.
1/26
© 2011 Brian Crane, dist. by Washington Post Writers Group

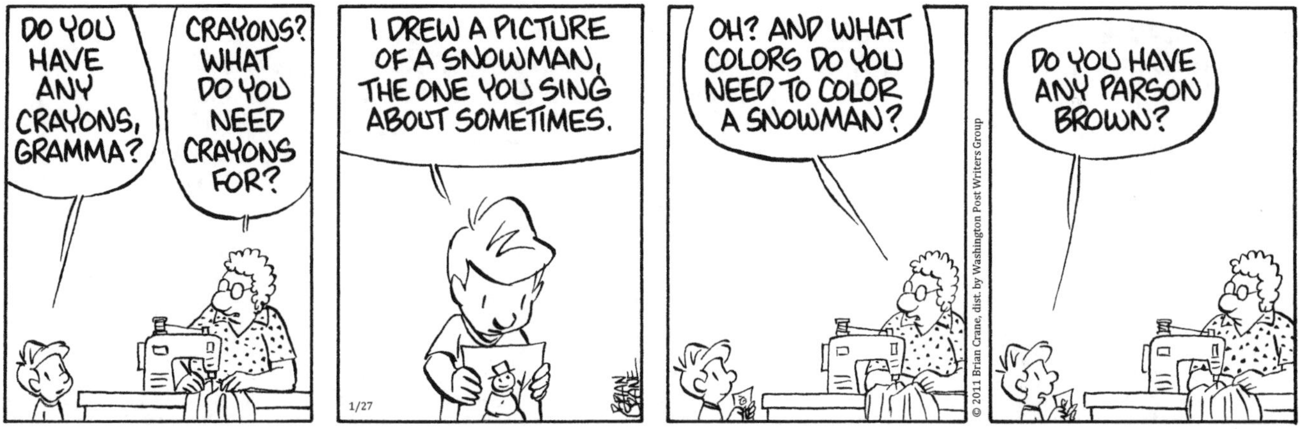
DO YOU HAVE ANY CRAYONS, GRAMMA?
CRAYONS? WHAT DO YOU NEED CRAYONS FOR?
I DREW A PICTURE OF A SNOWMAN, THE ONE YOU SING ABOUT SOMETIMES.
1/27
OH? AND WHAT COLORS DO YOU NEED TO COLOR A SNOWMAN?
DO YOU HAVE ANY PARSON BROWN?
© 2011 Brian Crane, dist. by Washington Post Writers Group

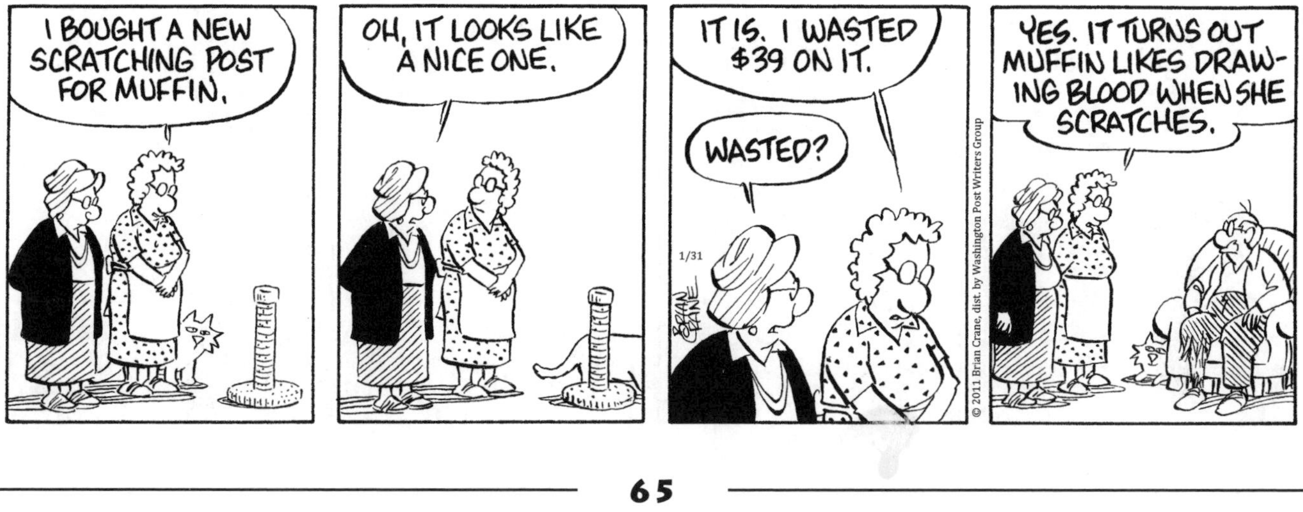
I BOUGHT A NEW SCRATCHING POST FOR MUFFIN.
OH, IT LOOKS LIKE A NICE ONE.
IT IS. I WASTED $39 ON IT.
WASTED?
1/31
YES. IT TURNS OUT MUFFIN LIKES DRAWING BLOOD WHEN SHE SCRATCHES.
© 2011 Brian Crane, dist. by Washington Post Writers Group

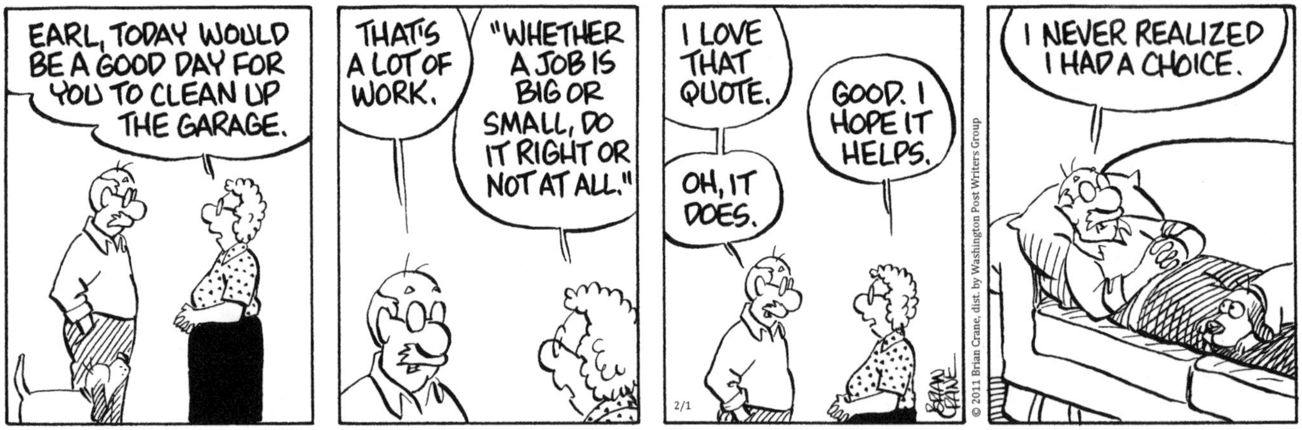
EARL, TODAY WOULD BE A GOOD DAY FOR YOU TO CLEAN UP THE GARAGE.
THAT'S A LOT OF WORK.
"WHETHER A JOB IS BIG OR SMALL, DO IT RIGHT OR NOT AT ALL."
I LOVE THAT QUOTE.
GOOD. I HOPE IT HELPS.
OH, IT DOES.
2/1
I NEVER REALIZED I HAD A CHOICE.

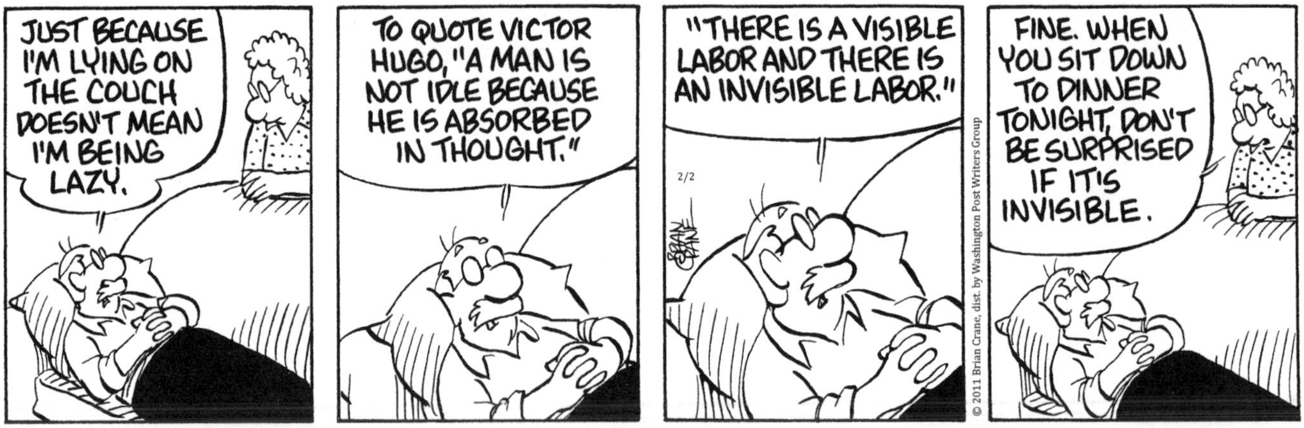
JUST BECAUSE I'M LYING ON THE COUCH DOESN'T MEAN I'M BEING LAZY.
TO QUOTE VICTOR HUGO, "A MAN IS NOT IDLE BECAUSE HE IS ABSORBED IN THOUGHT."
"THERE IS A VISIBLE LABOR AND THERE IS AN INVISIBLE LABOR."
2/2
FINE. WHEN YOU SIT DOWN TO DINNER TONIGHT, DON'T BE SURPRISED IF IT'S INVISIBLE.

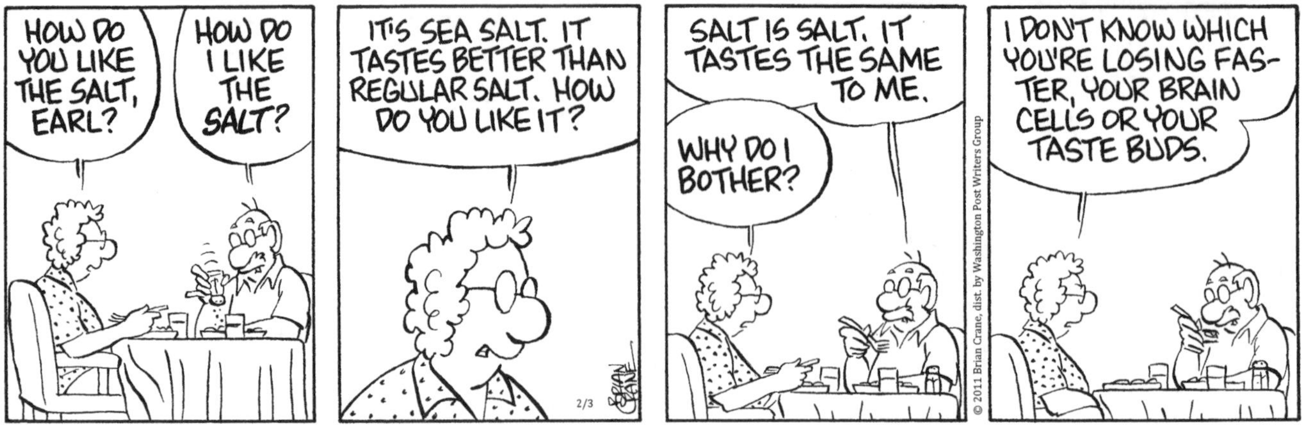
HOW DO YOU LIKE THE SALT, EARL?
HOW DO I LIKE THE SALT?
IT'S SEA SALT. IT TASTES BETTER THAN REGULAR SALT. HOW DO YOU LIKE IT?
2/3
SALT IS SALT. IT TASTES THE SAME TO ME.
WHY DO I BOTHER?
I DON'T KNOW WHICH YOU'RE LOSING FASTER, YOUR BRAIN CELLS OR YOUR TASTE BUDS.

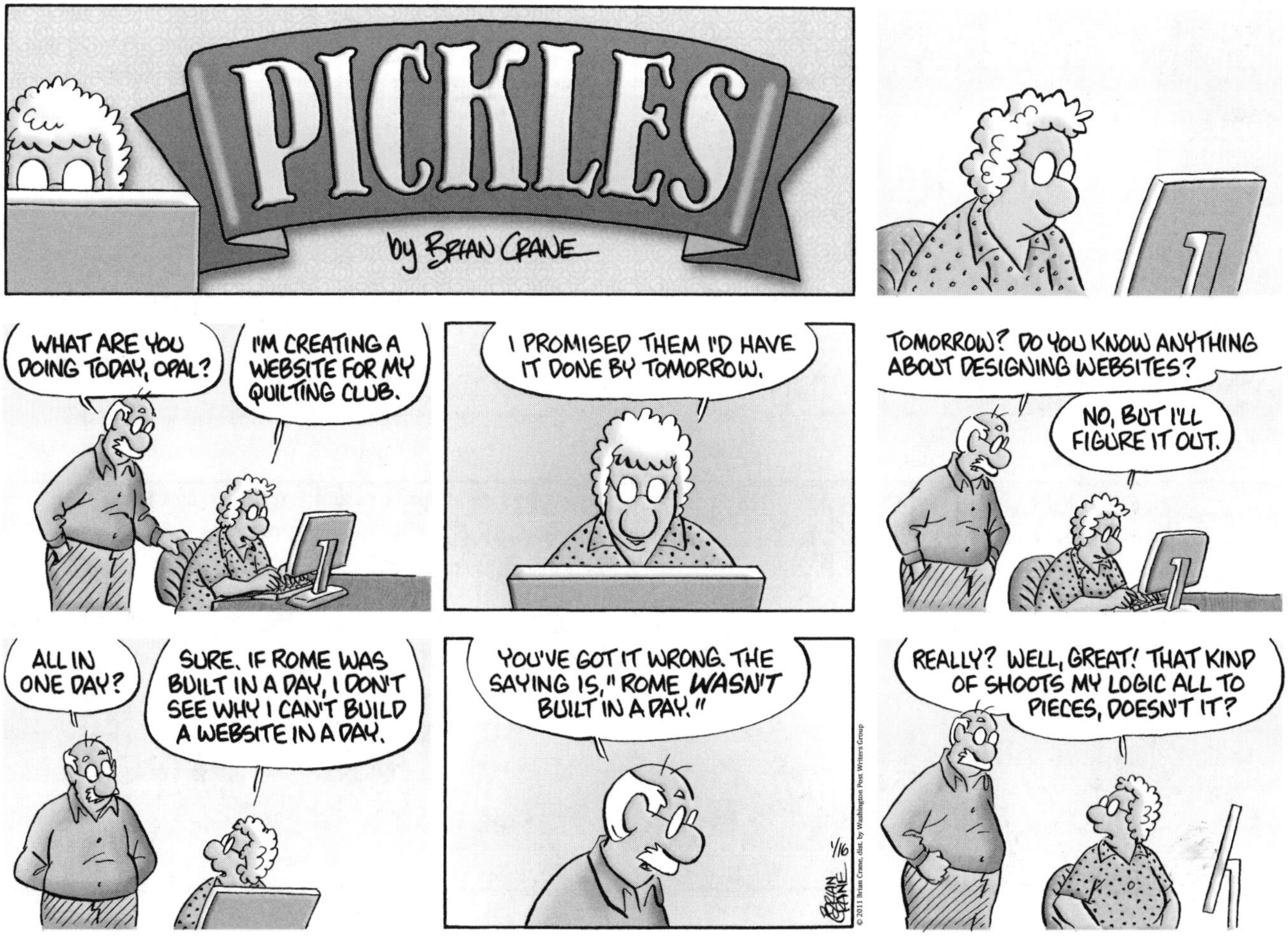
PICKLES
by BRIAN CRANE
WHAT ARE YOU DOING TODAY, OPAL?
I'M CREATING A WEBSITE FOR MY QUILTING CLUB.
I PROMISED THEM I'D HAVE IT DONE BY TOMORROW.
TOMORROW? DO YOU KNOW ANYTHING ABOUT DESIGNING WEBSITES?
NO, BUT I'LL FIGURE IT OUT.
ALL IN ONE DAY?
SURE. IF ROME WAS BUILT IN A DAY, I DON'T SEE WHY I CAN'T BUILD A WEBSITE IN A DAY.
YOU'VE GOT IT WRONG. THE SAYING IS, "ROME *WASN'T* BUILT IN A DAY."
1/16
BRIAN CRANE
© 2011 Brian Crane, dist. by Washington Post Writers Group
REALLY? WELL, GREAT! THAT KIND OF SHOOTS MY LOGIC ALL TO PIECES, DOESN'T IT?

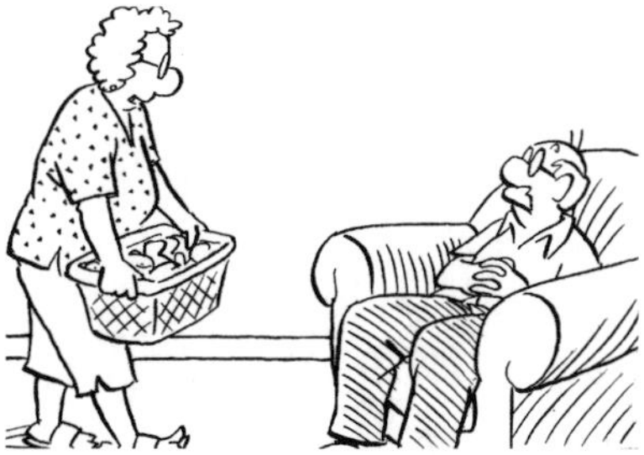

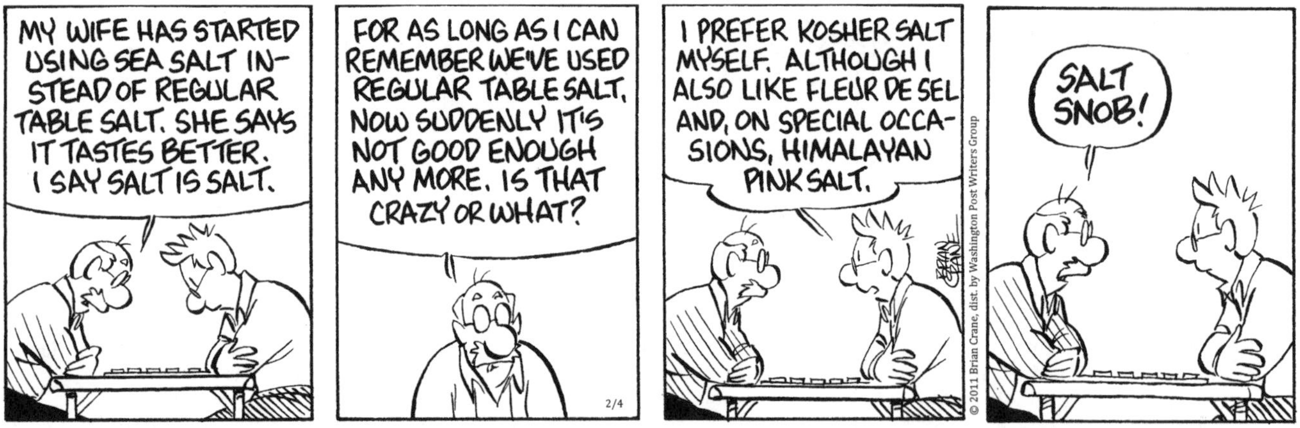
MY WIFE HAS STARTED USING SEA SALT INSTEAD OF REGULAR TABLE SALT. SHE SAYS IT TASTES BETTER. I SAY SALT IS SALT.
FOR AS LONG AS I CAN REMEMBER WE'VE USED REGULAR TABLE SALT. NOW SUDDENLY IT'S NOT GOOD ENOUGH ANY MORE. IS THAT CRAZY OR WHAT?
2/4
I PREFER KOSHER SALT MYSELF. ALTHOUGH I ALSO LIKE FLEUR DE SEL AND, ON SPECIAL OCCASIONS, HIMALAYAN PINK SALT.
BRIAN CRANE
© 2011 Brian Crane, dist. by Washington Post Writers Group
SALT SNOB!

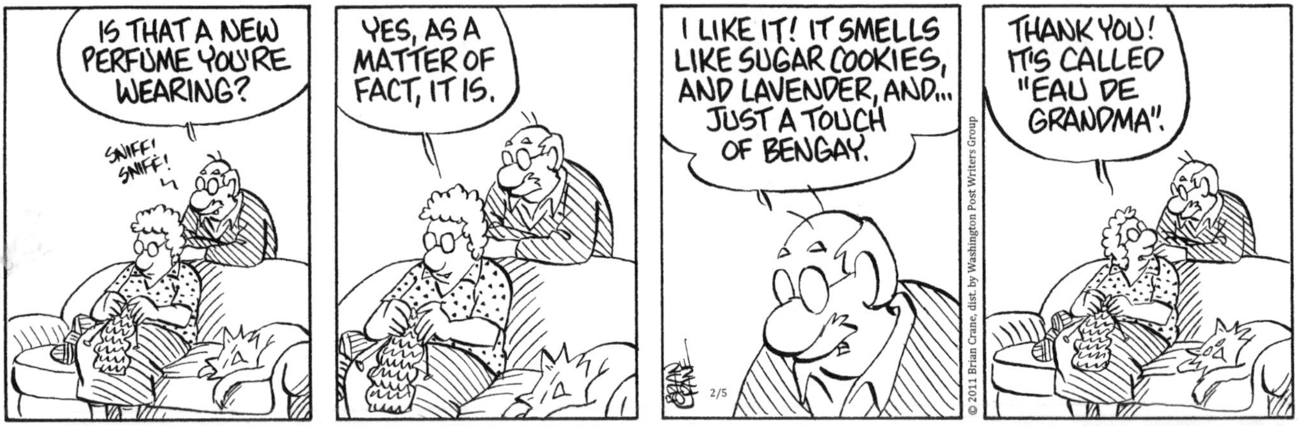
IS THAT A NEW PERFUME YOU'RE WEARING?
SNIFF! SNIFF!
YES, AS A MATTER OF FACT, IT IS.
I LIKE IT! IT SMELLS LIKE SUGAR COOKIES, AND LAVENDER, AND... JUST A TOUCH OF BENGAY.
BRIAN CRANE
2/5
© 2011 Brian Crane, dist. by Washington Post Writers Group
THANK YOU! IT'S CALLED "EAU DE GRANDMA".

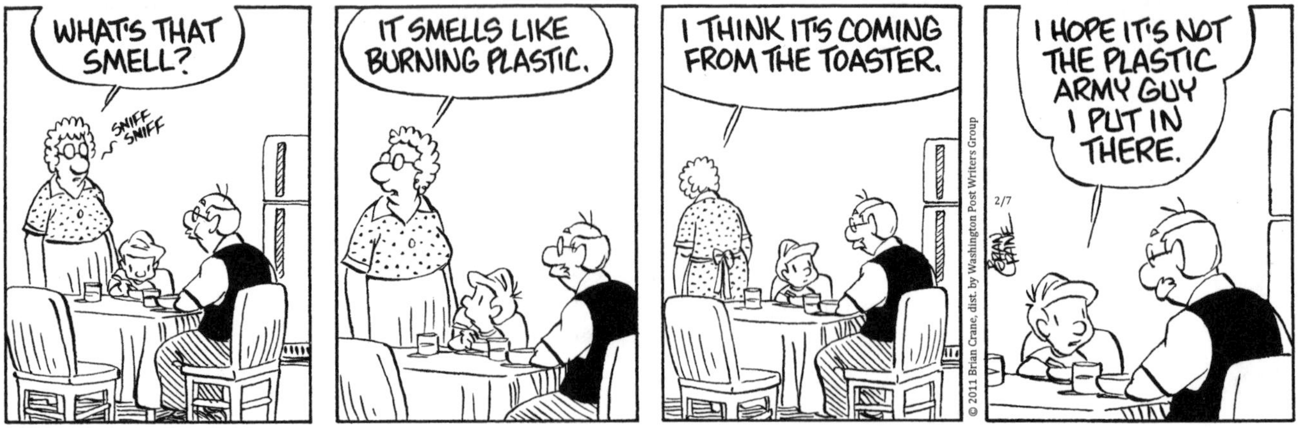
WHAT'S THAT SMELL?
SNIFF SNIFF
IT SMELLS LIKE BURNING PLASTIC.
I THINK IT'S COMING FROM THE TOASTER.
© 2011 Brian Crane, dist. by Washington Post Writers Group
2/7
BRIAN CRANE
I HOPE IT'S NOT THE PLASTIC ARMY GUY I PUT IN THERE.

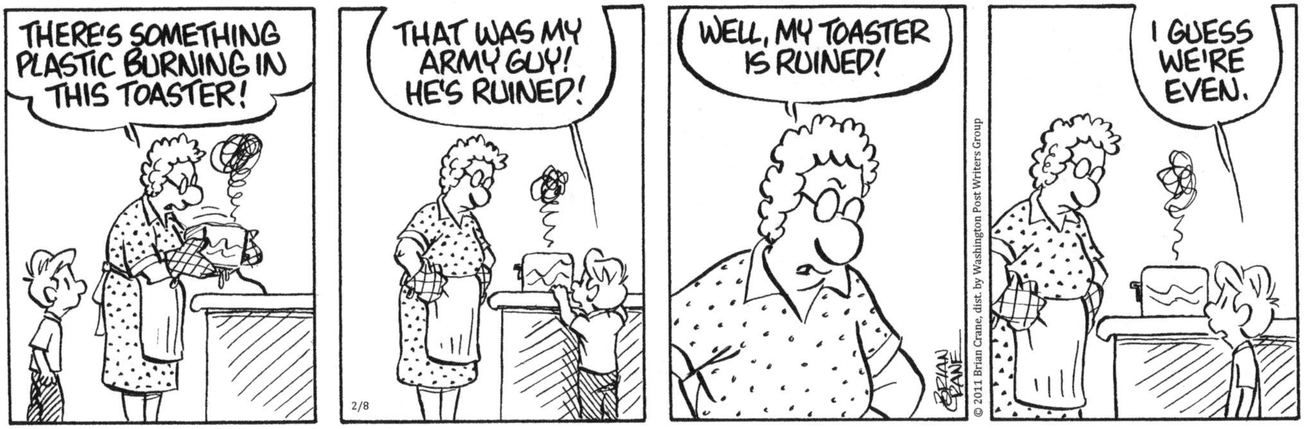
THERE'S SOMETHING PLASTIC BURNING IN THIS TOASTER!
THAT WAS MY ARMY GUY! HE'S RUINED!
2/8
WELL, MY TOASTER IS RUINED!
BRIAN CRANE
I GUESS WE'RE EVEN.

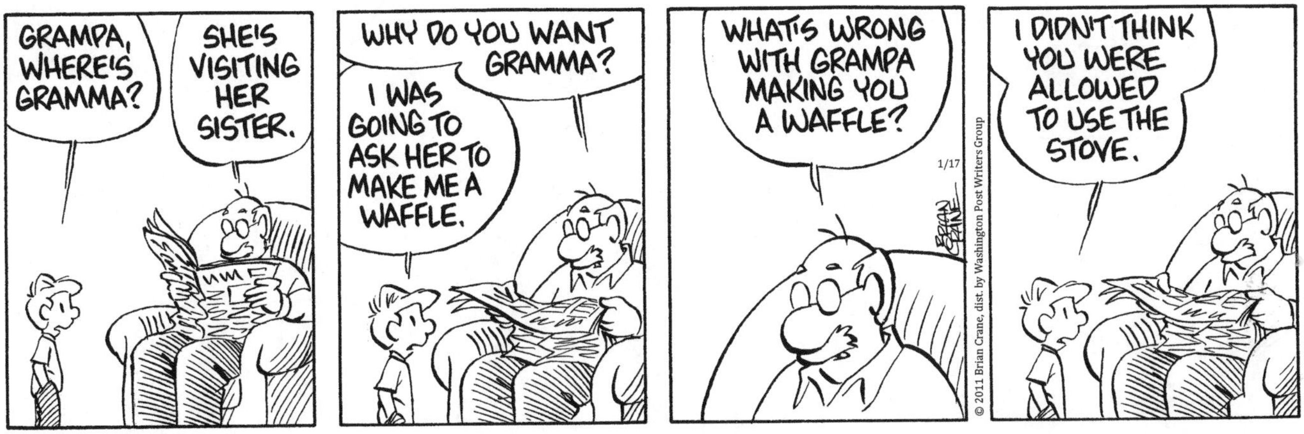
GRAMPA, WHERE'S GRAMMA?
SHE'S VISITING HER SISTER.
WHY DO YOU WANT GRAMMA?
I WAS GOING TO ASK HER TO MAKE ME A WAFFLE.
WHAT'S WRONG WITH GRAMPA MAKING YOU A WAFFLE?
1/17
BRIAN CRANE
I DIDN'T THINK YOU WERE ALLOWED TO USE THE STOVE.

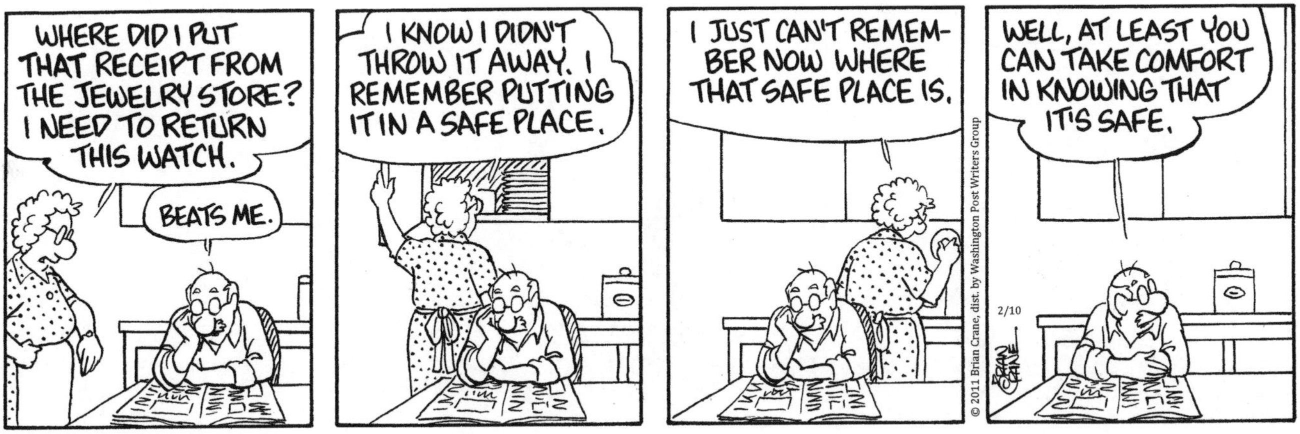
WHERE DID I PUT THAT RECEIPT FROM THE JEWELRY STORE? I NEED TO RETURN THIS WATCH.
BEATS ME.
I KNOW I DIDN'T THROW IT AWAY. I REMEMBER PUTTING IT IN A SAFE PLACE.
I JUST CAN'T REMEMBER NOW WHERE THAT SAFE PLACE IS.
2/10
BRIAN CRANE
WELL, AT LEAST YOU CAN TAKE COMFORT IN KNOWING THAT IT'S SAFE.

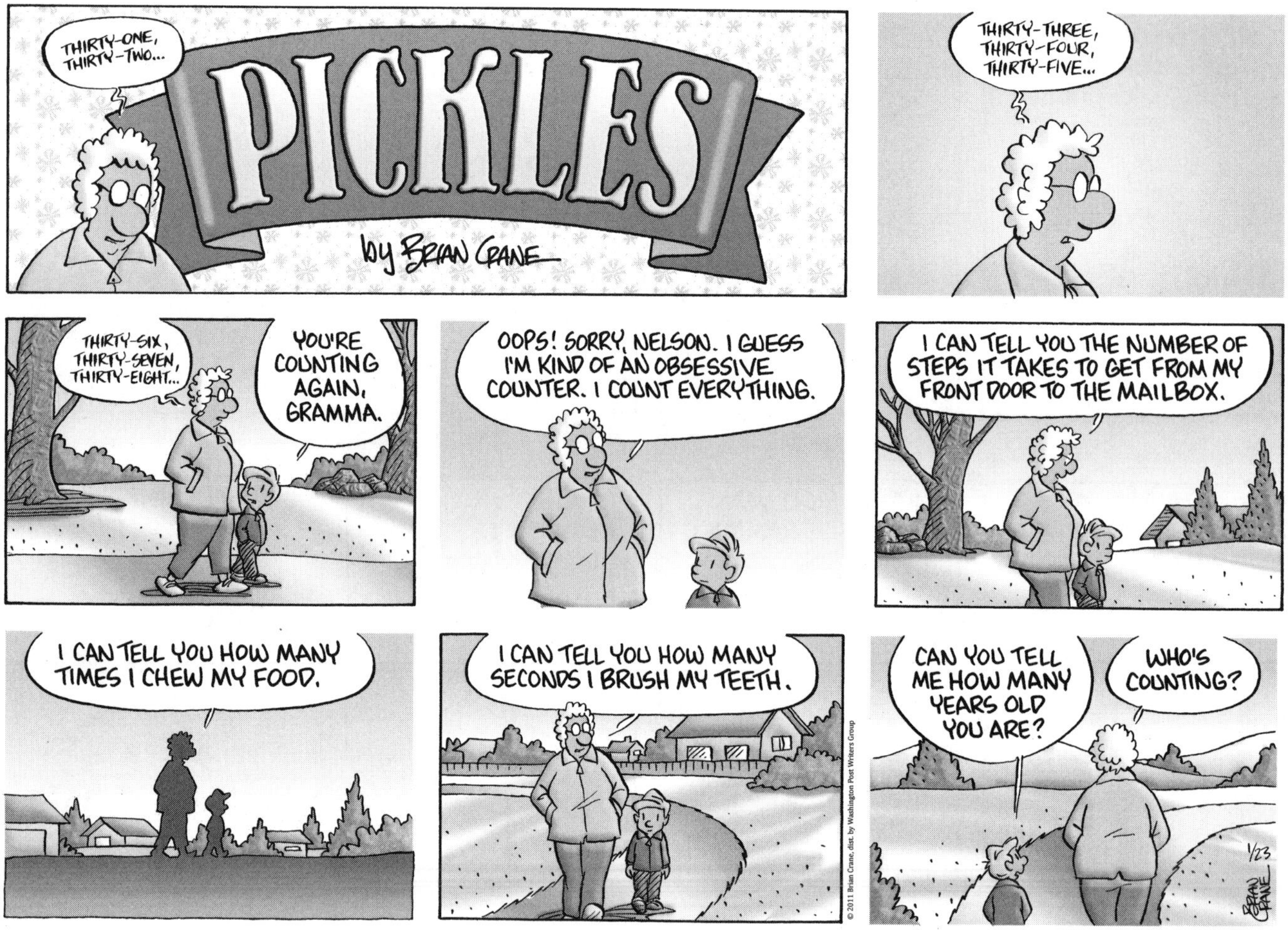
PICKLES
by BRIAN CRANE
THIRTY-ONE, THIRTY-TWO...
THIRTY-THREE, THIRTY-FOUR, THIRTY-FIVE...
THIRTY-SIX, THIRTY-SEVEN, THIRTY-EIGHT...
YOU'RE COUNTING AGAIN, GRAMMA.
OOPS! SORRY, NELSON. I GUESS I'M KIND OF AN OBSESSIVE COUNTER. I COUNT EVERYTHING.
I CAN TELL YOU THE NUMBER OF STEPS IT TAKES TO GET FROM MY FRONT DOOR TO THE MAILBOX.
I CAN TELL YOU HOW MANY TIMES I CHEW MY FOOD.
I CAN TELL YOU HOW MANY SECONDS I BRUSH MY TEETH.
CAN YOU TELL ME HOW MANY YEARS OLD YOU ARE?
WHO'S COUNTING?
1/23
BRIAN CRANE
© 2011 Brian Crane, dist. by Washington Post Writers Group

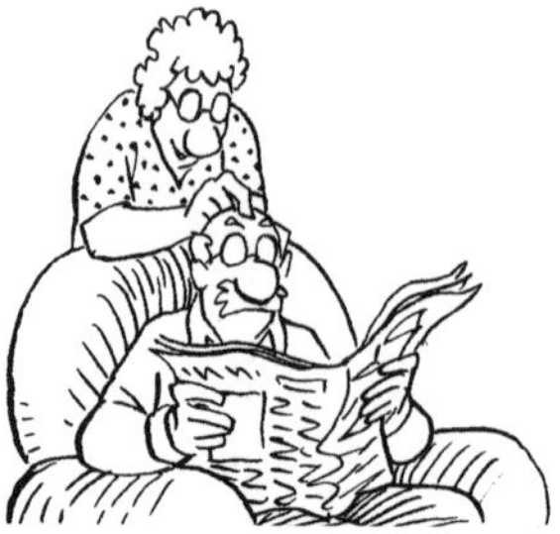

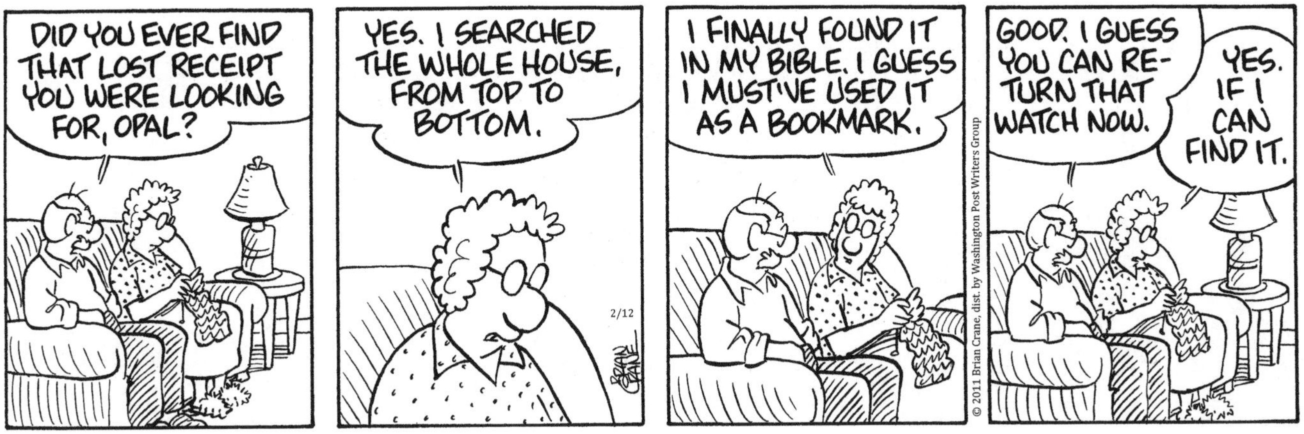
DID YOU EVER FIND THAT LOST RECEIPT YOU WERE LOOKING FOR, OPAL?
YES. I SEARCHED THE WHOLE HOUSE, FROM TOP TO BOTTOM.
2/12
I FINALLY FOUND IT IN MY BIBLE. I GUESS I MUST'VE USED IT AS A BOOKMARK.
© 2011 Brian Crane, dist. by Washington Post Writers Group
GOOD. I GUESS YOU CAN RE-TURN THAT WATCH NOW.
YES. IF I CAN FIND IT.

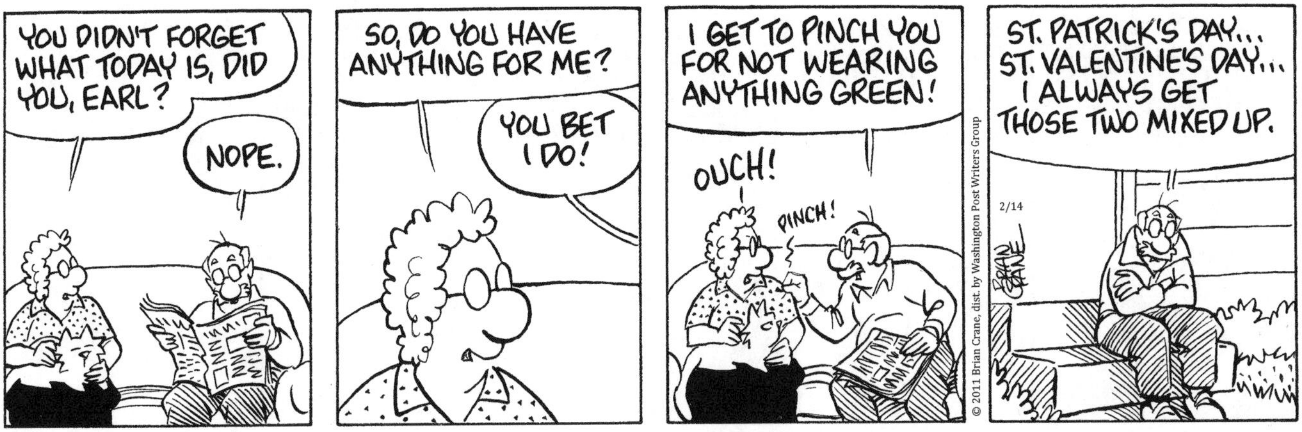
YOU DIDN'T FORGET WHAT TODAY IS, DID YOU, EARL?
NOPE.
SO, DO YOU HAVE ANYTHING FOR ME?
YOU BET I DO!
I GET TO PINCH YOU FOR NOT WEARING ANYTHING GREEN!
OUCH!
PINCH!
© 2011 Brian Crane, dist. by Washington Post Writers Group
ST. PATRICK'S DAY... ST. VALENTINE'S DAY... I ALWAYS GET THOSE TWO MIXED UP.
2/14

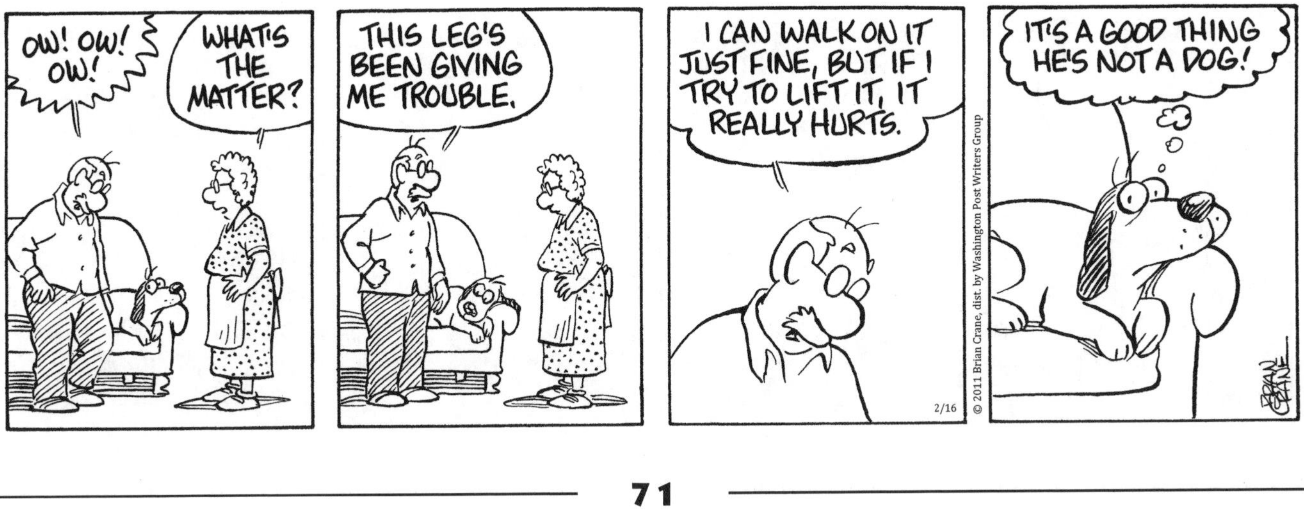
OW! OW! OW!
WHAT'S THE MATTER?
THIS LEG'S BEEN GIVING ME TROUBLE.
I CAN WALK ON IT JUST FINE, BUT IF I TRY TO LIFT IT, IT REALLY HURTS.
2/16
© 2011 Brian Crane, dist. by Washington Post Writers Group
IT'S A GOOD THING HE'S NOT A DOG!

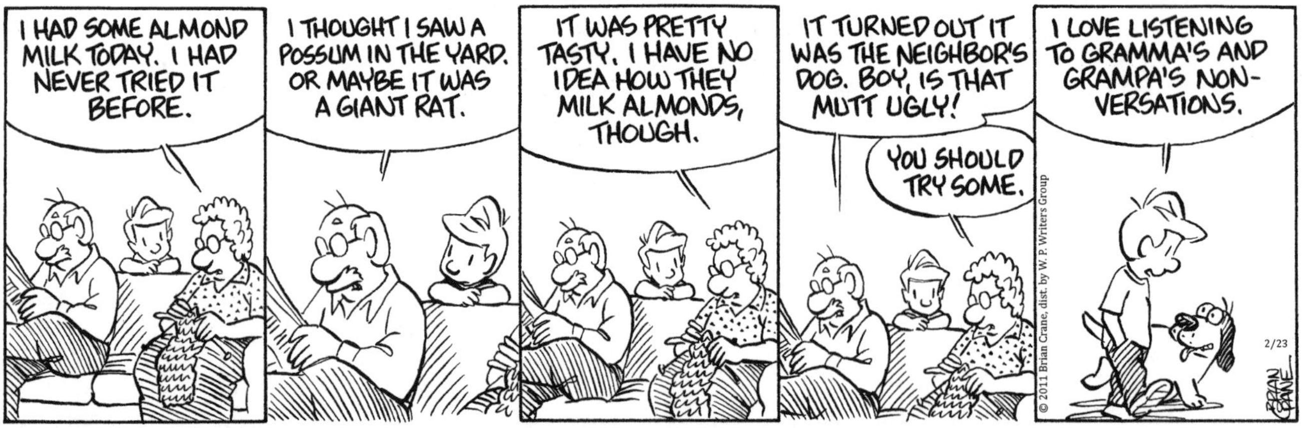
I HAD SOME ALMOND MILK TODAY. I HAD NEVER TRIED IT BEFORE.
I THOUGHT I SAW A POSSUM IN THE YARD. OR MAYBE IT WAS A GIANT RAT.
IT WAS PRETTY TASTY. I HAVE NO IDEA HOW THEY MILK ALMONDS, THOUGH.
IT TURNED OUT IT WAS THE NEIGHBOR'S DOG. BOY, IS THAT MUTT UGLY!
YOU SHOULD TRY SOME.
I LOVE LISTENING TO GRAMMA'S AND GRAMPA'S NON-VERSATIONS.
© 2011 Brian Crane, dist. by W. P. Writers Group
2/23
BRIAN CRANE

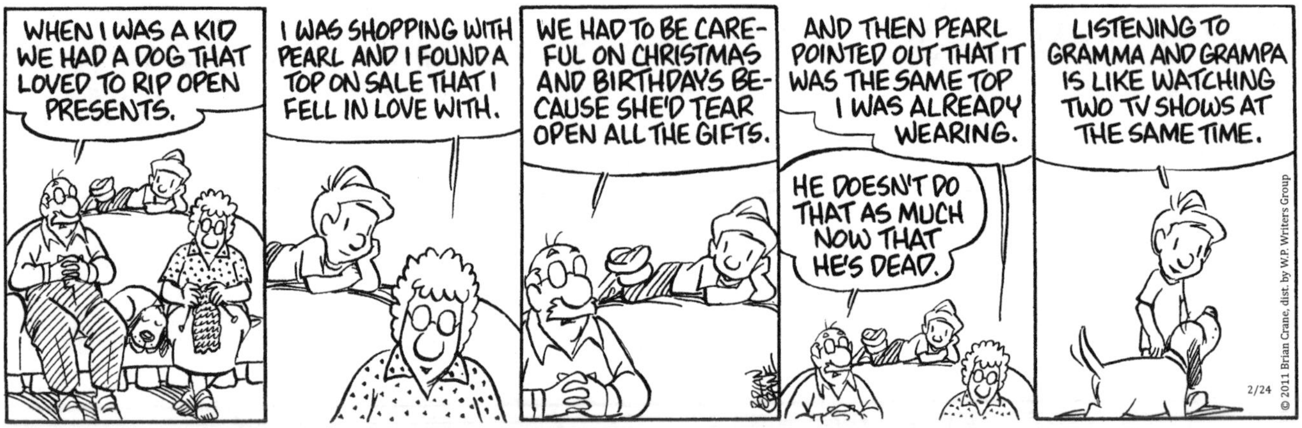
WHEN I WAS A KID WE HAD A DOG THAT LOVED TO RIP OPEN PRESENTS.
I WAS SHOPPING WITH PEARL AND I FOUND A TOP ON SALE THAT I FELL IN LOVE WITH.
WE HAD TO BE CARE-FUL ON CHRISTMAS AND BIRTHDAYS BE-CAUSE SHE'D TEAR OPEN ALL THE GIFTS.
AND THEN PEARL POINTED OUT THAT IT WAS THE SAME TOP I WAS ALREADY WEARING.
HE DOESN'T DO THAT AS MUCH NOW THAT HE'S DEAD.
LISTENING TO GRAMMA AND GRAMPA IS LIKE WATCHING TWO TV SHOWS AT THE SAME TIME.
BRIAN CRANE
© 2011 Brian Crane, dist. by W.P. Writers Group
2/24

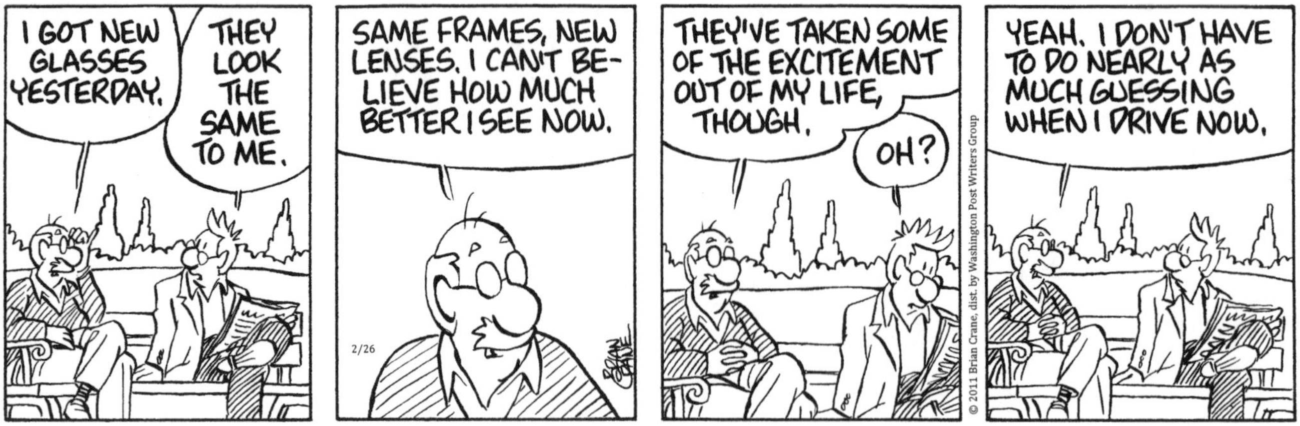
I GOT NEW GLASSES YESTERDAY.
THEY LOOK THE SAME TO ME.
SAME FRAMES, NEW LENSES. I CAN'T BE-LIEVE HOW MUCH BETTER I SEE NOW.
2/26
BRIAN CRANE
THEY'VE TAKEN SOME OF THE EXCITEMENT OUT OF MY LIFE, THOUGH.
OH?
© 2011 Brian Crane, dist. by Washington Post Writers Group
YEAH. I DON'T HAVE TO DO NEARLY AS MUCH GUESSING WHEN I DRIVE NOW.

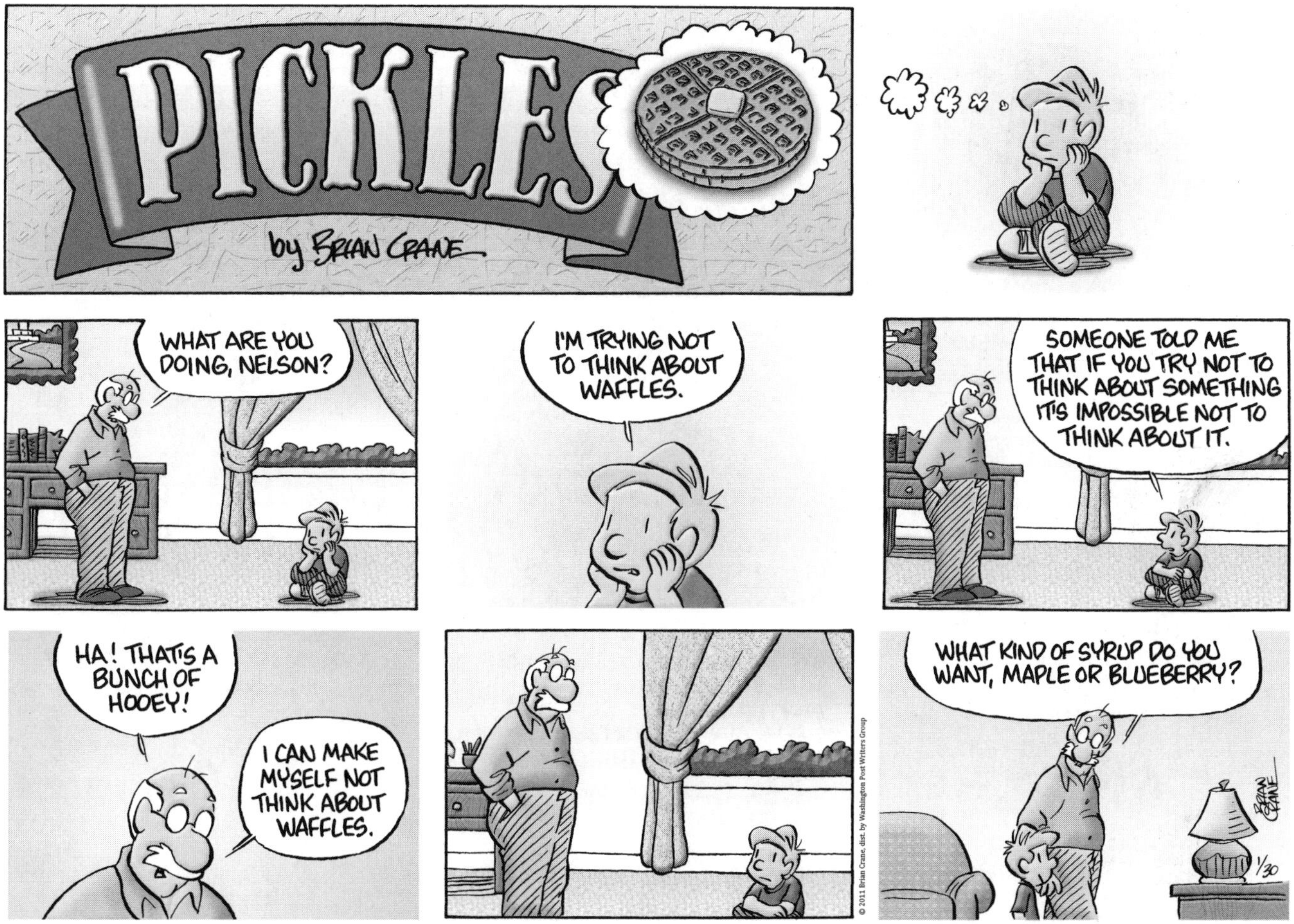
PICKLES
by BRIAN CRANE
WHAT ARE YOU DOING, NELSON?
I'M TRYING NOT TO THINK ABOUT WAFFLES.
SOMEONE TOLD ME THAT IF YOU TRY NOT TO THINK ABOUT SOMETHING IT'S IMPOSSIBLE NOT TO THINK ABOUT IT.
HA! THAT'S A BUNCH OF HOOEY!
I CAN MAKE MYSELF NOT THINK ABOUT WAFFLES.
© 2011 Brian Crane, dist. by Washington Post Writers Group
WHAT KIND OF SYRUP DO YOU WANT, MAPLE OR BLUEBERRY?
BRIAN CRANE
1/30

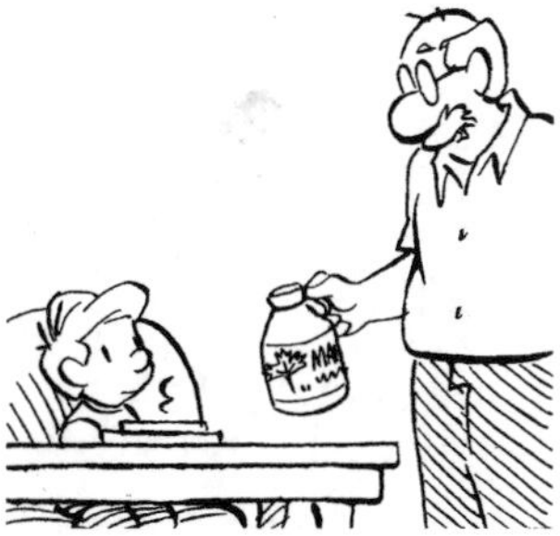

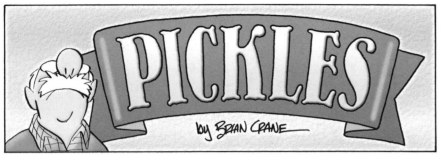

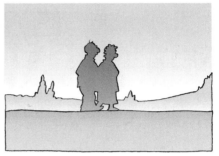

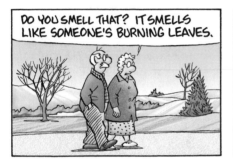

PICKLES
by BRIAN CRANE
DO YOU SMELL THAT? IT SMELLS LIKE SOMEONE'S BURNING LEAVES.
SNIFF SNIFF
SNIFF! SNAFFLE! SNORF!!
YEAH. I THINK YOU'RE RIGHT.
WHY DO YOU HAVE TO SNIFF LIKE THAT BEFORE YOU CAN SMELL ANYTHING? CAN'T YOU JUST SMELL THINGS THROUGH YOUR NORMAL BREATHING?
YOU KNOW I DON'T SMELL VERY GOOD.
YOU SAID IT, NOT ME.
© 2011 Brian Crane, dist. by Washington Post Writers Group

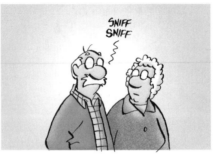

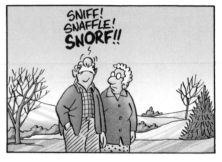

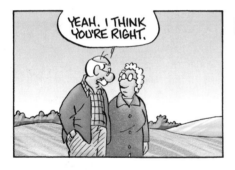

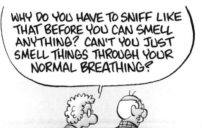

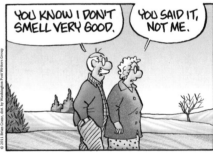

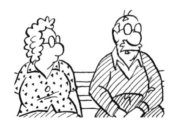

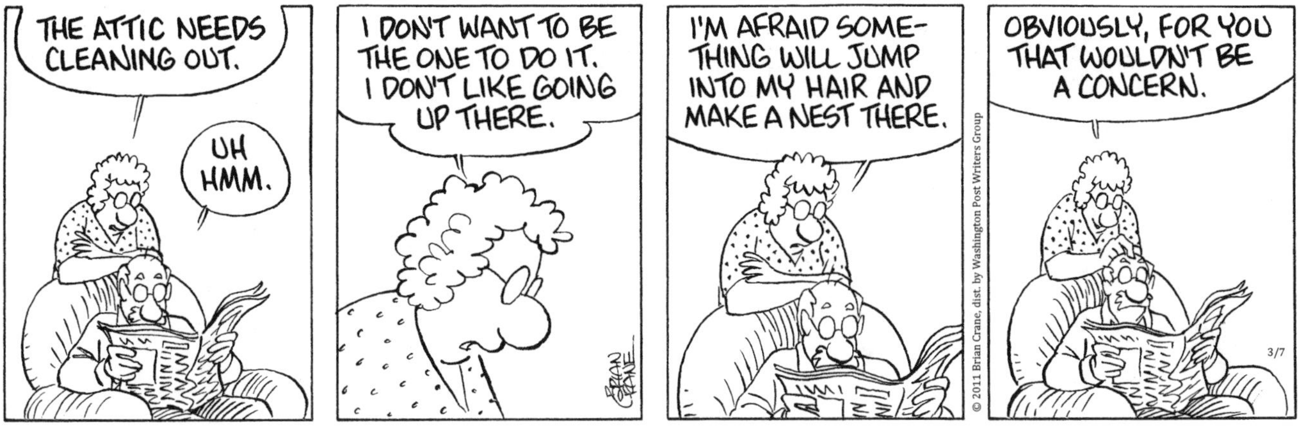
THE ATTIC NEEDS CLEANING OUT.
UH HMM.
I DON'T WANT TO BE THE ONE TO DO IT. I DON'T LIKE GOING UP THERE.
BRIAN CRANE
I'M AFRAID SOME-THING WILL JUMP INTO MY HAIR AND MAKE A NEST THERE.
© 2011 Brian Crane, dist. by Washington Post Writers Group
OBVIOUSLY, FOR YOU THAT WOULDN'T BE A CONCERN.
3/7

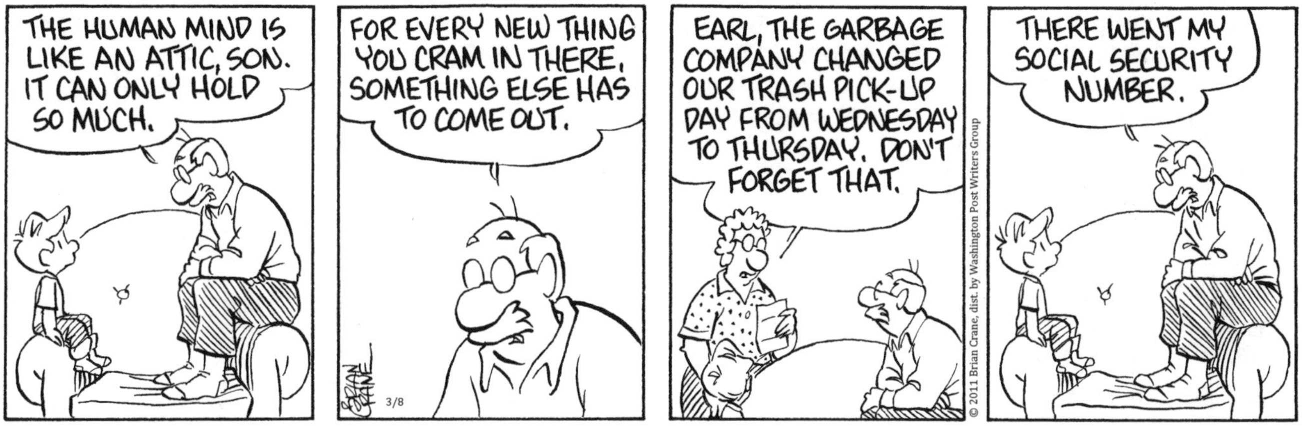
THE HUMAN MIND IS LIKE AN ATTIC, SON. IT CAN ONLY HOLD SO MUCH.
FOR EVERY NEW THING YOU CRAM IN THERE, SOMETHING ELSE HAS TO COME OUT.
BRIAN CRANE
3/8
EARL, THE GARBAGE COMPANY CHANGED OUR TRASH PICK-UP DAY FROM WEDNESDAY TO THURSDAY. DON'T FORGET THAT.
© 2011 Brian Crane, dist. by Washington Post Writers Group
THERE WENT MY SOCIAL SECURITY NUMBER.

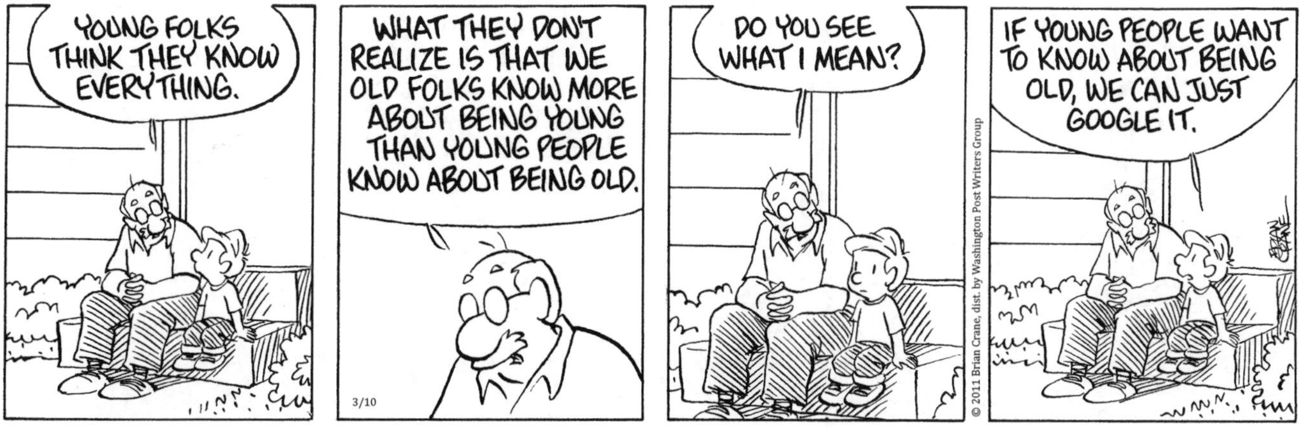
YOUNG FOLKS THINK THEY KNOW EVERYTHING.
WHAT THEY DON'T REALIZE IS THAT WE OLD FOLKS KNOW MORE ABOUT BEING YOUNG THAN YOUNG PEOPLE KNOW ABOUT BEING OLD.
3/10
DO YOU SEE WHAT I MEAN?
© 2011 Brian Crane, dist. by Washington Post Writers Group
IF YOUNG PEOPLE WANT TO KNOW ABOUT BEING OLD, WE CAN JUST GOOGLE IT.
BRIAN CRANE

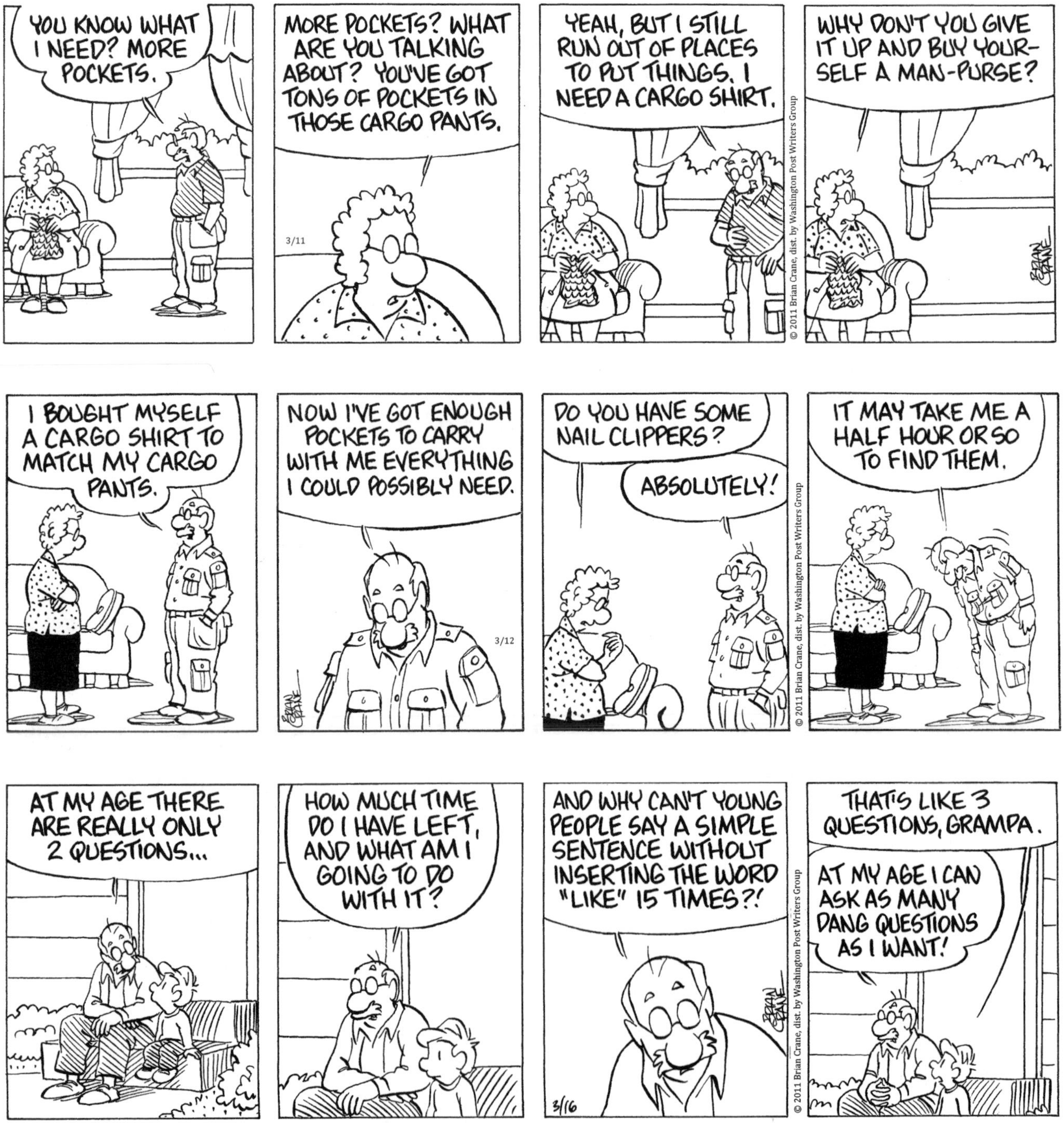
YOU KNOW WHAT I NEED? MORE POCKETS.
MORE POCKETS? WHAT ARE YOU TALKING ABOUT? YOU'VE GOT TONS OF POCKETS IN THOSE CARGO PANTS.
3/11
YEAH, BUT I STILL RUN OUT OF PLACES TO PUT THINGS. I NEED A CARGO SHIRT.
© 2011 Brian Crane, dist. by Washington Post Writers Group
WHY DON'T YOU GIVE IT UP AND BUY YOURSELF A MAN-PURSE?
BRIAN CRANE
I BOUGHT MYSELF A CARGO SHIRT TO MATCH MY CARGO PANTS.
NOW I'VE GOT ENOUGH POCKETS TO CARRY WITH ME EVERYTHING I COULD POSSIBLY NEED.
3/12
BRIAN CRANE
DO YOU HAVE SOME NAIL CLIPPERS?
ABSOLUTELY!
© 2011 Brian Crane, dist. by Washington Post Writers Group
IT MAY TAKE ME A HALF HOUR OR SO TO FIND THEM.
AT MY AGE THERE ARE REALLY ONLY 2 QUESTIONS...
HOW MUCH TIME DO I HAVE LEFT, AND WHAT AM I GOING TO DO WITH IT?
AND WHY CAN'T YOUNG PEOPLE SAY A SIMPLE SENTENCE WITHOUT INSERTING THE WORD "LIKE" 15 TIMES?!
3/16
BRIAN CRANE
© 2011 Brian Crane, dist. by Washington Post Writers Group
THAT'S LIKE 3 QUESTIONS, GRAMPA.
AT MY AGE I CAN ASK AS MANY DANG QUESTIONS AS I WANT!

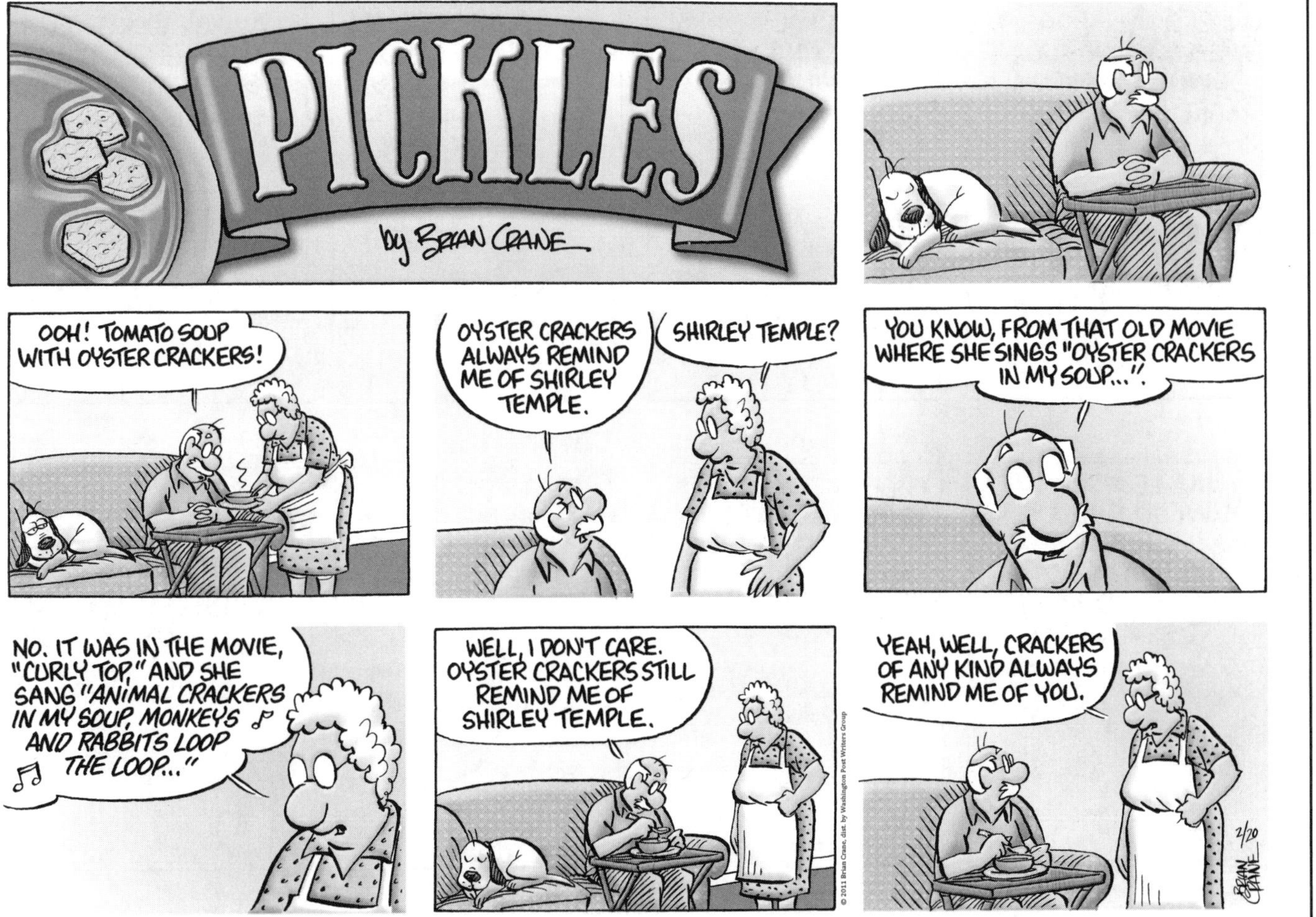
PICKLES
by BRIAN CRANE
OOH! TOMATO SOUP WITH OYSTER CRACKERS!
OYSTER CRACKERS ALWAYS REMIND ME OF SHIRLEY TEMPLE.
SHIRLEY TEMPLE?
YOU KNOW, FROM THAT OLD MOVIE WHERE SHE SINGS "OYSTER CRACKERS IN MY SOUP...".
NO. IT WAS IN THE MOVIE, "CURLY TOP," AND SHE SANG "ANIMAL CRACKERS IN MY SOUP, MONKEYS AND RABBITS LOOP THE LOOP..."
WELL, I DON'T CARE. OYSTER CRACKERS STILL REMIND ME OF SHIRLEY TEMPLE.
YEAH, WELL, CRACKERS OF ANY KIND ALWAYS REMIND ME OF YOU.
© 2011 Brian Crane, dist. by Washington Post Writers Group
2/20
BRIAN CRANE

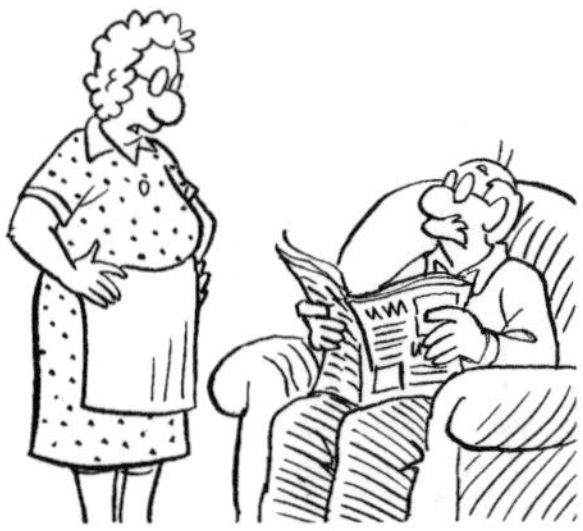

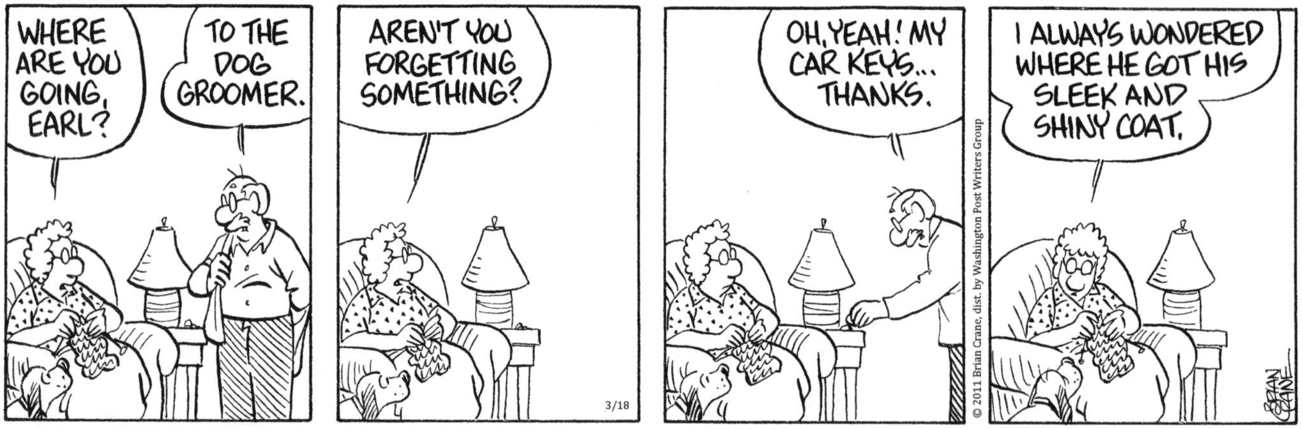
WHERE ARE YOU GOING, EARL?
TO THE DOG GROOMER.
AREN'T YOU FORGETTING SOMETHING?
3/18
OH, YEAH! MY CAR KEYS... THANKS.
© 2011 Brian Crane, dist. by Washington Post Writers Group
I ALWAYS WONDERED WHERE HE GOT HIS SLEEK AND SHINY COAT.
BRIAN CRANE

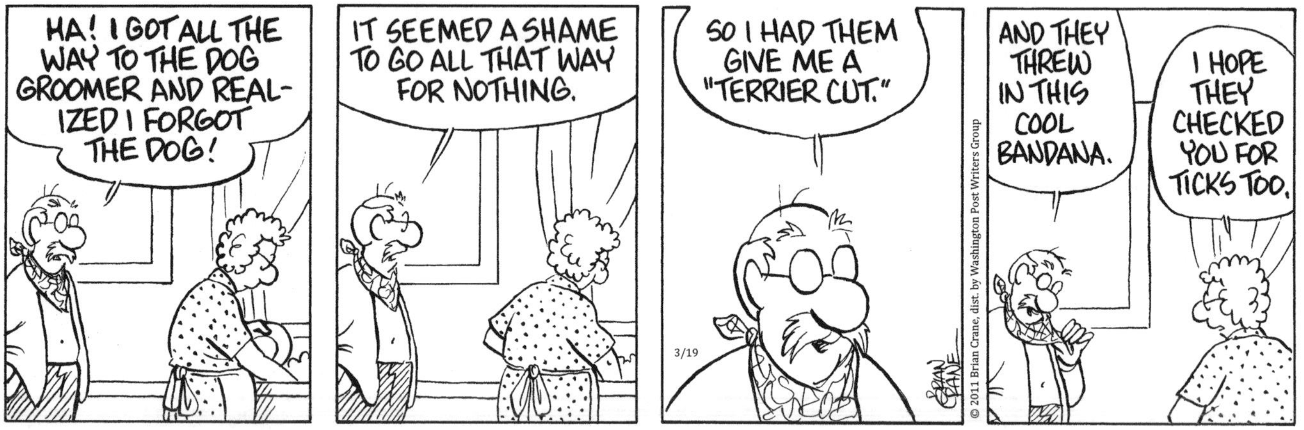
HA! I GOT ALL THE WAY TO THE DOG GROOMER AND REALIZED I FORGOT THE DOG!
IT SEEMED A SHAME TO GO ALL THAT WAY FOR NOTHING.
SO I HAD THEM GIVE ME A "TERRIER CUT."
3/19
BRIAN CRANE
© 2011 Brian Crane, dist. by Washington Post Writers Group
AND THEY THREW IN THIS COOL BANDANA.
I HOPE THEY CHECKED YOU FOR TICKS TOO.

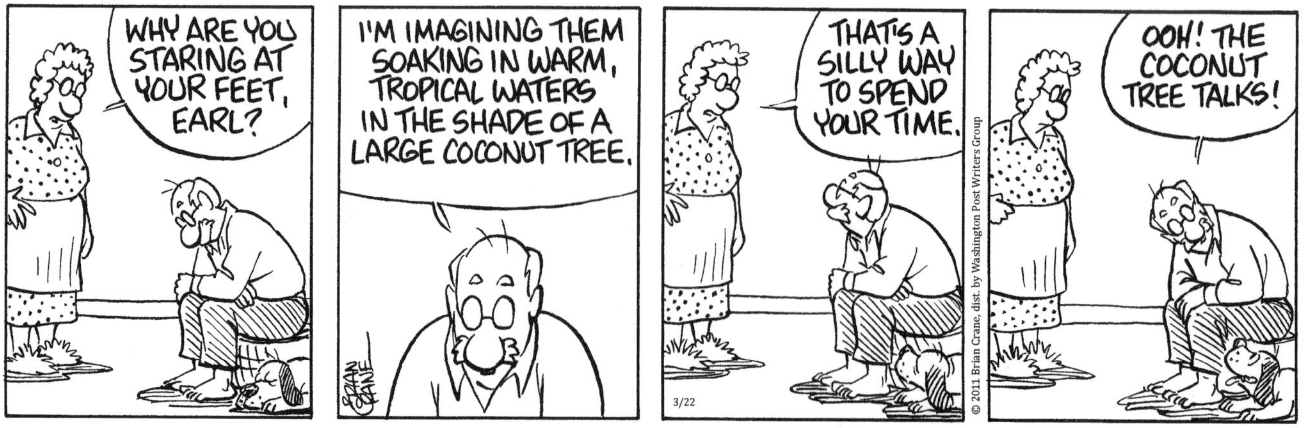
WHY ARE YOU STARING AT YOUR FEET, EARL?
I'M IMAGINING THEM SOAKING IN WARM, TROPICAL WATERS IN THE SHADE OF A LARGE COCONUT TREE.
BRIAN CRANE
THAT'S A SILLY WAY TO SPEND YOUR TIME.
3/22
© 2011 Brian Crane, dist. by Washington Post Writers Group
OOH! THE COCONUT TREE TALKS!

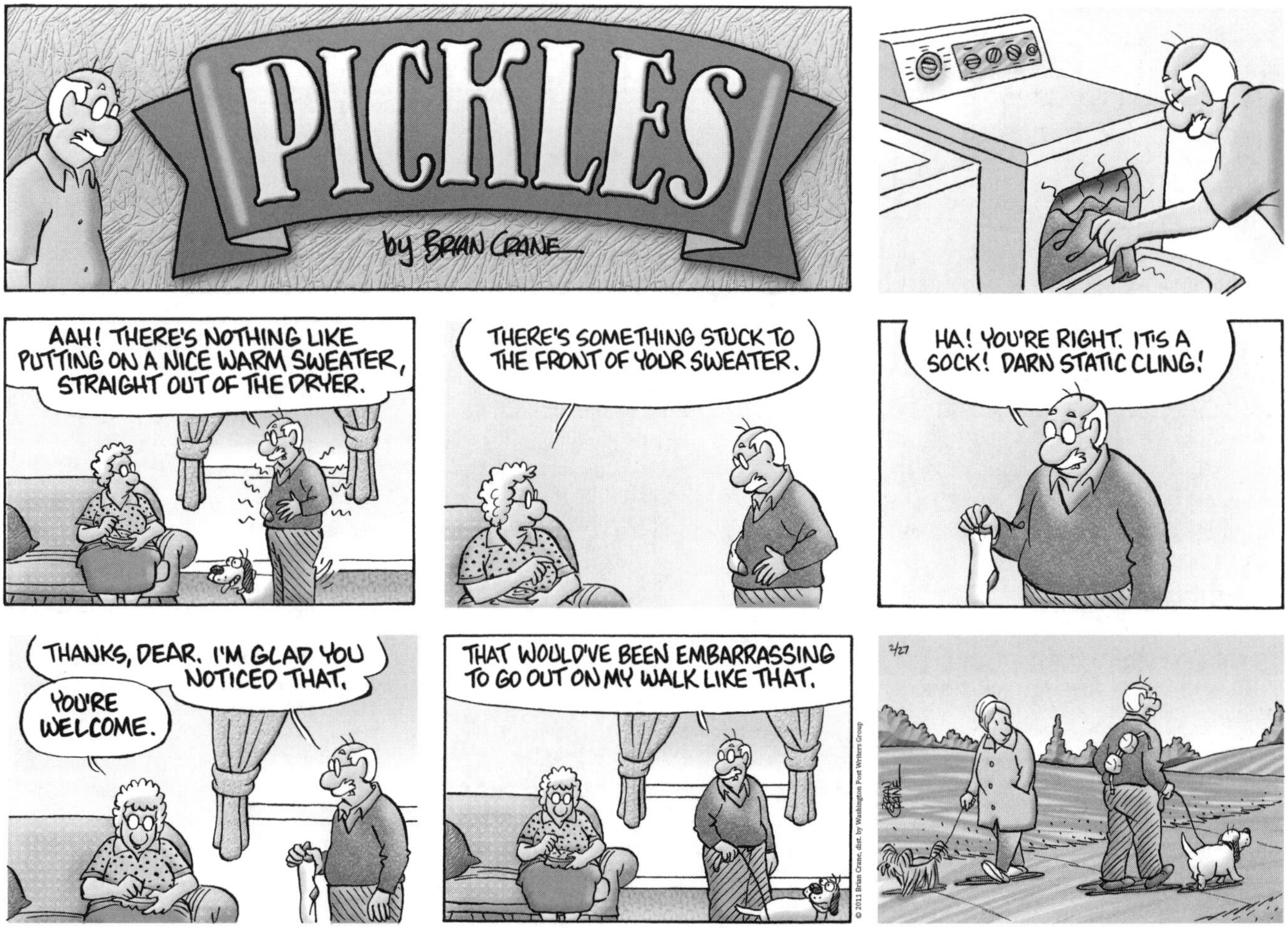
PICKLES
by BRIAN CRANE
AAH! THERE'S NOTHING LIKE PUTTING ON A NICE WARM SWEATER, STRAIGHT OUT OF THE DRYER.
THERE'S SOMETHING STUCK TO THE FRONT OF YOUR SWEATER.
HA! YOU'RE RIGHT. IT'S A SOCK! DARN STATIC CLING!
THANKS, DEAR. I'M GLAD YOU NOTICED THAT.
YOU'RE WELCOME.
THAT WOULD'VE BEEN EMBARRASSING TO GO OUT ON MY WALK LIKE THAT.
© 2011 Brian Crane, dist. by Washington Post Writers Group
2/27

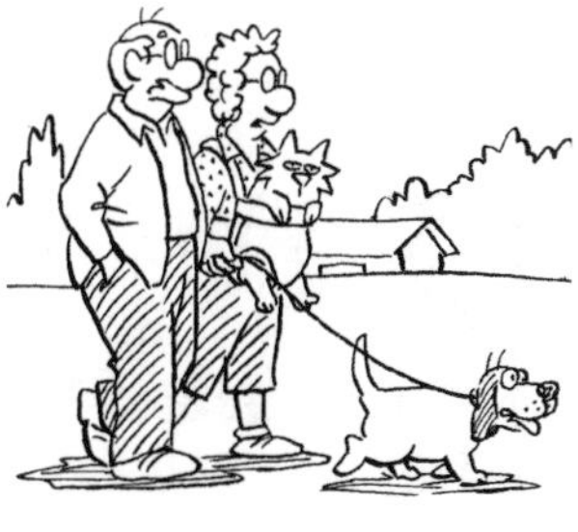

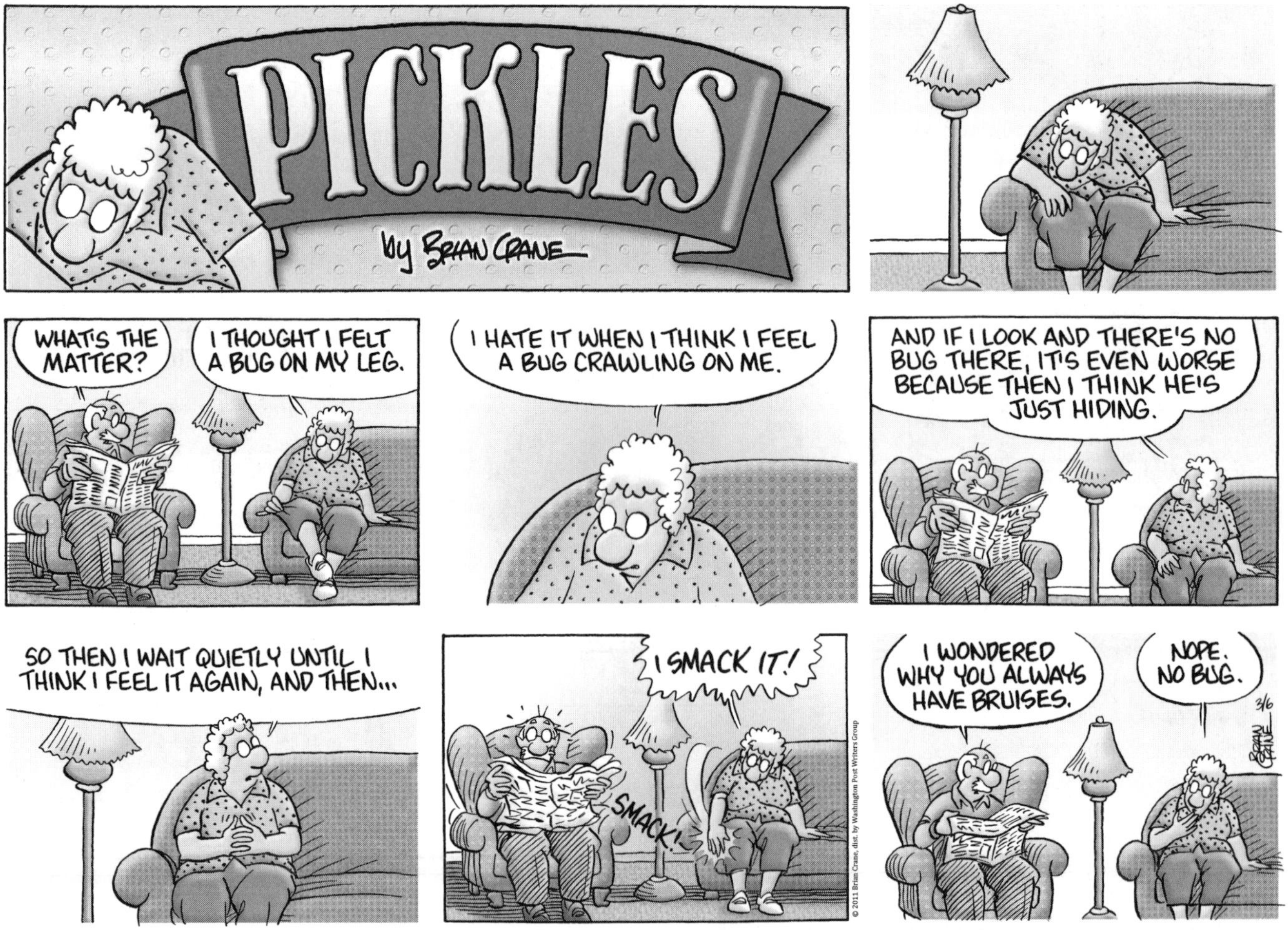
PICKLES
by BRIAN CRANE
WHAT'S THE MATTER?
I THOUGHT I FELT A BUG ON MY LEG.
I HATE IT WHEN I THINK I FEEL A BUG CRAWLING ON ME.
AND IF I LOOK AND THERE'S NO BUG THERE, IT'S EVEN WORSE BECAUSE THEN I THINK HE'S JUST HIDING.
SO THEN I WAIT QUIETLY UNTIL I THINK I FEEL IT AGAIN, AND THEN...
I SMACK IT!
SMACK!
I WONDERED WHY YOU ALWAYS HAVE BRUISES.
NOPE. NO BUG.
3/6
BRIAN CRANE
© 2011 Brian Crane, dist. by Washington Post Writers Group

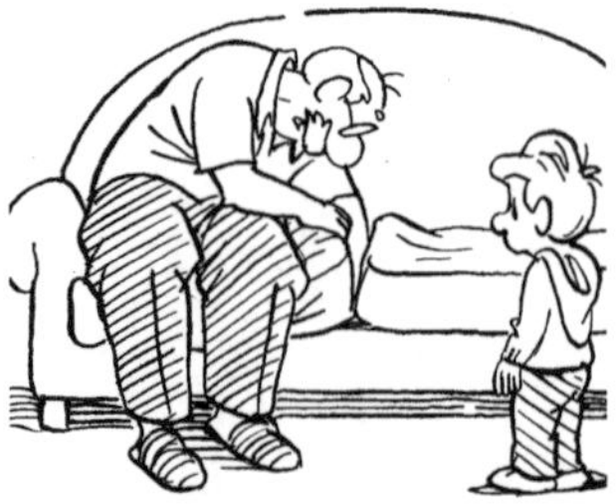

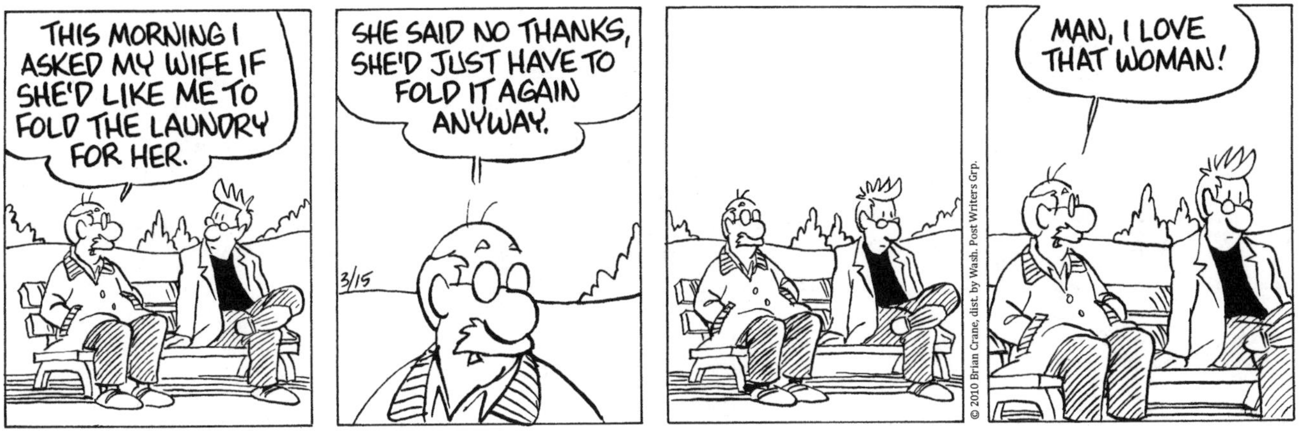
THIS MORNING I ASKED MY WIFE IF SHE'D LIKE ME TO FOLD THE LAUNDRY FOR HER.
SHE SAID NO THANKS, SHE'D JUST HAVE TO FOLD IT AGAIN ANYWAY.
3/15
MAN, I LOVE THAT WOMAN!

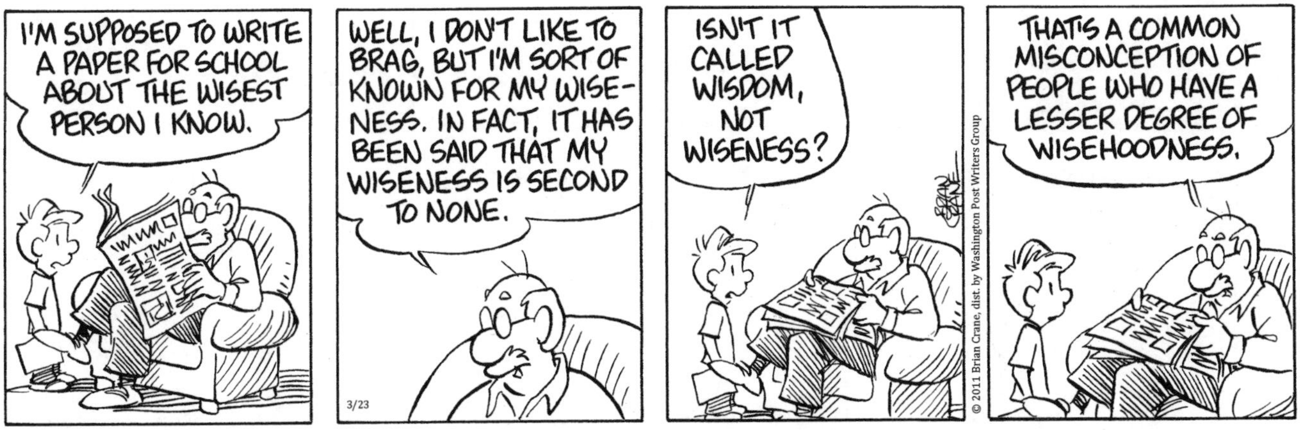
I'M SUPPOSED TO WRITE A PAPER FOR SCHOOL ABOUT THE WISEST PERSON I KNOW.
WELL, I DON'T LIKE TO BRAG, BUT I'M SORT OF KNOWN FOR MY WISENESS. IN FACT, IT HAS BEEN SAID THAT MY WISENESS IS SECOND TO NONE.
3/23
ISN'T IT CALLED WISDOM, NOT WISENESS?
THAT'S A COMMON MISCONCEPTION OF PEOPLE WHO HAVE A LESSER DEGREE OF WISEHOODNESS.

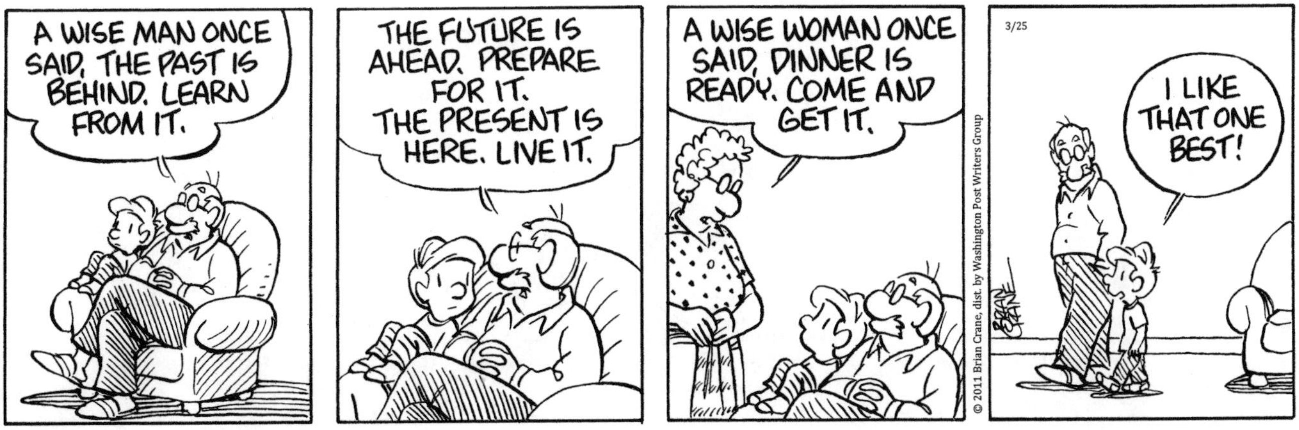
A WISE MAN ONCE SAID, THE PAST IS BEHIND. LEARN FROM IT.
THE FUTURE IS AHEAD. PREPARE FOR IT. THE PRESENT IS HERE. LIVE IT.
A WISE WOMAN ONCE SAID, DINNER IS READY. COME AND GET IT.
3/25
I LIKE THAT ONE BEST!

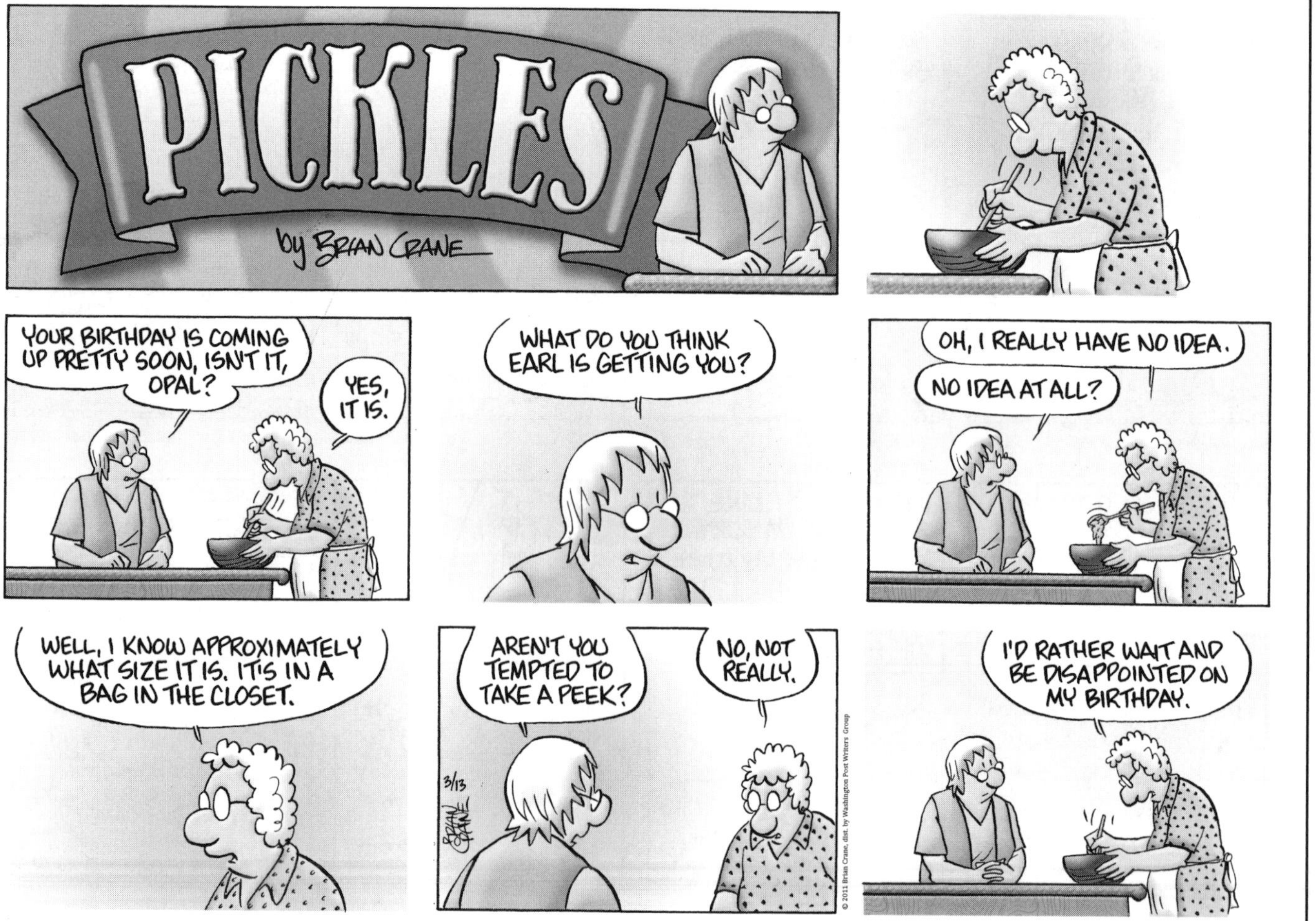
PICKLES
by BRIAN CRANE
YOUR BIRTHDAY IS COMING UP PRETTY SOON, ISN'T IT, OPAL?
YES, IT IS.
WHAT DO YOU THINK EARL IS GETTING YOU?
OH, I REALLY HAVE NO IDEA.
NO IDEA AT ALL?
WELL, I KNOW APPROXIMATELY WHAT SIZE IT IS. IT'S IN A BAG IN THE CLOSET.
AREN'T YOU TEMPTED TO TAKE A PEEK?
NO, NOT REALLY.
3/13
BRIAN CRANE
© 2011 Brian Crane, dist. by Washington Post Writers Group
I'D RATHER WAIT AND BE DISAPPOINTED ON MY BIRTHDAY.

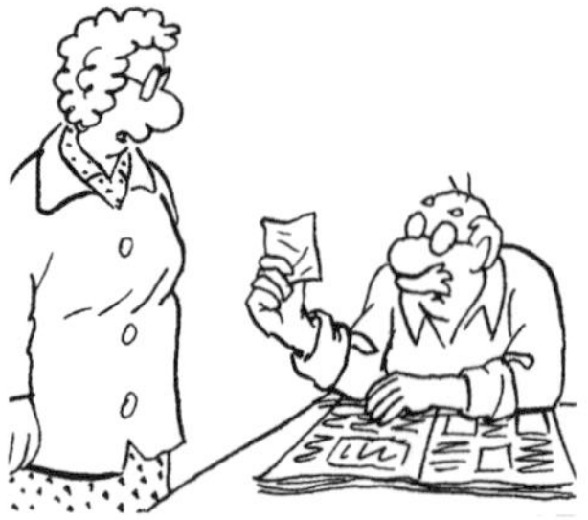

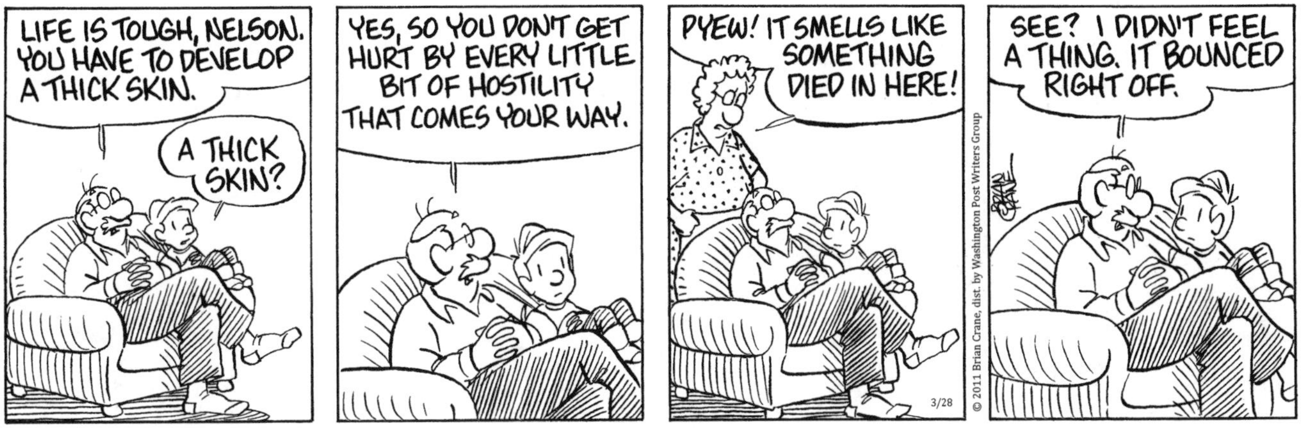
LIFE IS TOUGH, NELSON. YOU HAVE TO DEVELOP A THICK SKIN.
A THICK SKIN?
YES, SO YOU DON'T GET HURT BY EVERY LITTLE BIT OF HOSTILITY THAT COMES YOUR WAY.
PYEW! IT SMELLS LIKE SOMETHING DIED IN HERE!
3/28
© 2011 Brian Crane, dist. by Washington Post Writers Group
SEE? I DIDN'T FEEL A THING. IT BOUNCED RIGHT OFF.

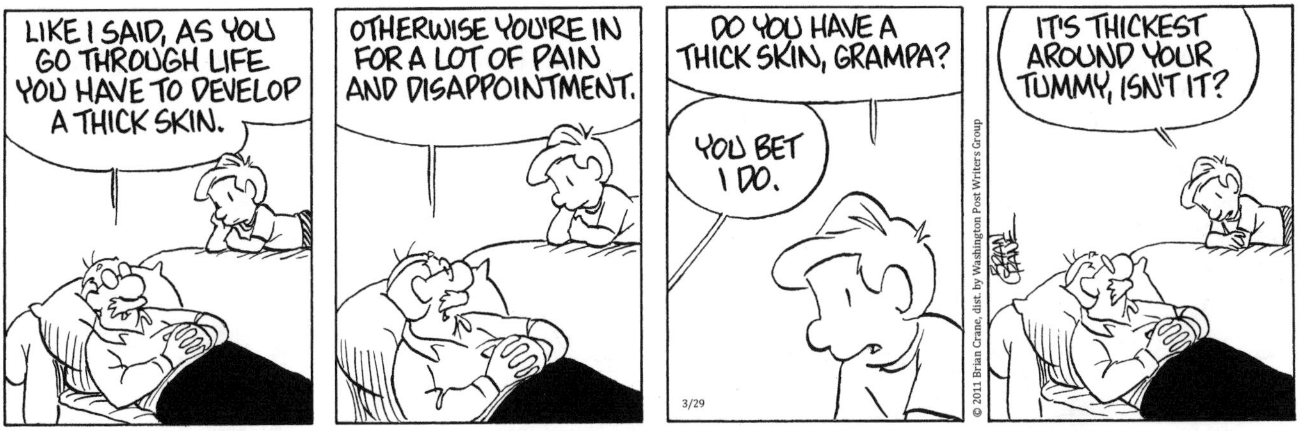
LIKE I SAID, AS YOU GO THROUGH LIFE YOU HAVE TO DEVELOP A THICK SKIN.
OTHERWISE YOU'RE IN FOR A LOT OF PAIN AND DISAPPOINTMENT.
DO YOU HAVE A THICK SKIN, GRAMPA?
YOU BET I DO.
3/29
© 2011 Brian Crane, dist. by Washington Post Writers Group
IT'S THICKEST AROUND YOUR TUMMY, ISN'T IT?

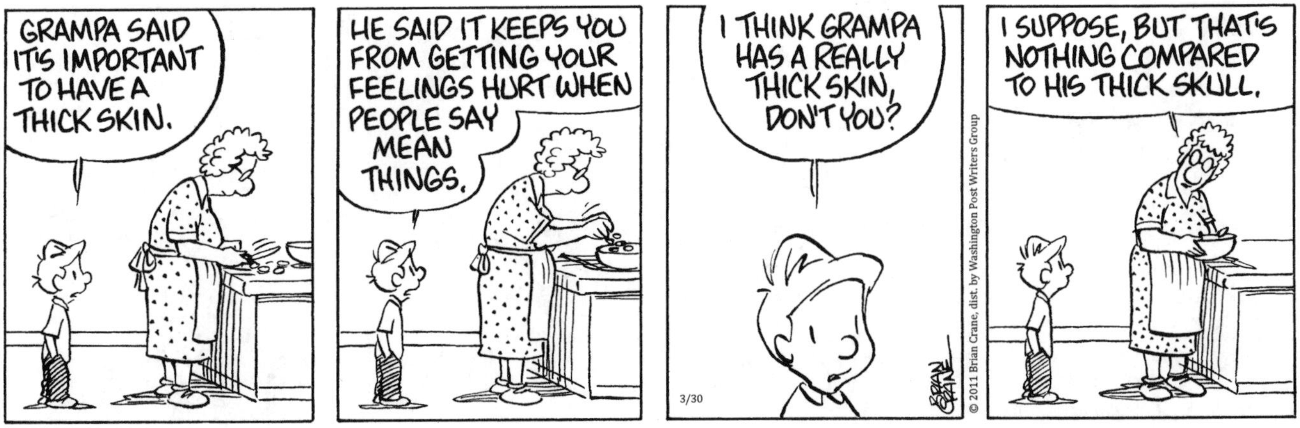
GRAMPA SAID IT'S IMPORTANT TO HAVE A THICK SKIN.
HE SAID IT KEEPS YOU FROM GETTING YOUR FEELINGS HURT WHEN PEOPLE SAY MEAN THINGS.
I THINK GRAMPA HAS A REALLY THICK SKIN, DON'T YOU?
3/30
© 2011 Brian Crane, dist. by Washington Post Writers Group
I SUPPOSE, BUT THAT'S NOTHING COMPARED TO HIS THICK SKULL.

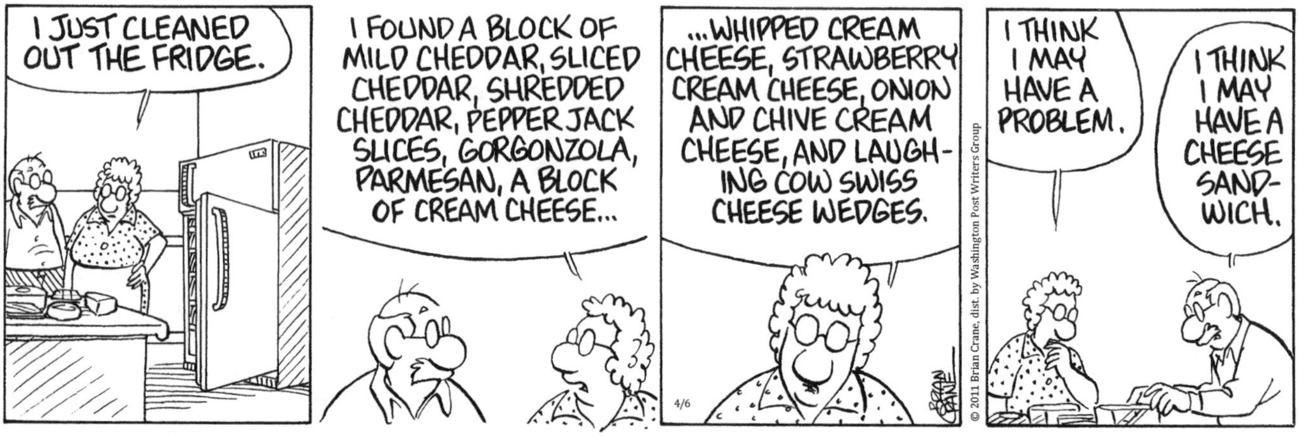
I JUST CLEANED OUT THE FRIDGE.
I FOUND A BLOCK OF MILD CHEDDAR, SLICED CHEDDAR, SHREDDED CHEDDAR, PEPPER JACK SLICES, GORGONZOLA, PARMESAN, A BLOCK OF CREAM CHEESE...
...WHIPPED CREAM CHEESE, STRAWBERRY CREAM CHEESE, ONION AND CHIVE CREAM CHEESE, AND LAUGHING COW SWISS CHEESE WEDGES.
I THINK I MAY HAVE A PROBLEM.
I THINK I MAY HAVE A CHEESE SANDWICH.

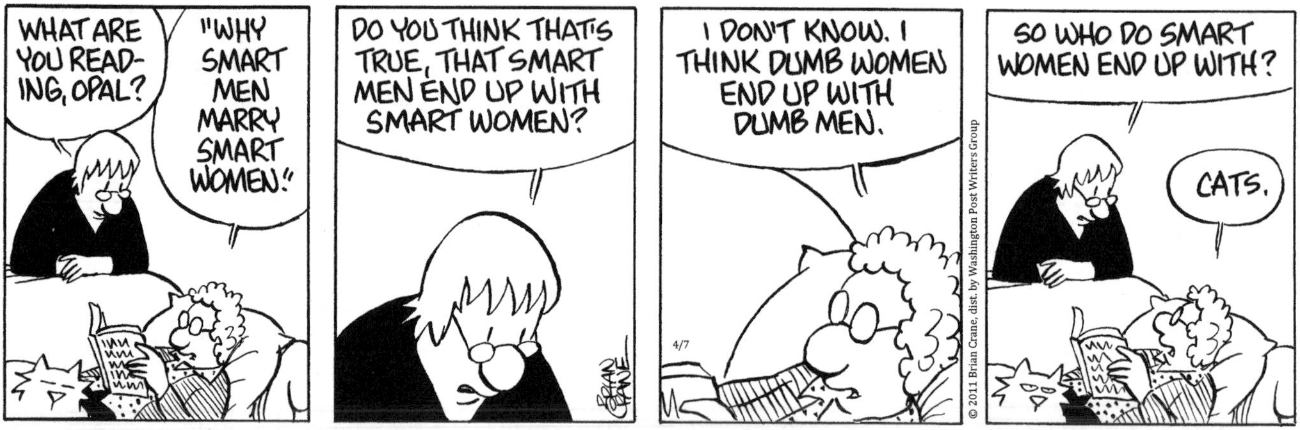
WHAT ARE YOU READING, OPAL?
"WHY SMART MEN MARRY SMART WOMEN."
DO YOU THINK THAT'S TRUE, THAT SMART MEN END UP WITH SMART WOMEN?
I DON'T KNOW. I THINK DUMB WOMEN END UP WITH DUMB MEN.
SO WHO DO SMART WOMEN END UP WITH?
CATS.

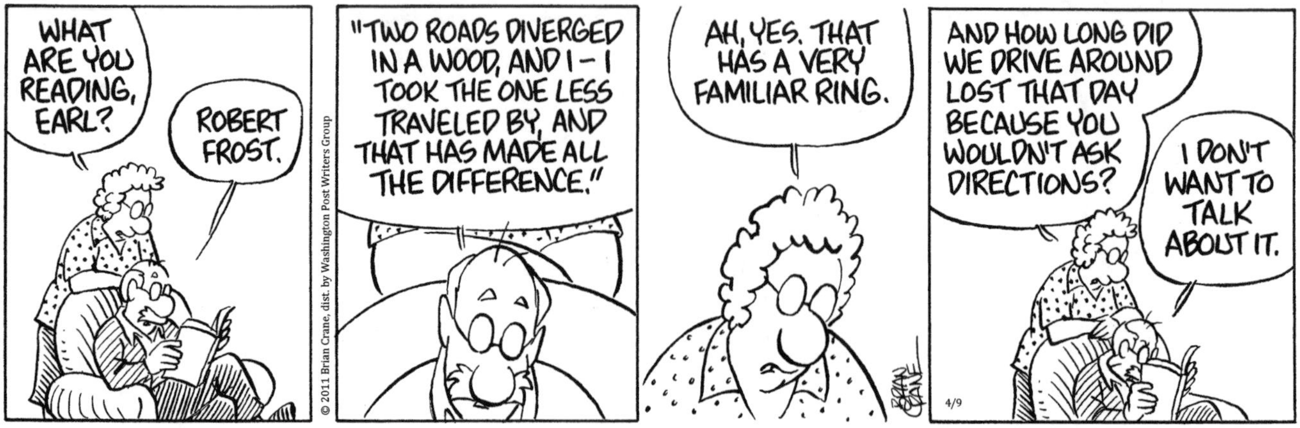
WHAT ARE YOU READING, EARL?
ROBERT FROST.
"TWO ROADS DIVERGED IN A WOOD, AND I – I TOOK THE ONE LESS TRAVELED BY, AND THAT HAS MADE ALL THE DIFFERENCE."
AH, YES. THAT HAS A VERY FAMILIAR RING.
AND HOW LONG DID WE DRIVE AROUND LOST THAT DAY BECAUSE YOU WOULDN'T ASK DIRECTIONS?
I DON'T WANT TO TALK ABOUT IT.

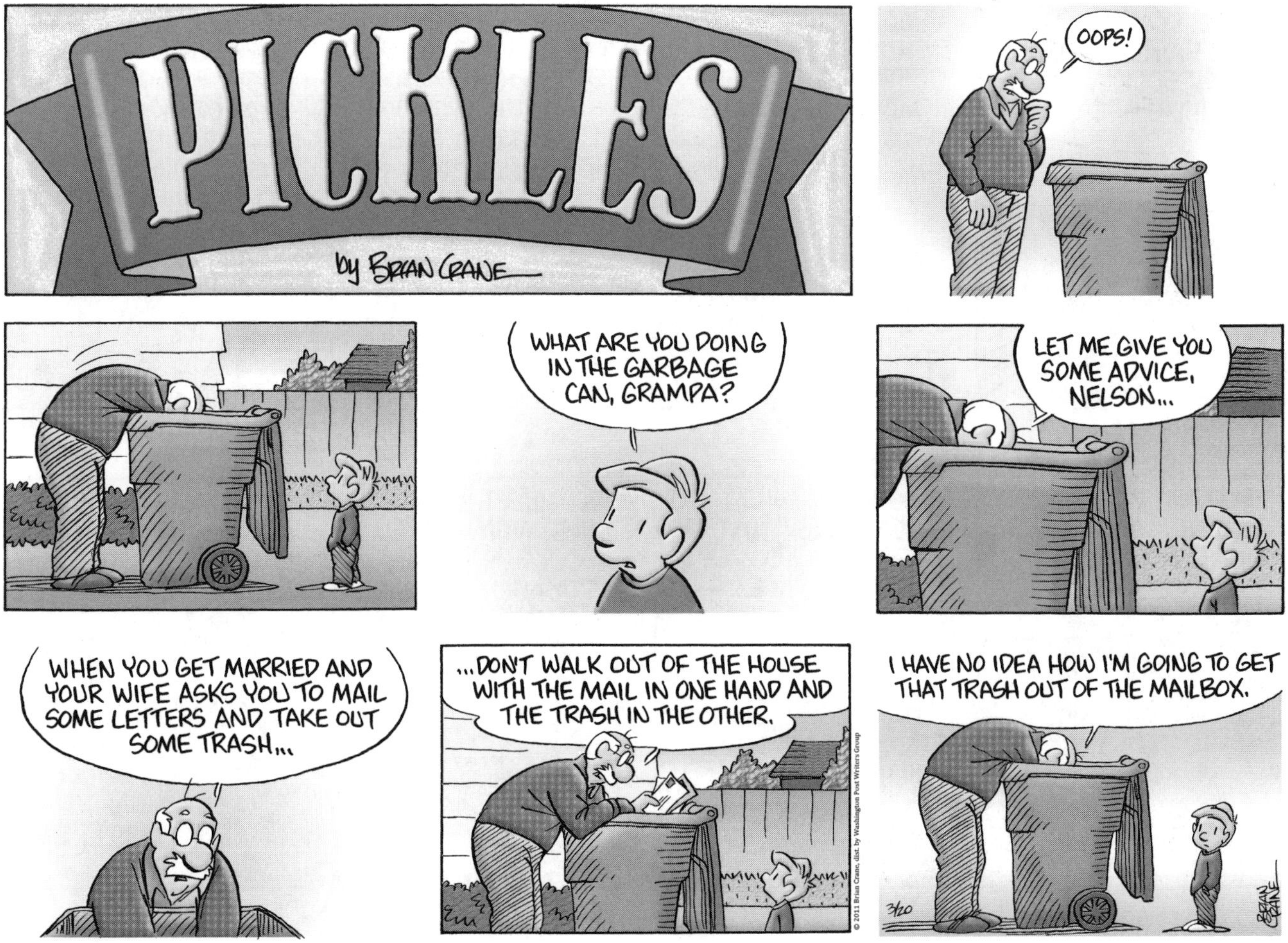
PICKLES
by BRIAN CRANE
OOPS!
WHAT ARE YOU DOING IN THE GARBAGE CAN, GRAMPA?
LET ME GIVE YOU SOME ADVICE, NELSON...
WHEN YOU GET MARRIED AND YOUR WIFE ASKS YOU TO MAIL SOME LETTERS AND TAKE OUT SOME TRASH...
...DON'T WALK OUT OF THE HOUSE WITH THE MAIL IN ONE HAND AND THE TRASH IN THE OTHER.
© 2011 Brian Crane, dist. by Washington Post Writers Group
I HAVE NO IDEA HOW I'M GOING TO GET THAT TRASH OUT OF THE MAILBOX.
3/20
BRIAN CRANE

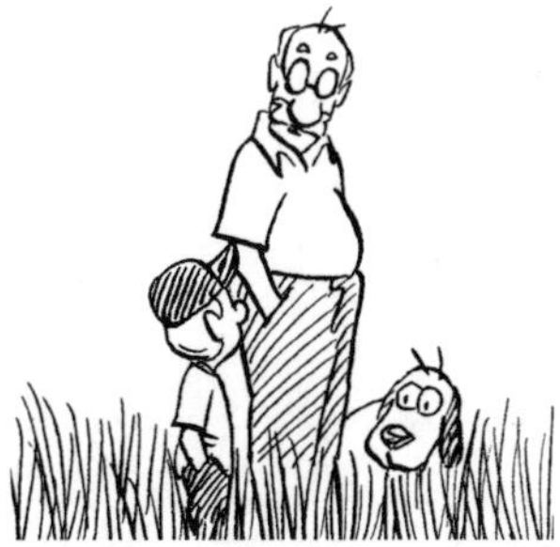

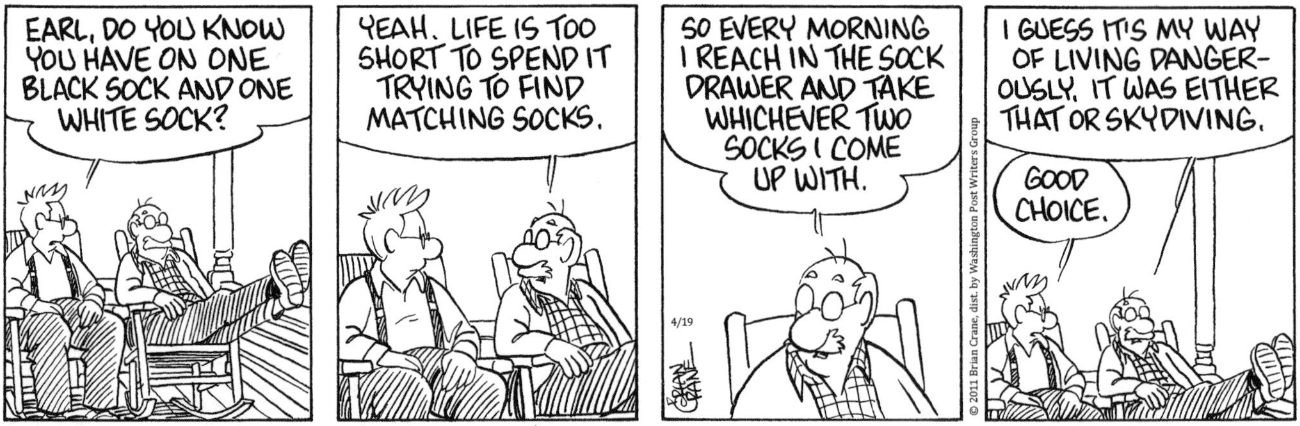
EARL, DO YOU KNOW YOU HAVE ON ONE BLACK SOCK AND ONE WHITE SOCK?
YEAH. LIFE IS TOO SHORT TO SPEND IT TRYING TO FIND MATCHING SOCKS.
SO EVERY MORNING I REACH IN THE SOCK DRAWER AND TAKE WHICHEVER TWO SOCKS I COME UP WITH.
4/19
I GUESS IT'S MY WAY OF LIVING DANGEROUSLY. IT WAS EITHER THAT OR SKYDIVING.
GOOD CHOICE.
© 2011 Brian Crane, dist. by Washington Post Writers Group

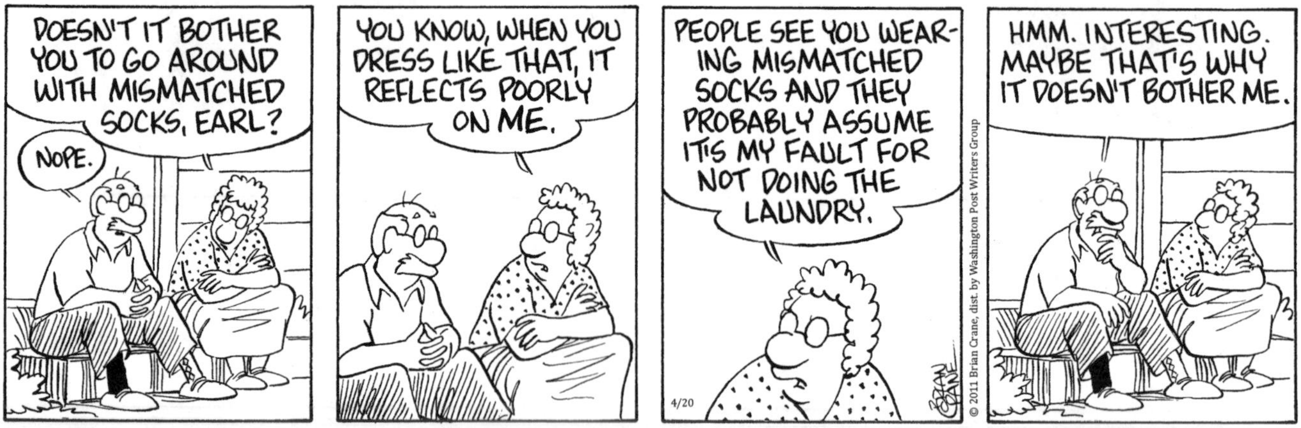
DOESN'T IT BOTHER YOU TO GO AROUND WITH MISMATCHED SOCKS, EARL?
NOPE.
YOU KNOW, WHEN YOU DRESS LIKE THAT, IT REFLECTS POORLY ON ME.
PEOPLE SEE YOU WEARING MISMATCHED SOCKS AND THEY PROBABLY ASSUME IT'S MY FAULT FOR NOT DOING THE LAUNDRY.
4/20
HMM. INTERESTING. MAYBE THAT'S WHY IT DOESN'T BOTHER ME.
© 2011 Brian Crane, dist. by Washington Post Writers Group

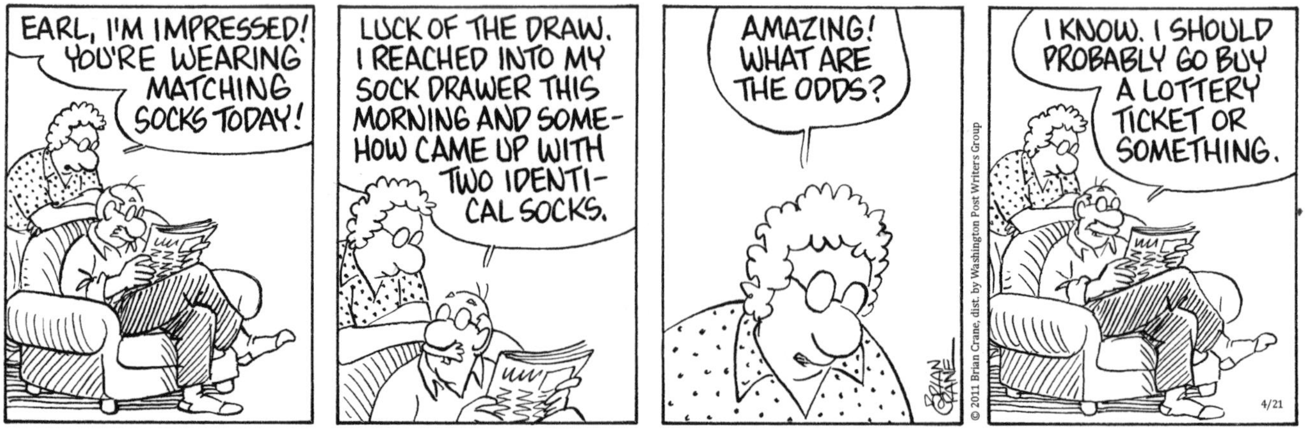
EARL, I'M IMPRESSED! YOU'RE WEARING MATCHING SOCKS TODAY!
LUCK OF THE DRAW. I REACHED INTO MY SOCK DRAWER THIS MORNING AND SOMEHOW CAME UP WITH TWO IDENTICAL SOCKS.
AMAZING! WHAT ARE THE ODDS?
I KNOW. I SHOULD PROBABLY GO BUY A LOTTERY TICKET OR SOMETHING.
© 2011 Brian Crane, dist. by Washington Post Writers Group
4/21

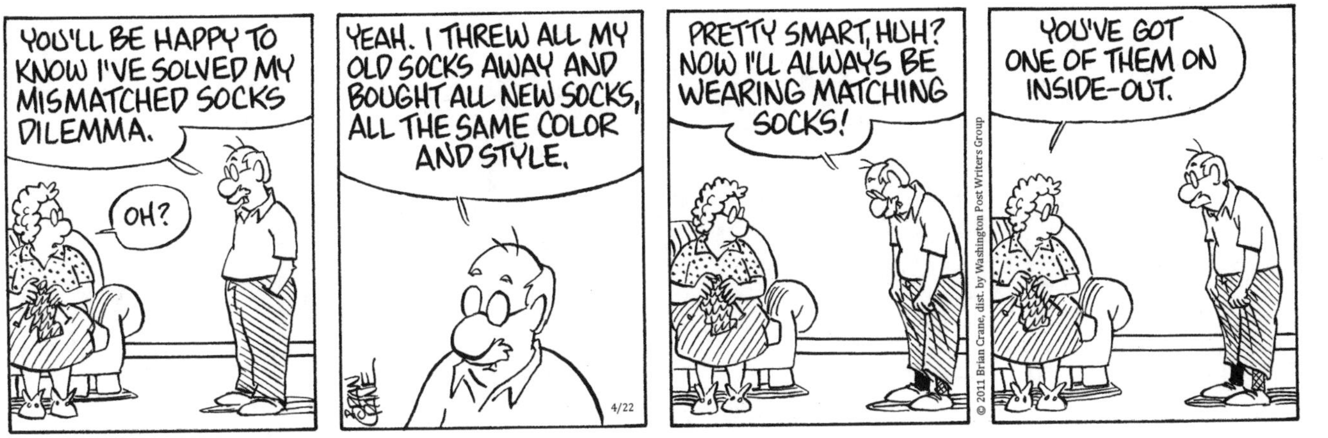
YOU'LL BE HAPPY TO KNOW I'VE SOLVED MY MISMATCHED SOCKS DILEMMA.
OH?
YEAH. I THREW ALL MY OLD SOCKS AWAY AND BOUGHT ALL NEW SOCKS, ALL THE SAME COLOR AND STYLE.
4/22
PRETTY SMART, HUH? NOW I'LL ALWAYS BE WEARING MATCHING SOCKS!
YOU'VE GOT ONE OF THEM ON INSIDE-OUT.
© 2011 Brian Crane, dist. by Washington Post Writers Group

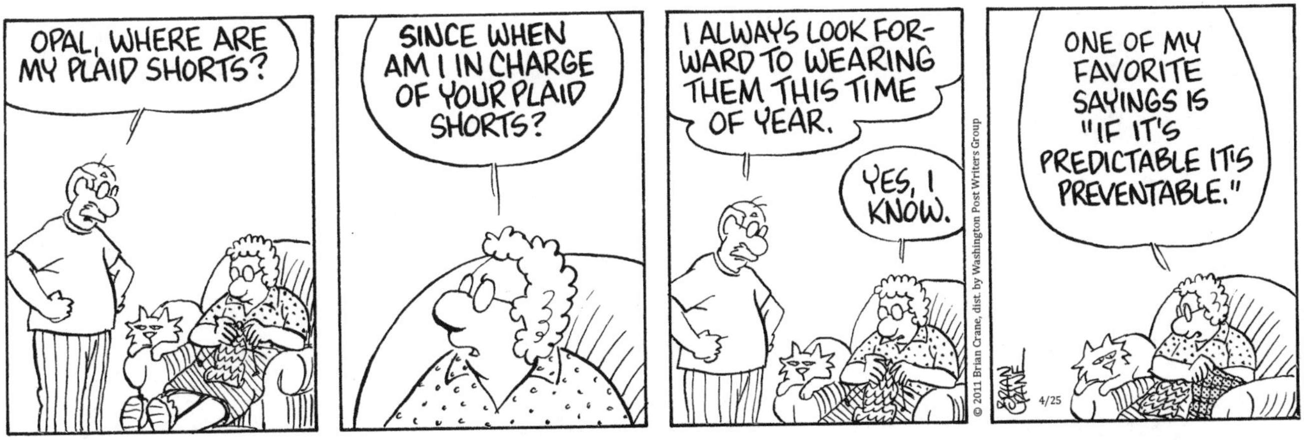
OPAL, WHERE ARE MY PLAID SHORTS?
SINCE WHEN AM I IN CHARGE OF YOUR PLAID SHORTS?
I ALWAYS LOOK FORWARD TO WEARING THEM THIS TIME OF YEAR.
YES, I KNOW.
ONE OF MY FAVORITE SAYINGS IS "IF IT'S PREDICTABLE IT'S PREVENTABLE."
4/25
© 2011 Brian Crane, dist. by Washington Post Writers Group

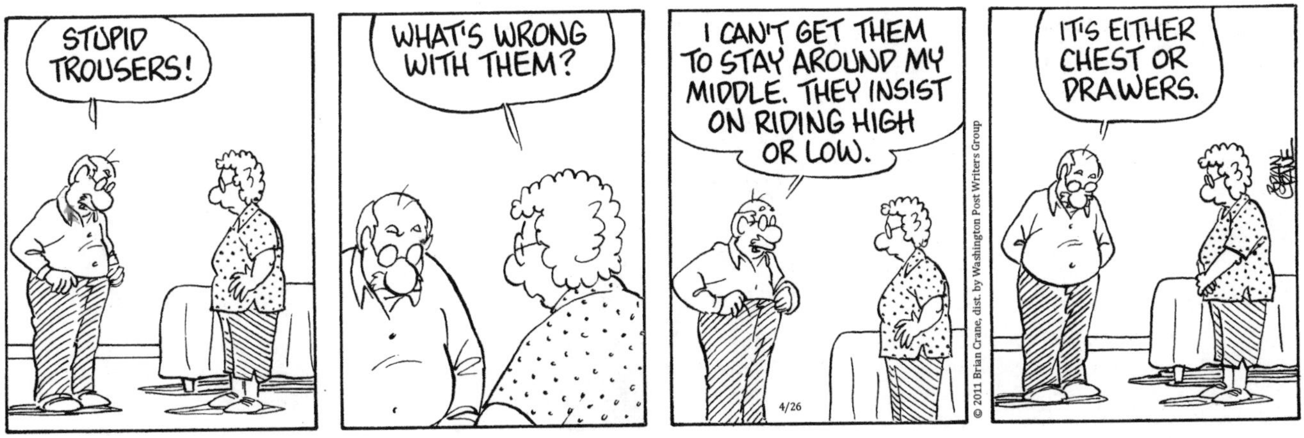
STUPID TROUSERS!
WHAT'S WRONG WITH THEM?
I CAN'T GET THEM TO STAY AROUND MY MIDDLE. THEY INSIST ON RIDING HIGH OR LOW.
4/26
IT'S EITHER CHEST OR DRAWERS.
© 2011 Brian Crane, dist. by Washington Post Writers Group

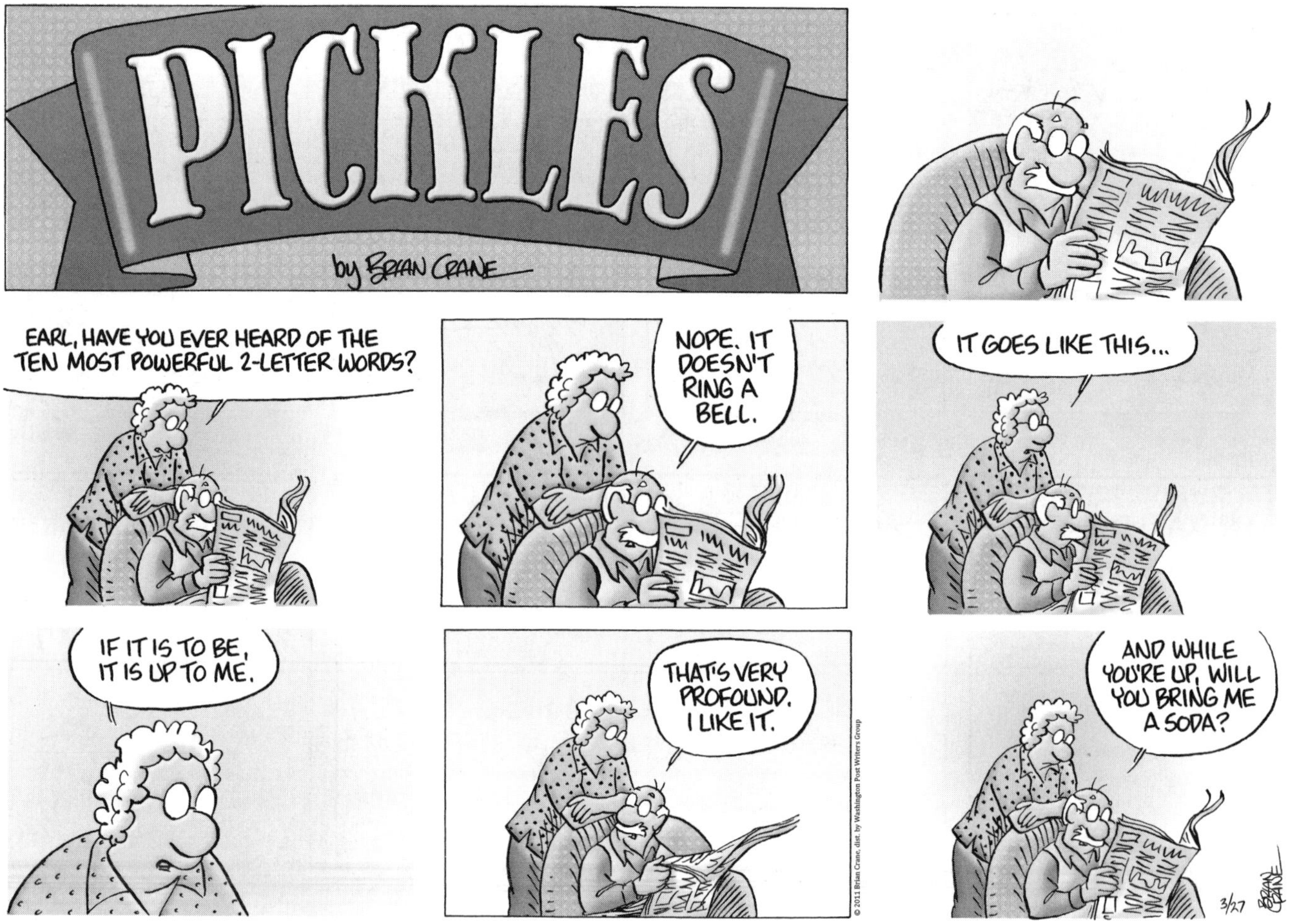
PICKLES
by BRIAN CRANE
EARL, HAVE YOU EVER HEARD OF THE TEN MOST POWERFUL 2-LETTER WORDS?
NOPE. IT DOESN'T RING A BELL.
IT GOES LIKE THIS...
IF IT IS TO BE, IT IS UP TO ME.
THAT'S VERY PROFOUND. I LIKE IT.
© 2011 Brian Crane, dist. by Washington Post Writers Group
AND WHILE YOU'RE UP, WILL YOU BRING ME A SODA?
3/27
BRIAN CRANE

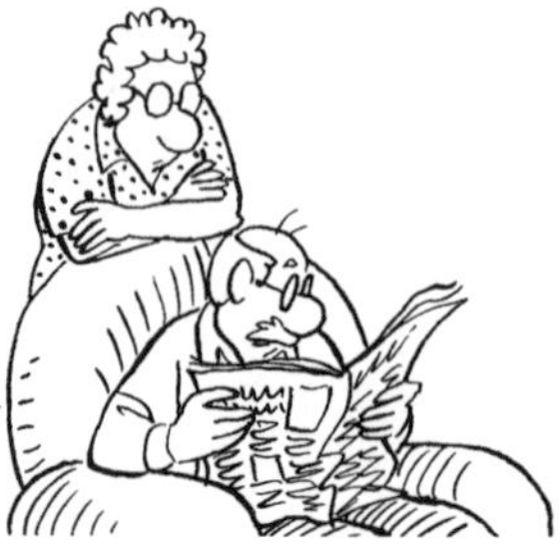

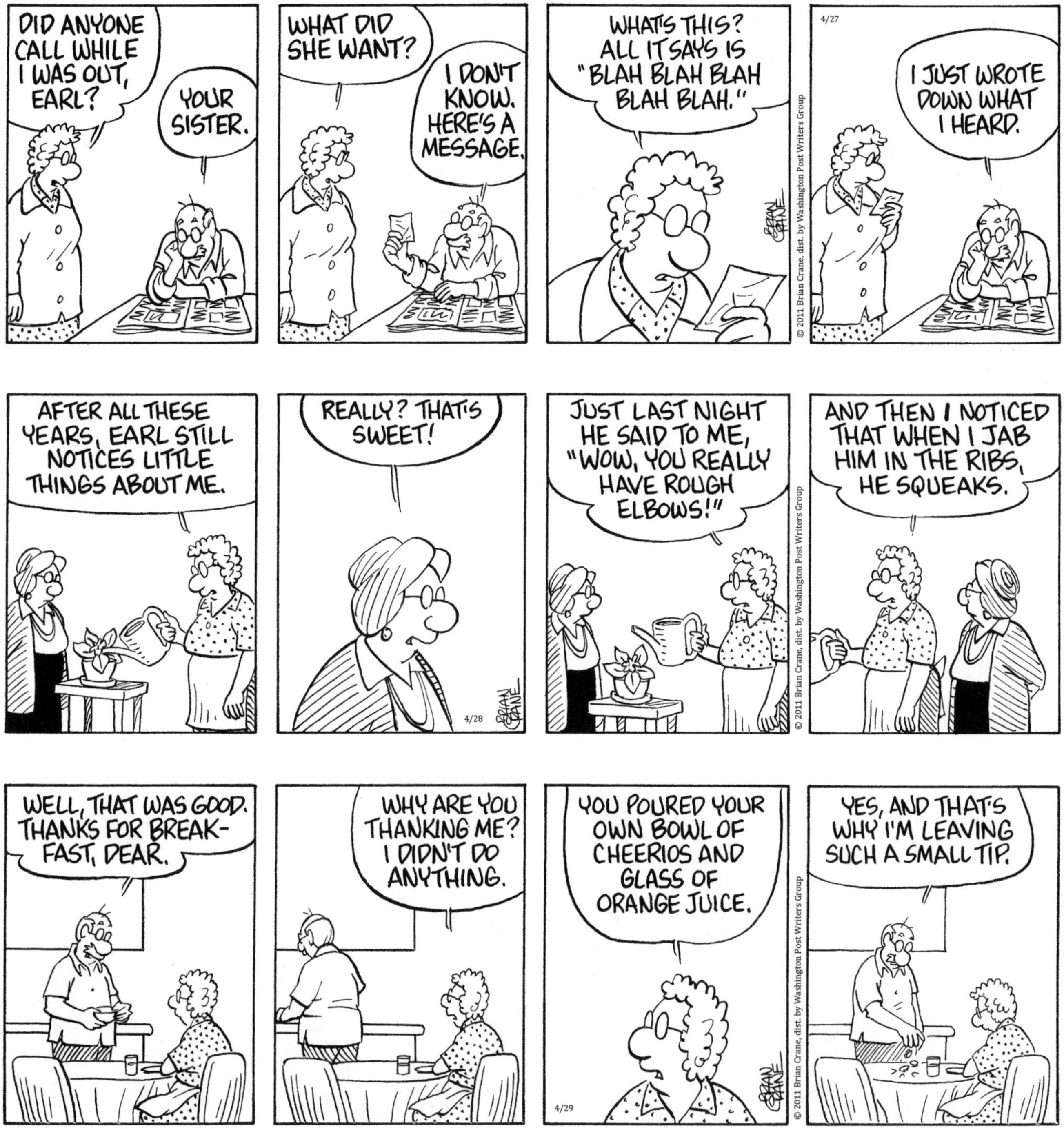
DID ANYONE CALL WHILE I WAS OUT, EARL?
YOUR SISTER.
WHAT DID SHE WANT?
I DON'T KNOW. HERE'S A MESSAGE.
WHAT'S THIS? ALL IT SAYS IS "BLAH BLAH BLAH BLAH BLAH."
4/27
I JUST WROTE DOWN WHAT I HEARD.
© 2011 Brian Crane, dist. by Washington Post Writers Group
AFTER ALL THESE YEARS, EARL STILL NOTICES LITTLE THINGS ABOUT ME.
REALLY? THAT'S SWEET!
4/28
JUST LAST NIGHT HE SAID TO ME, "WOW, YOU REALLY HAVE ROUGH ELBOWS!"
AND THEN I NOTICED THAT WHEN I JAB HIM IN THE RIBS, HE SQUEAKS.
© 2011 Brian Crane, dist. by Washington Post Writers Group
WELL, THAT WAS GOOD. THANKS FOR BREAK-FAST, DEAR.
WHY ARE YOU THANKING ME? I DIDN'T DO ANYTHING.
YOU POURED YOUR OWN BOWL OF CHEERIOS AND GLASS OF ORANGE JUICE.
4/29
YES, AND THAT'S WHY I'M LEAVING SUCH A SMALL TIP.
© 2011 Brian Crane, dist. by Washington Post Writers Group

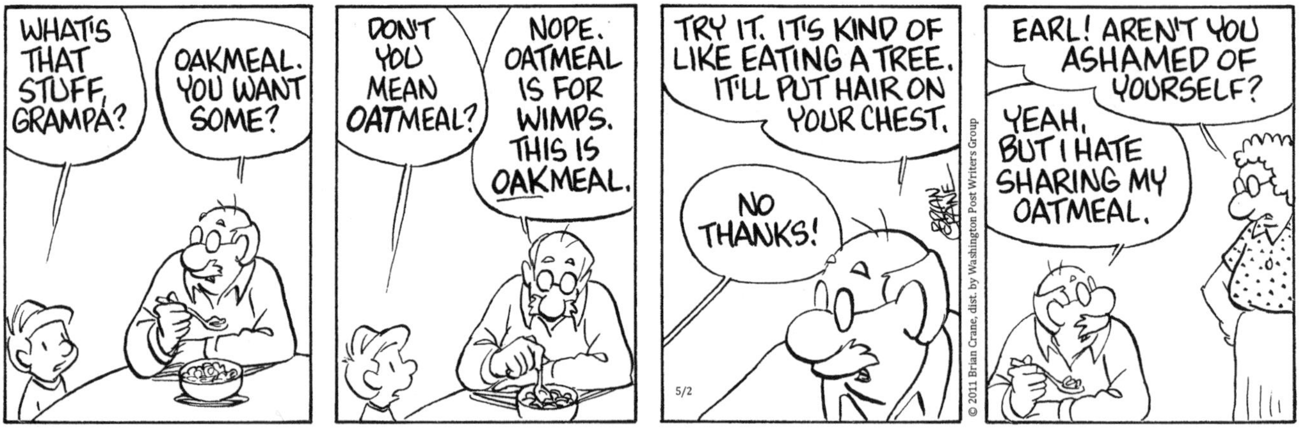
WHAT'S THAT STUFF, GRAMPA?
OAKMEAL. YOU WANT SOME?
DON'T YOU MEAN OATMEAL?
NOPE. OATMEAL IS FOR WIMPS. THIS IS OAKMEAL.
TRY IT. IT'S KIND OF LIKE EATING A TREE. IT'LL PUT HAIR ON YOUR CHEST.
NO THANKS!
5/2
EARL! AREN'T YOU ASHAMED OF YOURSELF?
YEAH, BUT I HATE SHARING MY OATMEAL.

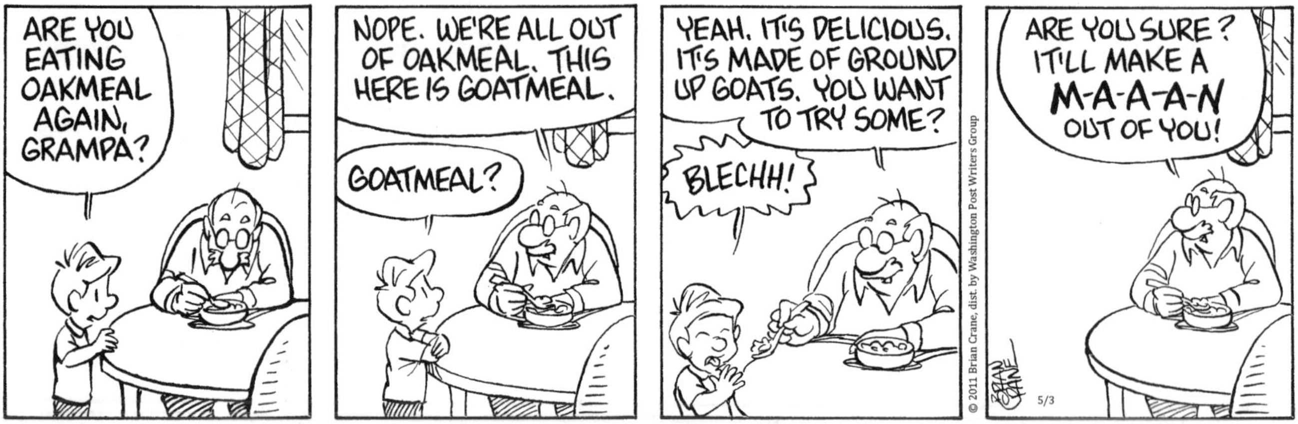
ARE YOU EATING OAKMEAL AGAIN, GRAMPA?
NOPE. WE'RE ALL OUT OF OAKMEAL. THIS HERE IS GOATMEAL.
GOATMEAL?
YEAH. IT'S DELICIOUS. IT'S MADE OF GROUND UP GOATS. YOU WANT TO TRY SOME?
BLECHH!
ARE YOU SURE? IT'LL MAKE A M-A-A-A-N OUT OF YOU!
5/3

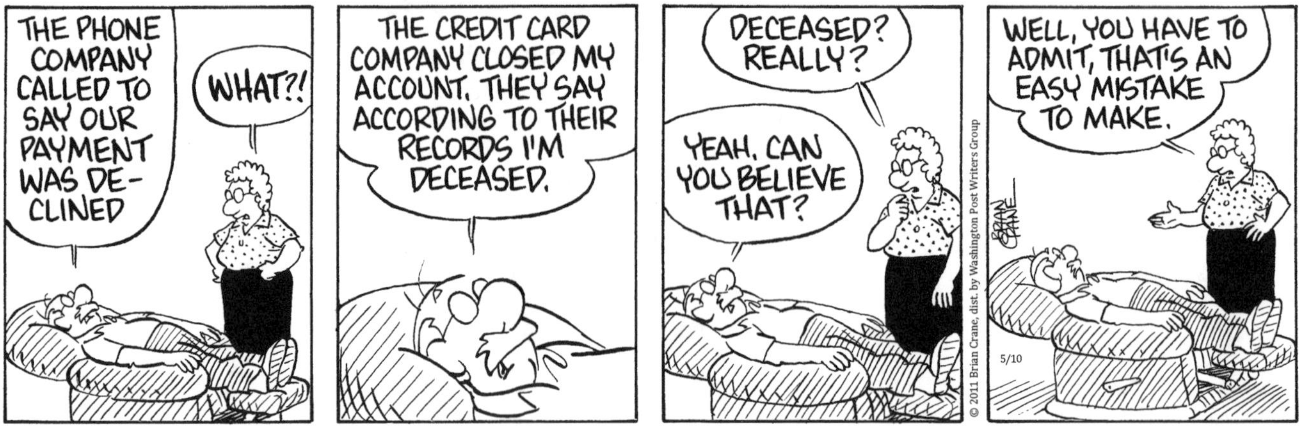
THE PHONE COMPANY CALLED TO SAY OUR PAYMENT WAS DE-CLINED
WHAT?!
THE CREDIT CARD COMPANY CLOSED MY ACCOUNT. THEY SAY ACCORDING TO THEIR RECORDS I'M DECEASED.
DECEASED? REALLY?
YEAH. CAN YOU BELIEVE THAT?
WELL, YOU HAVE TO ADMIT, THAT'S AN EASY MISTAKE TO MAKE.
5/10

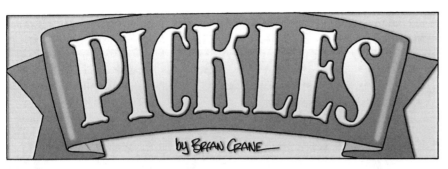

PICKLES
by BRIAN CRANE
WHAT ARE YOU EATING, GRAMPA?
I'M NOT SURE. THEY'RE EITHER PRUNES OR DRIED PLUMS.
I WAS TRYING FIND SOME PRUNES AT THE STORE TODAY, BUT THEY DIDN'T HAVE ANY. ALL THEY HAD WERE DRIED PLUMS.
AND THEN SUDDENLY IT DAWNED ON ME... DUH! DRIED PLUMS ARE PRUNES!
I DON'T KNOW WHY THEY HAVE A DIFFERENT NAME FOR PLUMS WHEN THEY'RE DRIED, BUT THEY DO.
SAME THING WITH RAISINS. RAISINS ARE JUST DRIED-UP GRAPES.
ARE GRAMPAS JUST DRIED-UP MEN?
© 2011 Brian Crane, dist. by Washington Post Writers Group
4/10
BRIAN CRANE

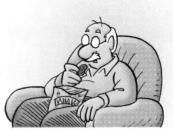

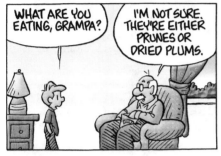

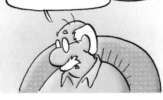

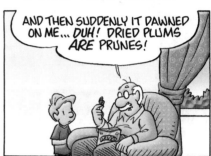

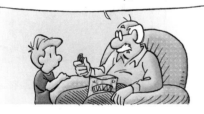

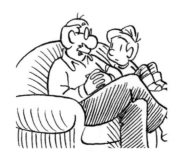

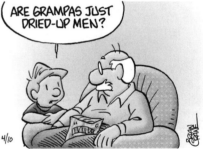

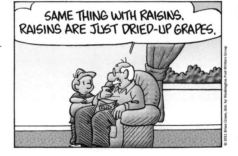

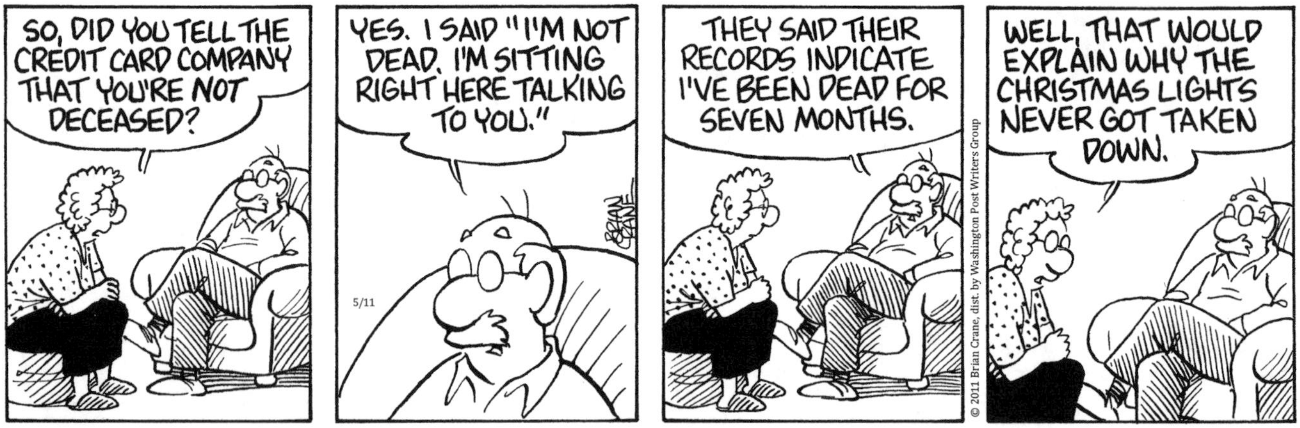
SO, DID YOU TELL THE CREDIT CARD COMPANY THAT YOU'RE NOT DECEASED?
YES. I SAID "I'M NOT DEAD. I'M SITTING RIGHT HERE TALKING TO YOU."
BRIAN CRANE
5/11
THEY SAID THEIR RECORDS INDICATE I'VE BEEN DEAD FOR SEVEN MONTHS.
© 2011 Brian Crane, dist. by Washington Post Writers Group
WELL, THAT WOULD EXPLAIN WHY THE CHRISTMAS LIGHTS NEVER GOT TAKEN DOWN.

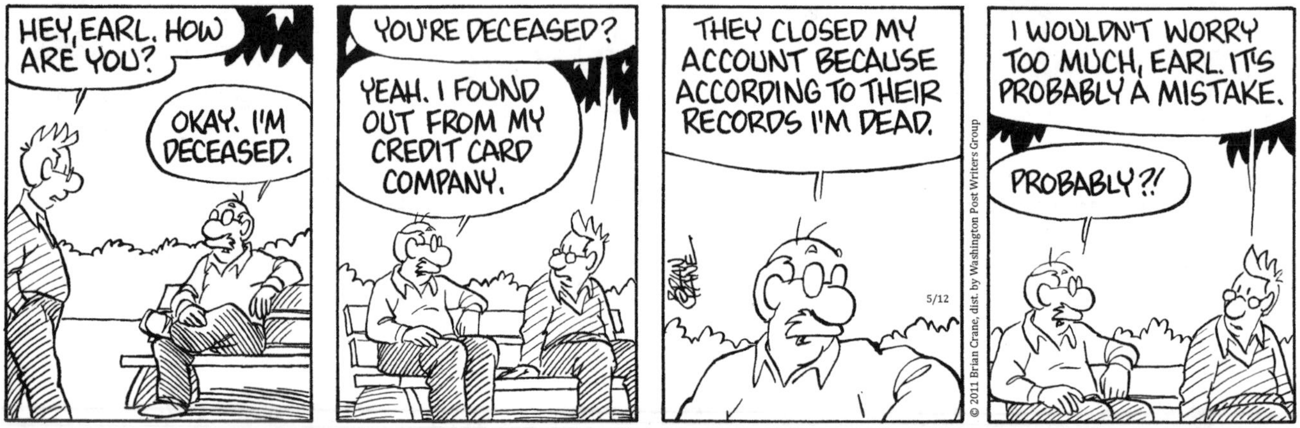
HEY, EARL. HOW ARE YOU?
OKAY. I'M DECEASED.
YOU'RE DECEASED?
YEAH. I FOUND OUT FROM MY CREDIT CARD COMPANY.
THEY CLOSED MY ACCOUNT BECAUSE ACCORDING TO THEIR RECORDS I'M DEAD.
BRIAN CRANE
5/12
© 2011 Brian Crane, dist. by Washington Post Writers Group
I WOULDN'T WORRY TOO MUCH, EARL. IT'S PROBABLY A MISTAKE.
PROBABLY?!

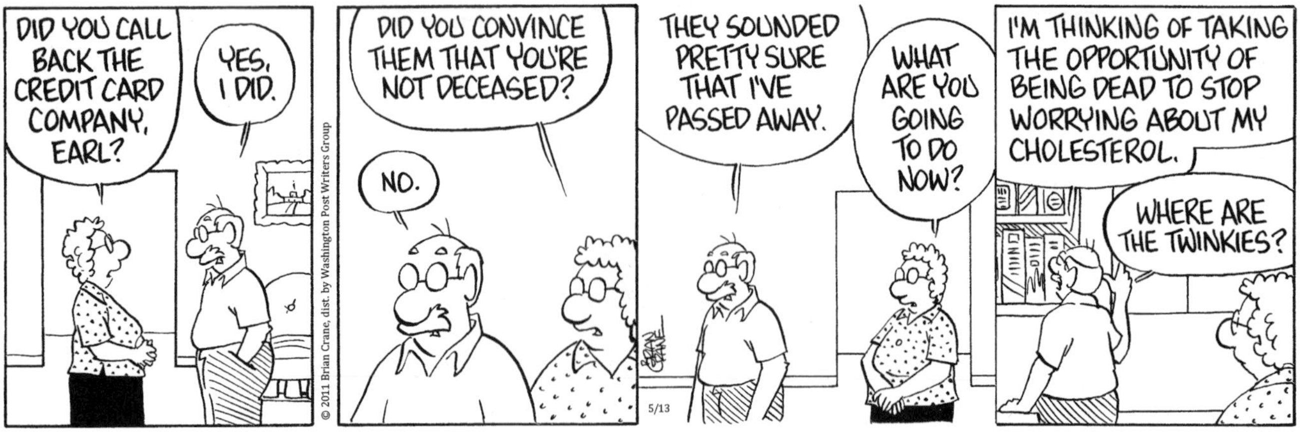
DID YOU CALL BACK THE CREDIT CARD COMPANY, EARL?
YES, I DID.
© 2011 Brian Crane, dist. by Washington Post Writers Group
DID YOU CONVINCE THEM THAT YOU'RE NOT DECEASED?
NO.
BRIAN CRANE
5/13
THEY SOUNDED PRETTY SURE THAT I'VE PASSED AWAY.
WHAT ARE YOU GOING TO DO NOW?
I'M THINKING OF TAKING THE OPPORTUNITY OF BEING DEAD TO STOP WORRYING ABOUT MY CHOLESTEROL.
WHERE ARE THE TWINKIES?

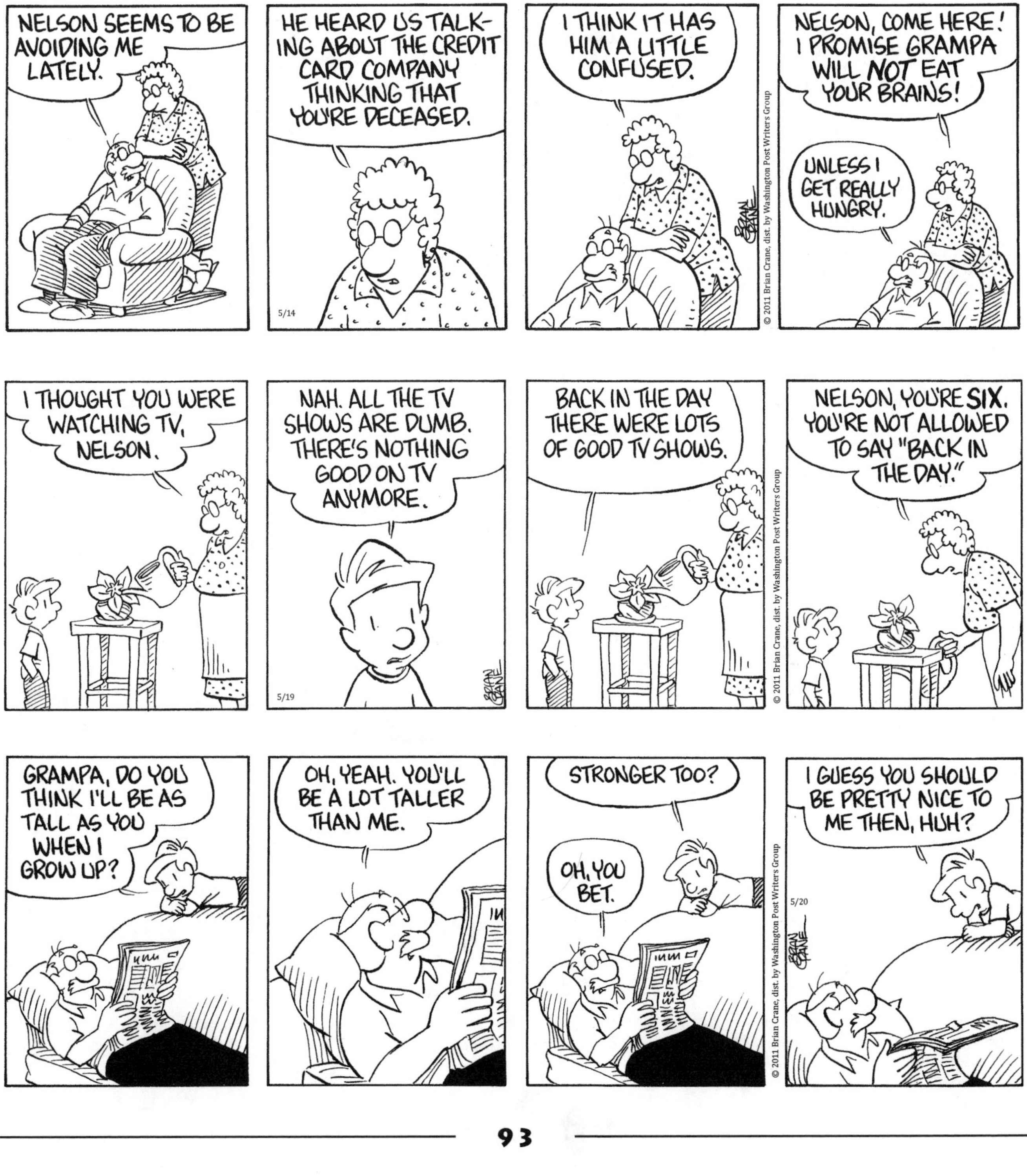
NELSON SEEMS TO BE AVOIDING ME LATELY.
HE HEARD US TALKING ABOUT THE CREDIT CARD COMPANY THINKING THAT YOU'RE DECEASED.
5/14
I THINK IT HAS HIM A LITTLE CONFUSED.
NELSON, COME HERE! I PROMISE GRAMPA WILL NOT EAT YOUR BRAINS!
UNLESS I GET REALLY HUNGRY.
© 2011 Brian Crane, dist. by Washington Post Writers Group
I THOUGHT YOU WERE WATCHING TV, NELSON.
NAH. ALL THE TV SHOWS ARE DUMB. THERE'S NOTHING GOOD ON TV ANYMORE.
5/19
BACK IN THE DAY THERE WERE LOTS OF GOOD TV SHOWS.
NELSON, YOU'RE SIX. YOU'RE NOT ALLOWED TO SAY "BACK IN THE DAY."
© 2011 Brian Crane, dist. by Washington Post Writers Group
GRAMPA, DO YOU THINK I'LL BE AS TALL AS YOU WHEN I GROW UP?
OH, YEAH. YOU'LL BE A LOT TALLER THAN ME.
STRONGER TOO?
OH, YOU BET.
I GUESS YOU SHOULD BE PRETTY NICE TO ME THEN, HUH?
5/20
© 2011 Brian Crane, dist. by Washington Post Writers Group

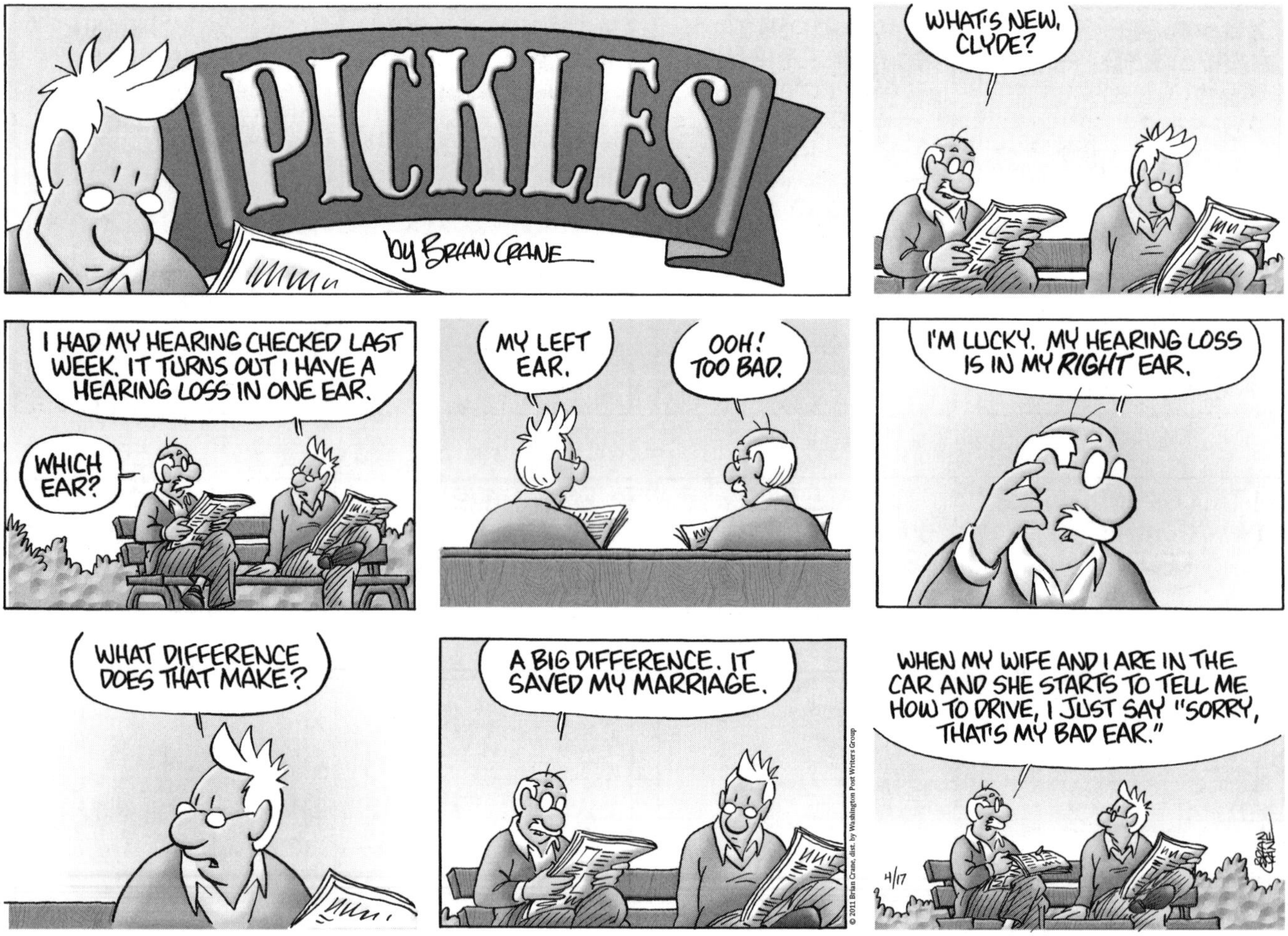
PICKLES
by Brian Crane
WHAT'S NEW, CLYDE?
I HAD MY HEARING CHECKED LAST WEEK. IT TURNS OUT I HAVE A HEARING LOSS IN ONE EAR.
WHICH EAR?
MY LEFT EAR.
OOH! TOO BAD.
I'M LUCKY. MY HEARING LOSS IS IN MY *RIGHT* EAR.
WHAT DIFFERENCE DOES THAT MAKE?
A BIG DIFFERENCE. IT SAVED MY MARRIAGE.
WHEN MY WIFE AND I ARE IN THE CAR AND SHE STARTS TO TELL ME HOW TO DRIVE, I JUST SAY "SORRY, THAT'S MY BAD EAR."
4/17
© 2011 Brian Crane, dist. by Washington Post Writers Group

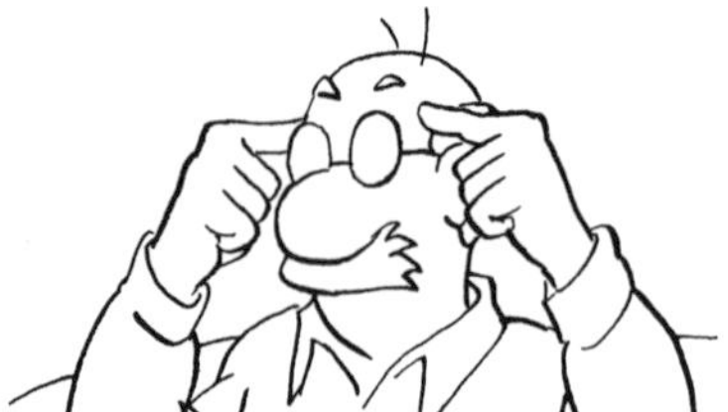

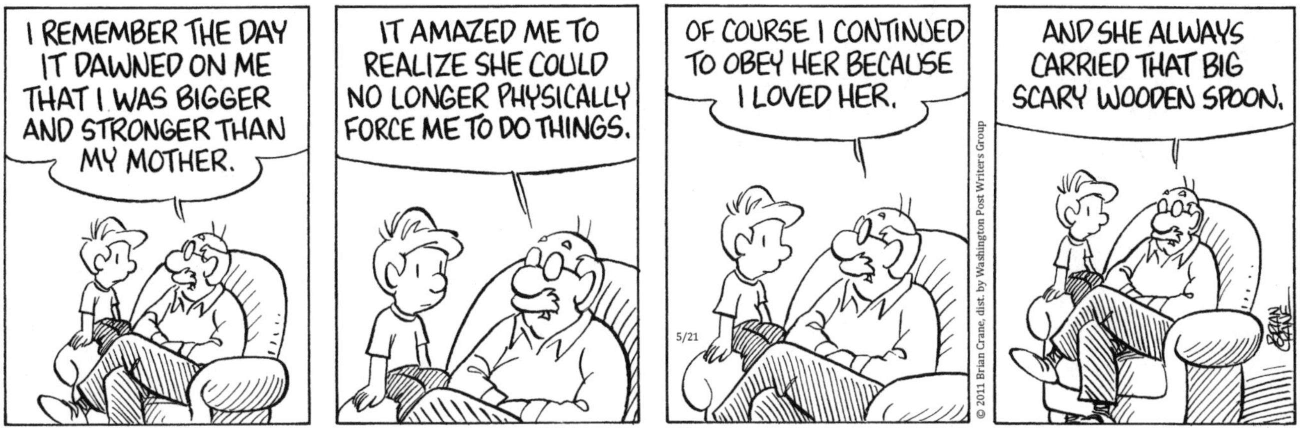

I REMEMBER THE DAY IT DAWNED ON ME THAT I WAS BIGGER AND STRONGER THAN MY MOTHER.
IT AMAZED ME TO REALIZE SHE COULD NO LONGER PHYSICALLY FORCE ME TO DO THINGS.
OF COURSE I CONTINUED TO OBEY HER BECAUSE I LOVED HER.
5/21
AND SHE ALWAYS CARRIED THAT BIG SCARY WOODEN SPOON.
BRIAN CRANE

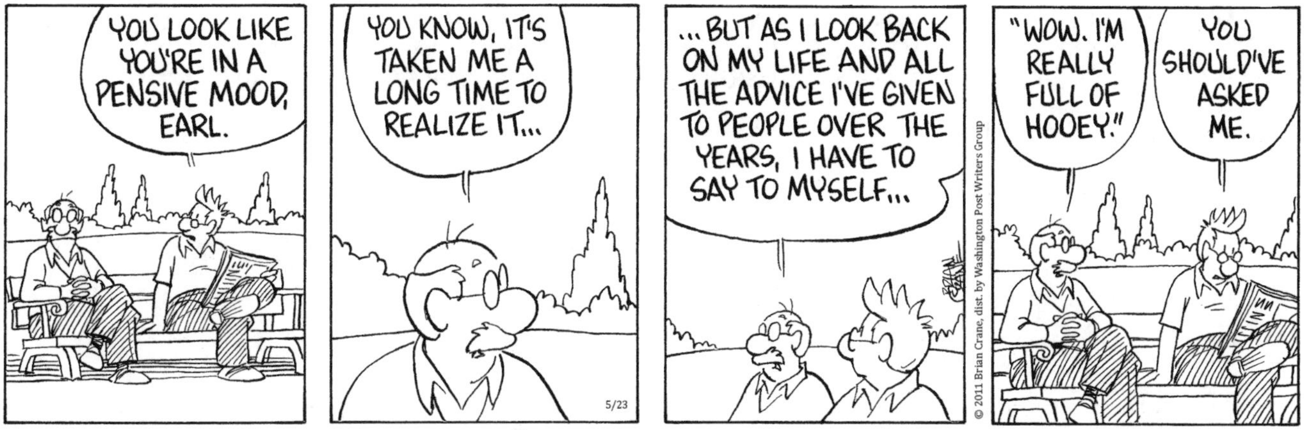

YOU LOOK LIKE YOU'RE IN A PENSIVE MOOD, EARL.
YOU KNOW, IT'S TAKEN ME A LONG TIME TO REALIZE IT...
5/23
...BUT AS I LOOK BACK ON MY LIFE AND ALL THE ADVICE I'VE GIVEN TO PEOPLE OVER THE YEARS, I HAVE TO SAY TO MYSELF...
BRIAN CRANE
"WOW. I'M REALLY FULL OF HOOEY."
YOU SHOULD'VE ASKED ME.

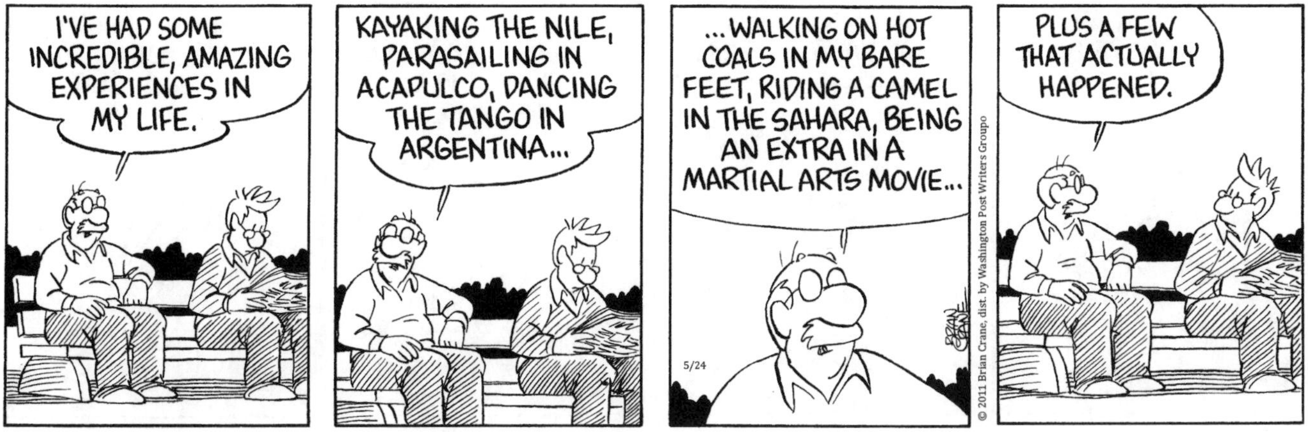

I'VE HAD SOME INCREDIBLE, AMAZING EXPERIENCES IN MY LIFE.
KAYAKING THE NILE, PARASAILING IN ACAPULCO, DANCING THE TANGO IN ARGENTINA...
...WALKING ON HOT COALS IN MY BARE FEET, RIDING A CAMEL IN THE SAHARA, BEING AN EXTRA IN A MARTIAL ARTS MOVIE...
5/24
BRIAN CRANE
PLUS A FEW THAT ACTUALLY HAPPENED.

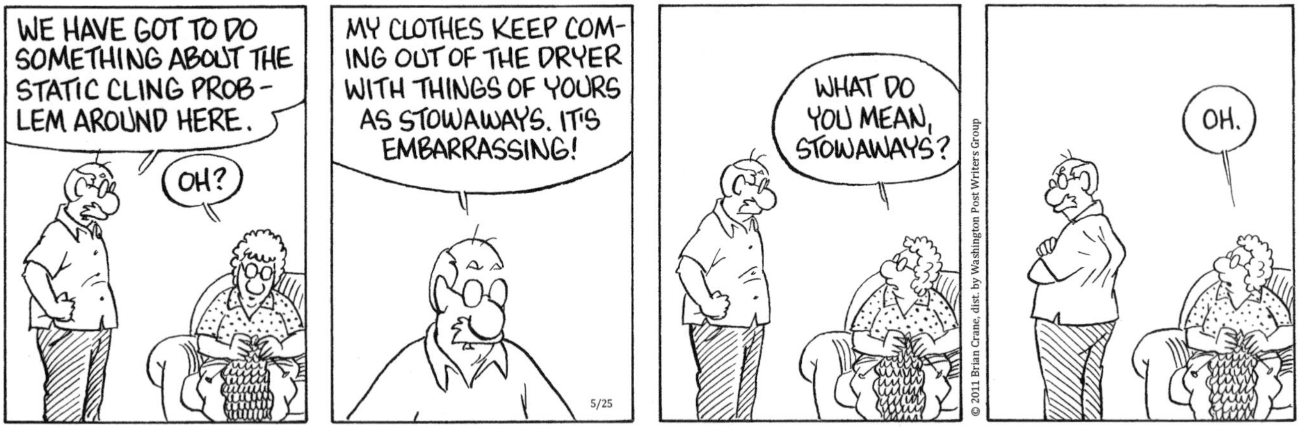
WE HAVE GOT TO DO SOMETHING ABOUT THE STATIC CLING PROB-LEM AROUND HERE.
OH?
MY CLOTHES KEEP COM-ING OUT OF THE DRYER WITH THINGS OF YOURS AS STOWAWAYS. IT'S EMBARRASSING!
5/25
WHAT DO YOU MEAN, STOWAWAYS?
OH.

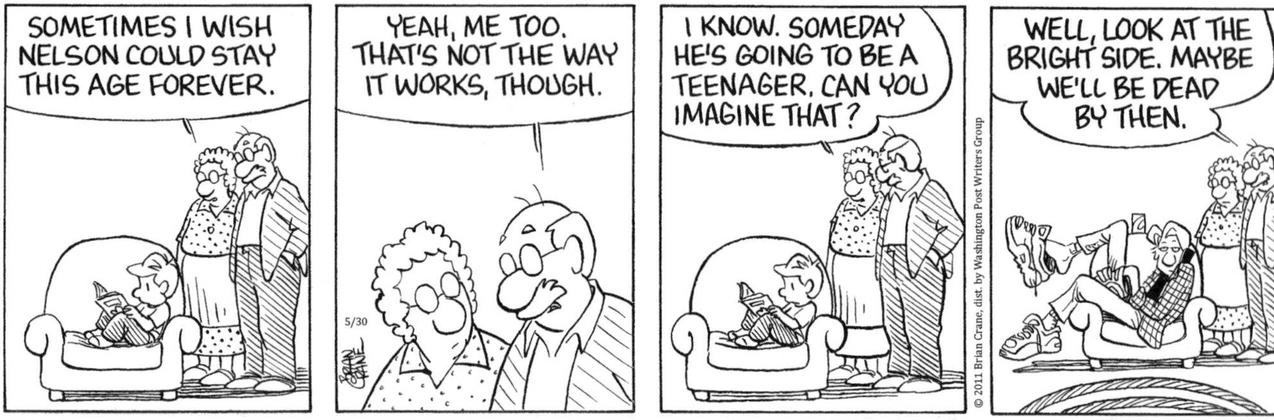
SOMETIMES I WISH NELSON COULD STAY THIS AGE FOREVER.
YEAH, ME TOO. THAT'S NOT THE WAY IT WORKS, THOUGH.
5/30
I KNOW. SOMEDAY HE'S GOING TO BE A TEENAGER. CAN YOU IMAGINE THAT?
WELL, LOOK AT THE BRIGHT SIDE. MAYBE WE'LL BE DEAD BY THEN.

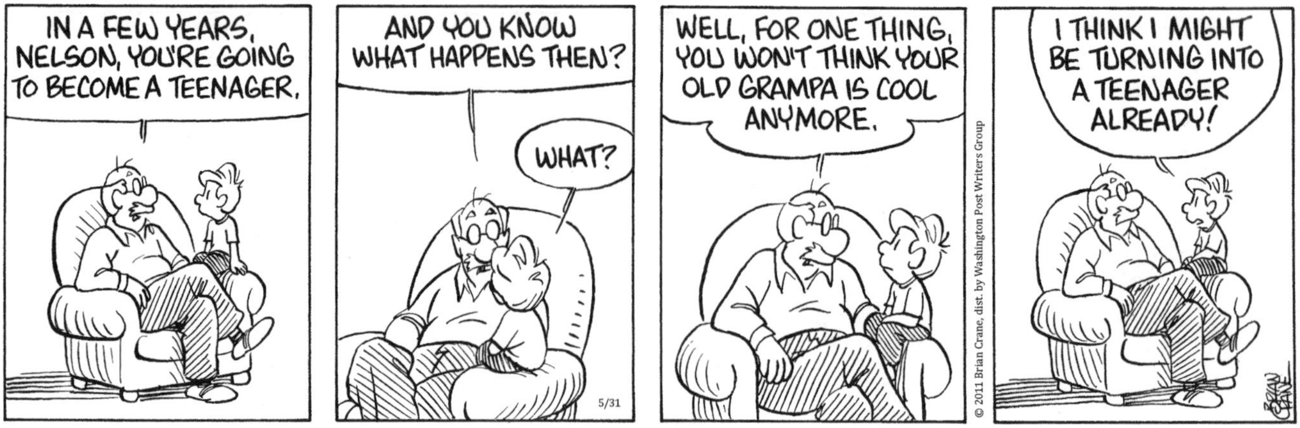
IN A FEW YEARS, NELSON, YOU'RE GOING TO BECOME A TEENAGER.
AND YOU KNOW WHAT HAPPENS THEN?
WHAT?
5/31
WELL, FOR ONE THING, YOU WON'T THINK YOUR OLD GRAMPA IS COOL ANYMORE.
I THINK I MIGHT BE TURNING INTO A TEENAGER ALREADY!

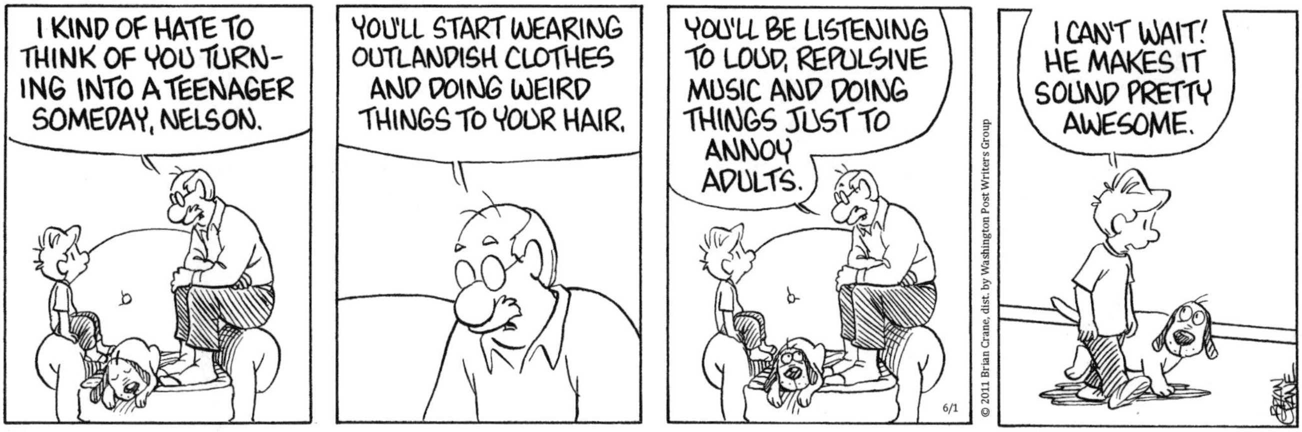
I KIND OF HATE TO THINK OF YOU TURNING INTO A TEENAGER SOMEDAY, NELSON.
YOU'LL START WEARING OUTLANDISH CLOTHES AND DOING WEIRD THINGS TO YOUR HAIR.
YOU'LL BE LISTENING TO LOUD, REPULSIVE MUSIC AND DOING THINGS JUST TO ANNOY ADULTS.
6/1
I CAN'T WAIT! HE MAKES IT SOUND PRETTY AWESOME.

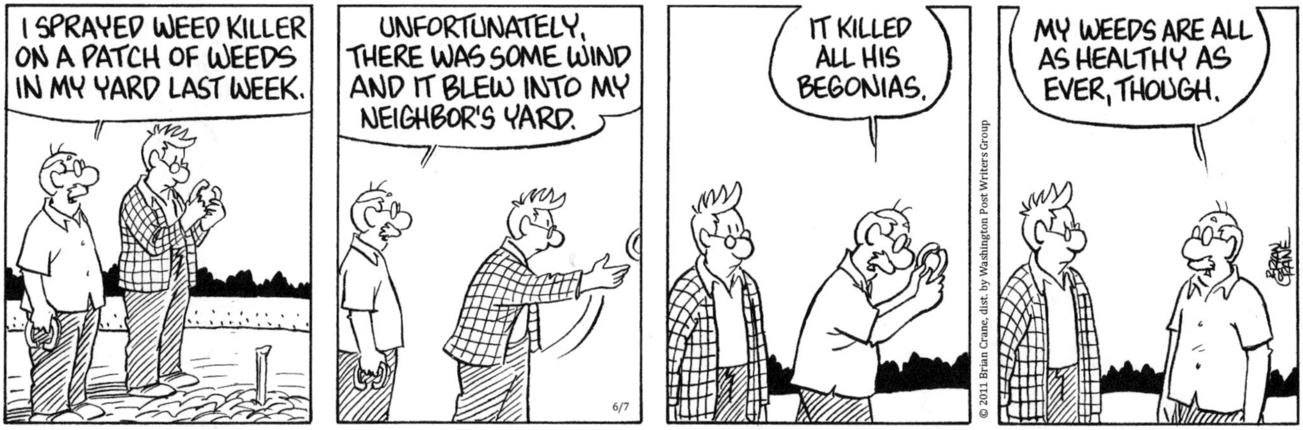
I SPRAYED WEED KILLER ON A PATCH OF WEEDS IN MY YARD LAST WEEK.
UNFORTUNATELY, THERE WAS SOME WIND AND IT BLEW INTO MY NEIGHBOR'S YARD.
6/7
IT KILLED ALL HIS BEGONIAS.
MY WEEDS ARE ALL AS HEALTHY AS EVER, THOUGH.

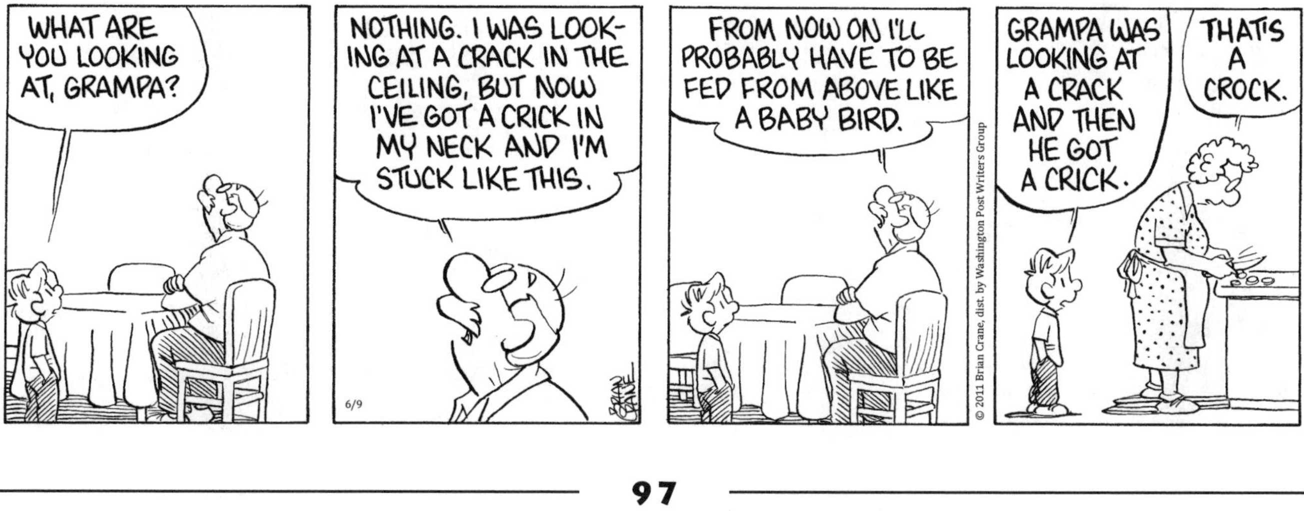
WHAT ARE YOU LOOKING AT, GRAMPA?
NOTHING. I WAS LOOKING AT A CRACK IN THE CEILING, BUT NOW I'VE GOT A CRICK IN MY NECK AND I'M STUCK LIKE THIS.
6/9
FROM NOW ON I'LL PROBABLY HAVE TO BE FED FROM ABOVE LIKE A BABY BIRD.
GRAMPA WAS LOOKING AT A CRACK AND THEN HE GOT A CRICK.
THAT'S A CROCK.

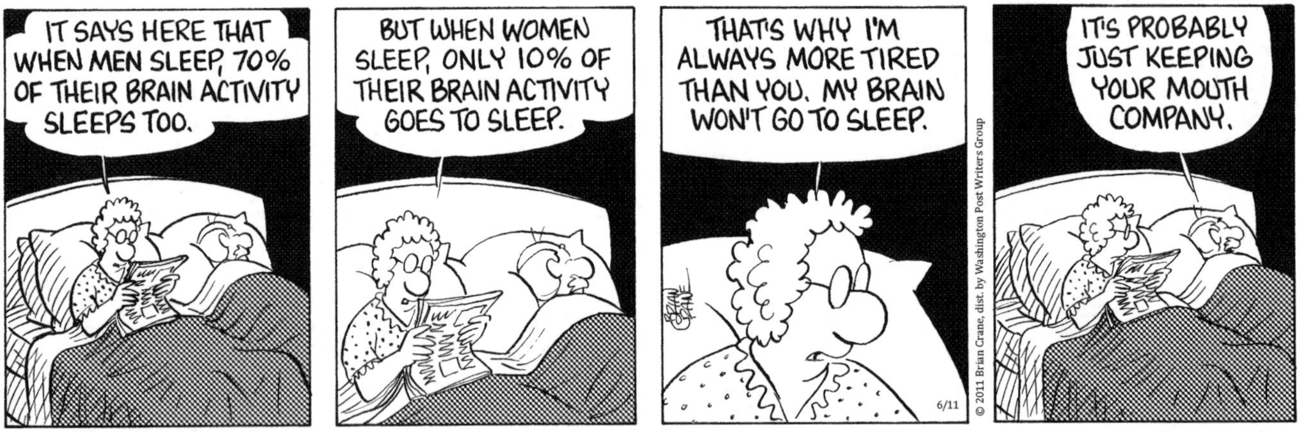
IT SAYS HERE THAT WHEN MEN SLEEP, 70% OF THEIR BRAIN ACTIVITY SLEEPS TOO.
BUT WHEN WOMEN SLEEP, ONLY 10% OF THEIR BRAIN ACTIVITY GOES TO SLEEP.
THAT'S WHY I'M ALWAYS MORE TIRED THAN YOU. MY BRAIN WON'T GO TO SLEEP.
IT'S PROBABLY JUST KEEPING YOUR MOUTH COMPANY.
6/11

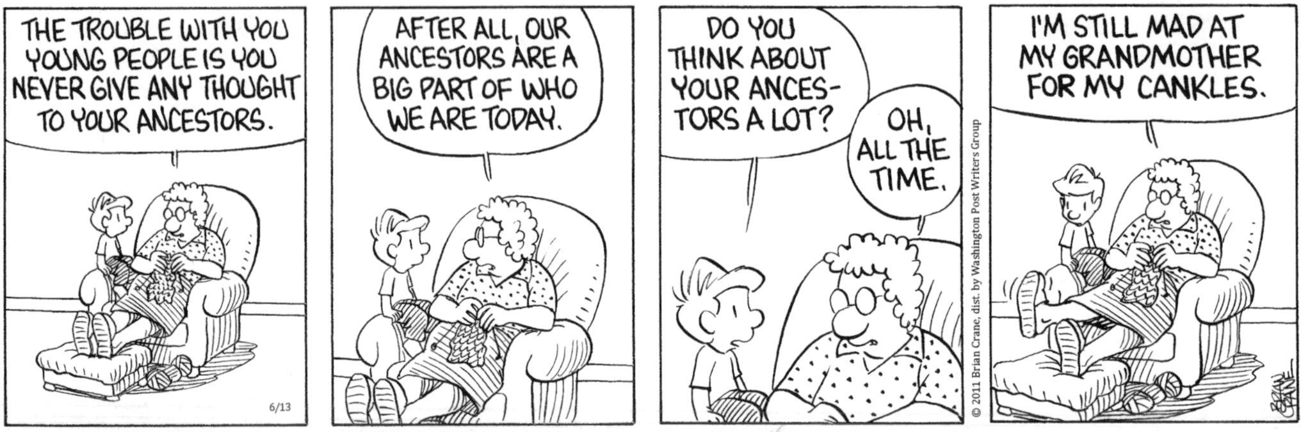
THE TROUBLE WITH YOU YOUNG PEOPLE IS YOU NEVER GIVE ANY THOUGHT TO YOUR ANCESTORS.
6/13
AFTER ALL, OUR ANCESTORS ARE A BIG PART OF WHO WE ARE TODAY.
DO YOU THINK ABOUT YOUR ANCES-TORS A LOT?
OH, ALL THE TIME.
I'M STILL MAD AT MY GRANDMOTHER FOR MY CANKLES.

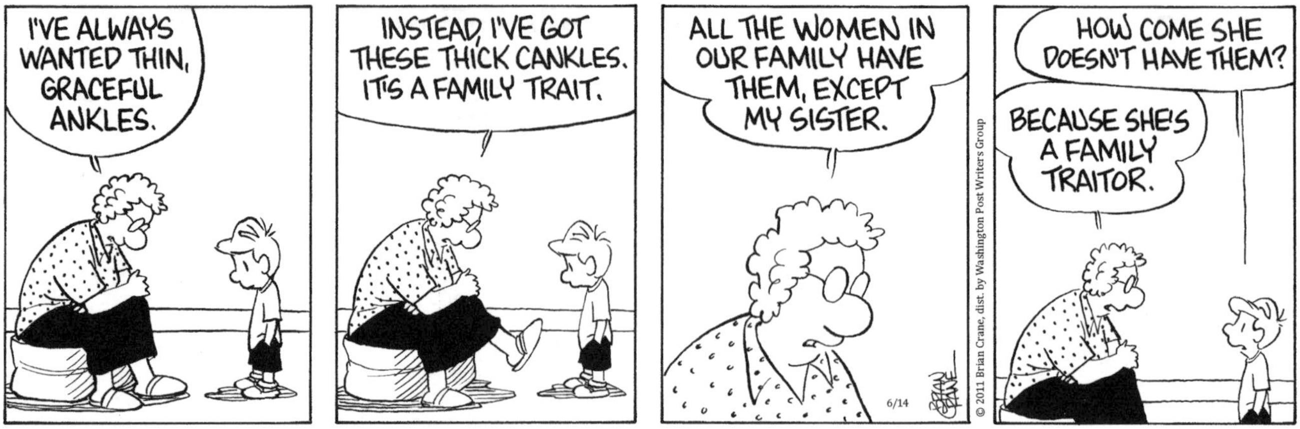
I'VE ALWAYS WANTED THIN, GRACEFUL ANKLES.
INSTEAD, I'VE GOT THESE THICK CANKLES. IT'S A FAMILY TRAIT.
ALL THE WOMEN IN OUR FAMILY HAVE THEM, EXCEPT MY SISTER.
6/14
HOW COME SHE DOESN'T HAVE THEM?
BECAUSE SHE'S A FAMILY TRAITOR.

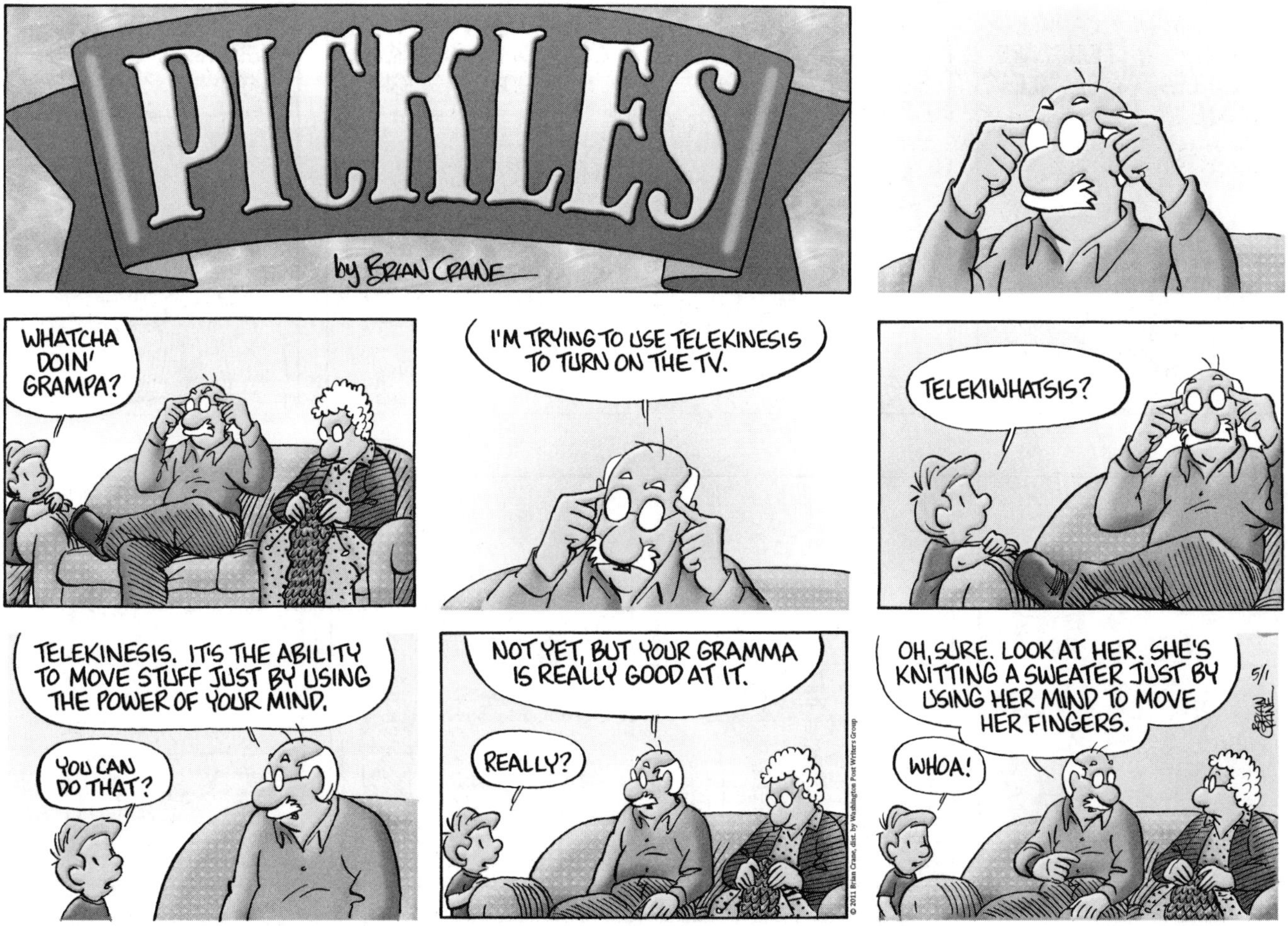
PICKLES
by BRIAN CRANE
WHATCHA DOIN' GRAMPA?
I'M TRYING TO USE TELEKINESIS TO TURN ON THE TV.
TELEKIWHATSIS?
TELEKINESIS. IT'S THE ABILITY TO MOVE STUFF JUST BY USING THE POWER OF YOUR MIND.
YOU CAN DO THAT?
NOT YET, BUT YOUR GRAMMA IS REALLY GOOD AT IT.
REALLY?
OH, SURE. LOOK AT HER. SHE'S KNITTING A SWEATER JUST BY USING HER MIND TO MOVE HER FINGERS.
WHOA!
5/1
© 2011 Brian Crane, dist. by Washington Post Writers Group

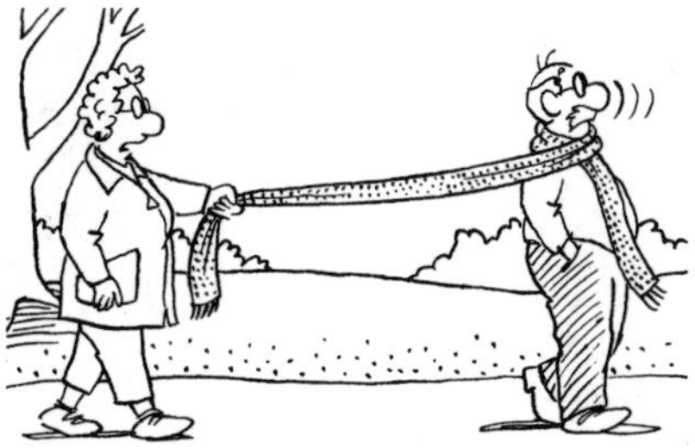

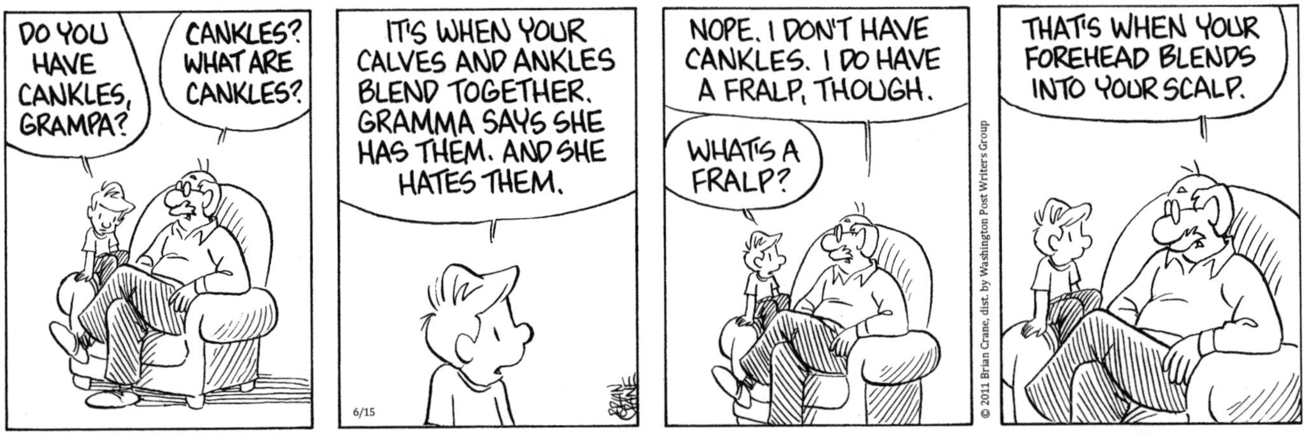
DO YOU HAVE CANKLES, GRAMPA?
CANKLES? WHAT ARE CANKLES?
IT'S WHEN YOUR CALVES AND ANKLES BLEND TOGETHER. GRAMMA SAYS SHE HAS THEM. AND SHE HATES THEM.
6/15
NOPE. I DON'T HAVE CANKLES. I DO HAVE A FRALP, THOUGH.
WHAT'S A FRALP?
© 2011 Brian Crane, dist. by Washington Post Writers Group
THAT'S WHEN YOUR FOREHEAD BLENDS INTO YOUR SCALP.

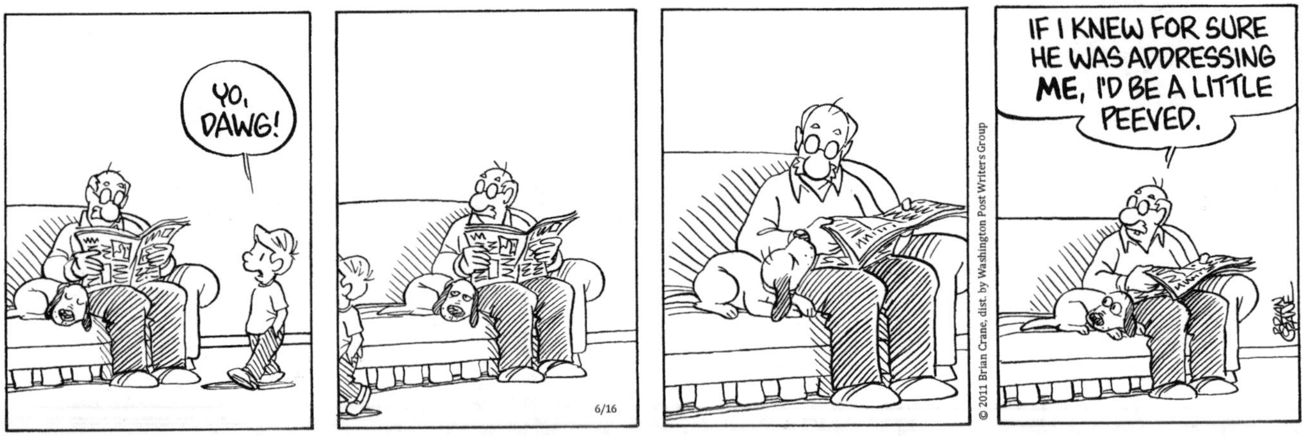
YO, DAWG!
6/16
© 2011 Brian Crane, dist. by Washington Post Writers Group
IF I KNEW FOR SURE HE WAS ADDRESSING ME, I'D BE A LITTLE PEEVED.

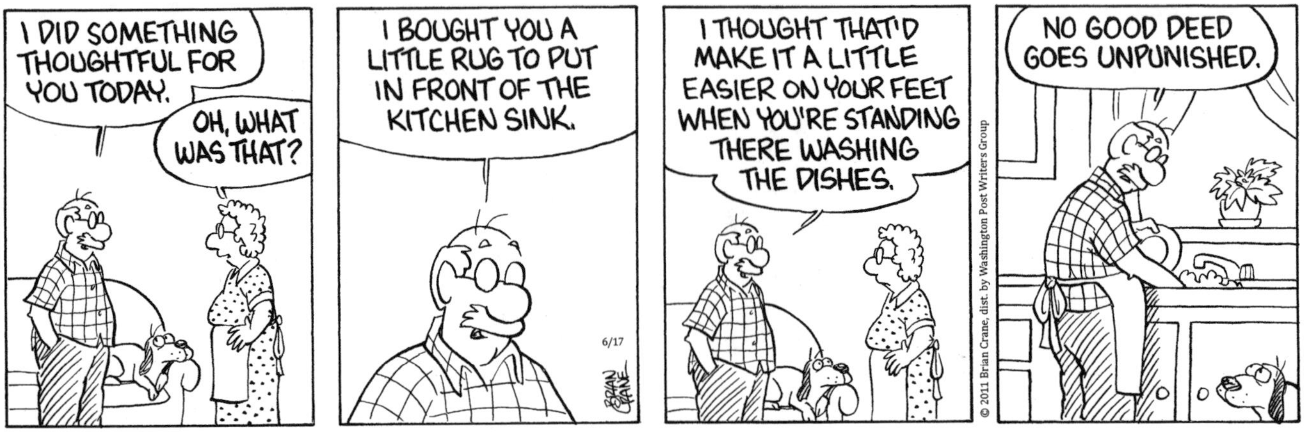
I DID SOMETHING THOUGHTFUL FOR YOU TODAY.
OH, WHAT WAS THAT?
I BOUGHT YOU A LITTLE RUG TO PUT IN FRONT OF THE KITCHEN SINK.
6/17
I THOUGHT THAT'D MAKE IT A LITTLE EASIER ON YOUR FEET WHEN YOU'RE STANDING THERE WASHING THE DISHES.
© 2011 Brian Crane, dist. by Washington Post Writers Group
NO GOOD DEED GOES UNPUNISHED.

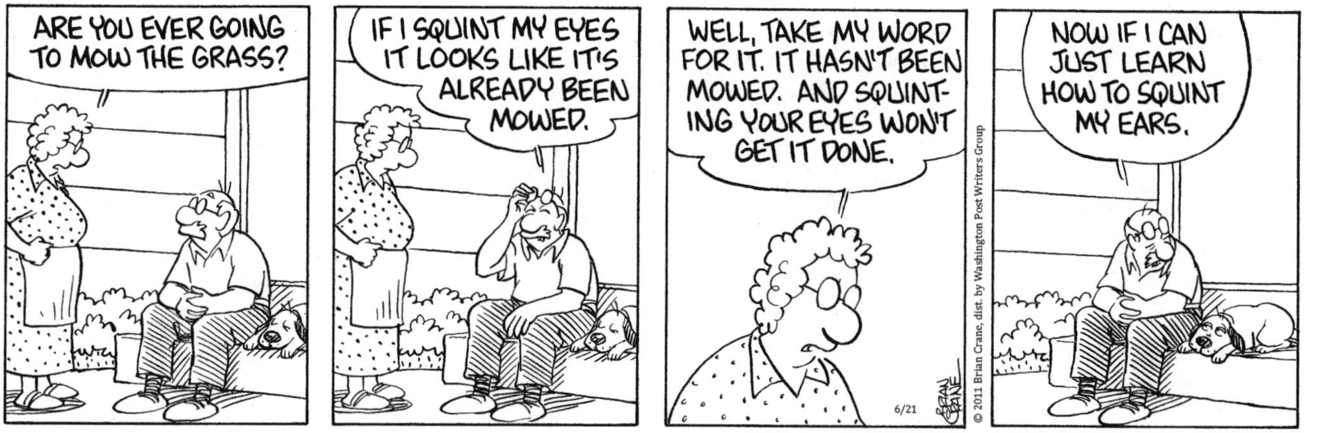
ARE YOU EVER GOING TO MOW THE GRASS?
IF I SQUINT MY EYES IT LOOKS LIKE IT'S ALREADY BEEN MOWED.
WELL, TAKE MY WORD FOR IT. IT HASN'T BEEN MOWED. AND SQUINTING YOUR EYES WON'T GET IT DONE.
NOW IF I CAN JUST LEARN HOW TO SQUINT MY EARS.
6/21
BRIAN CRANE
© 2011 Brian Crane, dist. by Washington Post Writers Group

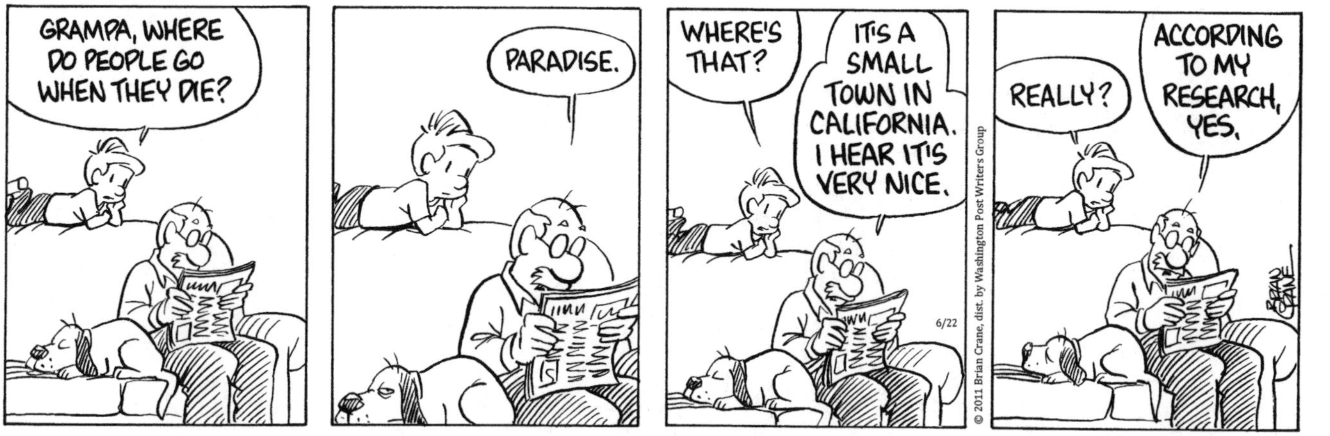
GRAMPA, WHERE DO PEOPLE GO WHEN THEY DIE?
PARADISE.
WHERE'S THAT?
IT'S A SMALL TOWN IN CALIFORNIA. I HEAR IT'S VERY NICE.
REALLY?
ACCORDING TO MY RESEARCH, YES.
6/22
BRIAN CRANE
© 2011 Brian Crane, dist. by Washington Post Writers Group

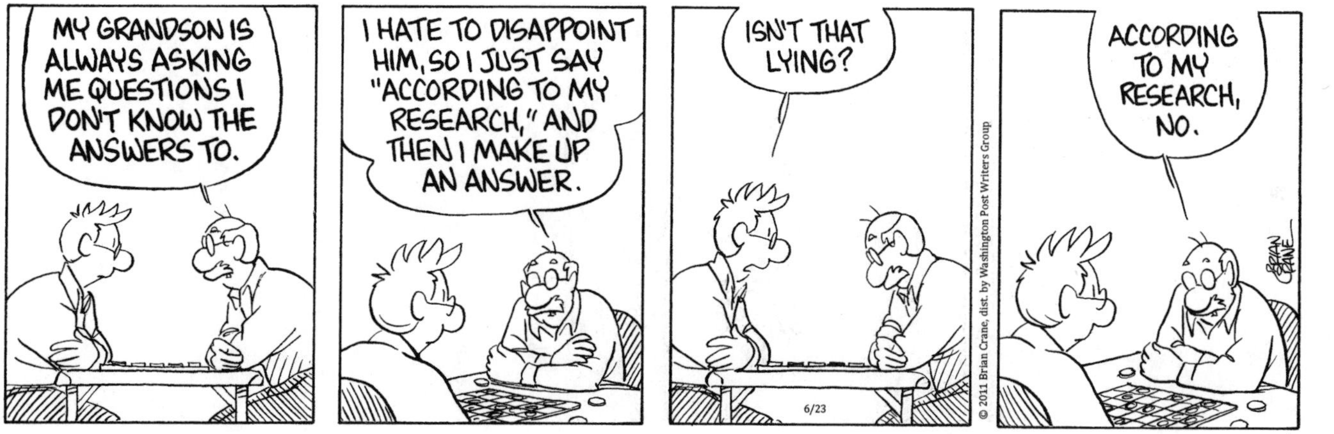
MY GRANDSON IS ALWAYS ASKING ME QUESTIONS I DON'T KNOW THE ANSWERS TO.
I HATE TO DISAPPOINT HIM, SO I JUST SAY "ACCORDING TO MY RESEARCH," AND THEN I MAKE UP AN ANSWER.
ISN'T THAT LYING?
ACCORDING TO MY RESEARCH, NO.
6/23
BRIAN CRANE
© 2011 Brian Crane, dist. by Washington Post Writers Group

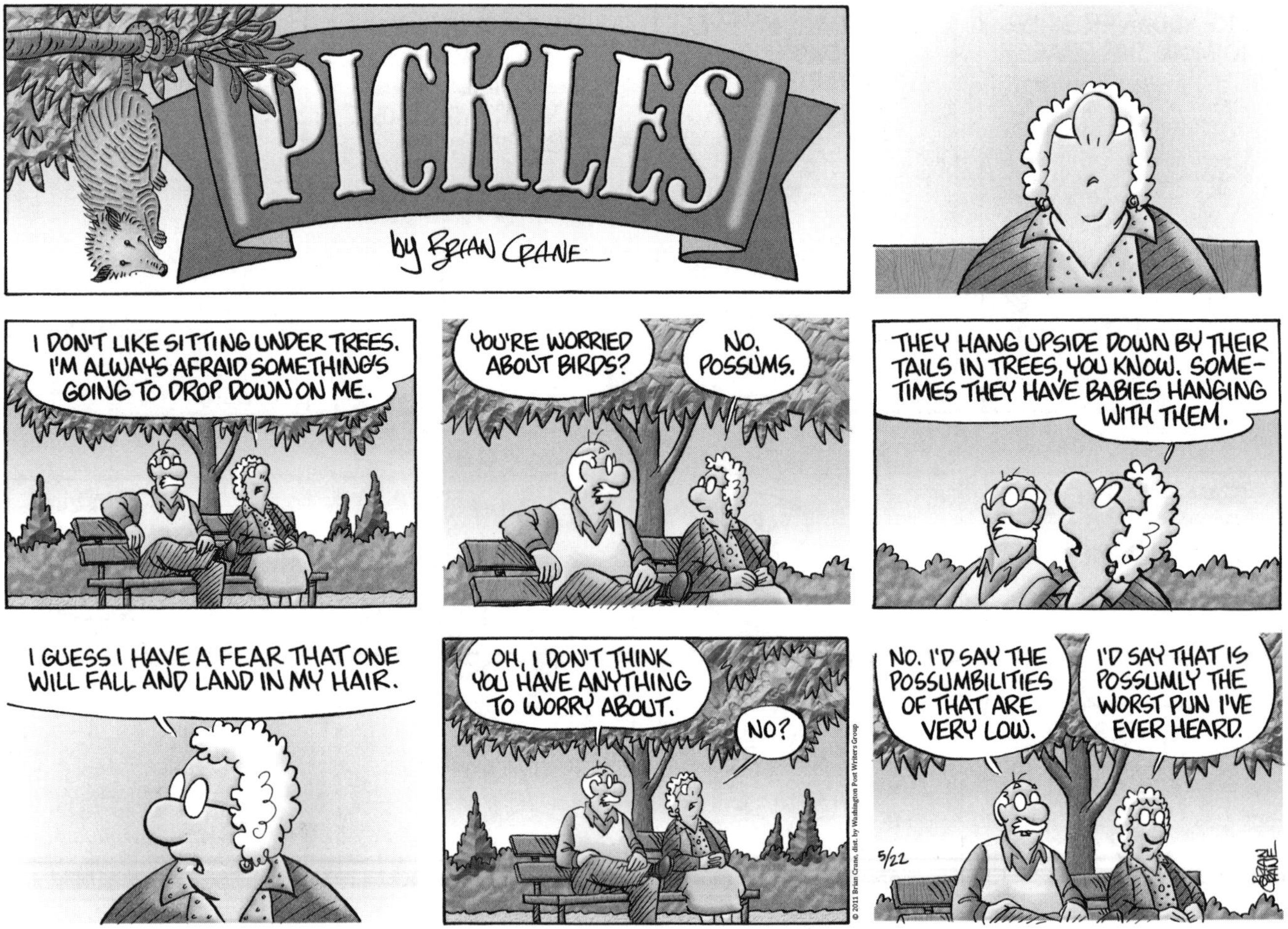
PICKLES
by BRIAN CRANE
I DON'T LIKE SITTING UNDER TREES. I'M ALWAYS AFRAID SOMETHING'S GOING TO DROP DOWN ON ME.
YOU'RE WORRIED ABOUT BIRDS?
NO. POSSUMS.
THEY HANG UPSIDE DOWN BY THEIR TAILS IN TREES, YOU KNOW. SOMETIMES THEY HAVE BABIES HANGING WITH THEM.
I GUESS I HAVE A FEAR THAT ONE WILL FALL AND LAND IN MY HAIR.
OH, I DON'T THINK YOU HAVE ANYTHING TO WORRY ABOUT.
NO?
© 2011 Brian Crane, dist. by Washington Post Writers Group
NO. I'D SAY THE POSSUMBILITIES OF THAT ARE VERY LOW.
I'D SAY THAT IS POSSUMLY THE WORST PUN I'VE EVER HEARD.
5/22
BRIAN CRANE

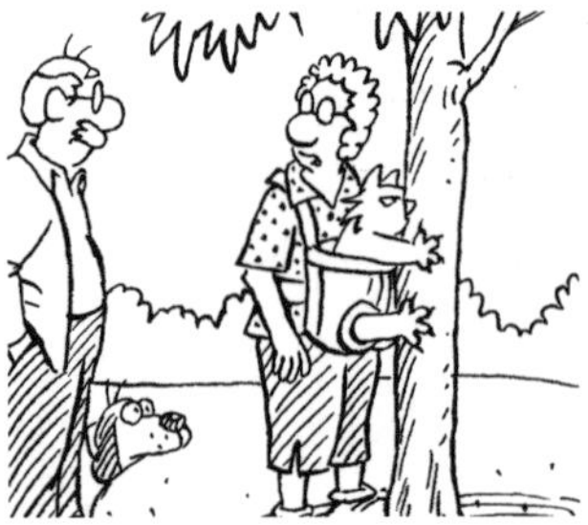

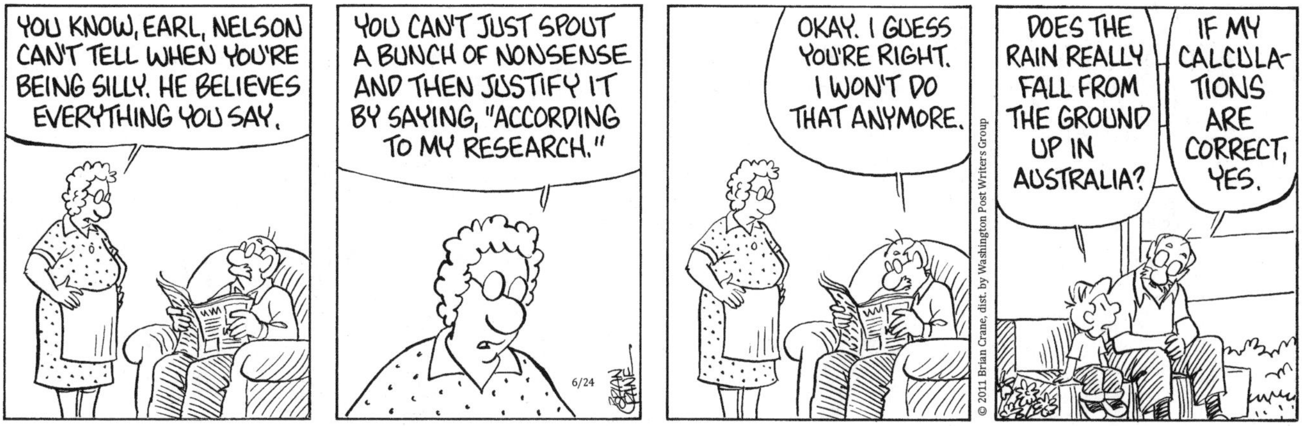
YOU KNOW, EARL, NELSON CAN'T TELL WHEN YOU'RE BEING SILLY. HE BELIEVES EVERYTHING YOU SAY.
YOU CAN'T JUST SPOUT A BUNCH OF NONSENSE AND THEN JUSTIFY IT BY SAYING, "ACCORDING TO MY RESEARCH."
6/24
OKAY. I GUESS YOU'RE RIGHT. I WON'T DO THAT ANYMORE.
DOES THE RAIN REALLY FALL FROM THE GROUND UP IN AUSTRALIA?
IF MY CALCULATIONS ARE CORRECT, YES.

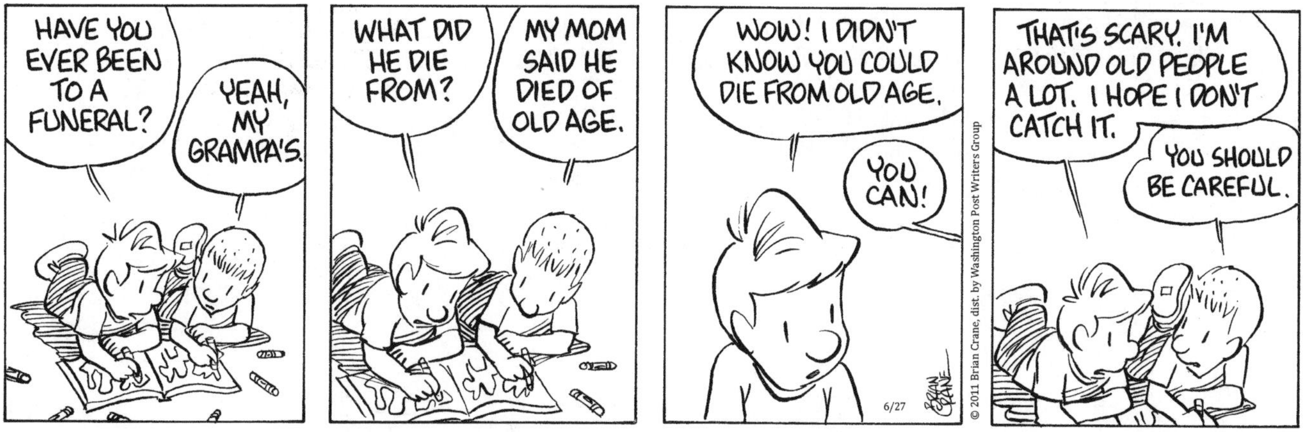
HAVE YOU EVER BEEN TO A FUNERAL?
YEAH, MY GRAMPA'S.
WHAT DID HE DIE FROM?
MY MOM SAID HE DIED OF OLD AGE.
WOW! I DIDN'T KNOW YOU COULD DIE FROM OLD AGE.
YOU CAN!
6/27
THAT'S SCARY. I'M AROUND OLD PEOPLE A LOT. I HOPE I DON'T CATCH IT.
YOU SHOULD BE CAREFUL.

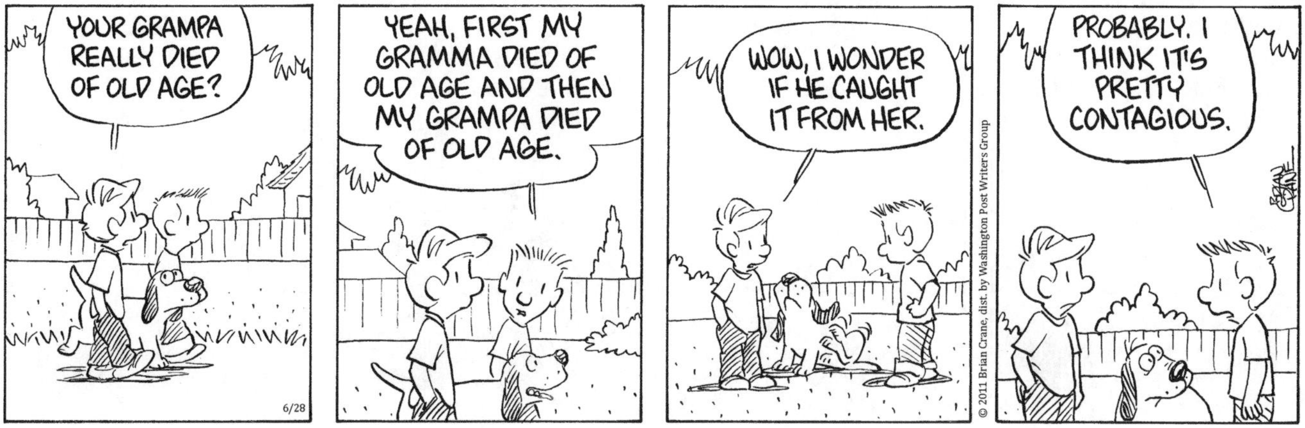
YOUR GRAMPA REALLY DIED OF OLD AGE?
6/28
YEAH, FIRST MY GRAMMA DIED OF OLD AGE AND THEN MY GRAMPA DIED OF OLD AGE.
WOW, I WONDER IF HE CAUGHT IT FROM HER.
PROBABLY. I THINK IT'S PRETTY CONTAGIOUS.

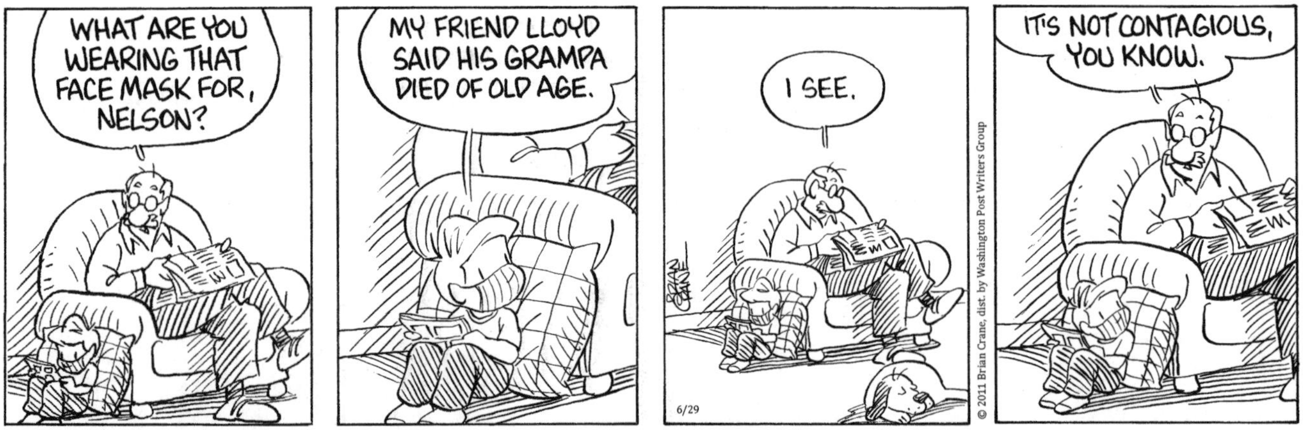
WHAT ARE YOU WEARING THAT FACE MASK FOR, NELSON?
MY FRIEND LLOYD SAID HIS GRAMPA DIED OF OLD AGE.
I SEE.
IT'S NOT CONTAGIOUS, YOU KNOW.
6/29
© 2011 Brian Crane, dist. by Washington Post Writers Group

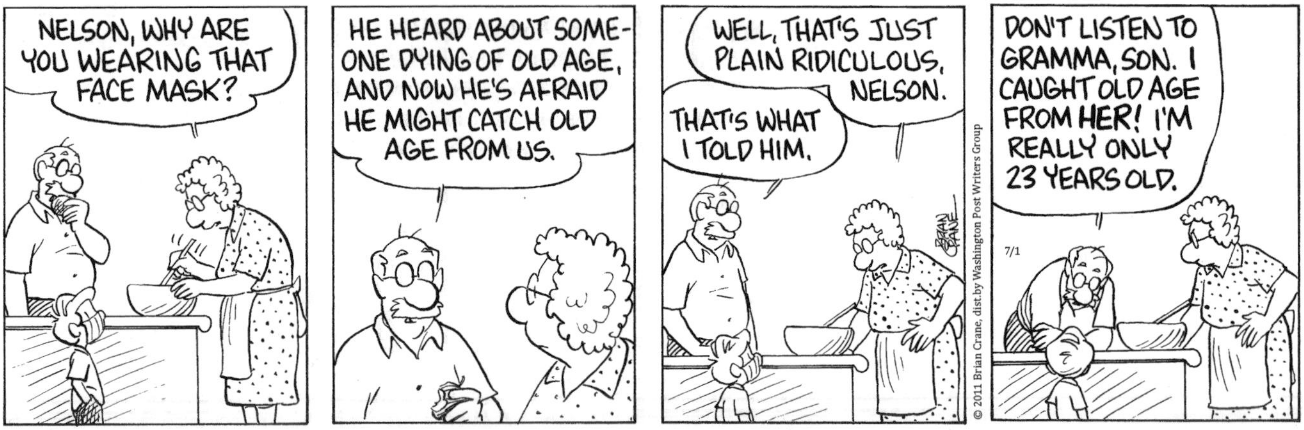
NELSON, WHY ARE YOU WEARING THAT FACE MASK?
HE HEARD ABOUT SOMEONE DYING OF OLD AGE, AND NOW HE'S AFRAID HE MIGHT CATCH OLD AGE FROM US.
WELL, THAT'S JUST PLAIN RIDICULOUS, NELSON.
THAT'S WHAT I TOLD HIM.
DON'T LISTEN TO GRAMMA, SON. I CAUGHT OLD AGE FROM HER! I'M REALLY ONLY 23 YEARS OLD.
7/1
© 2011 Brian Crane, dist. by Washington Post Writers Group

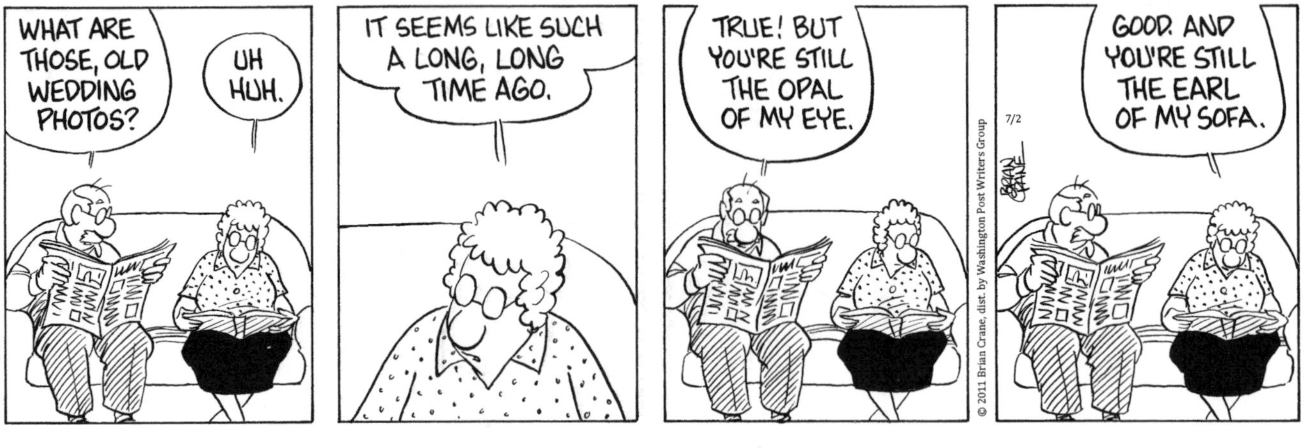
WHAT ARE THOSE, OLD WEDDING PHOTOS?
UH HUH.
IT SEEMS LIKE SUCH A LONG, LONG TIME AGO.
TRUE! BUT YOU'RE STILL THE OPAL OF MY EYE.
GOOD. AND YOU'RE STILL THE EARL OF MY SOFA.
7/2
© 2011 Brian Crane, dist. by Washington Post Writers Group

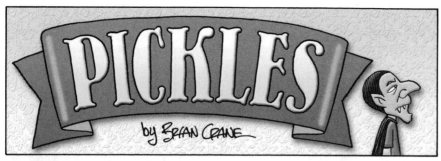

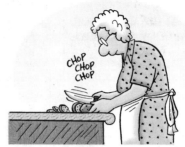

PICKLES
by BRIAN CRANE
CHOP CHOP CHOP
NELSON, WHY ARE YOU WEARING THAT MASK?
BECAUSE I MISS HALLOWEEN.
TRICK OR TREAT!
OKAY. HERE YOU GO.
CUCUMBER SLICES?
© 2011 Brian Crane, dist. by Washington Post Writers Group
7/3
THAT'S BETTER THAN THE POCKET LINT GRAMPA GAVE ME.
BRIAN CRANE

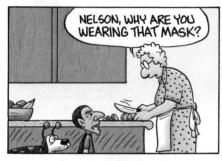

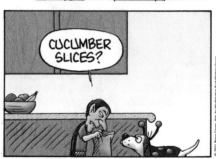

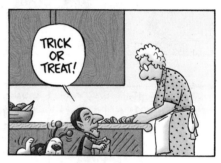

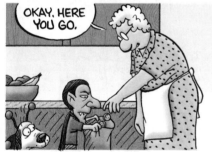

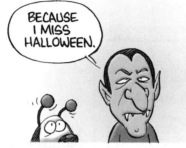

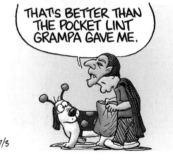

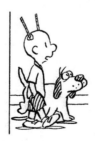

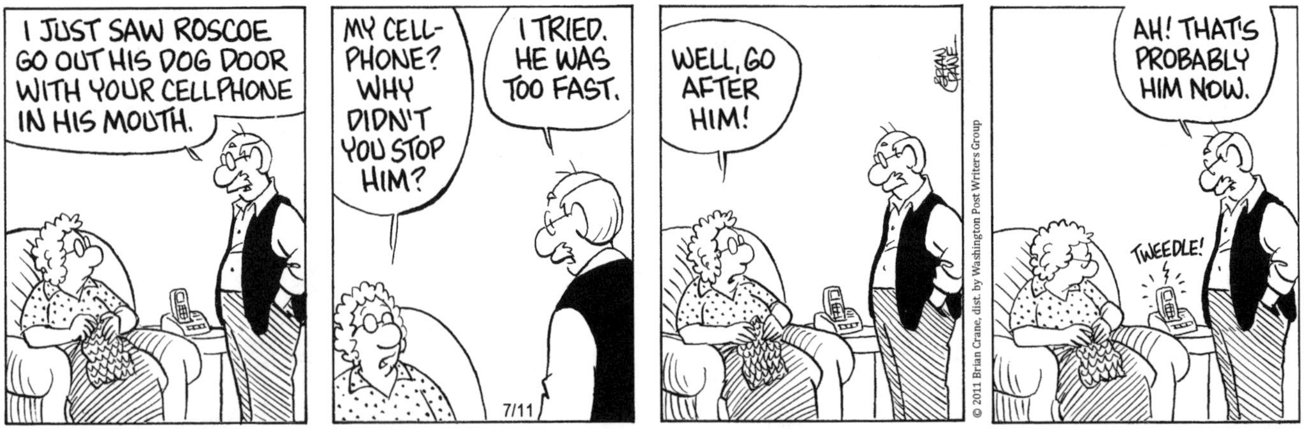
I JUST SAW ROSCOE GO OUT HIS DOG DOOR WITH YOUR CELLPHONE IN HIS MOUTH.
MY CELL-PHONE? WHY DIDN'T YOU STOP HIM?
I TRIED. HE WAS TOO FAST.
7/11
WELL, GO AFTER HIM!
© 2011 Brian Crane, dist. by Washington Post Writers Group
AH! THAT'S PROBABLY HIM NOW.
TWEEDLE!

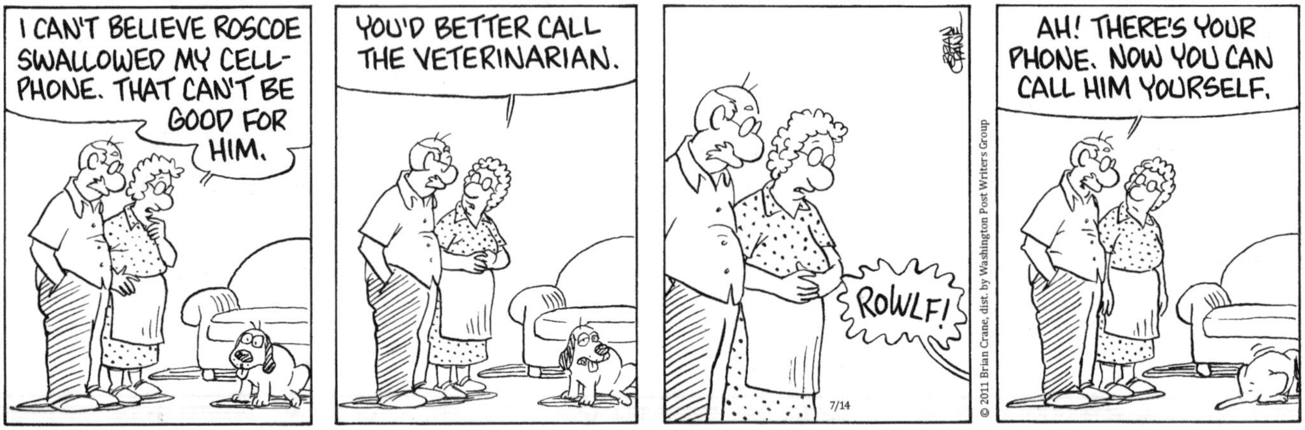
I CAN'T BELIEVE ROSCOE SWALLOWED MY CELL-PHONE. THAT CAN'T BE GOOD FOR HIM.
YOU'D BETTER CALL THE VETERINARIAN.
ROWLF!
7/14
© 2011 Brian Crane, dist. by Washington Post Writers Group
AH! THERE'S YOUR PHONE. NOW YOU CAN CALL HIM YOURSELF.

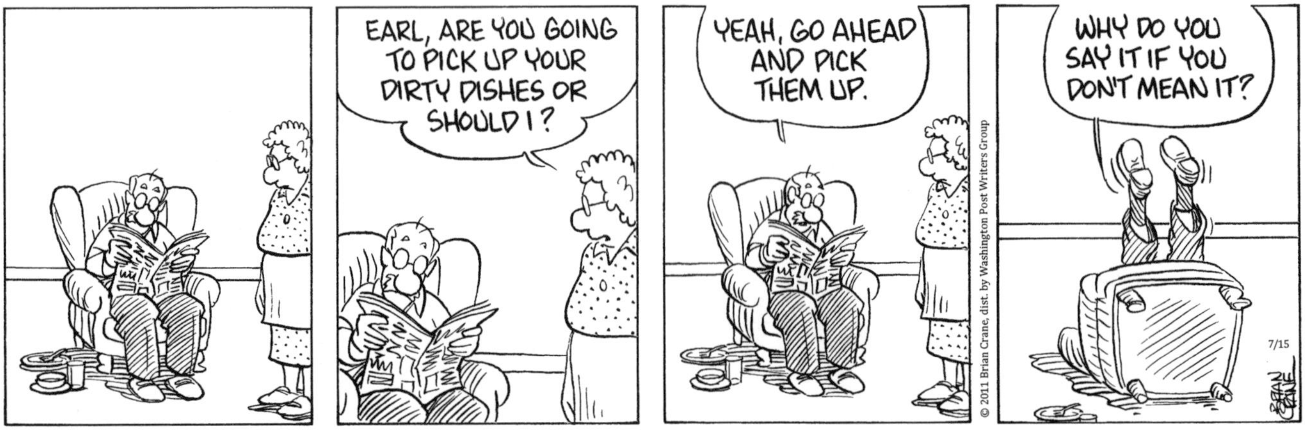
EARL, ARE YOU GOING TO PICK UP YOUR DIRTY DISHES OR SHOULD I?
YEAH, GO AHEAD AND PICK THEM UP.
© 2011 Brian Crane, dist. by Washington Post Writers Group
WHY DO YOU SAY IT IF YOU DON'T MEAN IT?
7/15

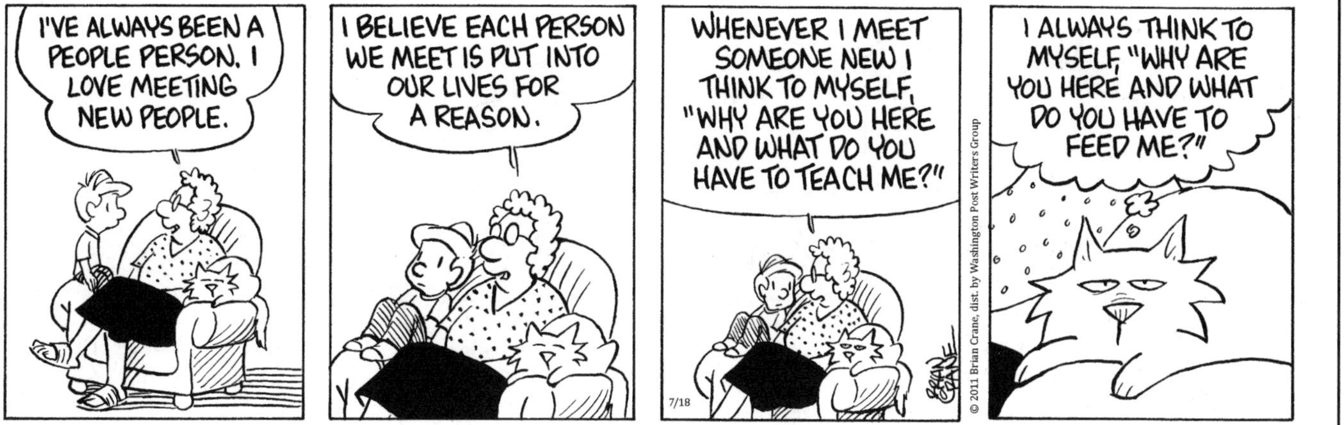
I'VE ALWAYS BEEN A PEOPLE PERSON. I LOVE MEETING NEW PEOPLE.
I BELIEVE EACH PERSON WE MEET IS PUT INTO OUR LIVES FOR A REASON.
WHENEVER I MEET SOMEONE NEW I THINK TO MYSELF, "WHY ARE YOU HERE AND WHAT DO YOU HAVE TO TEACH ME?"
7/18
© 2011 Brian Crane, dist. by Washington Post Writers Group
I ALWAYS THINK TO MYSELF, "WHY ARE YOU HERE AND WHAT DO YOU HAVE TO FEED ME?"

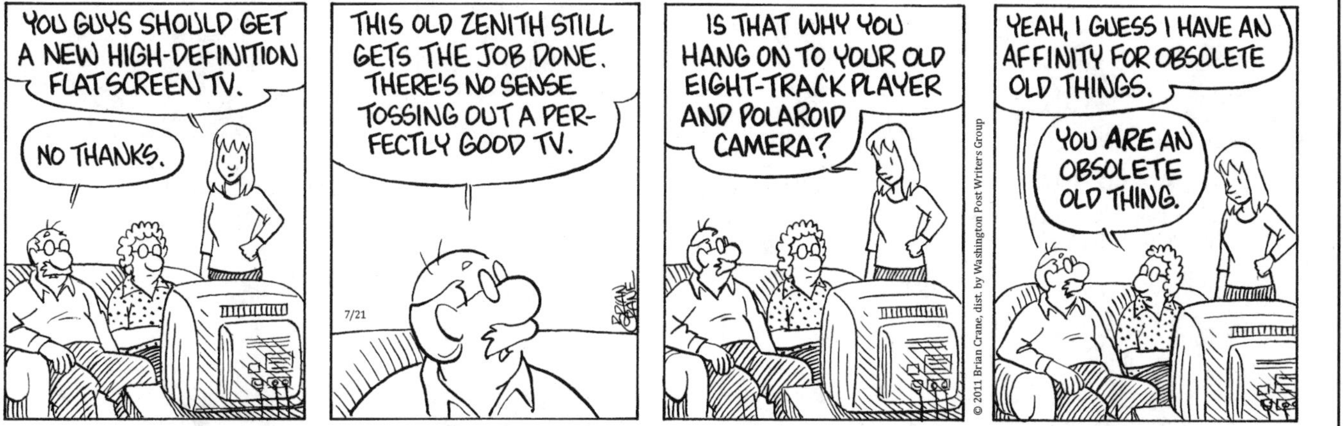
YOU GUYS SHOULD GET A NEW HIGH-DEFINITION FLATSCREEN TV.
NO THANKS.
THIS OLD ZENITH STILL GETS THE JOB DONE. THERE'S NO SENSE TOSSING OUT A PERFECTLY GOOD TV.
7/21
IS THAT WHY YOU HANG ON TO YOUR OLD EIGHT-TRACK PLAYER AND POLAROID CAMERA?
© 2011 Brian Crane, dist. by Washington Post Writers Group
YEAH, I GUESS I HAVE AN AFFINITY FOR OBSOLETE OLD THINGS.
YOU ARE AN OBSOLETE OLD THING.

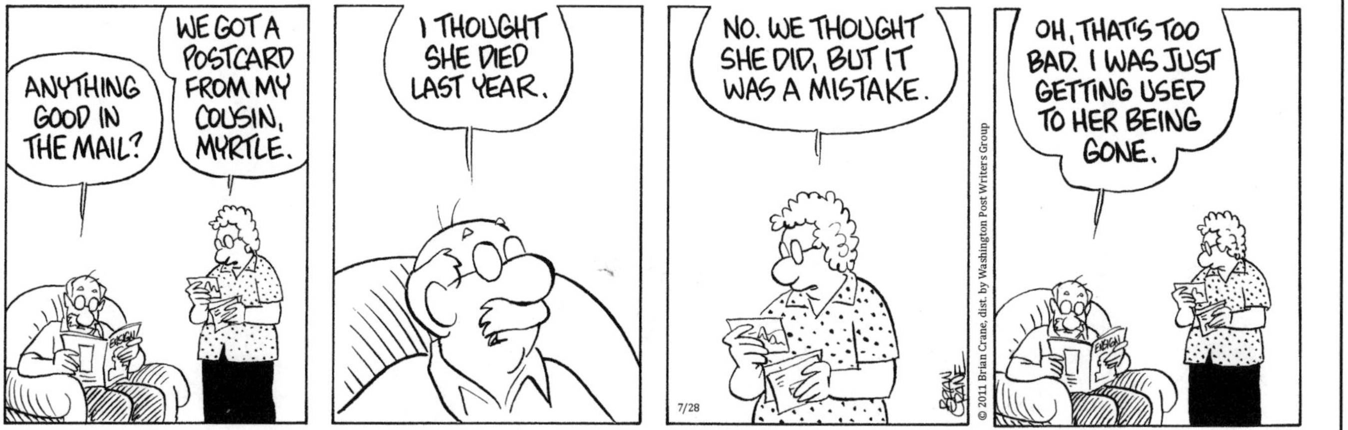
ANYTHING GOOD IN THE MAIL?
WE GOT A POSTCARD FROM MY COUSIN, MYRTLE.
I THOUGHT SHE DIED LAST YEAR.
NO. WE THOUGHT SHE DID, BUT IT WAS A MISTAKE.
7/28
© 2011 Brian Crane, dist. by Washington Post Writers Group
OH, THAT'S TOO BAD. I WAS JUST GETTING USED TO HER BEING GONE.

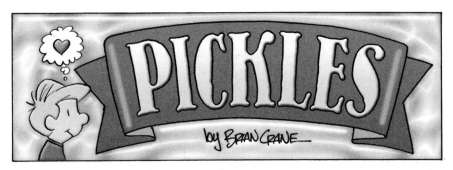

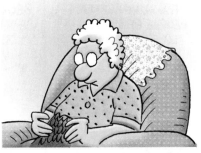

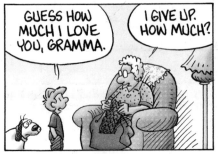

PICKLES
by BRIAN CRANE
GUESS HOW MUCH I LOVE YOU, GRAMMA.
I GIVE UP. HOW MUCH?
ONE HUNDRED!
REALLY? THAT'S VERY SWEET.
BUT JUST A HUNDRED, HUH? NOT EVEN TWO HUNDRED?
YEAH, TWO HUNDRED!
TWO HUNDRED, THAT'S ALL? NOT FIVE HUNDRED, OR MAYBE A THOUSAND?
OKAY, A THOUSAND, BUT I HAVE TO GO NOW.
© 2011 Brian Crane, dist. by Washington Post Writers Group
7/31
I WAS GETTING IN WAY OVER MY HEAD!

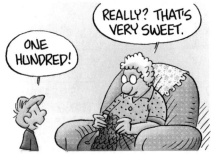

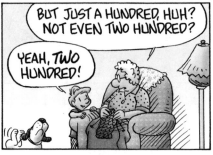

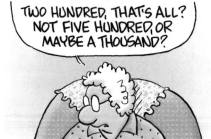

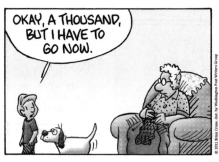

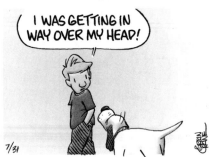

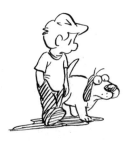

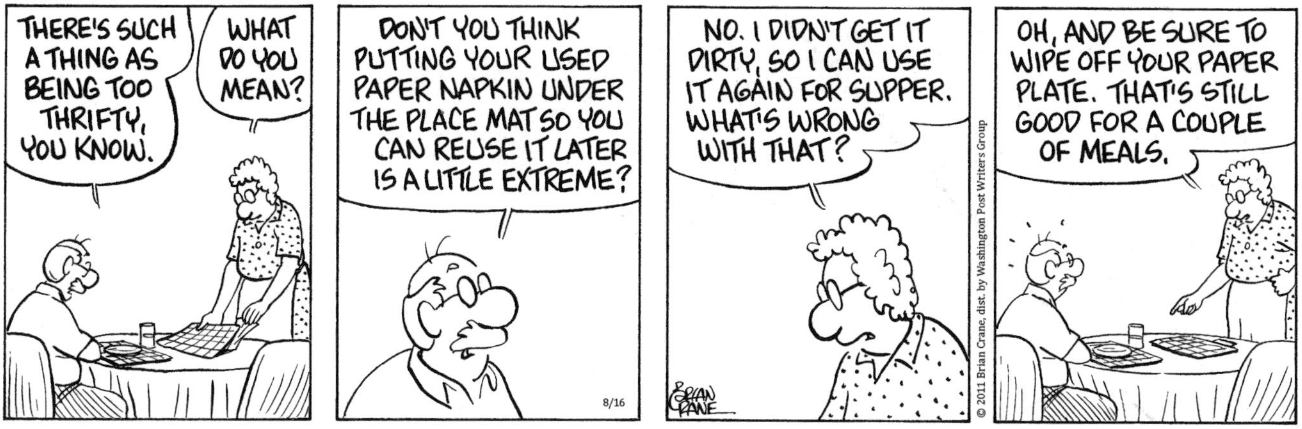
THERE'S SUCH A THING AS BEING TOO THRIFTY, YOU KNOW.
WHAT DO YOU MEAN?
DON'T YOU THINK PUTTING YOUR USED PAPER NAPKIN UNDER THE PLACE MAT SO YOU CAN REUSE IT LATER IS A LITTLE EXTREME?
8/16
NO. I DIDN'T GET IT DIRTY, SO I CAN USE IT AGAIN FOR SUPPER. WHAT'S WRONG WITH THAT?
BRIAN CRANE
OH, AND BE SURE TO WIPE OFF YOUR PAPER PLATE. THAT'S STILL GOOD FOR A COUPLE OF MEALS.
© 2011 Brian Crane, dist. by Washington Post Writers Group

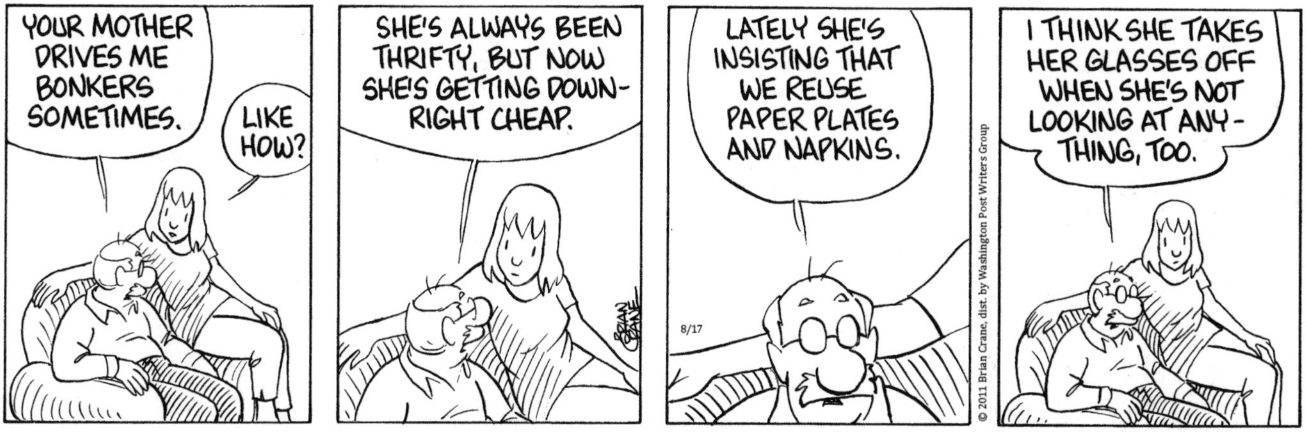
YOUR MOTHER DRIVES ME BONKERS SOMETIMES.
LIKE HOW?
SHE'S ALWAYS BEEN THRIFTY, BUT NOW SHE'S GETTING DOWN-RIGHT CHEAP.
BRIAN CRANE
LATELY SHE'S INSISTING THAT WE REUSE PAPER PLATES AND NAPKINS.
8/17
I THINK SHE TAKES HER GLASSES OFF WHEN SHE'S NOT LOOKING AT ANY-THING, TOO.
© 2011 Brian Crane, dist. by Washington Post Writers Group

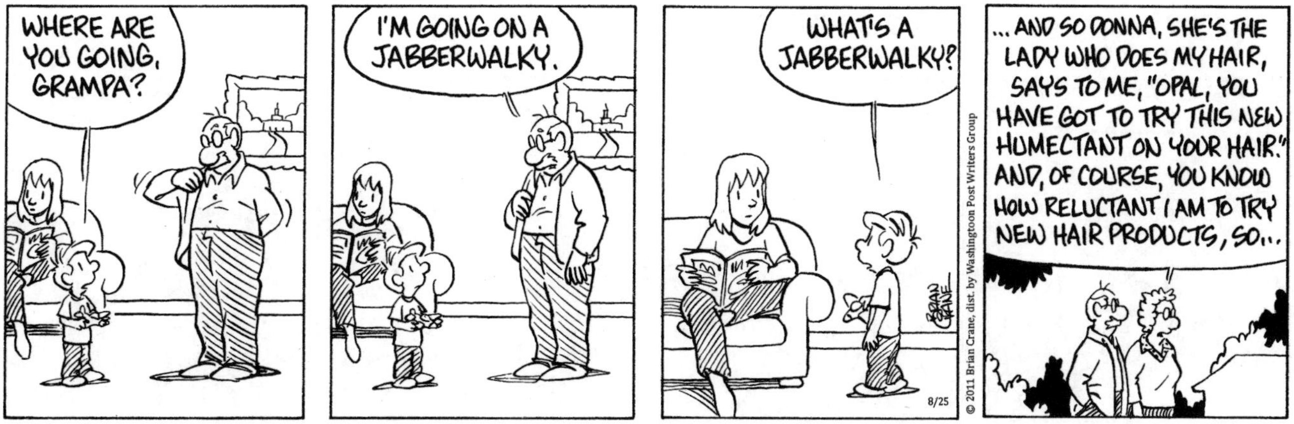
WHERE ARE YOU GOING, GRAMPA?
I'M GOING ON A JABBERWALKY.
WHAT'S A JABBERWALKY?
BRIAN CRANE
8/25
... AND SO DONNA, SHE'S THE LADY WHO DOES MY HAIR, SAYS TO ME, "OPAL, YOU HAVE GOT TO TRY THIS NEW HUMECTANT ON YOUR HAIR." AND, OF COURSE, YOU KNOW HOW RELUCTANT I AM TO TRY NEW HAIR PRODUCTS, SO...
© 2011 Brian Crane, dist. by Washingtoon Post Writers Group

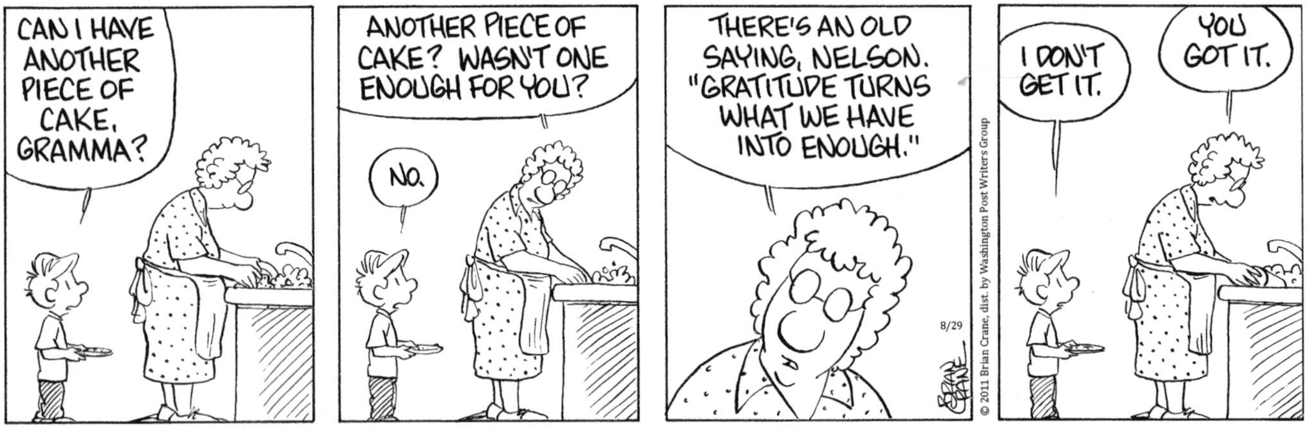
CAN I HAVE ANOTHER PIECE OF CAKE, GRAMMA?
ANOTHER PIECE OF CAKE? WASN'T ONE ENOUGH FOR YOU?
NO.
THERE'S AN OLD SAYING, NELSON. "GRATITUDE TURNS WHAT WE HAVE INTO ENOUGH."
8/29
I DON'T GET IT.
YOU GOT IT.

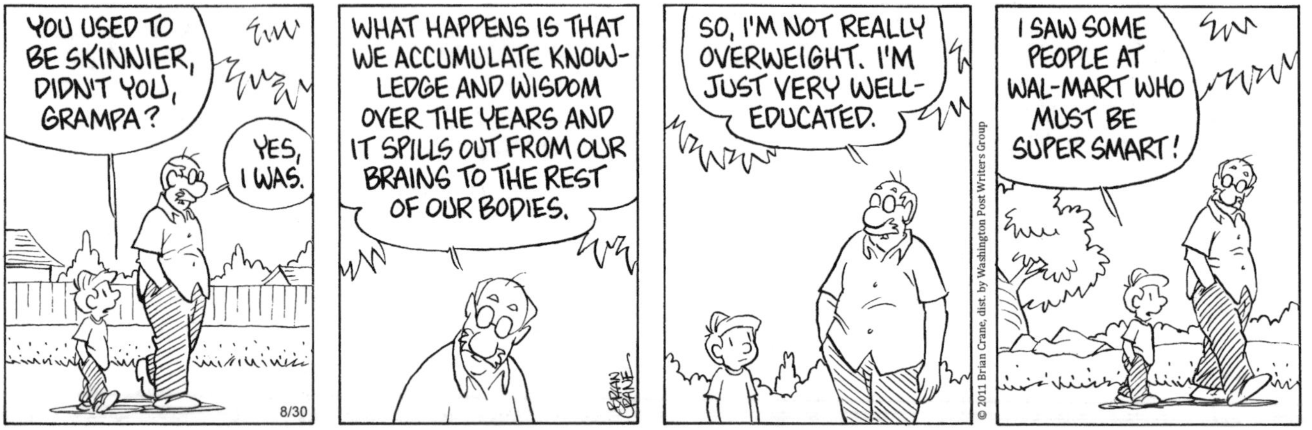
YOU USED TO BE SKINNIER, DIDN'T YOU, GRAMPA?
YES, I WAS.
8/30
WHAT HAPPENS IS THAT WE ACCUMULATE KNOWLEDGE AND WISDOM OVER THE YEARS AND IT SPILLS OUT FROM OUR BRAINS TO THE REST OF OUR BODIES.
SO, I'M NOT REALLY OVERWEIGHT. I'M JUST VERY WELL-EDUCATED.
I SAW SOME PEOPLE AT WAL-MART WHO MUST BE SUPER SMART!

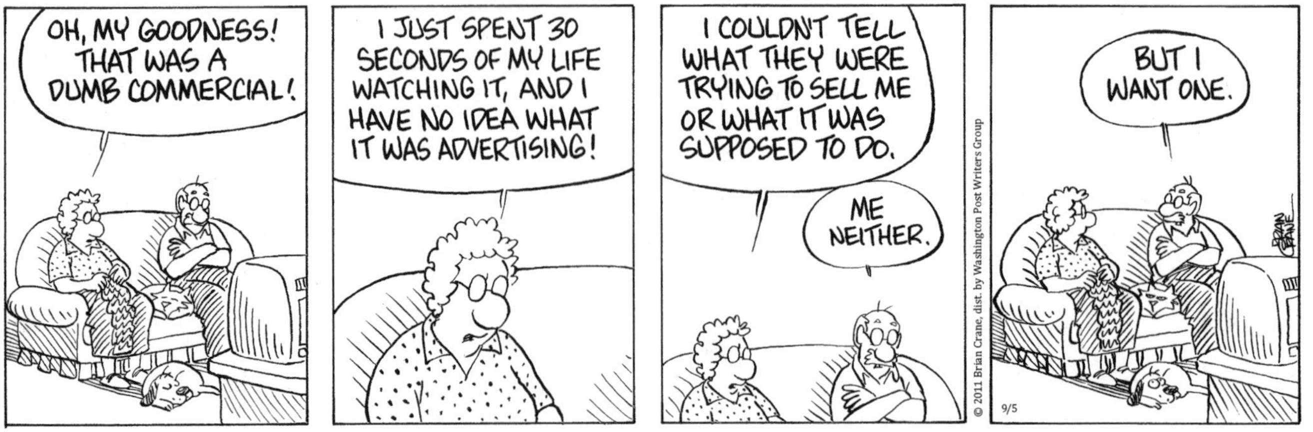
OH, MY GOODNESS! THAT WAS A DUMB COMMERCIAL!
I JUST SPENT 30 SECONDS OF MY LIFE WATCHING IT, AND I HAVE NO IDEA WHAT IT WAS ADVERTISING!
I COULDN'T TELL WHAT THEY WERE TRYING TO SELL ME OR WHAT IT WAS SUPPOSED TO DO.
ME NEITHER.
BUT I WANT ONE.
9/5

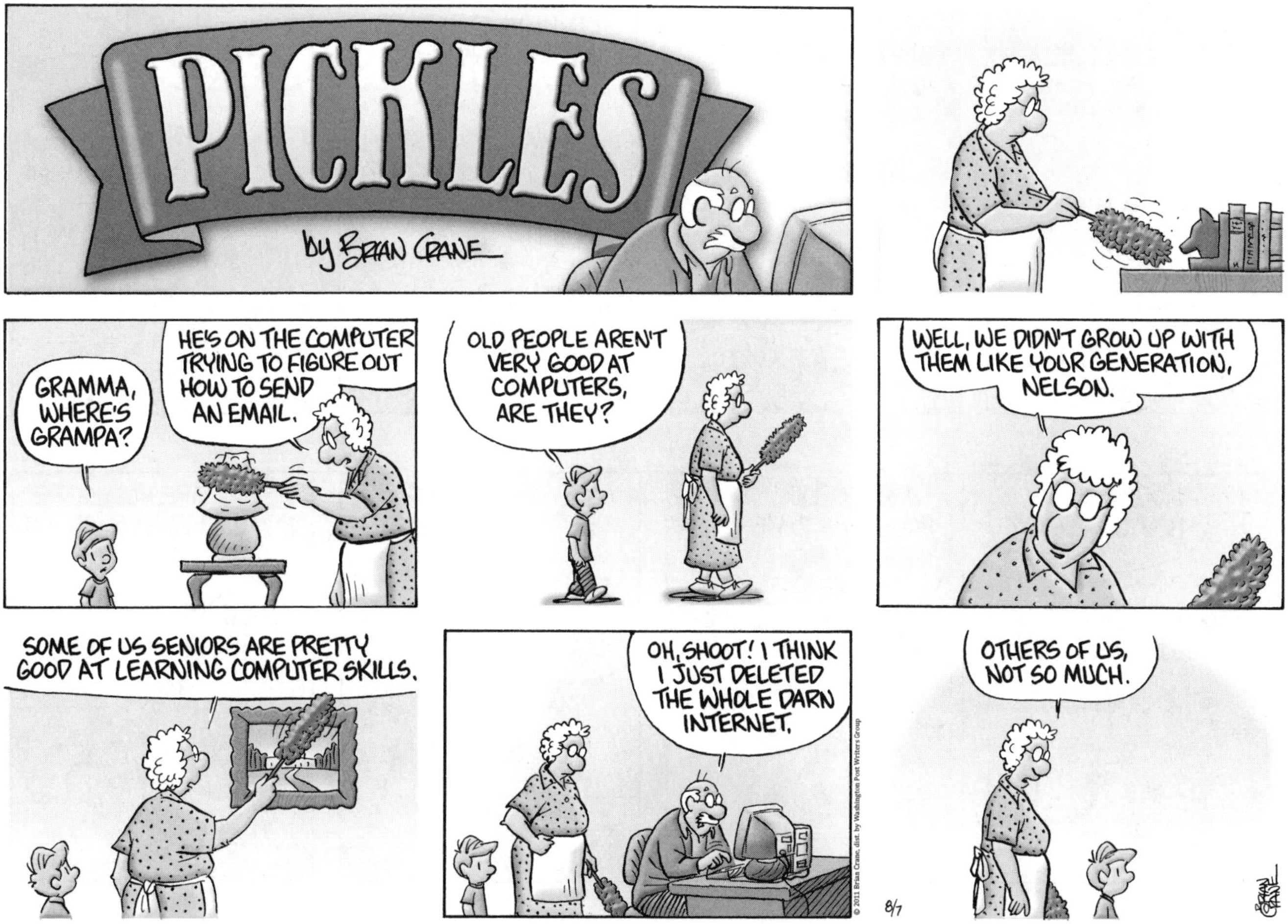
PICKLES
by Brian Crane
GRAMMA, WHERE'S GRAMPA?
HE'S ON THE COMPUTER TRYING TO FIGURE OUT HOW TO SEND AN EMAIL.
OLD PEOPLE AREN'T VERY GOOD AT COMPUTERS, ARE THEY?
WELL, WE DIDN'T GROW UP WITH THEM LIKE YOUR GENERATION, NELSON.
SOME OF US SENIORS ARE PRETTY GOOD AT LEARNING COMPUTER SKILLS.
OH, SHOOT! I THINK I JUST DELETED THE WHOLE DARN INTERNET.
© 2011 Brian Crane, dist. by Washington Post Writers Group
8/7
OTHERS OF US, NOT SO MUCH.
Brian Crane

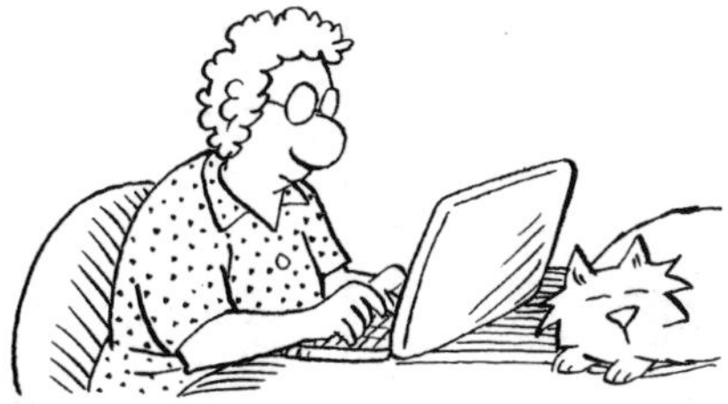

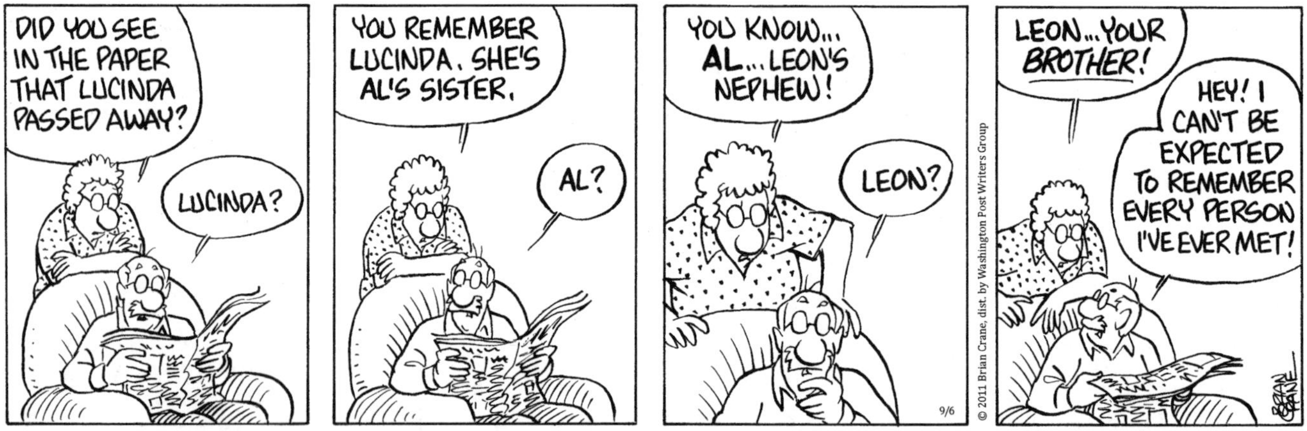
DID YOU SEE IN THE PAPER THAT LUCINDA PASSED AWAY?
LUCINDA?
YOU REMEMBER LUCINDA. SHE'S AL'S SISTER.
AL?
YOU KNOW... AL... LEON'S NEPHEW!
LEON?
9/6
LEON... YOUR BROTHER!
HEY! I CAN'T BE EXPECTED TO REMEMBER EVERY PERSON I'VE EVER MET!
BRIAN CRANE

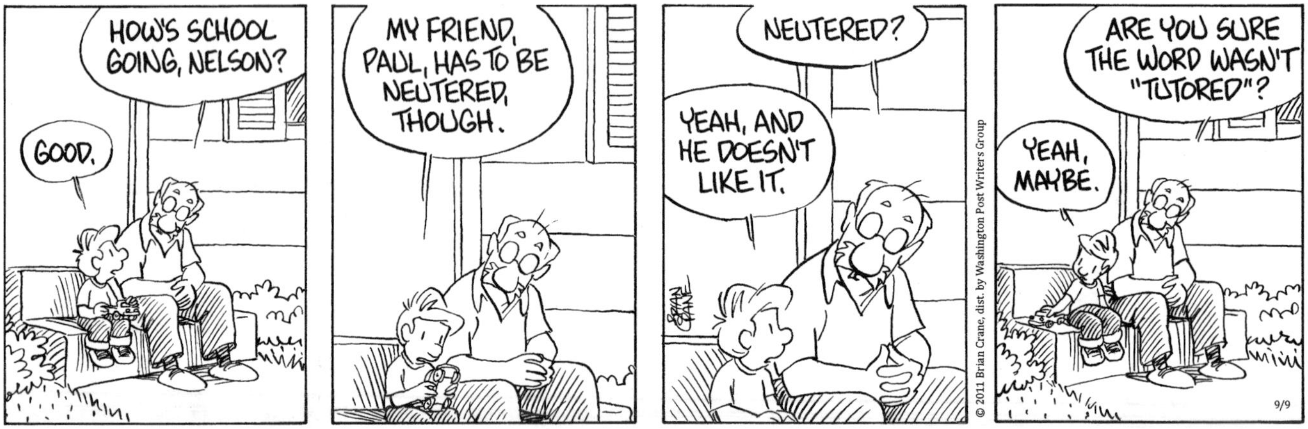
HOW'S SCHOOL GOING, NELSON?
GOOD.
MY FRIEND, PAUL, HAS TO BE NEUTERED, THOUGH.
NEUTERED?
YEAH, AND HE DOESN'T LIKE IT.
BRIAN CRANE
ARE YOU SURE THE WORD WASN'T "TUTORED"?
YEAH, MAYBE.
9/9

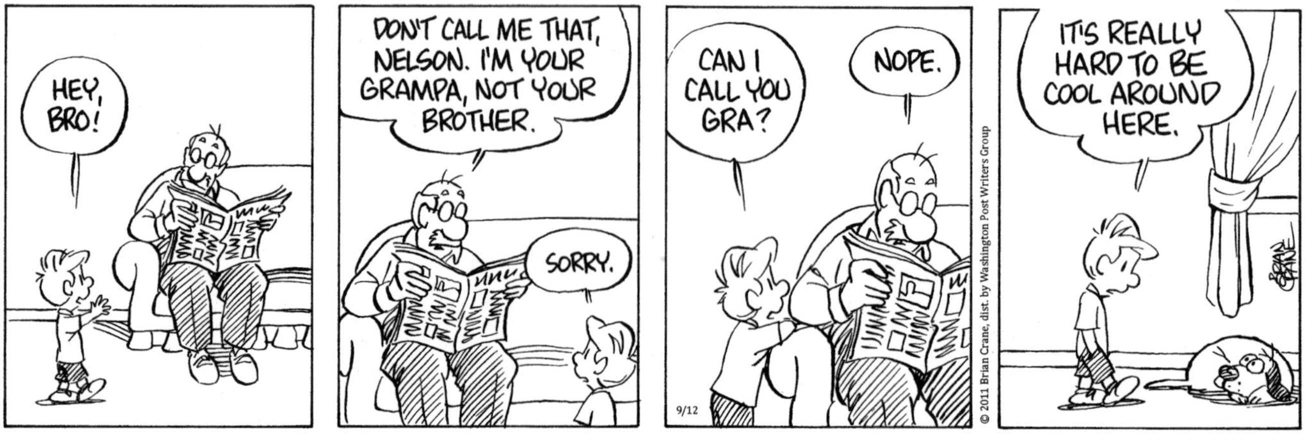
HEY, BRO!
DON'T CALL ME THAT, NELSON. I'M YOUR GRAMPA, NOT YOUR BROTHER.
SORRY.
CAN I CALL YOU GRA?
NOPE.
9/12
IT'S REALLY HARD TO BE COOL AROUND HERE.
BRIAN CRANE

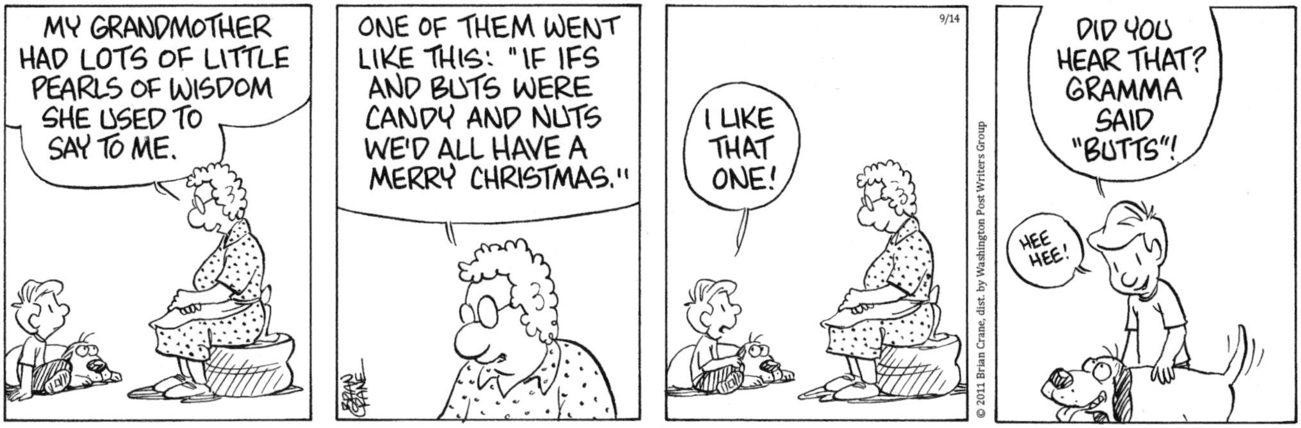
MY GRANDMOTHER HAD LOTS OF LITTLE PEARLS OF WISDOM SHE USED TO SAY TO ME.
ONE OF THEM WENT LIKE THIS: "IF IFS AND BUTS WERE CANDY AND NUTS WE'D ALL HAVE A MERRY CHRISTMAS."
9/14
I LIKE THAT ONE!
© 2011 Brian Crane, dist. by Washington Post Writers Group
DID YOU HEAR THAT? GRAMMA SAID "BUTTS"!
HEE HEE!

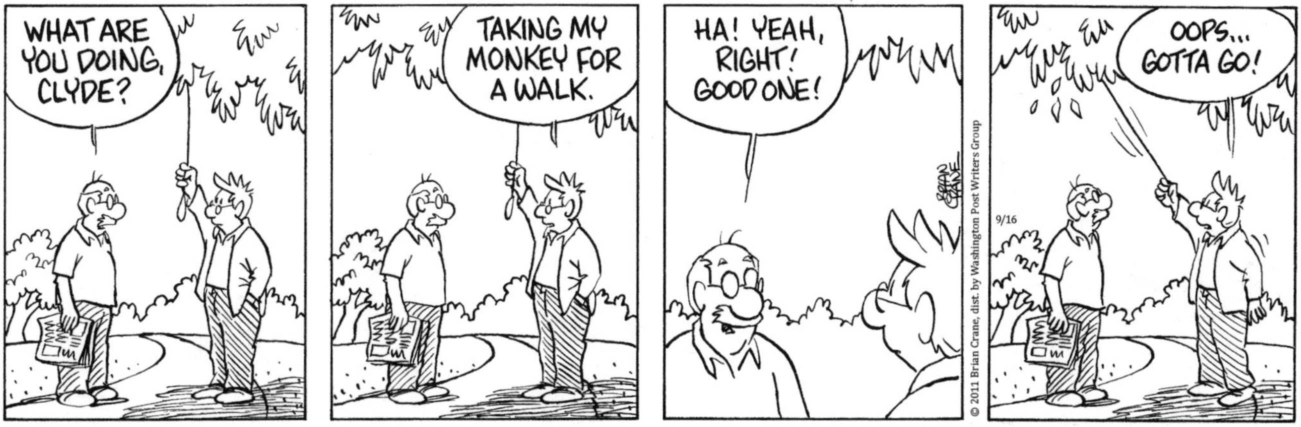
WHAT ARE YOU DOING, CLYDE?
TAKING MY MONKEY FOR A WALK.
HA! YEAH, RIGHT! GOOD ONE!
© 2011 Brian Crane, dist. by Washington Post Writers Group
9/16
OOPS... GOTTA GO!

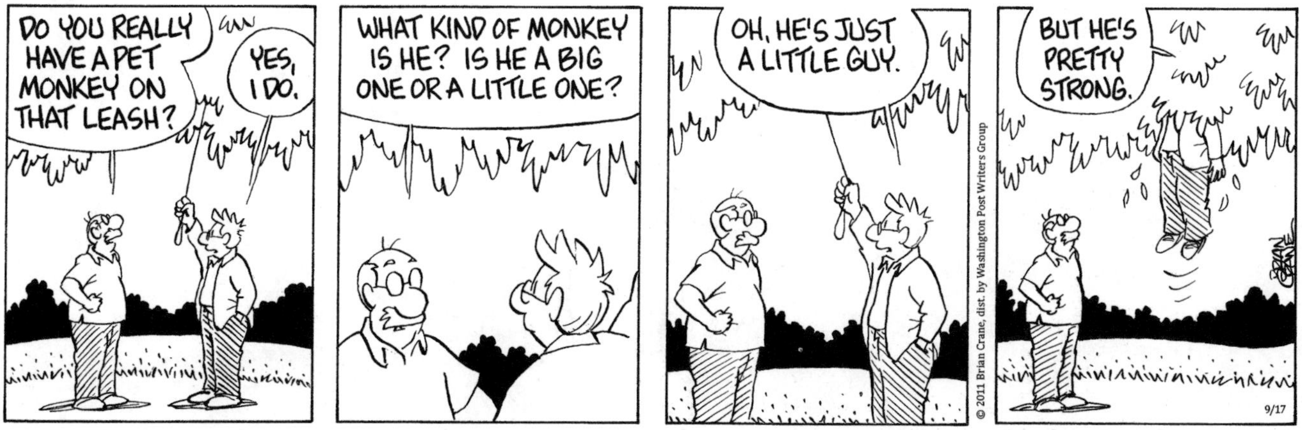
DO YOU REALLY HAVE A PET MONKEY ON THAT LEASH?
YES, I DO.
WHAT KIND OF MONKEY IS HE? IS HE A BIG ONE OR A LITTLE ONE?
© 2011 Brian Crane, dist. by Washington Post Writers Group
OH, HE'S JUST A LITTLE GUY.
© 2011 Brian Crane, dist. by Washington Post Writers Group
BUT HE'S PRETTY STRONG.
9/17

COULD IT BE? YES, IT COULD, SOMETHING'S COMING, SOMETHING GOOD...
PICKLES
by BRIAN CRANE
THERE'S A PLACE FOR US... SOMEWHERE A PLACE FOR US...
YOU LIKE TO SING, DON'T YOU, GRAMMA?
OH, YES. ESPECIALLY WHILE I DO HOUSEWORK. IT DRIVES GRAMPA CRAZY, THOUGH.
HE GETS THE SONGS STUCK IN HIS HEAD AND THEN HE FINDS HIMSELF SINGING THEM WITHOUT REALIZING IT.
LATELY I'VE BEEN SINGING SONGS FROM "WEST SIDE STORY."
8/14
BRIAN CRANE
© 2011 Brian Crane, dist. by Washington Post Writers Group
I FEEL PRETTY, OH, SO PRETTY. I FEEL PRETTY AND WITTY AND GAY...

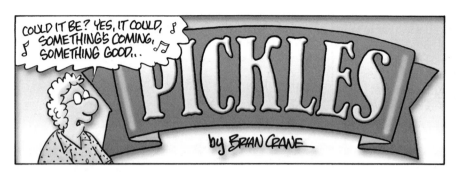

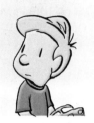

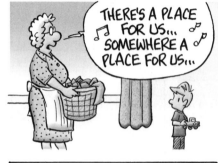

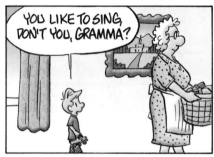

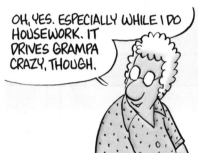

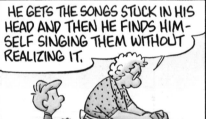

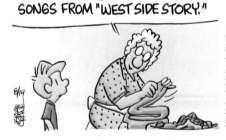

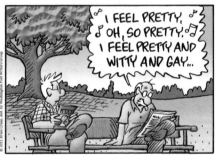

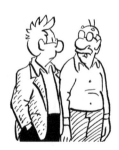

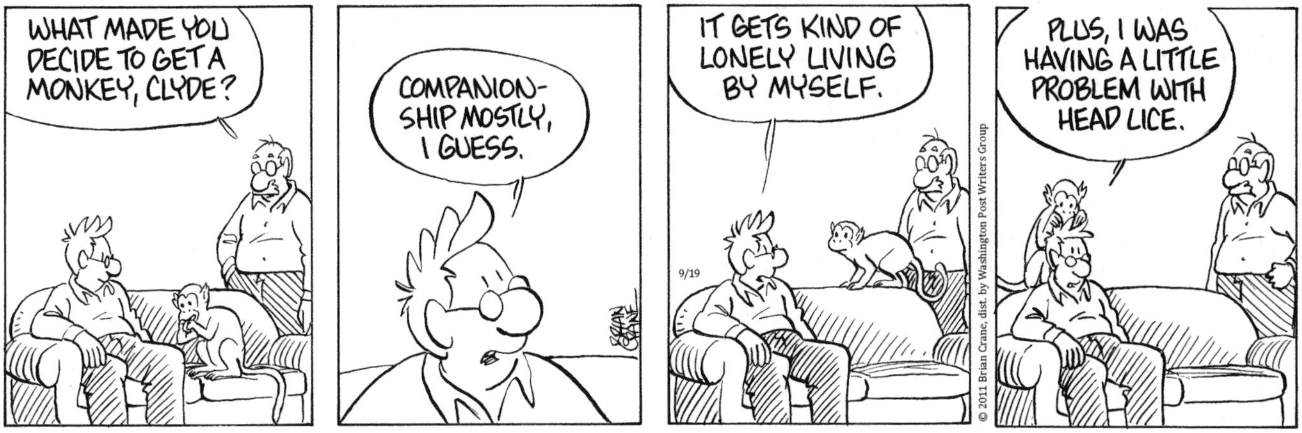
WHAT MADE YOU DECIDE TO GET A MONKEY, CLYDE?
COMPANION-SHIP MOSTLY, I GUESS.
IT GETS KIND OF LONELY LIVING BY MYSELF.
PLUS, I WAS HAVING A LITTLE PROBLEM WITH HEAD LICE.
9/19

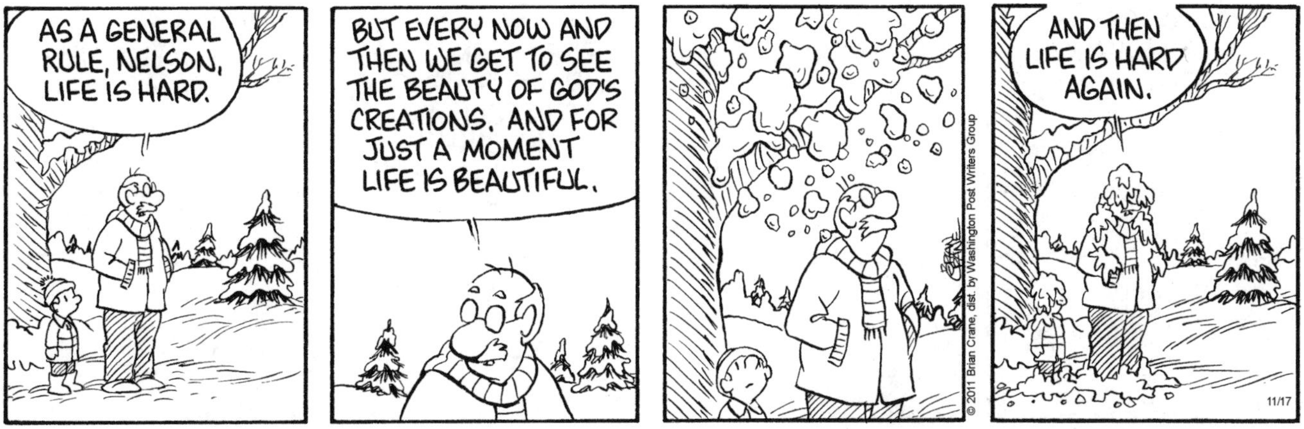
AS A GENERAL RULE, NELSON, LIFE IS HARD.
BUT EVERY NOW AND THEN WE GET TO SEE THE BEAUTY OF GOD'S CREATIONS. AND FOR JUST A MOMENT LIFE IS BEAUTIFUL.
AND THEN LIFE IS HARD AGAIN.
11/17

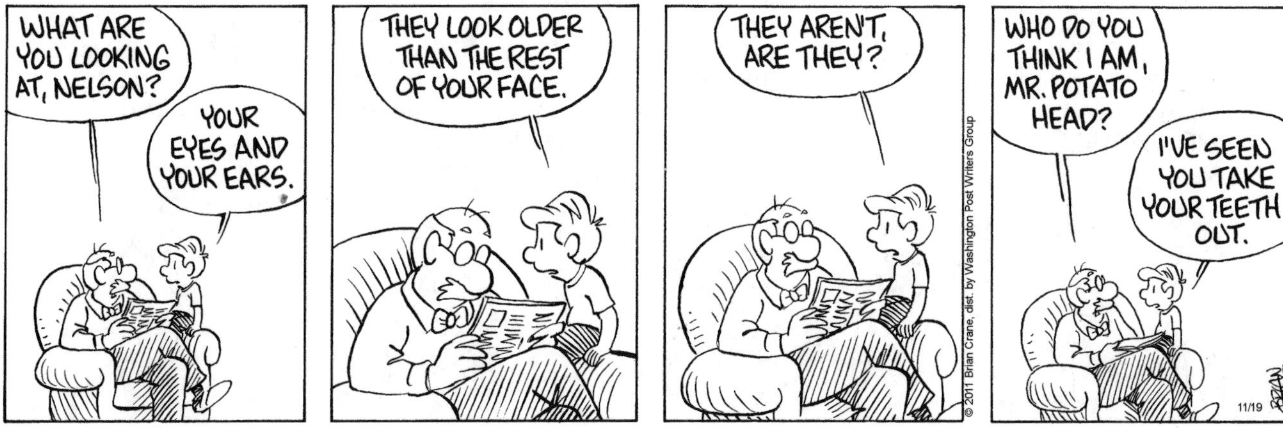
WHAT ARE YOU LOOKING AT, NELSON?
YOUR EYES AND YOUR EARS.
THEY LOOK OLDER THAN THE REST OF YOUR FACE.
THEY AREN'T, ARE THEY?
WHO DO YOU THINK I AM, MR. POTATO HEAD?
I'VE SEEN YOU TAKE YOUR TEETH OUT.
11/19

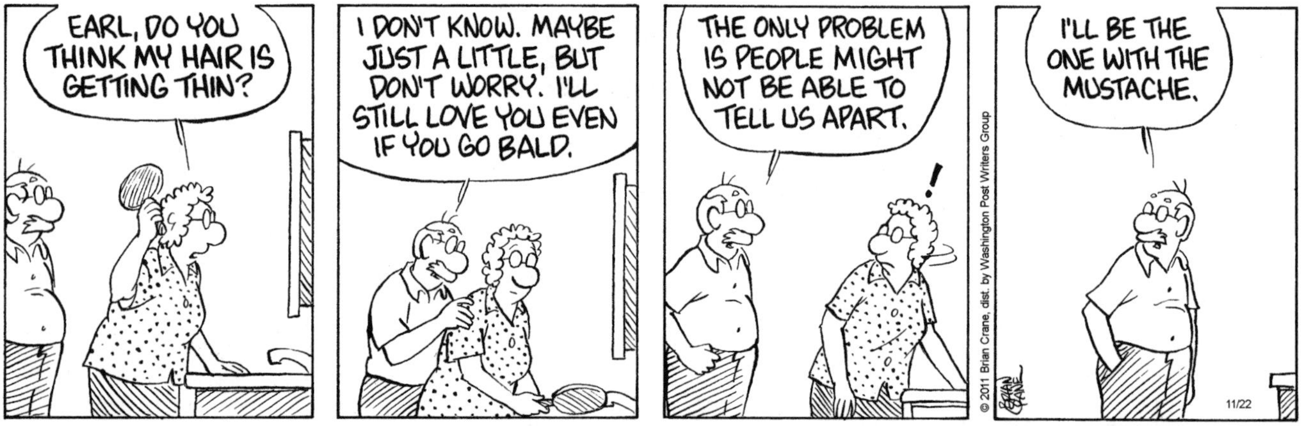
EARL, DO YOU THINK MY HAIR IS GETTING THIN?
I DON'T KNOW. MAYBE JUST A LITTLE, BUT DON'T WORRY. I'LL STILL LOVE YOU EVEN IF YOU GO BALD.
THE ONLY PROBLEM IS PEOPLE MIGHT NOT BE ABLE TO TELL US APART.
!
I'LL BE THE ONE WITH THE MUSTACHE.
© 2011 Brian Crane, dist. by Washington Post Writers Group
11/22

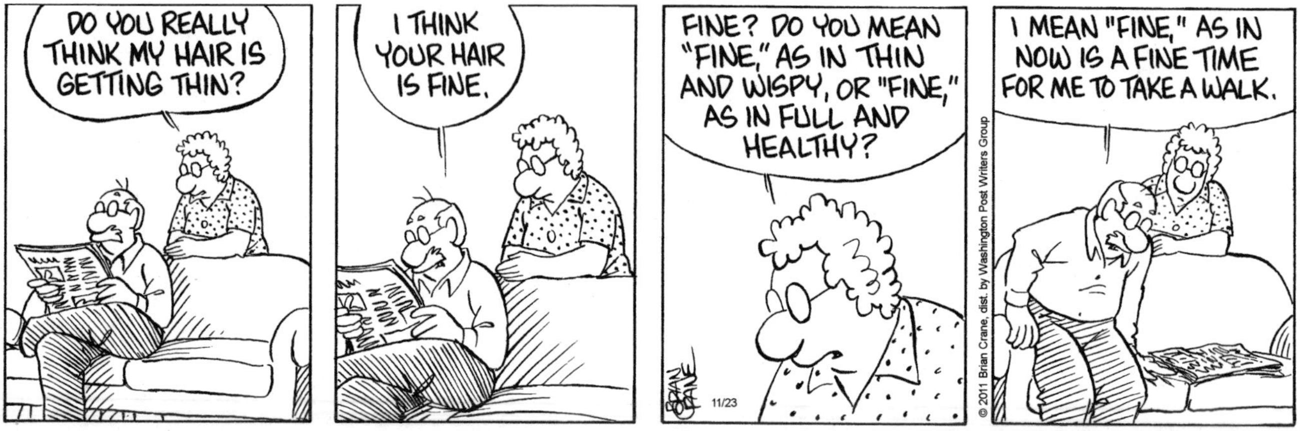
DO YOU REALLY THINK MY HAIR IS GETTING THIN?
I THINK YOUR HAIR IS FINE.
FINE? DO YOU MEAN "FINE," AS IN THIN AND WISPY, OR "FINE," AS IN FULL AND HEALTHY?
11/23
I MEAN "FINE," AS IN NOW IS A FINE TIME FOR ME TO TAKE A WALK.
© 2011 Brian Crane, dist. by Washington Post Writers Group

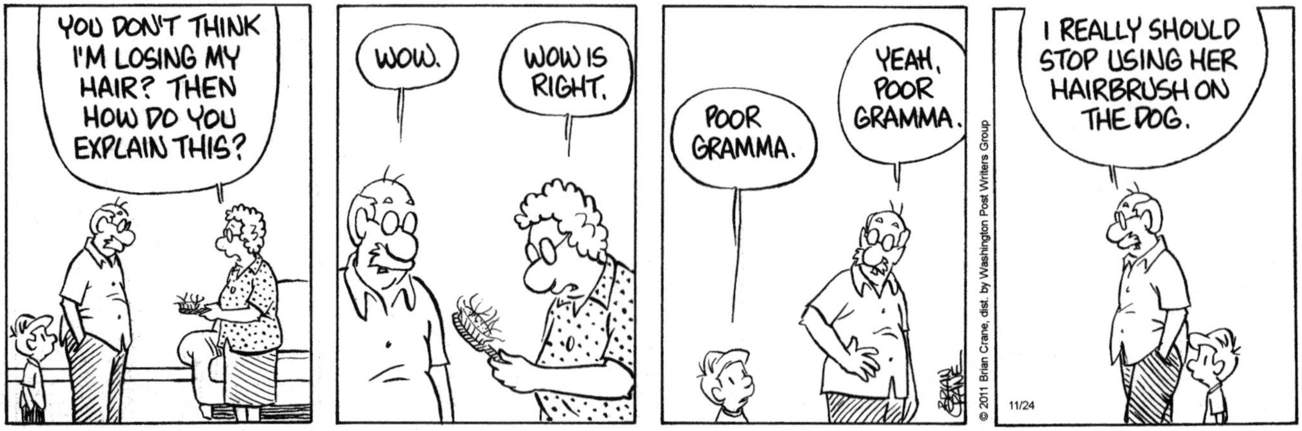
YOU DON'T THINK I'M LOSING MY HAIR? THEN HOW DO YOU EXPLAIN THIS?
WOW.
WOW IS RIGHT.
POOR GRAMMA.
YEAH, POOR GRAMMA.
© 2011 Brian Crane, dist. by Washington Post Writers Group
11/24
I REALLY SHOULD STOP USING HER HAIRBRUSH ON THE DOG.

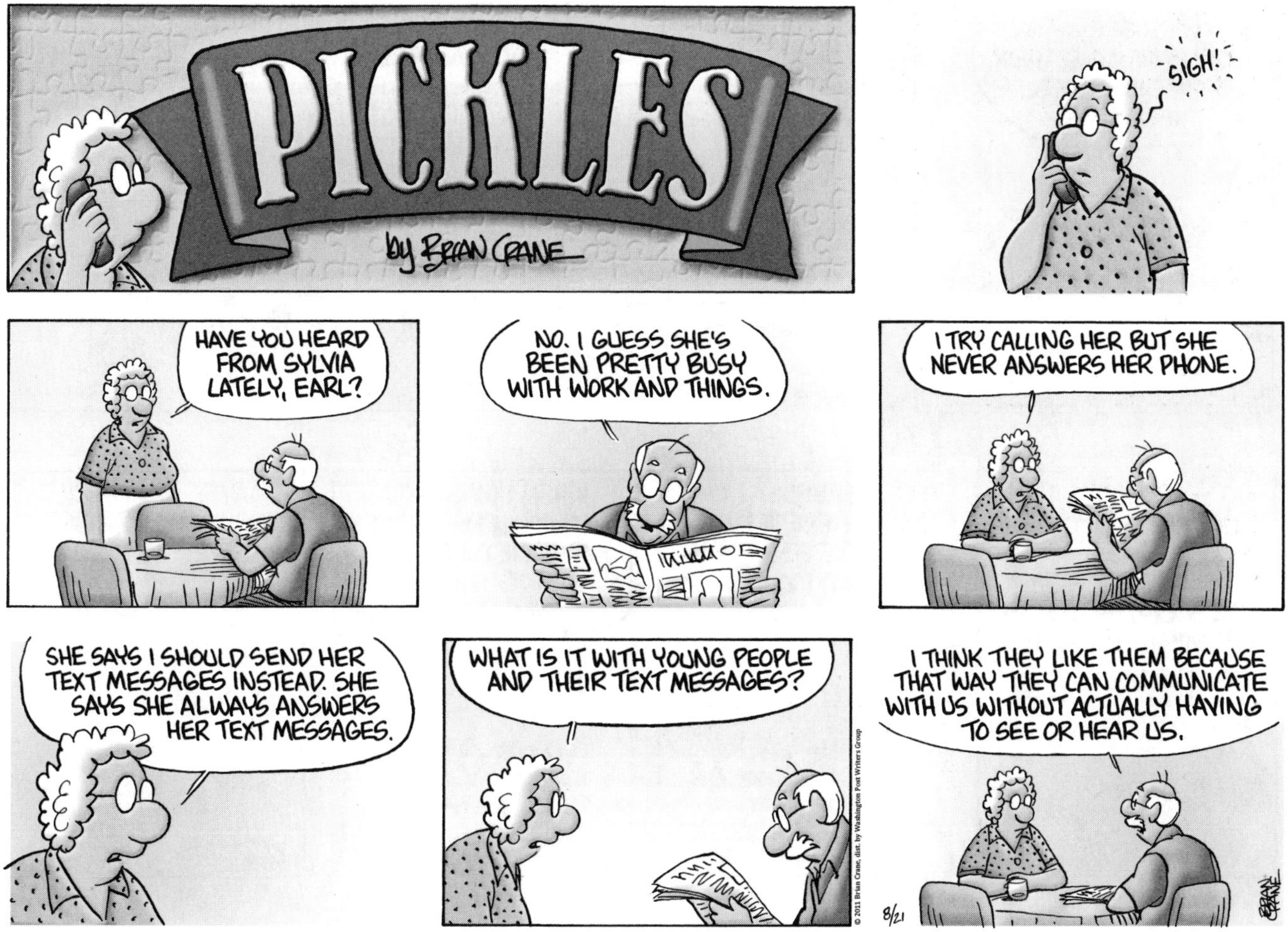
PICKLES
by Brian Crane
SIGH!
HAVE YOU HEARD FROM SYLVIA LATELY, EARL?
NO. I GUESS SHE'S BEEN PRETTY BUSY WITH WORK AND THINGS.
I TRY CALLING HER BUT SHE NEVER ANSWERS HER PHONE.
SHE SAYS I SHOULD SEND HER TEXT MESSAGES INSTEAD. SHE SAYS SHE ALWAYS ANSWERS HER TEXT MESSAGES.
WHAT IS IT WITH YOUNG PEOPLE AND THEIR TEXT MESSAGES?
I THINK THEY LIKE THEM BECAUSE THAT WAY THEY CAN COMMUNICATE WITH US WITHOUT ACTUALLY HAVING TO SEE OR HEAR US.
© 2011 Brian Crane, dist. by Washington Post Writers Group
8/21

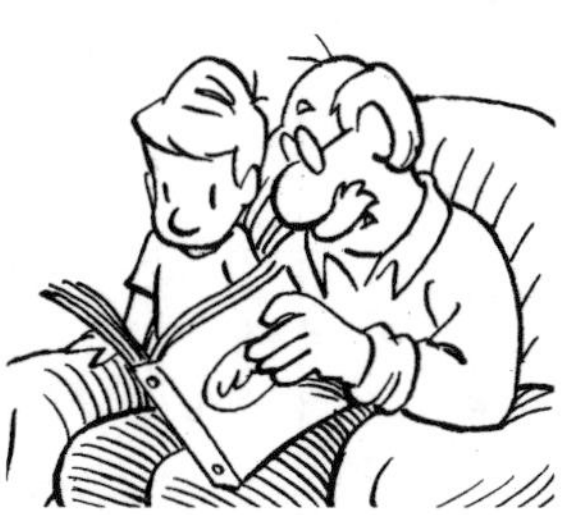

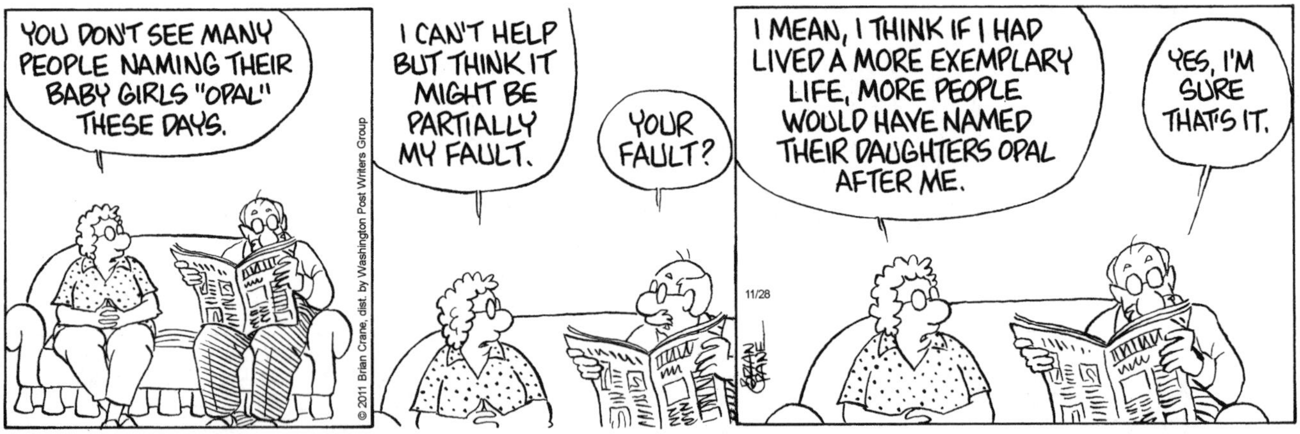
YOU DON'T SEE MANY PEOPLE NAMING THEIR BABY GIRLS "OPAL" THESE DAYS.
© 2011 Brian Crane, dist. by Washington Post Writers Group
I CAN'T HELP BUT THINK IT MIGHT BE PARTIALLY MY FAULT.
YOUR FAULT?
I MEAN, I THINK IF I HAD LIVED A MORE EXEMPLARY LIFE, MORE PEOPLE WOULD HAVE NAMED THEIR DAUGHTERS OPAL AFTER ME.
YES, I'M SURE THAT'S IT.
11/28

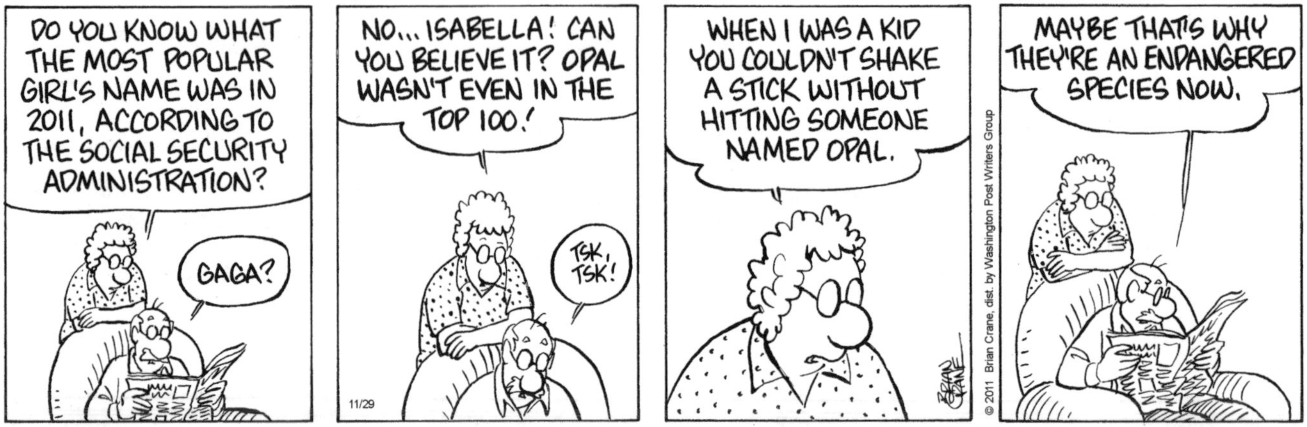
DO YOU KNOW WHAT THE MOST POPULAR GIRL'S NAME WAS IN 2011, ACCORDING TO THE SOCIAL SECURITY ADMINISTRATION?
GAGA?
NO... ISABELLA! CAN YOU BELIEVE IT? OPAL WASN'T EVEN IN THE TOP 100!
TSK, TSK!
11/29
WHEN I WAS A KID YOU COULDN'T SHAKE A STICK WITHOUT HITTING SOMEONE NAMED OPAL.
© 2011 Brian Crane, dist. by Washington Post Writers Group
MAYBE THAT'S WHY THEY'RE AN ENDANGERED SPECIES NOW.

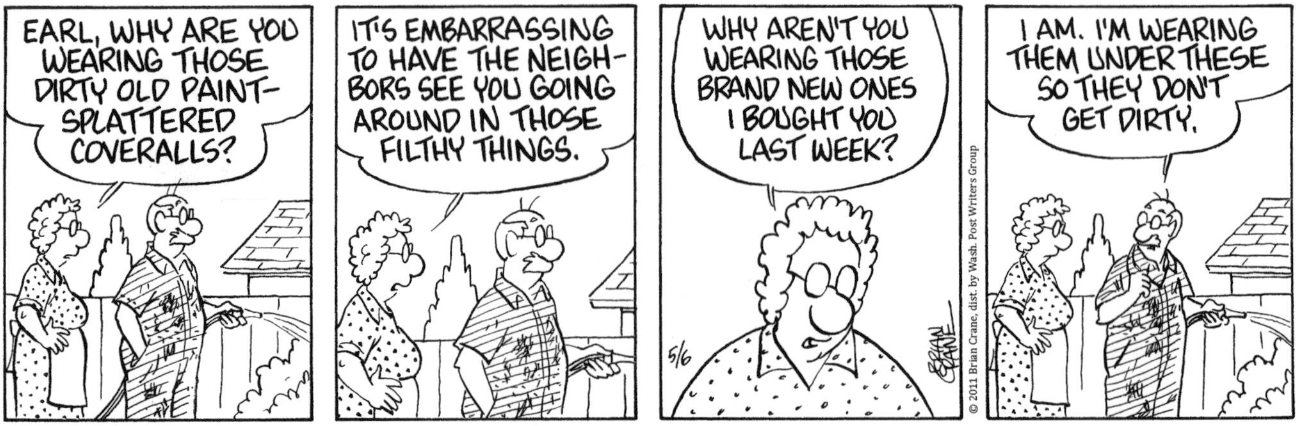
EARL, WHY ARE YOU WEARING THOSE DIRTY OLD PAINT-SPLATTERED COVERALLS?
IT'S EMBARRASSING TO HAVE THE NEIGH-BORS SEE YOU GOING AROUND IN THOSE FILTHY THINGS.
WHY AREN'T YOU WEARING THOSE BRAND NEW ONES I BOUGHT YOU LAST WEEK?
5/6
© 2011 Brian Crane, dist. by Wash. Post Writers Group
I AM. I'M WEARING THEM UNDER THESE SO THEY DON'T GET DIRTY.

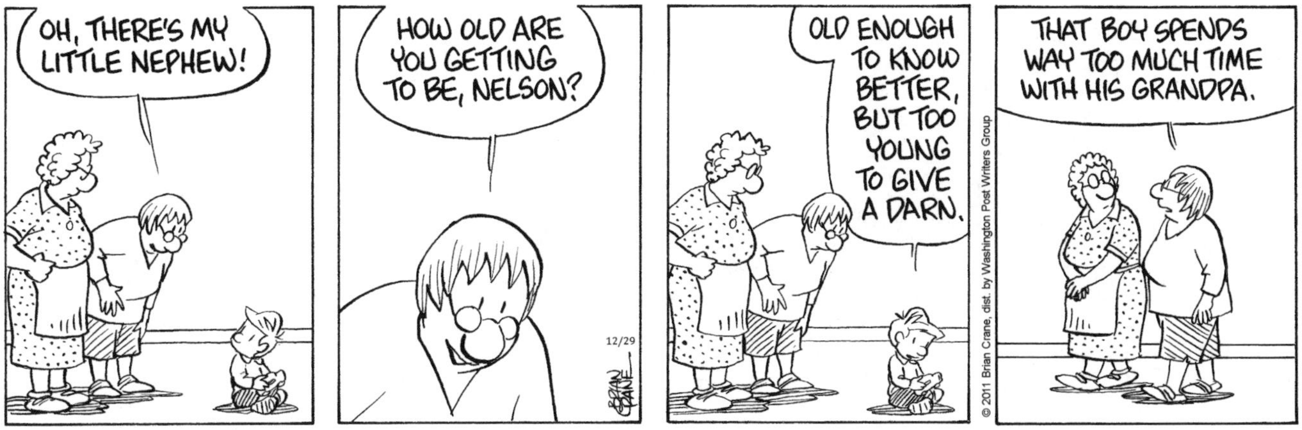
OH, THERE'S MY LITTLE NEPHEW!
HOW OLD ARE YOU GETTING TO BE, NELSON?
12/29
BRIAN CRANE
OLD ENOUGH TO KNOW BETTER, BUT TOO YOUNG TO GIVE A DARN.
THAT BOY SPENDS WAY TOO MUCH TIME WITH HIS GRANDPA.

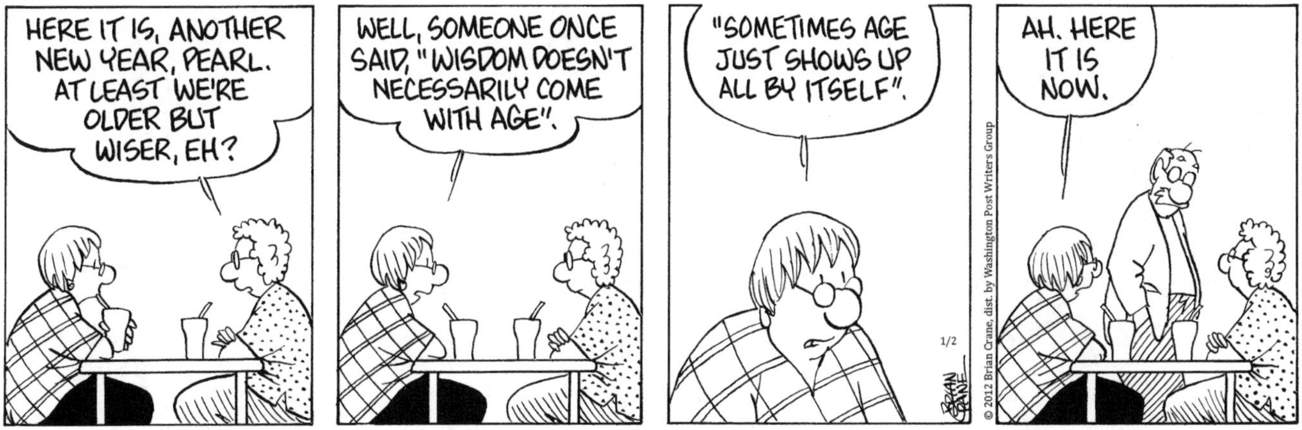
HERE IT IS, ANOTHER NEW YEAR, PEARL. AT LEAST WE'RE OLDER BUT WISER, EH?
WELL, SOMEONE ONCE SAID, "WISDOM DOESN'T NECESSARILY COME WITH AGE".
"SOMETIMES AGE JUST SHOWS UP ALL BY ITSELF".
1/2
BRIAN CRANE
AH. HERE IT IS NOW.

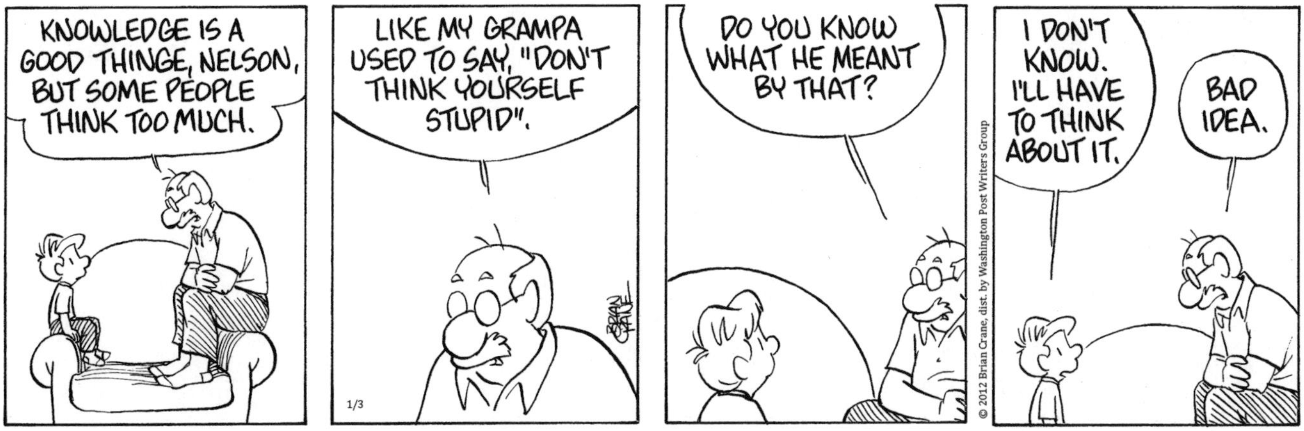
KNOWLEDGE IS A GOOD THINGE, NELSON, BUT SOME PEOPLE THINK TOO MUCH.
LIKE MY GRAMPA USED TO SAY, "DON'T THINK YOURSELF STUPID".
BRIAN CRANE
1/3
DO YOU KNOW WHAT HE MEANT BY THAT?
I DON'T KNOW. I'LL HAVE TO THINK ABOUT IT.
BAD IDEA.

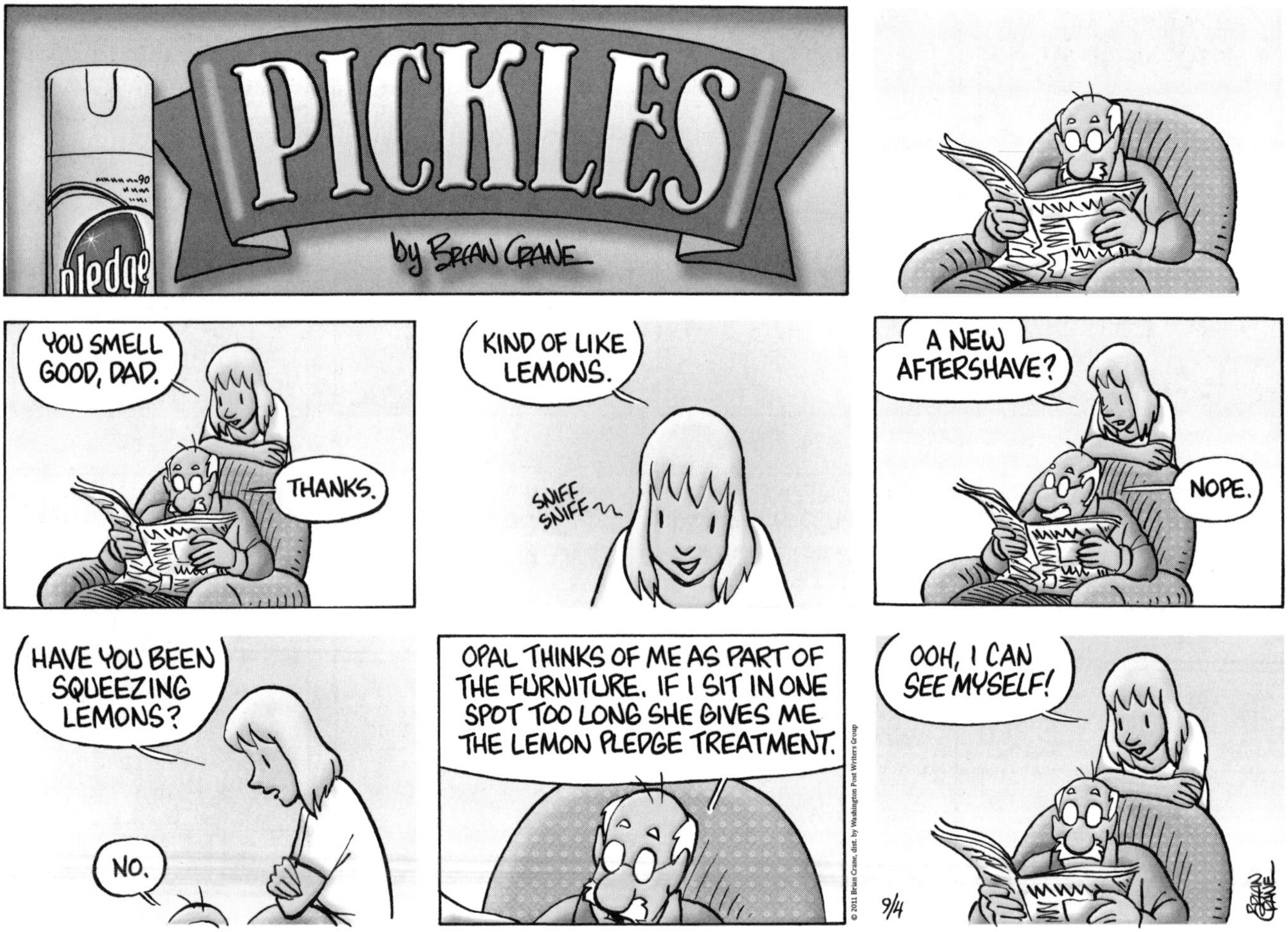
PICKLES
by BRIAN CRANE
pledge
YOU SMELL GOOD, DAD.
THANKS.
KIND OF LIKE LEMONS.
SNIFF SNIFF
A NEW AFTERSHAVE?
NOPE.
HAVE YOU BEEN SQUEEZING LEMONS?
NO.
OPAL THINKS OF ME AS PART OF THE FURNITURE. IF I SIT IN ONE SPOT TOO LONG SHE GIVES ME THE LEMON PLEDGE TREATMENT.
© 2011 Brian Crane, dist. by Washington Post Writers Group
9/4
OOH, I CAN SEE MYSELF!
BRIAN CRANE

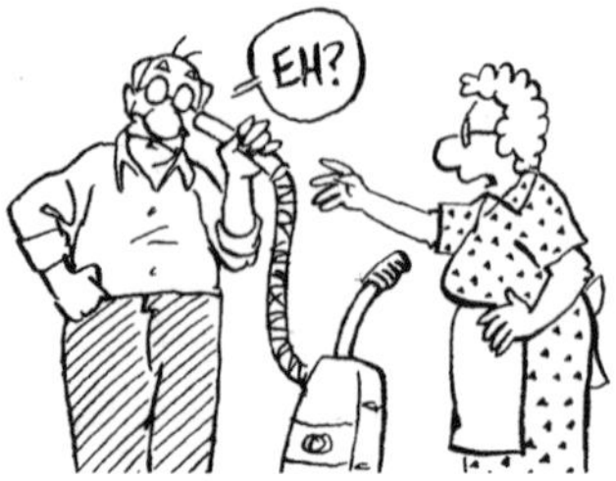
EH?

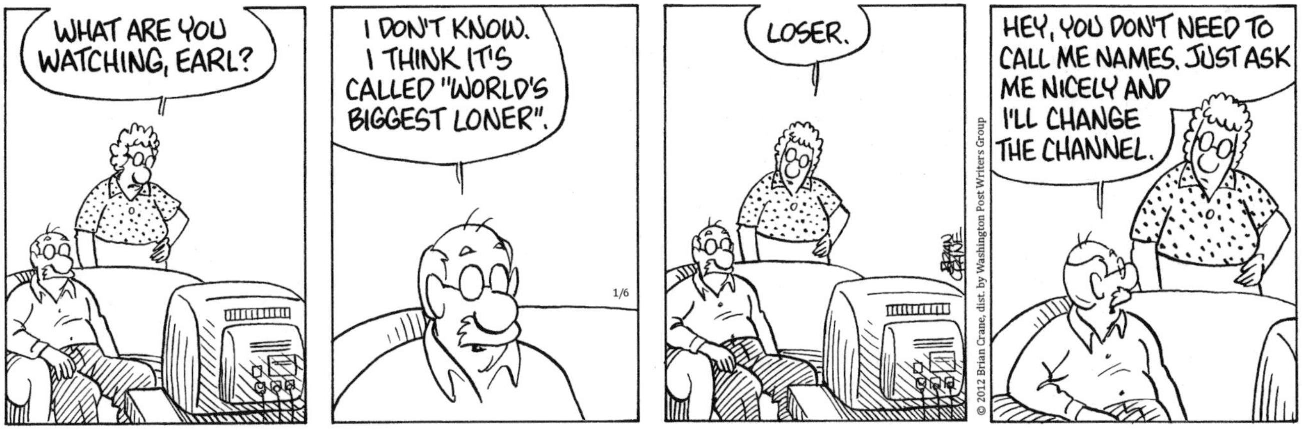
WHAT ARE YOU WATCHING, EARL?
I DON'T KNOW. I THINK IT'S CALLED "WORLD'S BIGGEST LONER".
1/6
LOSER.
HEY, YOU DON'T NEED TO CALL ME NAMES. JUST ASK ME NICELY AND I'LL CHANGE THE CHANNEL.

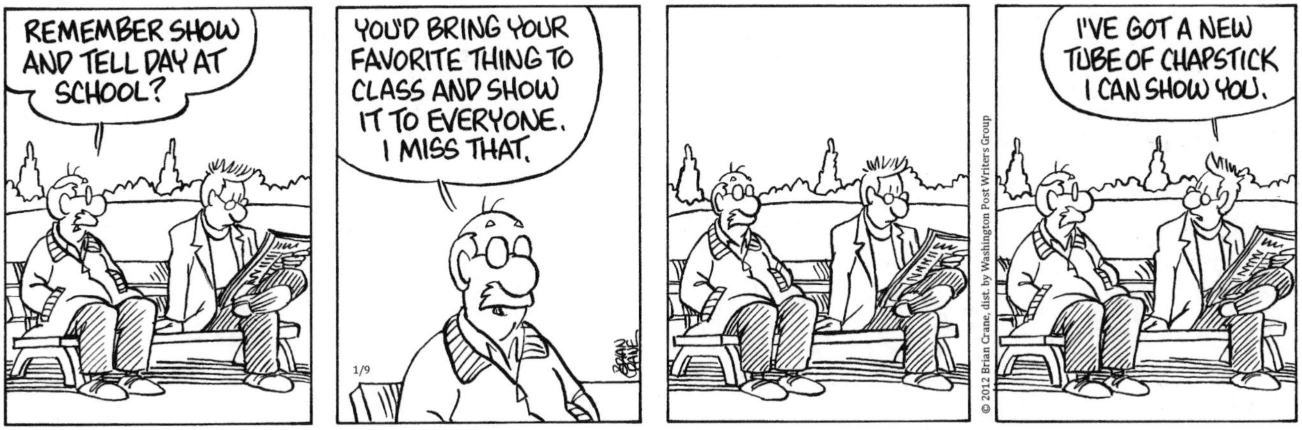
REMEMBER SHOW AND TELL DAY AT SCHOOL?
YOU'D BRING YOUR FAVORITE THING TO CLASS AND SHOW IT TO EVERYONE. I MISS THAT.
1/9
I'VE GOT A NEW TUBE OF CHAPSTICK I CAN SHOW YOU.

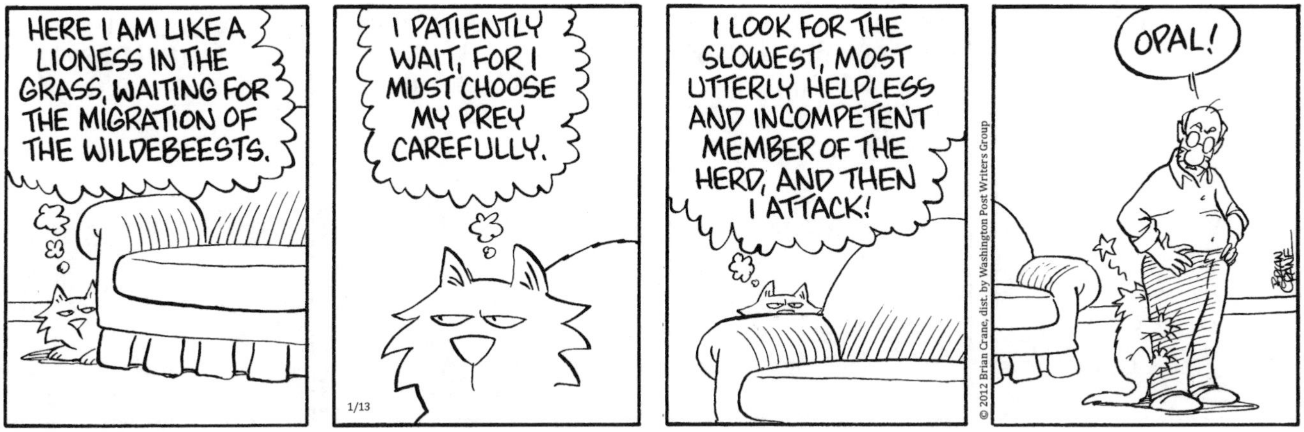
HERE I AM LIKE A LIONESS IN THE GRASS, WAITING FOR THE MIGRATION OF THE WILDEBEESTS.
I PATIENTLY WAIT, FOR I MUST CHOOSE MY PREY CAREFULLY.
1/13
I LOOK FOR THE SLOWEST, MOST UTTERLY HELPLESS AND INCOMPETENT MEMBER OF THE HERD, AND THEN I ATTACK!
OPAL!

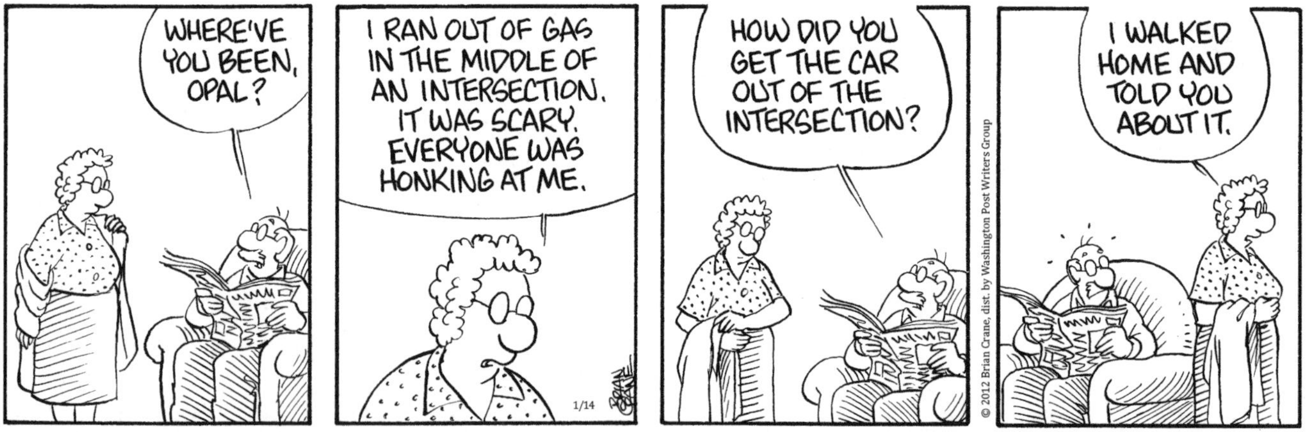
WHERE'VE YOU BEEN, OPAL?
I RAN OUT OF GAS IN THE MIDDLE OF AN INTERSECTION. IT WAS SCARY. EVERYONE WAS HONKING AT ME.
HOW DID YOU GET THE CAR OUT OF THE INTERSECTION?
I WALKED HOME AND TOLD YOU ABOUT IT.
1/14
© 2012 Brian Crane, dist. by Washington Post Writers Group

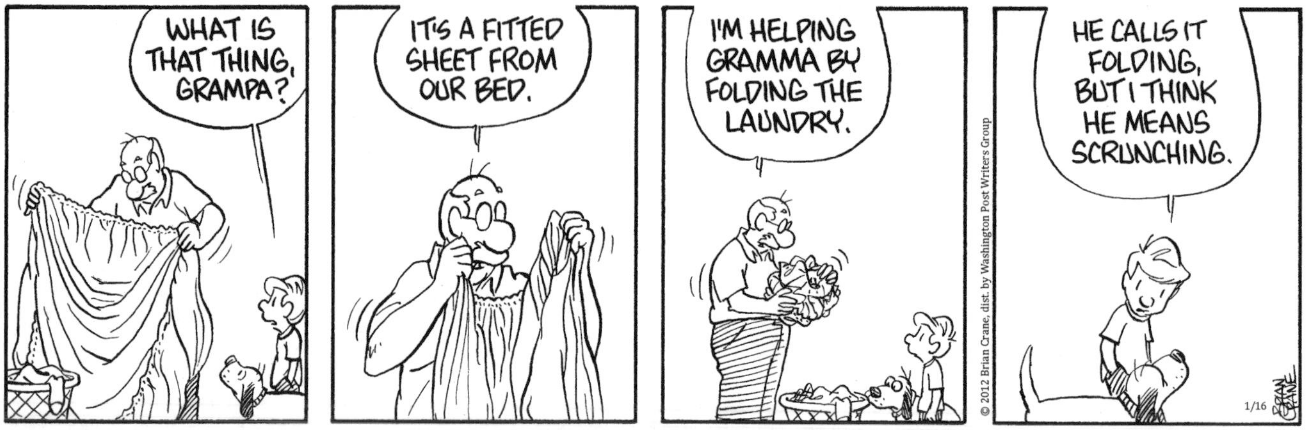
WHAT IS THAT THING, GRAMPA?
IT'S A FITTED SHEET FROM OUR BED.
I'M HELPING GRAMMA BY FOLDING THE LAUNDRY.
HE CALLS IT FOLDING, BUT I THINK HE MEANS SCRUNCHING.
1/16
© 2012 Brian Crane, dist. by Washington Post Writers Group

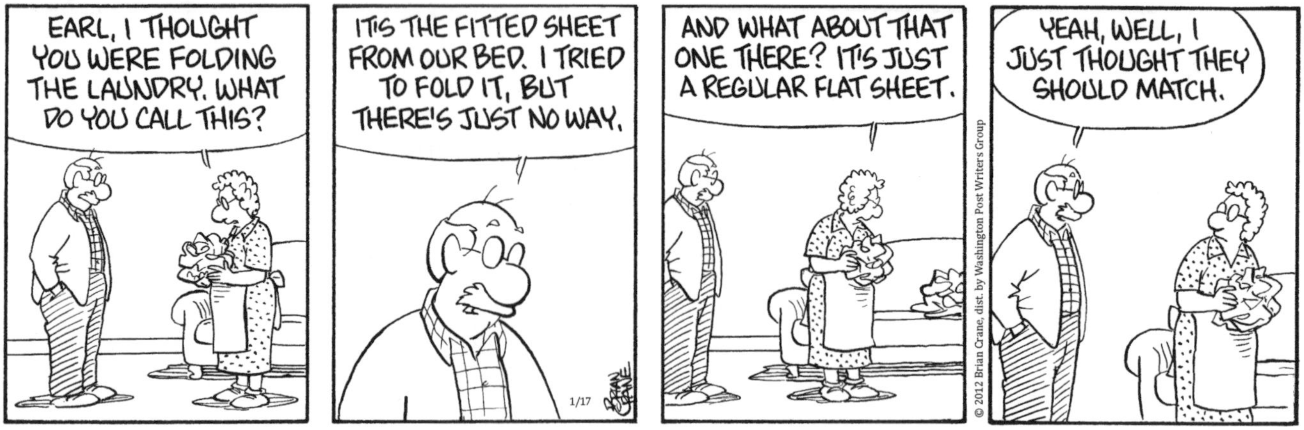
EARL, I THOUGHT YOU WERE FOLDING THE LAUNDRY. WHAT DO YOU CALL THIS?
IT'S THE FITTED SHEET FROM OUR BED. I TRIED TO FOLD IT, BUT THERE'S JUST NO WAY.
AND WHAT ABOUT THAT ONE THERE? IT'S JUST A REGULAR FLAT SHEET.
YEAH, WELL, I JUST THOUGHT THEY SHOULD MATCH.
1/17
© 2012 Brian Crane, dist. by Washington Post Writers Group

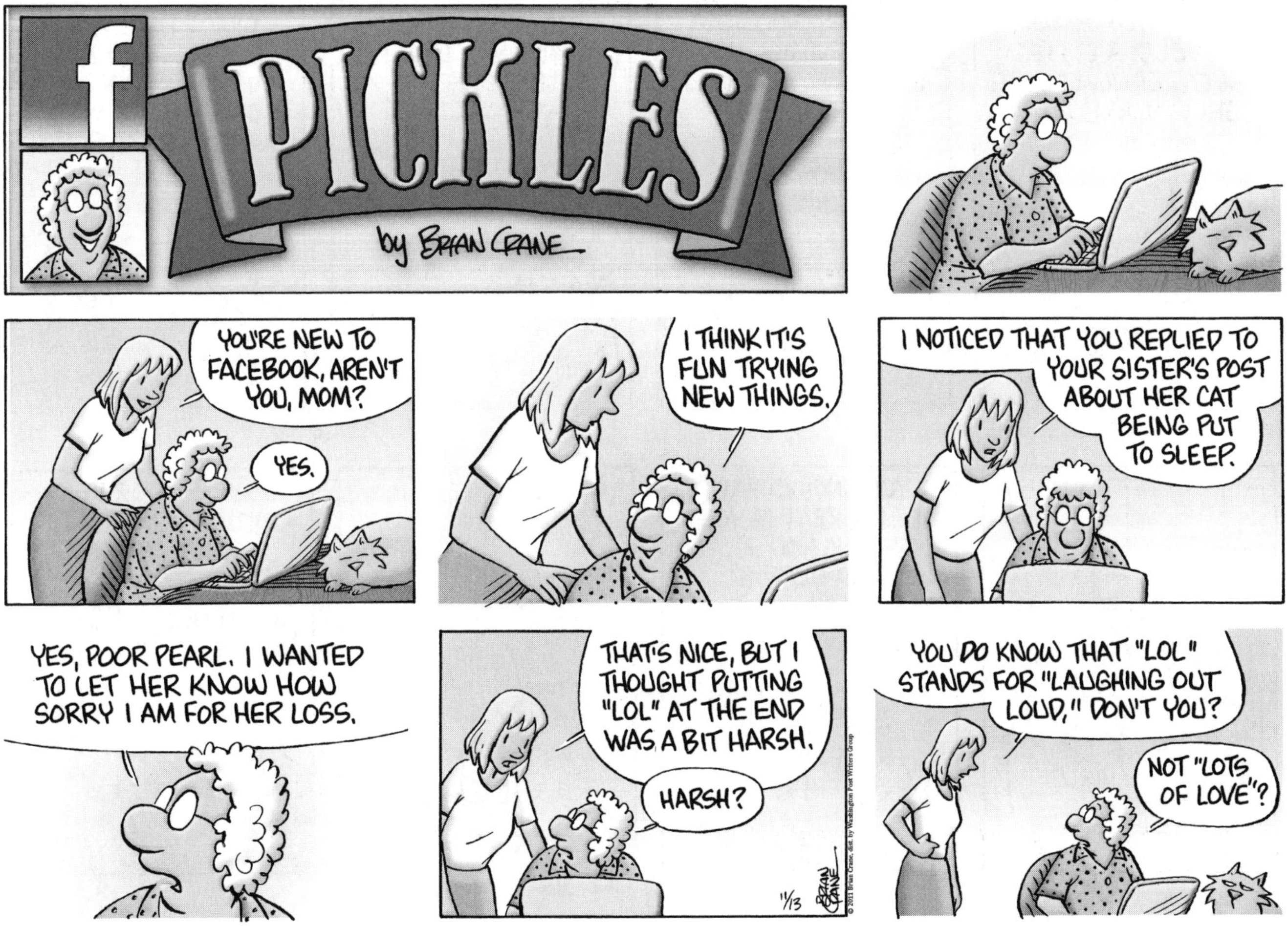
PICKLES
by BRIAN CRANE
YOU'RE NEW TO FACEBOOK, AREN'T YOU, MOM?
YES.
I THINK IT'S FUN TRYING NEW THINGS.
I NOTICED THAT YOU REPLIED TO YOUR SISTER'S POST ABOUT HER CAT BEING PUT TO SLEEP.
YES, POOR PEARL. I WANTED TO LET HER KNOW HOW SORRY I AM FOR HER LOSS.
THAT'S NICE, BUT I THOUGHT PUTTING "LOL" AT THE END WAS A BIT HARSH.
HARSH?
11/13
© 2011 Brian Crane, dist. by Washington Post Writers Group
YOU DO KNOW THAT "LOL" STANDS FOR "LAUGHING OUT LOUD," DON'T YOU?
NOT "LOTS OF LOVE"?

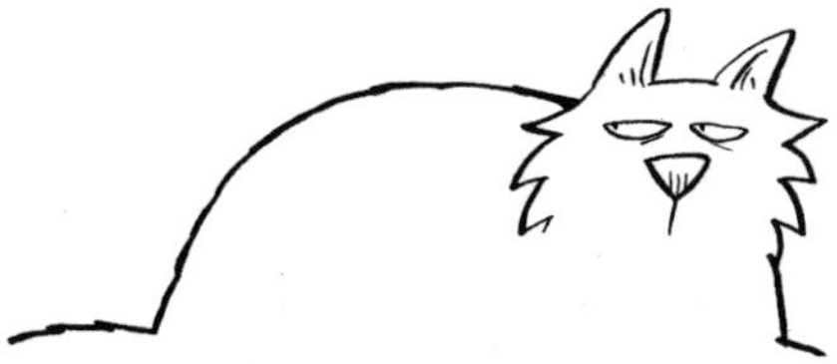

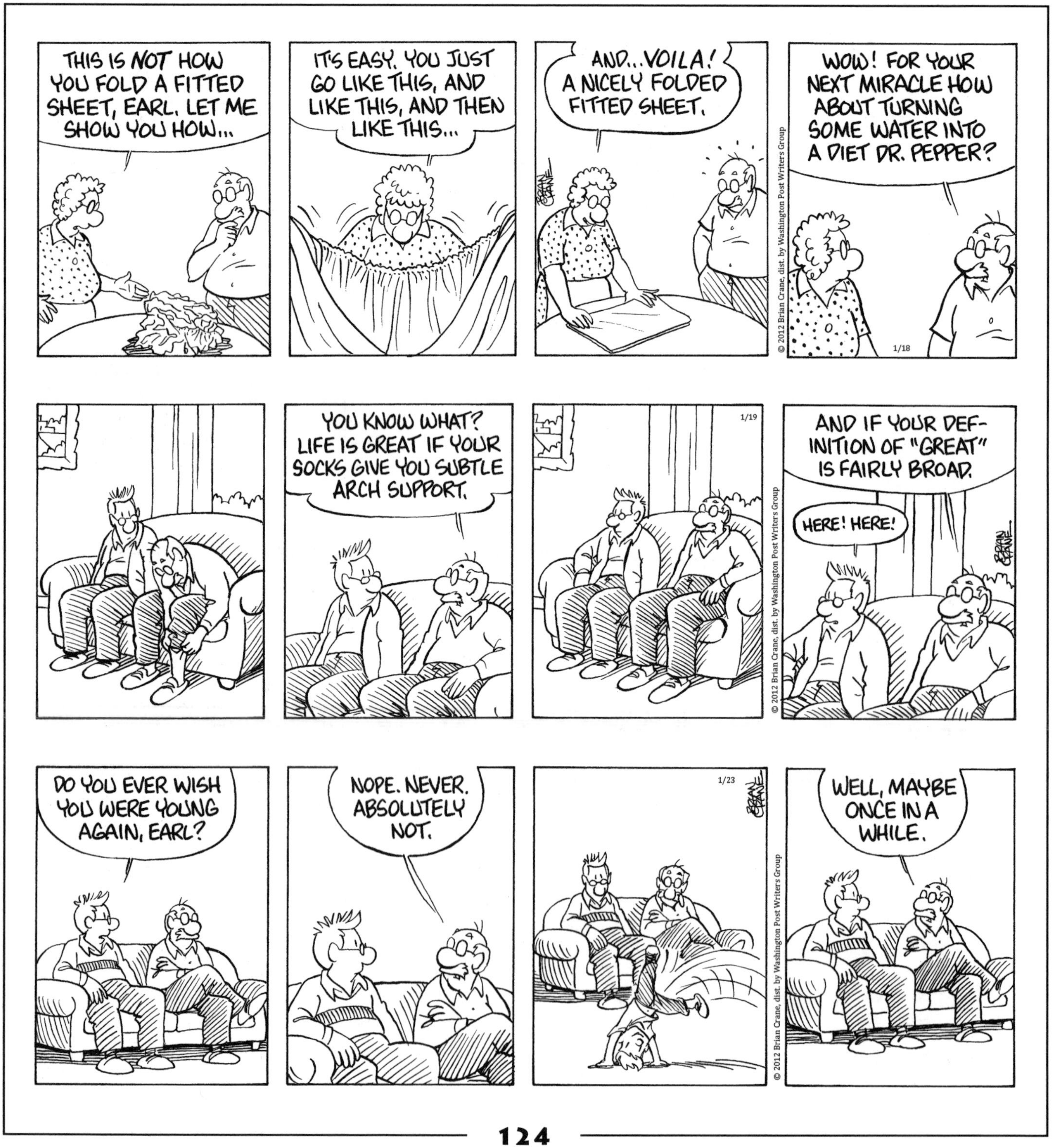
THIS IS NOT HOW YOU FOLD A FITTED SHEET, EARL. LET ME SHOW YOU HOW...
IT'S EASY. YOU JUST GO LIKE THIS, AND LIKE THIS, AND THEN LIKE THIS...
AND...VOILA! A NICELY FOLDED FITTED SHEET.
WOW! FOR YOUR NEXT MIRACLE HOW ABOUT TURNING SOME WATER INTO A DIET DR. PEPPER?
© 2012 Brian Crane, dist. by Washington Post Writers Group
1/18
YOU KNOW WHAT? LIFE IS GREAT IF YOUR SOCKS GIVE YOU SUBTLE ARCH SUPPORT.
1/19
AND IF YOUR DEFINITION OF "GREAT" IS FAIRLY BROAD.
HERE! HERE!
© 2012 Brian Crane, dist. by Washington Post Writers Group
DO YOU EVER WISH YOU WERE YOUNG AGAIN, EARL?
NOPE. NEVER. ABSOLUTELY NOT.
1/23
WELL, MAYBE ONCE IN A WHILE.
© 2012 Brian Crane, dist. by Washington Post Writers Group

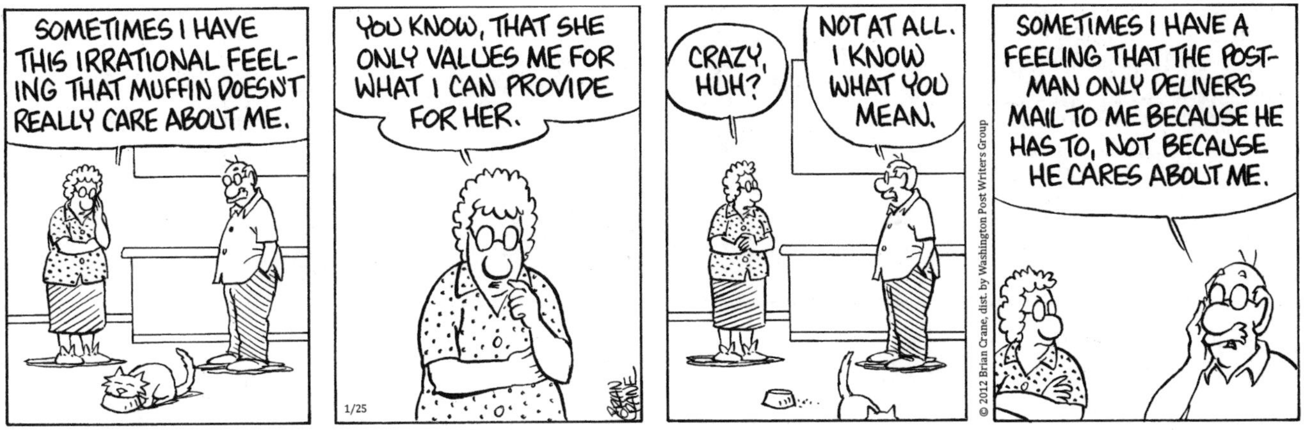
SOMETIMES I HAVE THIS IRRATIONAL FEELING THAT MUFFIN DOESN'T REALLY CARE ABOUT ME.
YOU KNOW, THAT SHE ONLY VALUES ME FOR WHAT I CAN PROVIDE FOR HER.
1/25
BRIAN CRANE
CRAZY, HUH?
NOT AT ALL. I KNOW WHAT YOU MEAN.
© 2012 Brian Crane, dist. by Washington Post Writers Group
SOMETIMES I HAVE A FEELING THAT THE POSTMAN ONLY DELIVERS MAIL TO ME BECAUSE HE HAS TO, NOT BECAUSE HE CARES ABOUT ME.

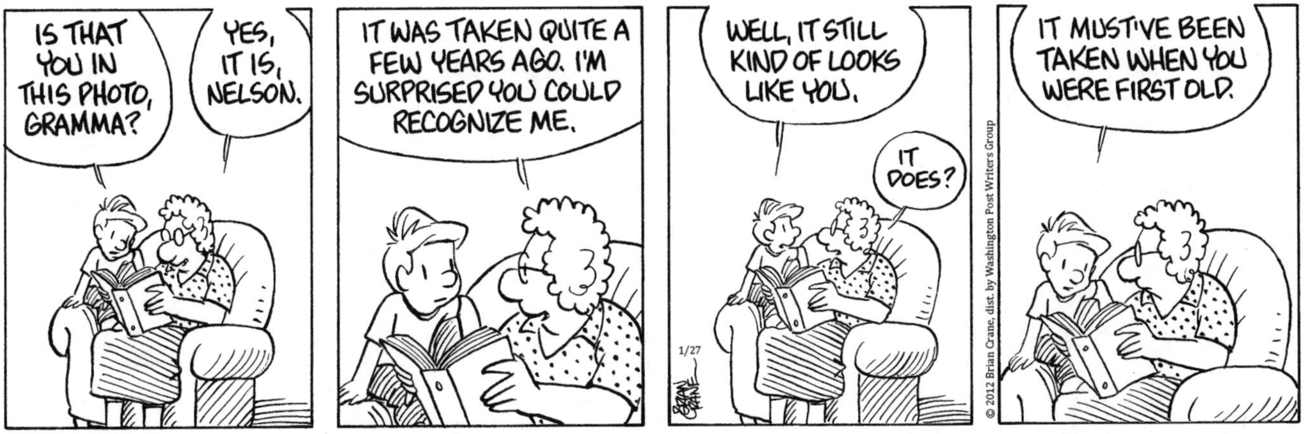
IS THAT YOU IN THIS PHOTO, GRAMMA?
YES, IT IS, NELSON.
IT WAS TAKEN QUITE A FEW YEARS AGO. I'M SURPRISED YOU COULD RECOGNIZE ME.
WELL, IT STILL KIND OF LOOKS LIKE YOU.
IT DOES?
1/27
BRIAN CRANE
© 2012 Brian Crane, dist. by Washington Post Writers Group
IT MUST'VE BEEN TAKEN WHEN YOU WERE FIRST OLD.

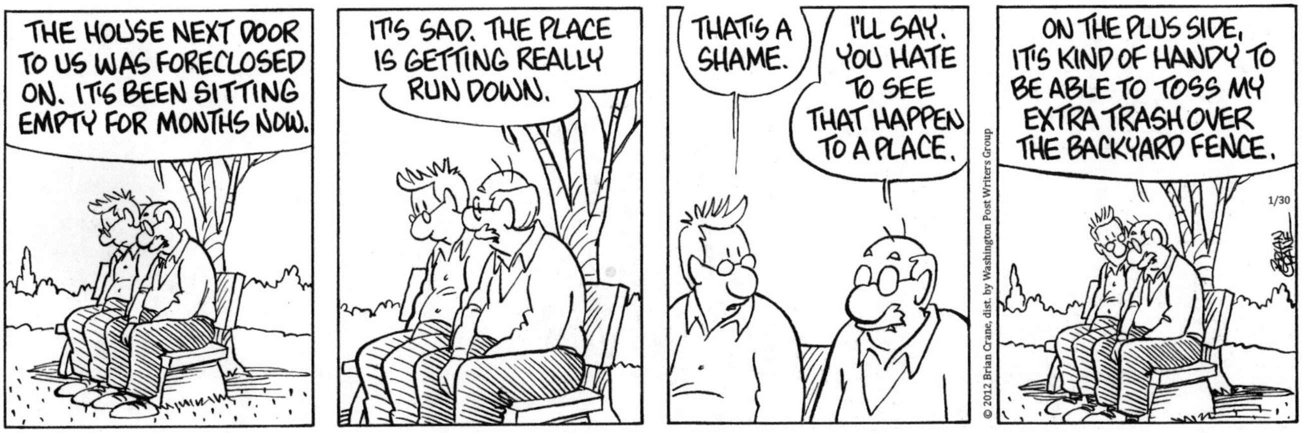
THE HOUSE NEXT DOOR TO US WAS FORECLOSED ON. IT'S BEEN SITTING EMPTY FOR MONTHS NOW.
IT'S SAD. THE PLACE IS GETTING REALLY RUN DOWN.
THAT'S A SHAME.
I'LL SAY. YOU HATE TO SEE THAT HAPPEN TO A PLACE.
© 2012 Brian Crane, dist. by Washington Post Writers Group
ON THE PLUS SIDE, IT'S KIND OF HANDY TO BE ABLE TO TOSS MY EXTRA TRASH OVER THE BACKYARD FENCE.
1/30
BRIAN CRANE

PICKLES
by BRIAN CRANE
WHAT ARE YOU MAKING, GRAMMA?
IT'S A SCARF, NELSON.
WHY IS IT SO LONG?
IT'S GOING TO HELP ME RIDE HERD ON GRAMPA.
12/11
EARL, HEEL!
© 2011 Brian Crane, dist. by Washington Post Writers Group

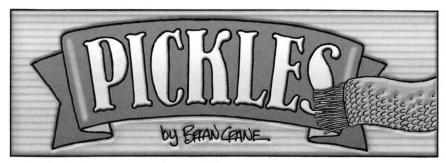

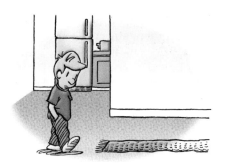

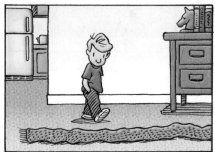

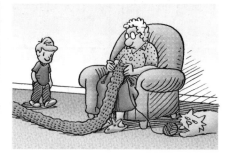

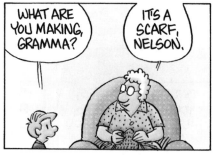

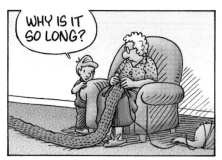

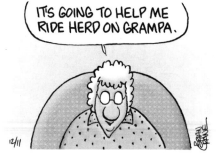

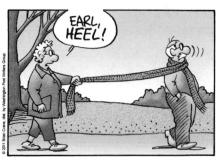

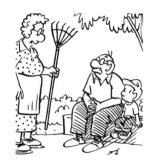

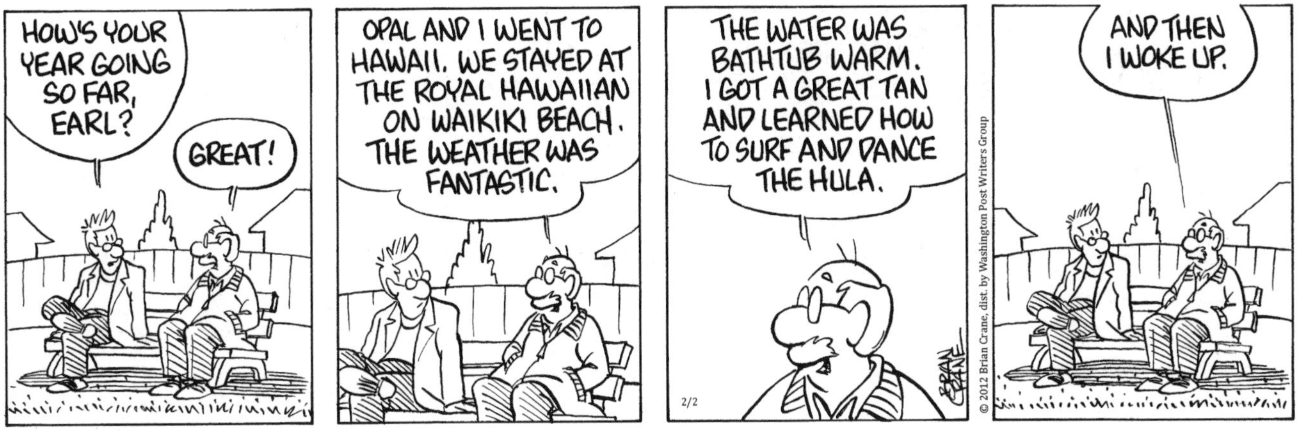
HOW'S YOUR YEAR GOING SO FAR, EARL?
GREAT!
OPAL AND I WENT TO HAWAII. WE STAYED AT THE ROYAL HAWAIIAN ON WAIKIKI BEACH. THE WEATHER WAS FANTASTIC.
THE WATER WAS BATHTUB WARM. I GOT A GREAT TAN AND LEARNED HOW TO SURF AND DANCE THE HULA.
2/2
© 2012 Brian Crane, dist. by Washington Post Writers Group
AND THEN I WOKE UP.

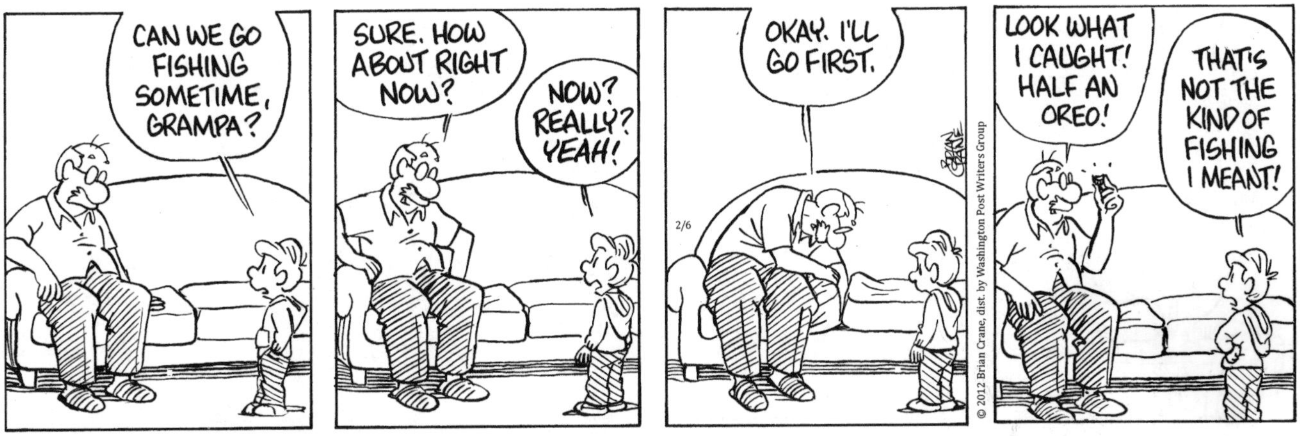
CAN WE GO FISHING SOMETIME, GRAMPA?
SURE. HOW ABOUT RIGHT NOW?
NOW? REALLY? YEAH!
OKAY. I'LL GO FIRST.
2/6
© 2012 Brian Crane, dist. by Washington Post Writers Group
LOOK WHAT I CAUGHT! HALF AN OREO!
THAT'S NOT THE KIND OF FISHING I MEANT!

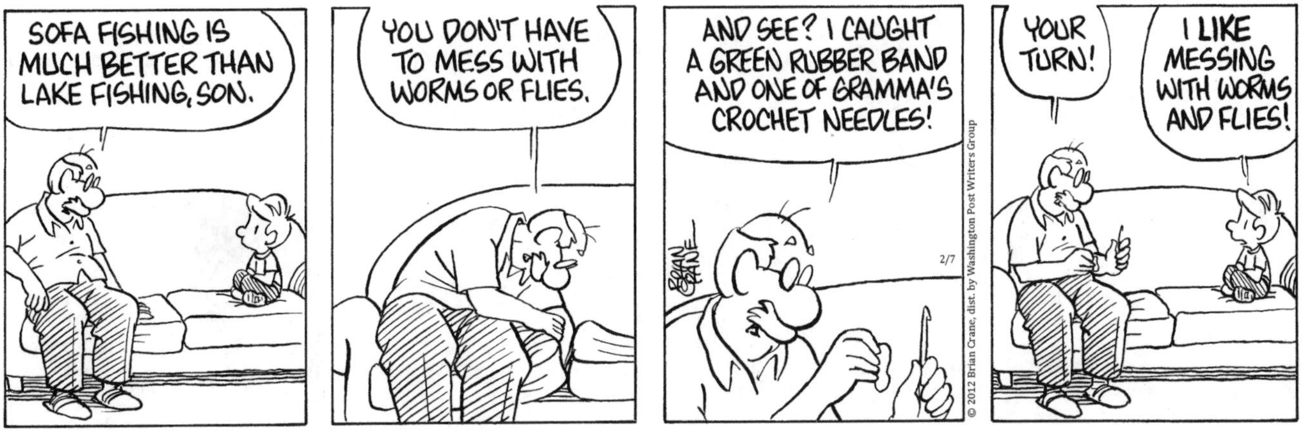
SOFA FISHING IS MUCH BETTER THAN LAKE FISHING, SON.
YOU DON'T HAVE TO MESS WITH WORMS OR FLIES.
AND SEE? I CAUGHT A GREEN RUBBER BAND AND ONE OF GRAMMA'S CROCHET NEEDLES!
2/7
© 2012 Brian Crane, dist. by Washington Post Writers Group
YOUR TURN!
I LIKE MESSING WITH WORMS AND FLIES!

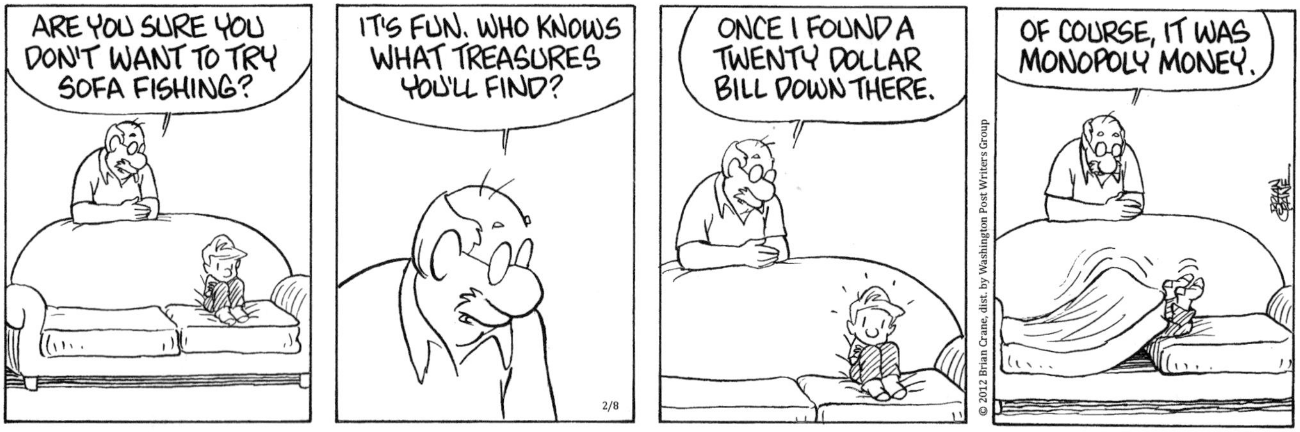
ARE YOU SURE YOU DON'T WANT TO TRY SOFA FISHING?
IT'S FUN. WHO KNOWS WHAT TREASURES YOU'LL FIND?
ONCE I FOUND A TWENTY DOLLAR BILL DOWN THERE.
OF COURSE, IT WAS MONOPOLY MONEY.
© 2012 Brian Crane, dist. by Washington Post Writers Group
2/8
BRIAN CRANE

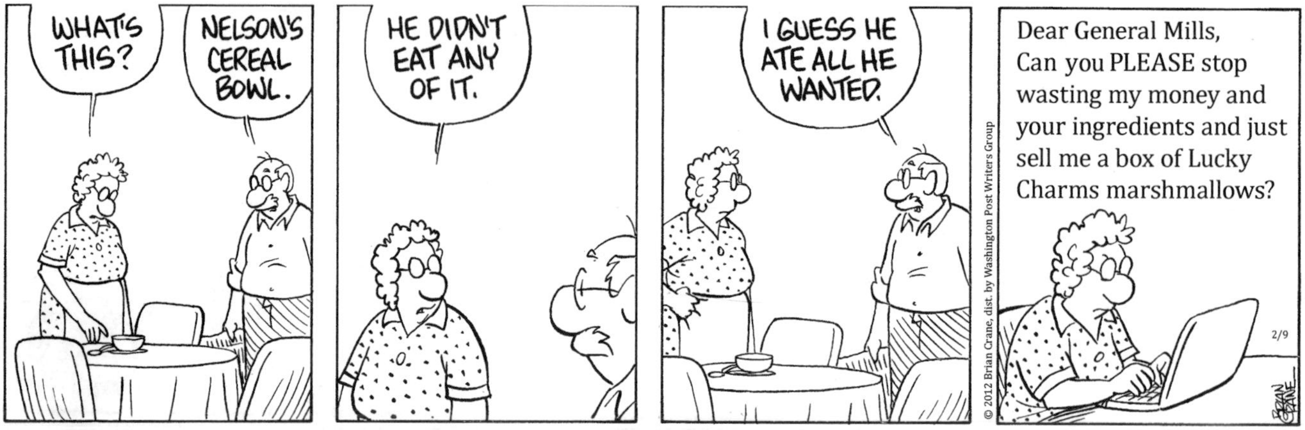
WHAT'S THIS?
NELSON'S CEREAL BOWL.
HE DIDN'T EAT ANY OF IT.
I GUESS HE ATE ALL HE WANTED.
Dear General Mills,
Can you PLEASE stop wasting my money and your ingredients and just sell me a box of Lucky Charms marshmallows?
© 2012 Brian Crane, dist. by Washington Post Writers Group
2/9
BRIAN CRANE

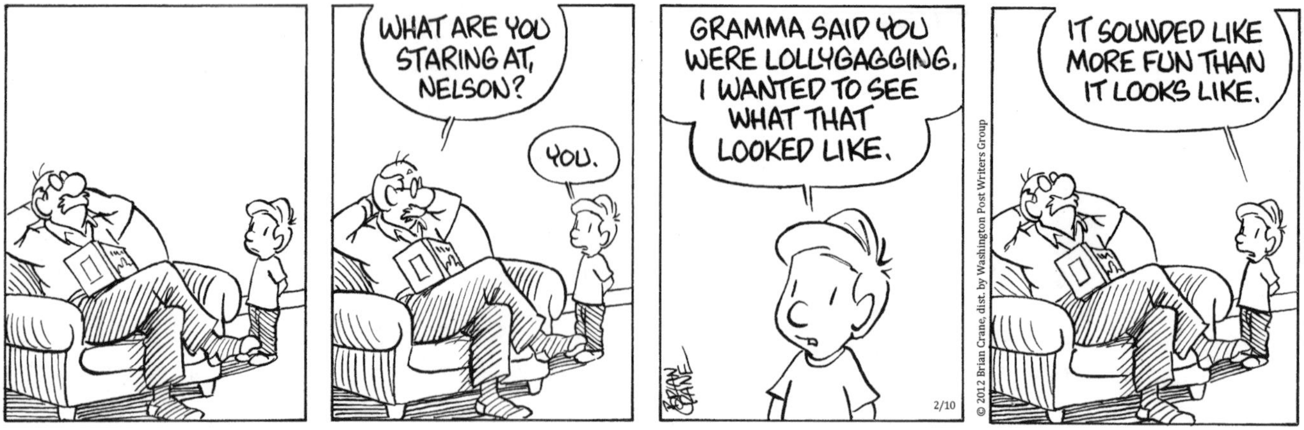
WHAT ARE YOU STARING AT, NELSON?
YOU.
GRAMMA SAID YOU WERE LOLLYGAGGING. I WANTED TO SEE WHAT THAT LOOKED LIKE.
IT SOUNDED LIKE MORE FUN THAN IT LOOKS LIKE.
© 2012 Brian Crane, dist. by Washington Post Writers Group
2/10
BRIAN CRANE

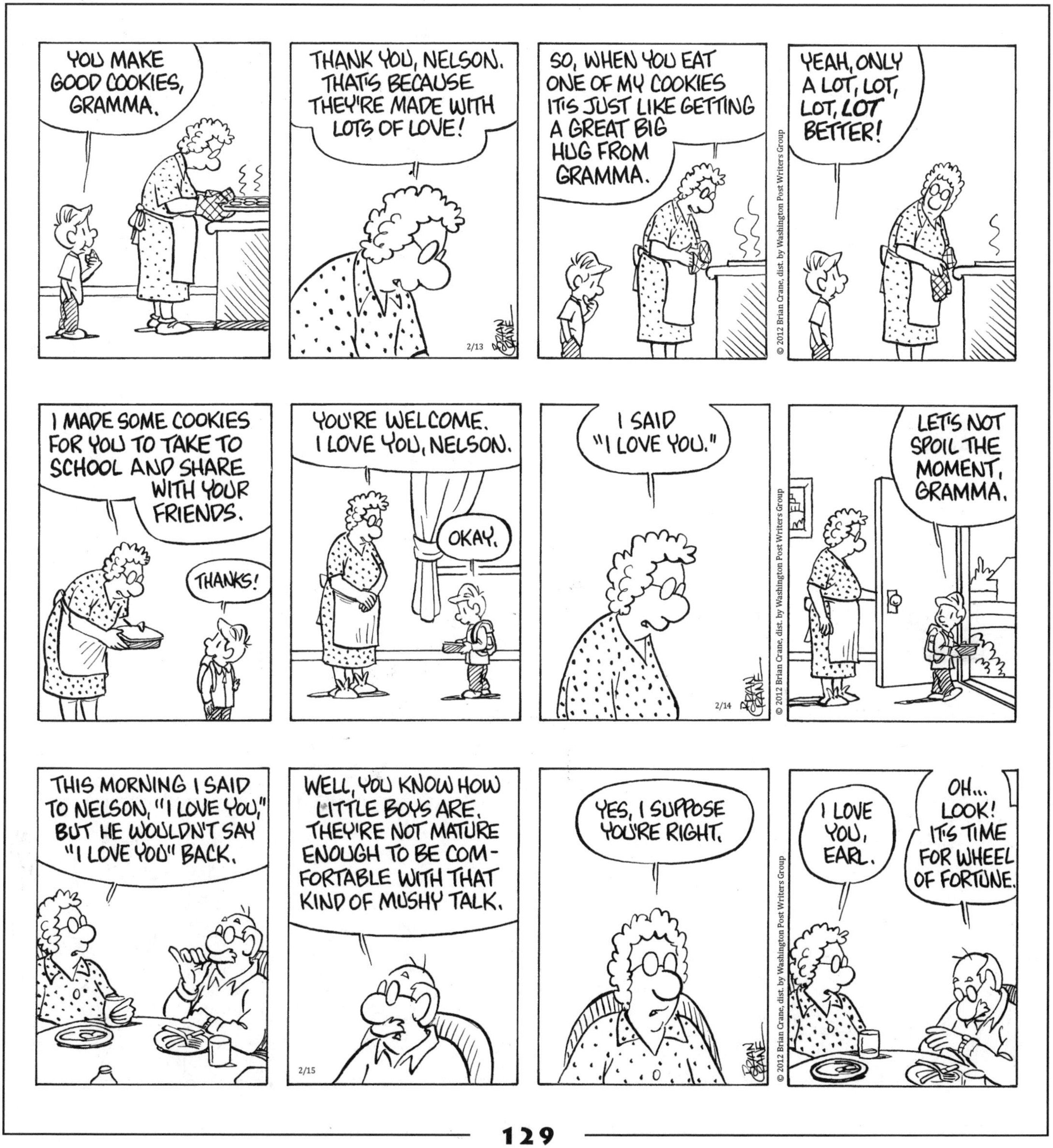
YOU MAKE GOOD COOKIES, GRAMMA.
THANK YOU, NELSON. THAT'S BECAUSE THEY'RE MADE WITH LOTS OF LOVE!
2/13
BRIAN CRANE
SO, WHEN YOU EAT ONE OF MY COOKIES IT'S JUST LIKE GETTING A GREAT BIG HUG FROM GRAMMA.
YEAH, ONLY A LOT, LOT, LOT, LOT BETTER!
© 2012 Brian Crane, dist. by Washington Post Writers Group
I MADE SOME COOKIES FOR YOU TO TAKE TO SCHOOL AND SHARE WITH YOUR FRIENDS.
THANKS!
YOU'RE WELCOME. I LOVE YOU, NELSON.
OKAY.
I SAID "I LOVE YOU."
2/14
BRIAN CRANE
LET'S NOT SPOIL THE MOMENT, GRAMMA.
© 2012 Brian Crane, dist. by Washington Post Writers Group
THIS MORNING I SAID TO NELSON, "I LOVE YOU," BUT HE WOULDN'T SAY "I LOVE YOU" BACK.
WELL, YOU KNOW HOW LITTLE BOYS ARE. THEY'RE NOT MATURE ENOUGH TO BE COM-FORTABLE WITH THAT KIND OF MUSHY TALK.
2/15
YES, I SUPPOSE YOU'RE RIGHT.
BRIAN CRANE
I LOVE YOU, EARL.
OH... LOOK! IT'S TIME FOR WHEEL OF FORTUNE.
© 2012 Brian Crane, dist. by Washington Post Writers Group

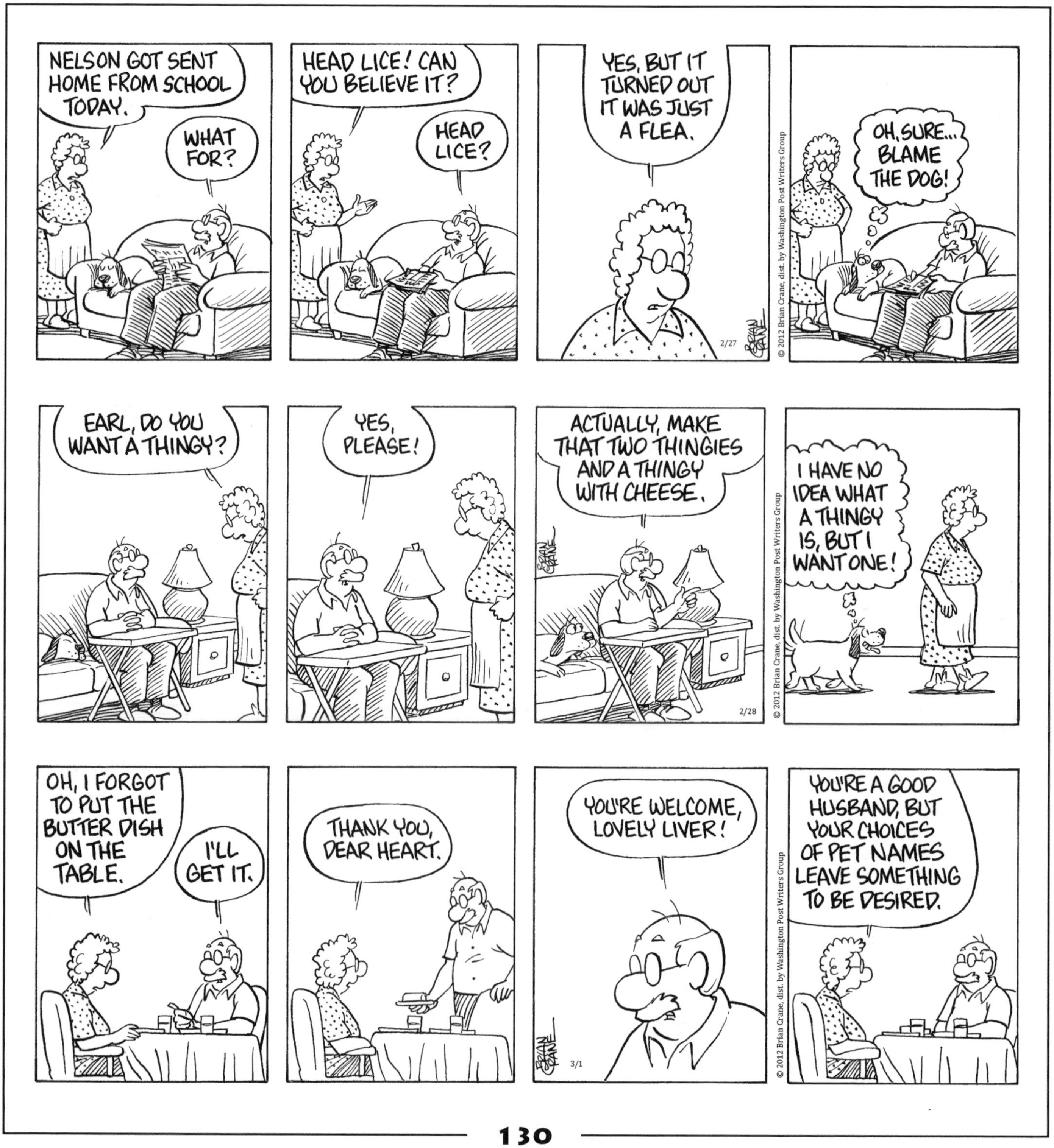
NELSON GOT SENT HOME FROM SCHOOL TODAY.
WHAT FOR?
HEAD LICE! CAN YOU BELIEVE IT?
HEAD LICE?
YES, BUT IT TURNED OUT IT WAS JUST A FLEA.
2/27
OH, SURE... BLAME THE DOG!
© 2012 Brian Crane, dist. by Washington Post Writers Group
EARL, DO YOU WANT A THINGY?
YES, PLEASE!
ACTUALLY, MAKE THAT TWO THINGIES AND A THINGY WITH CHEESE.
2/28
I HAVE NO IDEA WHAT A THINGY IS, BUT I WANT ONE!
© 2012 Brian Crane, dist. by Washington Post Writers Group
OH, I FORGOT TO PUT THE BUTTER DISH ON THE TABLE.
I'LL GET IT.
THANK YOU, DEAR HEART.
YOU'RE WELCOME, LOVELY LIVER!
3/1
YOU'RE A GOOD HUSBAND, BUT YOUR CHOICES OF PET NAMES LEAVE SOMETHING TO BE DESIRED.
© 2012 Brian Crane, dist. by Washington Post Writers Group

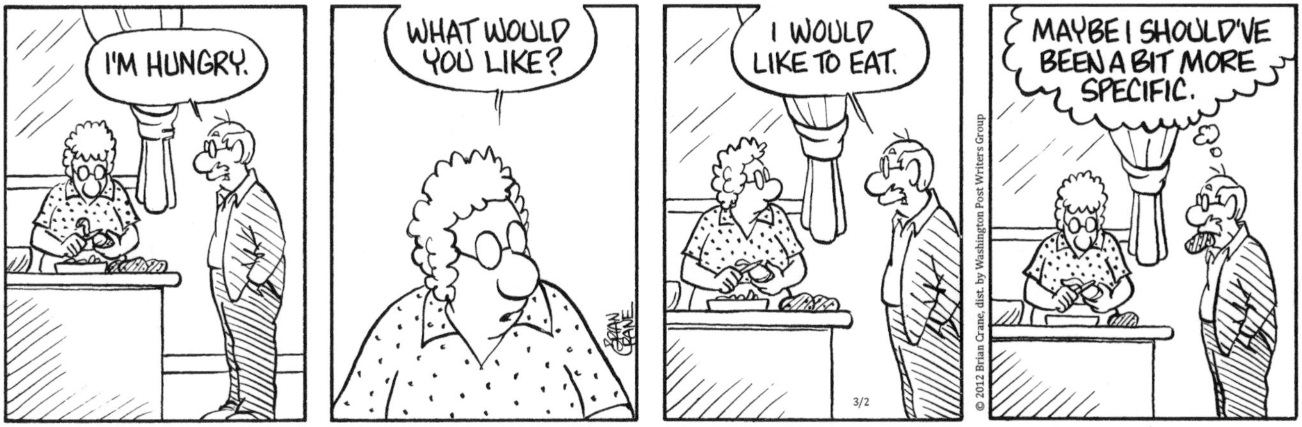
I'M HUNGRY.
WHAT WOULD YOU LIKE?
I WOULD LIKE TO EAT.
3/2
MAYBE I SHOULD'VE BEEN A BIT MORE SPECIFIC.

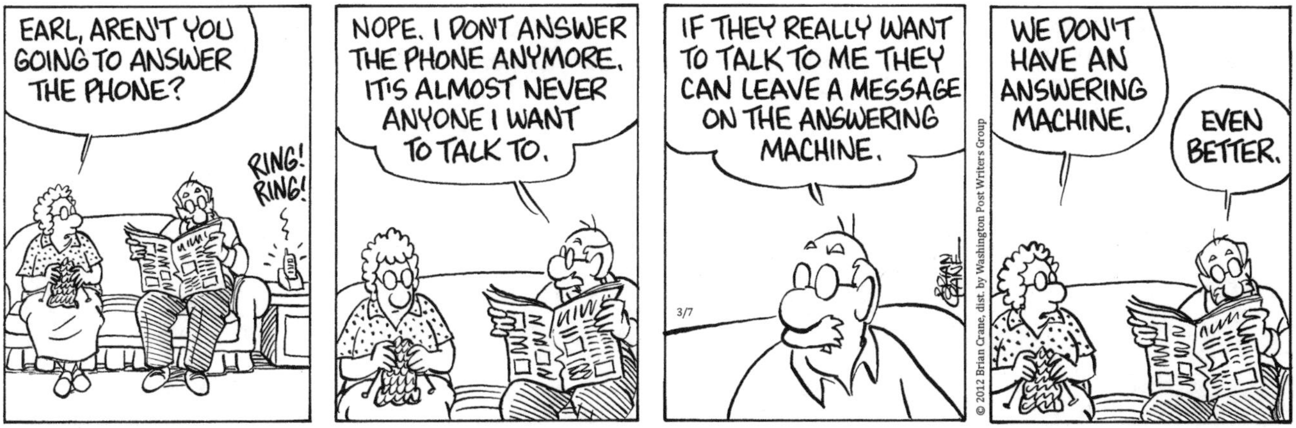
EARL, AREN'T YOU GOING TO ANSWER THE PHONE?
RING! RING!
NOPE. I DON'T ANSWER THE PHONE ANYMORE. IT'S ALMOST NEVER ANYONE I WANT TO TALK TO.
IF THEY REALLY WANT TO TALK TO ME THEY CAN LEAVE A MESSAGE ON THE ANSWERING MACHINE.
3/7
WE DON'T HAVE AN ANSWERING MACHINE.
EVEN BETTER.

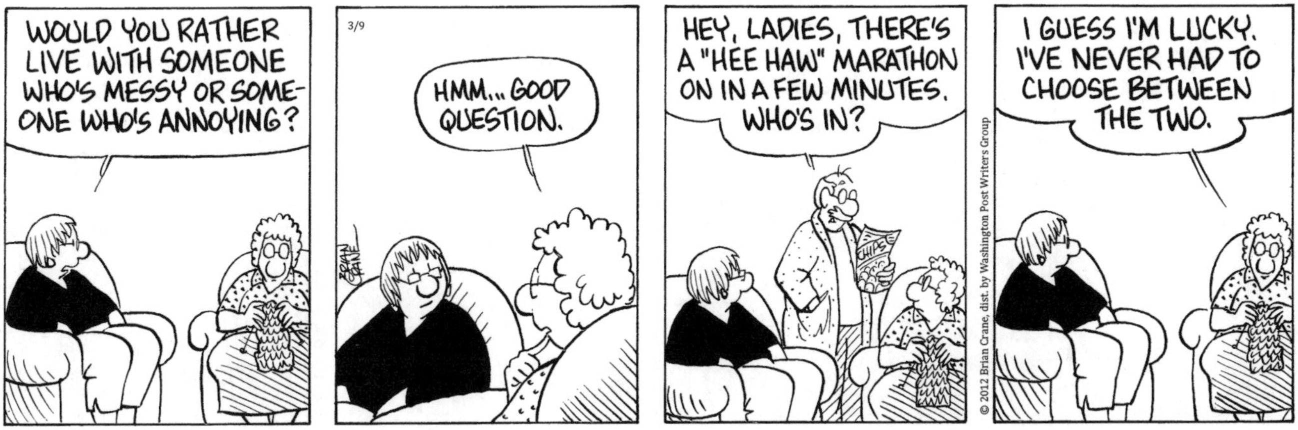
WOULD YOU RATHER LIVE WITH SOMEONE WHO'S MESSY OR SOME-ONE WHO'S ANNOYING?
3/9
HMM... GOOD QUESTION.
HEY, LADIES, THERE'S A "HEE HAW" MARATHON ON IN A FEW MINUTES. WHO'S IN?
CHIPS
I GUESS I'M LUCKY. I'VE NEVER HAD TO CHOOSE BETWEEN THE TWO.

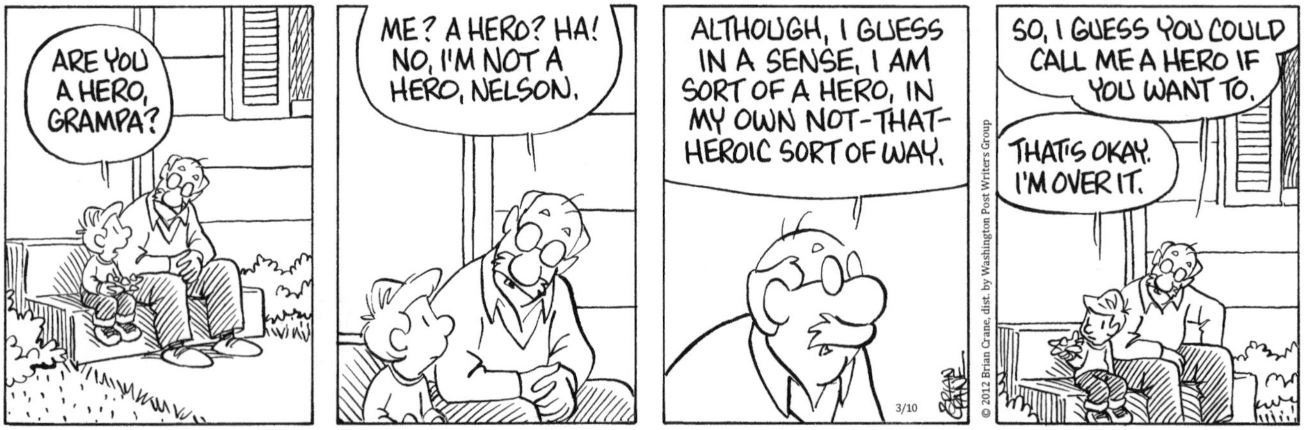
ARE YOU A HERO, GRAMPA?
ME? A HERO? HA! NO, I'M NOT A HERO, NELSON.
ALTHOUGH, I GUESS IN A SENSE, I AM SORT OF A HERO, IN MY OWN NOT-THAT-HEROIC SORT OF WAY.
3/10
SO, I GUESS YOU COULD CALL ME A HERO IF YOU WANT TO.
THAT'S OKAY. I'M OVER IT.

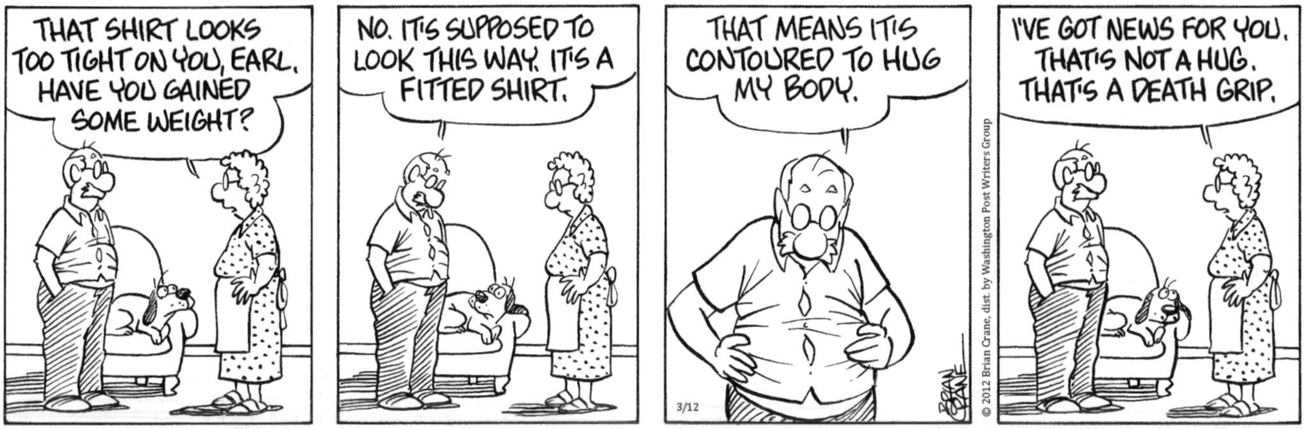
THAT SHIRT LOOKS TOO TIGHT ON YOU, EARL. HAVE YOU GAINED SOME WEIGHT?
NO. IT'S SUPPOSED TO LOOK THIS WAY. IT'S A FITTED SHIRT.
THAT MEANS IT'S CONTOURED TO HUG MY BODY.
3/12
I'VE GOT NEWS FOR YOU. THAT'S NOT A HUG. THAT'S A DEATH GRIP.

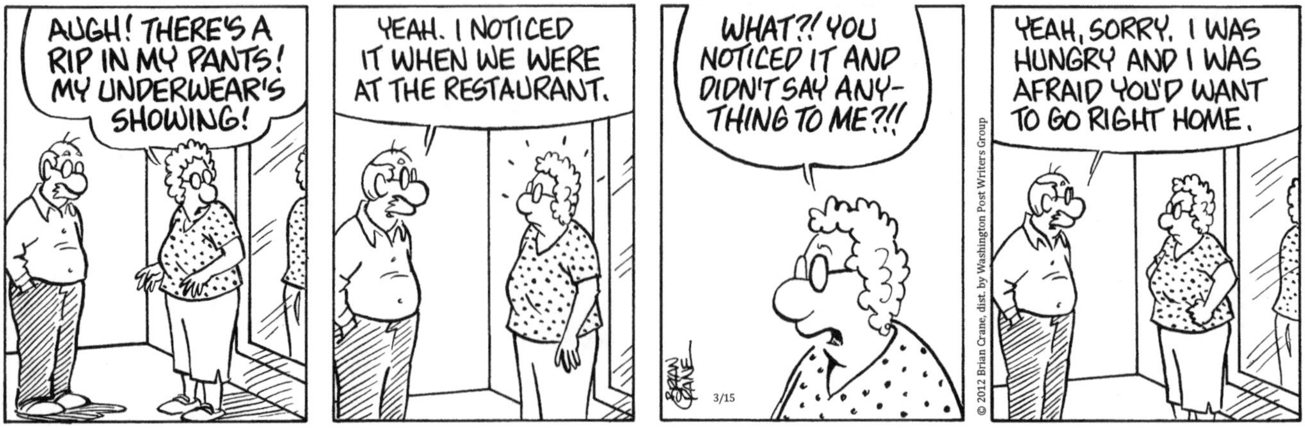
AUGH! THERE'S A RIP IN MY PANTS! MY UNDERWEAR'S SHOWING!
YEAH. I NOTICED IT WHEN WE WERE AT THE RESTAURANT.
WHAT?! YOU NOTICED IT AND DIDN'T SAY ANY-THING TO ME?!!
3/15
YEAH, SORRY. I WAS HUNGRY AND I WAS AFRAID YOU'D WANT TO GO RIGHT HOME.

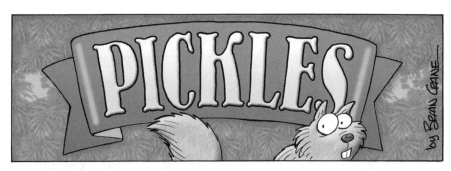

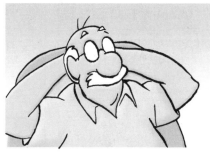

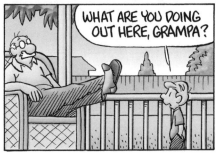

PICKLES
by BRIAN CRANE
WHAT ARE YOU DOING OUT HERE, GRAMPA?
NOTHING MUCH, NELSON. JUST RELAXING AND GETTING SOME EXERCISE.
RELAXING AND EXERCISING?
YEAH. I FIND IT VERY RELAXING TO LOOK AT MY APPLE TREE OVER THERE.
5/6
picklescomic@sbcglobal.net
HEY! STUPID SQUIRREL!! LEAVE MY APPLES ALONE!
© 2012 Brian Crane, dist. by Washington Post Writers Group
CAN I BORROW YOUR SHOES? I'M ABOUT OUT OF AMMO.

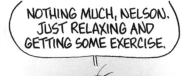

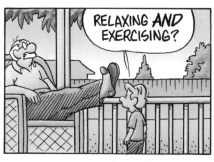

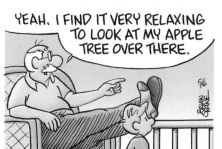

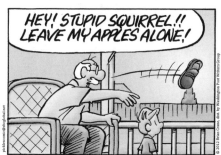

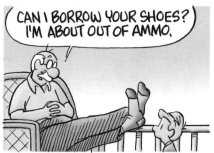

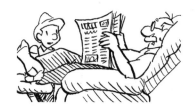

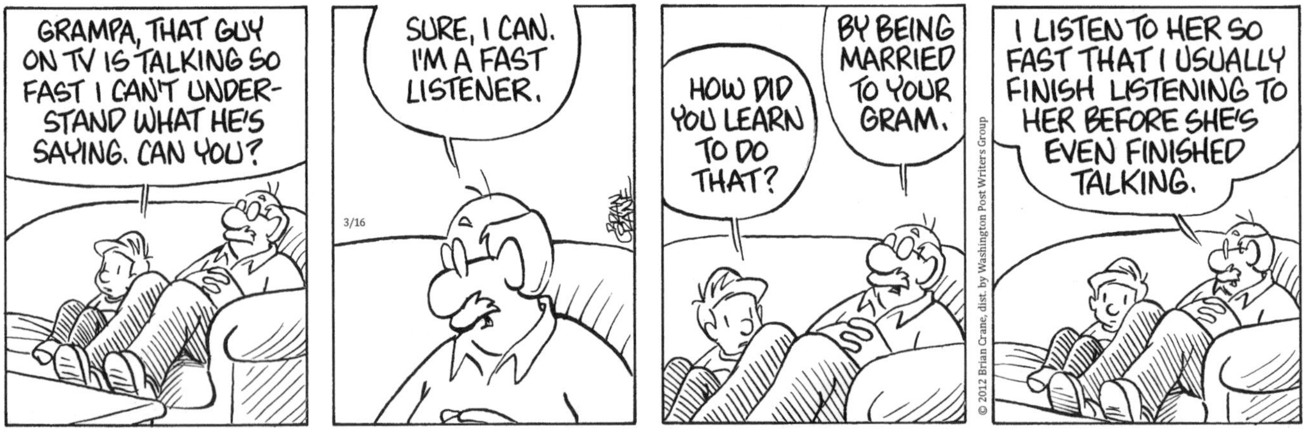
GRAMPA, THAT GUY ON TV IS TALKING SO FAST I CAN'T UNDERSTAND WHAT HE'S SAYING. CAN YOU?
SURE, I CAN. I'M A FAST LISTENER.
HOW DID YOU LEARN TO DO THAT?
BY BEING MARRIED TO YOUR GRAM.
I LISTEN TO HER SO FAST THAT I USUALLY FINISH LISTENING TO HER BEFORE SHE'S EVEN FINISHED TALKING.

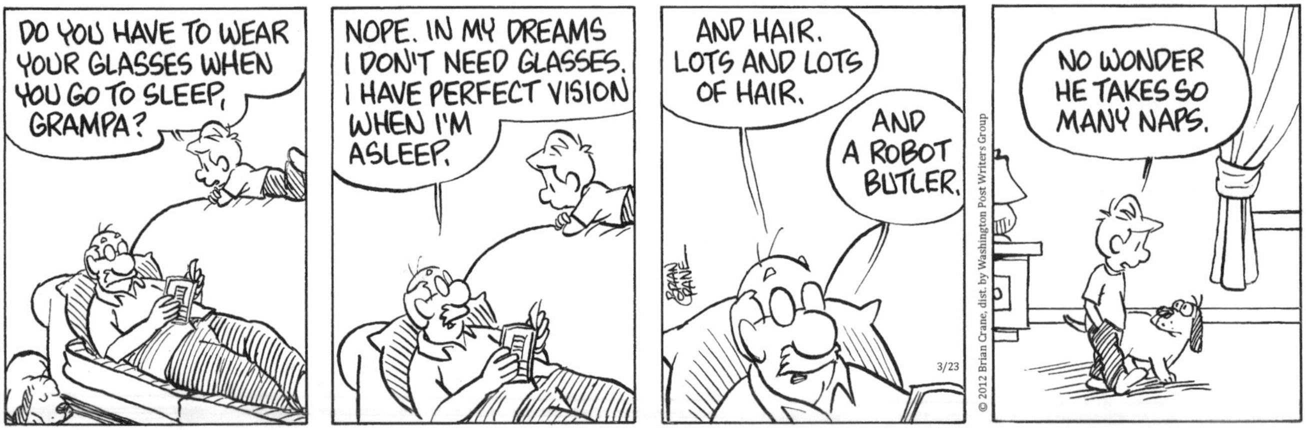
DO YOU HAVE TO WEAR YOUR GLASSES WHEN YOU GO TO SLEEP, GRAMPA?
NOPE. IN MY DREAMS I DON'T NEED GLASSES. I HAVE PERFECT VISION WHEN I'M ASLEEP.
AND HAIR. LOTS AND LOTS OF HAIR.
AND A ROBOT BUTLER.
NO WONDER HE TAKES SO MANY NAPS.

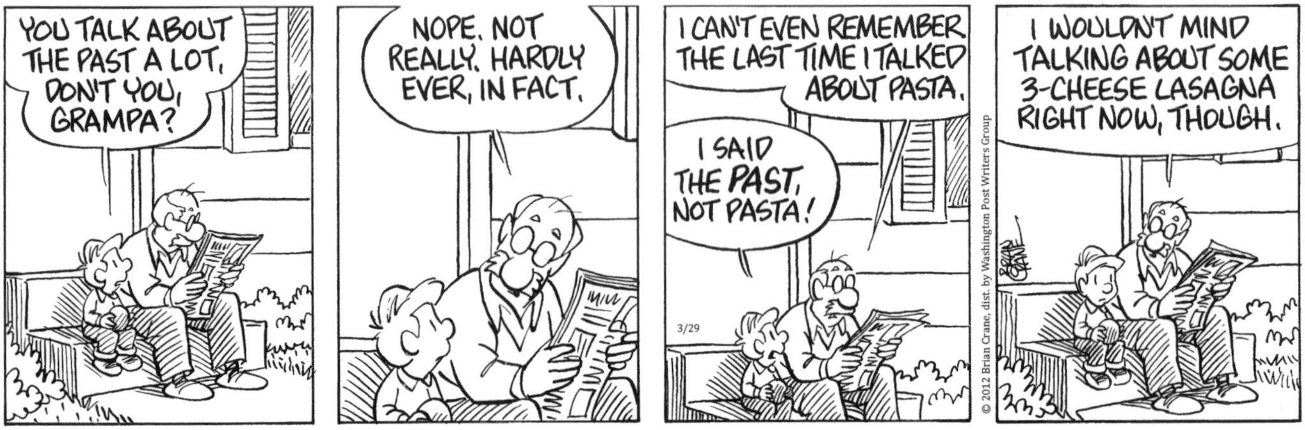
YOU TALK ABOUT THE PAST A LOT, DON'T YOU, GRAMPA?
NOPE. NOT REALLY. HARDLY EVER, IN FACT.
I CAN'T EVEN REMEMBER THE LAST TIME I TALKED ABOUT PASTA.
I SAID THE PAST, NOT PASTA!
I WOULDN'T MIND TALKING ABOUT SOME 3-CHEESE LASAGNA RIGHT NOW, THOUGH.

Panel 1
WHAT WAS IT LIKE LIVING IN THE PAST, GRAMPA?

IT WAS GREAT.

Panel 2
EVERYONE ADDRESSED THEIR ELDERS AS "SIR" AND YOU COULD BUY A NEW CAR FOR $600.

3/31

Panel 3
THERE WEREN'T MANY PHONES, BUT IT WAS ALWAYS A LIVE PERSON ON THE OTHER END, NOT A DARN ROBOT.

Panel 4
WERE THERE FLYING MONKEYS?

YUP. THAT'S WHY EVERYONE WORE HATS BACK THEN.

Panel 5
HOW COME WE HARDLY EVER HAVE MEANINGFUL CONVERSATIONS ANY MORE?

I DON'T KNOW.

Panel 6
LET'S HAVE A MEANINGFUL CONVERSATION.

OKAY.

Panel 7
BLACK JELLY BEANS ARE THE BEST JELLY BEANS.

4/2

Panel 8
NEVER MIND. I JUST REMEMBERED WHY.

Panel 9
WHO'S YOUR NEW FRIEND, NELSON?

Panel 10
HIS NAME IS NATE, BUT HE LIKES TO BE CALLED "CRASH".

4/7

Panel 11
HIS FAVORITE HOBBY IS DESTROYING THINGS.

Panel 12
I THOUGHT YOU SAID YOUR GRANDMOTHER WAS FRIENDLY.

EARL, WHAT ARE YOU EATING?

A BACON, LETTUCE AND TOMATO SANDWICH. DO YOU WANT ONE?

WHERE'D YOU GET THE BACON?

RIGHT HERE.

EARL, THIS ISN'T BACON. THIS IS "BEGGIN' STRIPS." IT'S FOR DOGS.

5/13

REALLY? HUH!

YOU SURE YOU DON'T WANT ONE?

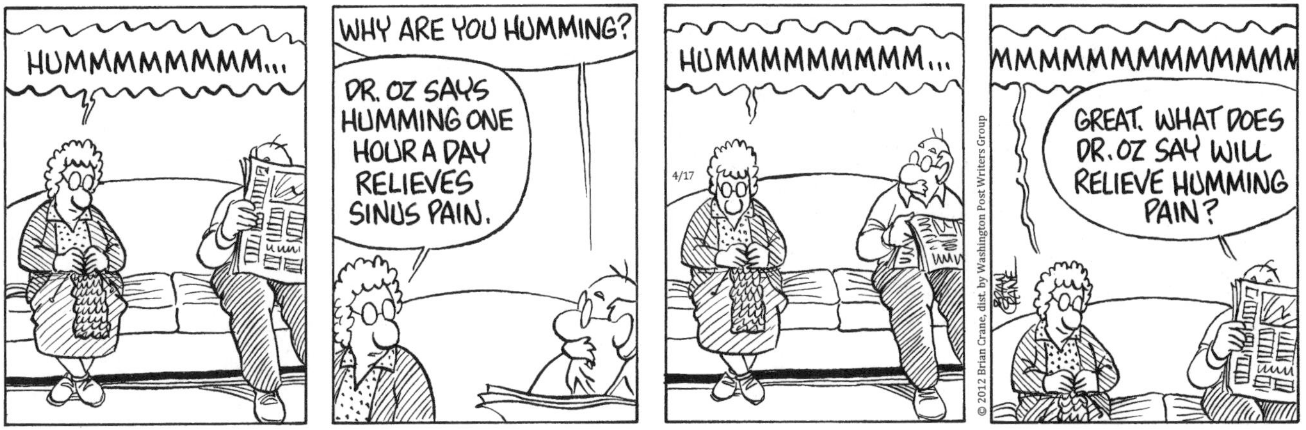
HUMMMMMMMM...
WHY ARE YOU HUMMING?
DR. OZ SAYS HUMMING ONE HOUR A DAY RELIEVES SINUS PAIN.
HUMMMMMMMMM...
4/17
MMMMMMMMMMMMMM
GREAT. WHAT DOES DR. OZ SAY WILL RELIEVE HUMMING PAIN?
© 2012 Brian Crane, dist. by Washington Post Writers Group

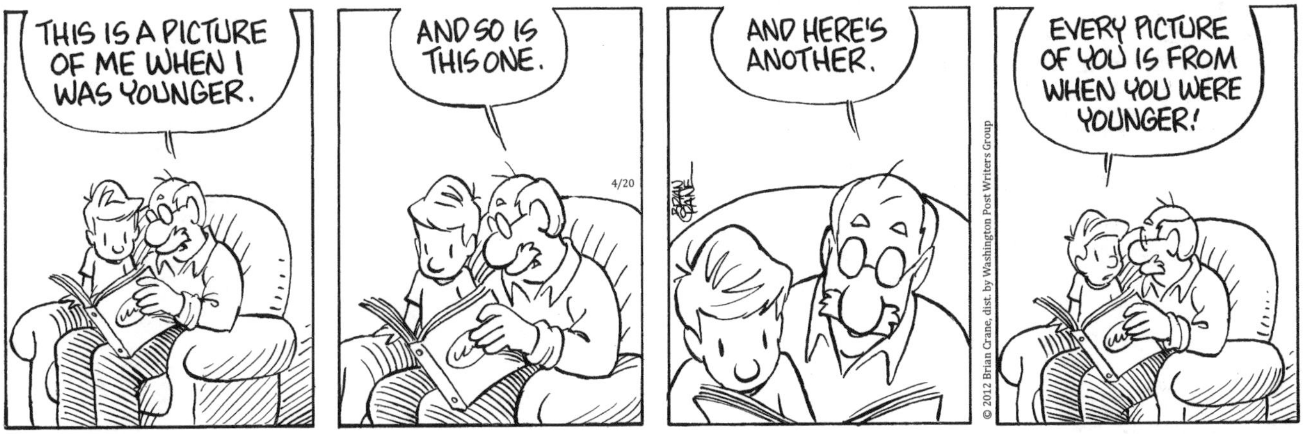
THIS IS A PICTURE OF ME WHEN I WAS YOUNGER.
AND SO IS THIS ONE.
4/20
AND HERE'S ANOTHER.
EVERY PICTURE OF YOU IS FROM WHEN YOU WERE YOUNGER!
© 2012 Brian Crane, dist. by Washington Post Writers Group

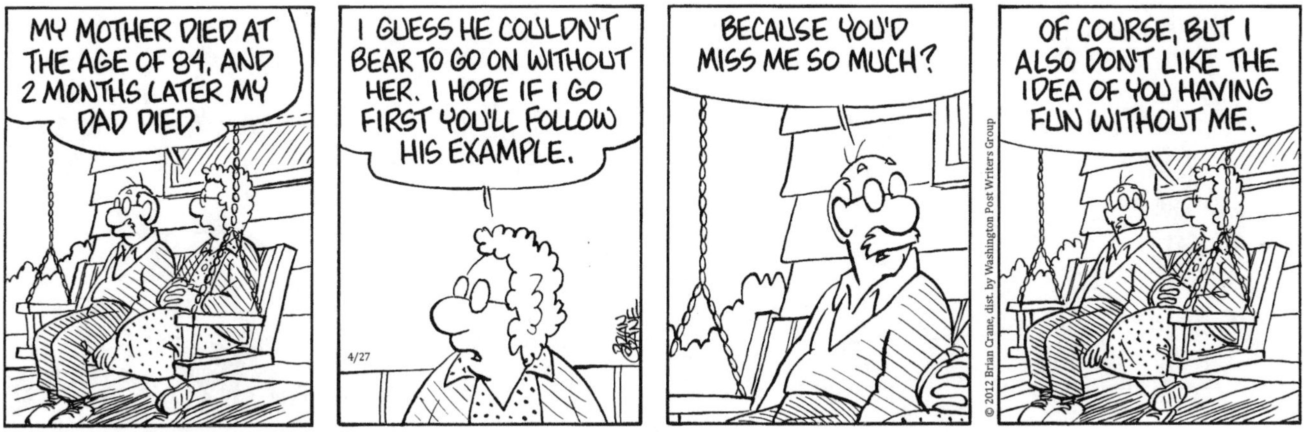
MY MOTHER DIED AT THE AGE OF 84, AND 2 MONTHS LATER MY DAD DIED.
I GUESS HE COULDN'T BEAR TO GO ON WITHOUT HER. I HOPE IF I GO FIRST YOU'LL FOLLOW HIS EXAMPLE.
4/27
BECAUSE YOU'D MISS ME SO MUCH?
OF COURSE, BUT I ALSO DON'T LIKE THE IDEA OF YOU HAVING FUN WITHOUT ME.
© 2012 Brian Crane, dist. by Washington Post Writers Group

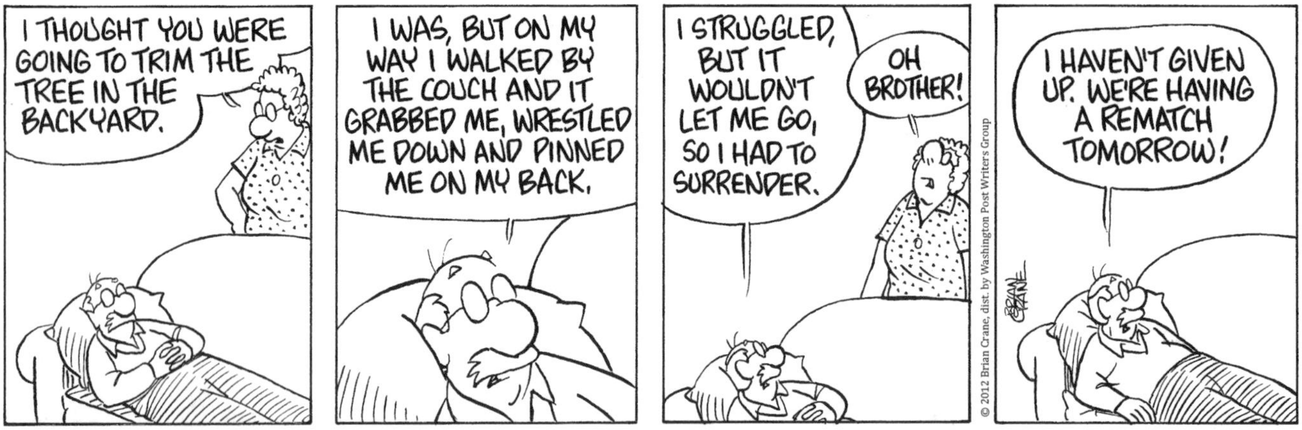
I THOUGHT YOU WERE GOING TO TRIM THE TREE IN THE BACKYARD.
I WAS, BUT ON MY WAY I WALKED BY THE COUCH AND IT GRABBED ME, WRESTLED ME DOWN AND PINNED ME ON MY BACK.
I STRUGGLED, BUT IT WOULDN'T LET ME GO, SO I HAD TO SURRENDER.
OH BROTHER!
I HAVEN'T GIVEN UP. WE'RE HAVING A REMATCH TOMORROW!
BRIAN CRANE
© 2012 Brian Crane, dist. by Washington Post Writers Group

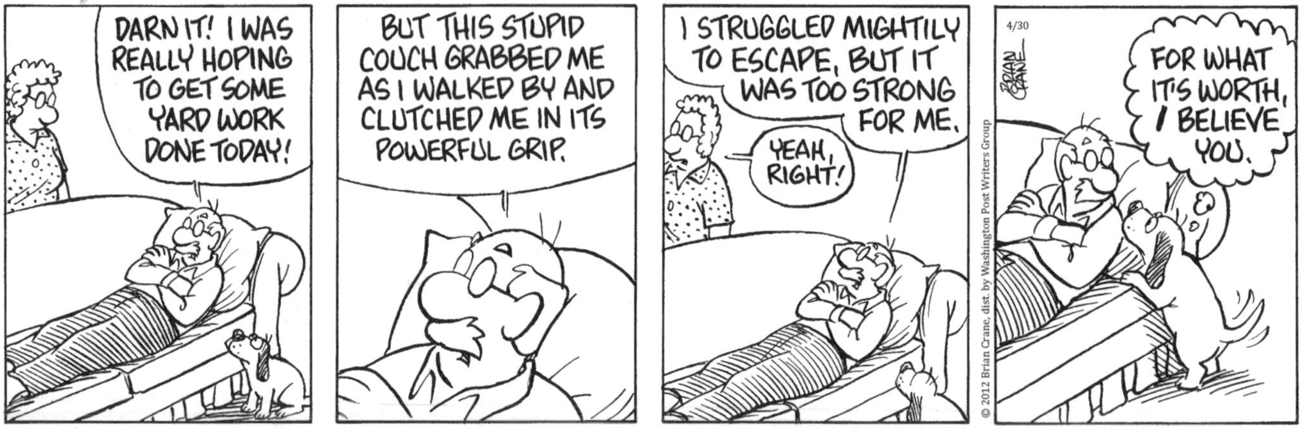
DARN IT! I WAS REALLY HOPING TO GET SOME YARD WORK DONE TODAY!
BUT THIS STUPID COUCH GRABBED ME AS I WALKED BY AND CLUTCHED ME IN ITS POWERFUL GRIP.
I STRUGGLED MIGHTILY TO ESCAPE, BUT IT WAS TOO STRONG FOR ME.
YEAH, RIGHT!
4/30
BRIAN CRANE
FOR WHAT IT'S WORTH, I BELIEVE YOU.
© 2012 Brian Crane, dist. by Washington Post Writers Group

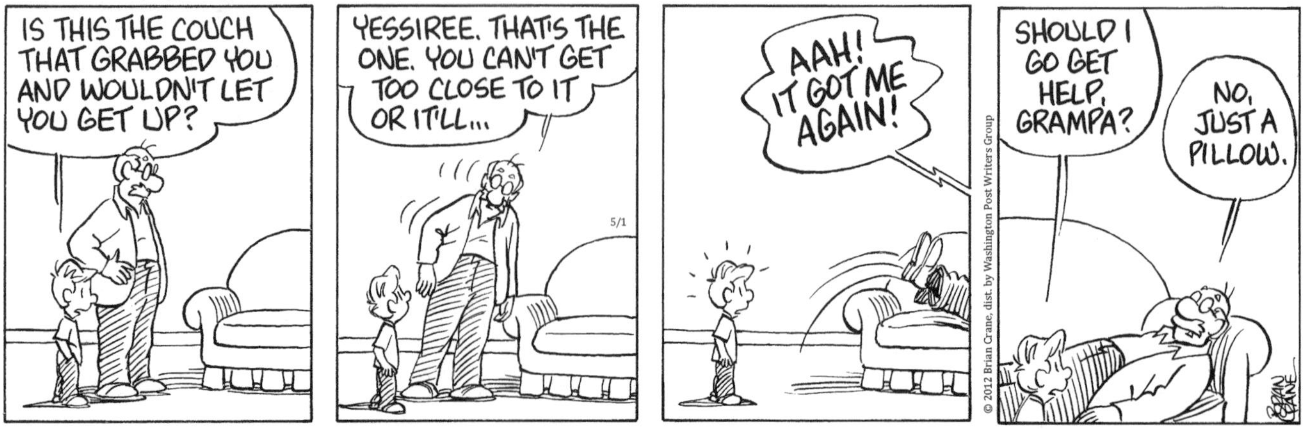
IS THIS THE COUCH THAT GRABBED YOU AND WOULDN'T LET YOU GET UP?
YESSIREE. THAT'S THE ONE. YOU CAN'T GET TOO CLOSE TO IT OR IT'LL...
5/1
AAH! IT GOT ME AGAIN!
SHOULD I GO GET HELP, GRAMPA?
NO, JUST A PILLOW.
BRIAN CRANE
© 2012 Brian Crane, dist. by Washington Post Writers Group

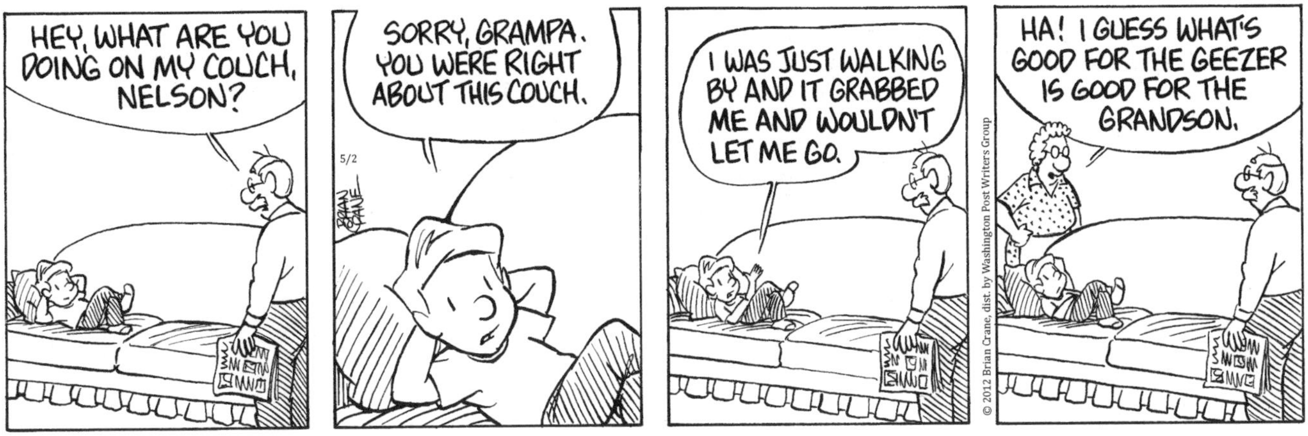
HEY, WHAT ARE YOU DOING ON MY COUCH, NELSON?
SORRY, GRAMPA. YOU WERE RIGHT ABOUT THIS COUCH.
5/2
I WAS JUST WALKING BY AND IT GRABBED ME AND WOULDN'T LET ME GO.
HA! I GUESS WHAT'S GOOD FOR THE GEEZER IS GOOD FOR THE GRANDSON.
© 2012 Brian Crane, dist. by Washington Post Writers Group

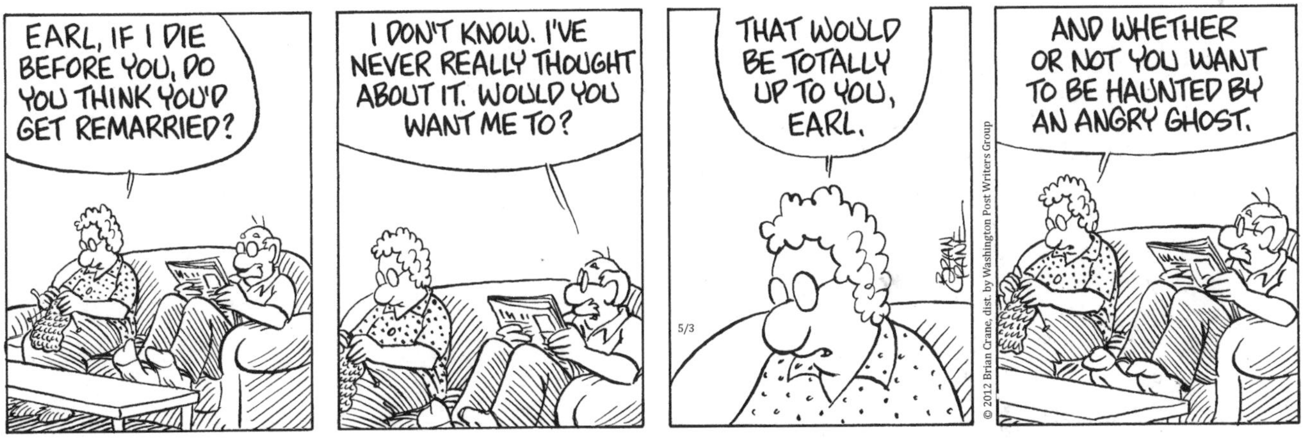
EARL, IF I DIE BEFORE YOU, DO YOU THINK YOU'D GET REMARRIED?
I DON'T KNOW. I'VE NEVER REALLY THOUGHT ABOUT IT. WOULD YOU WANT ME TO?
THAT WOULD BE TOTALLY UP TO YOU, EARL.
5/3
AND WHETHER OR NOT YOU WANT TO BE HAUNTED BY AN ANGRY GHOST.
© 2012 Brian Crane, dist. by Washington Post Writers Group

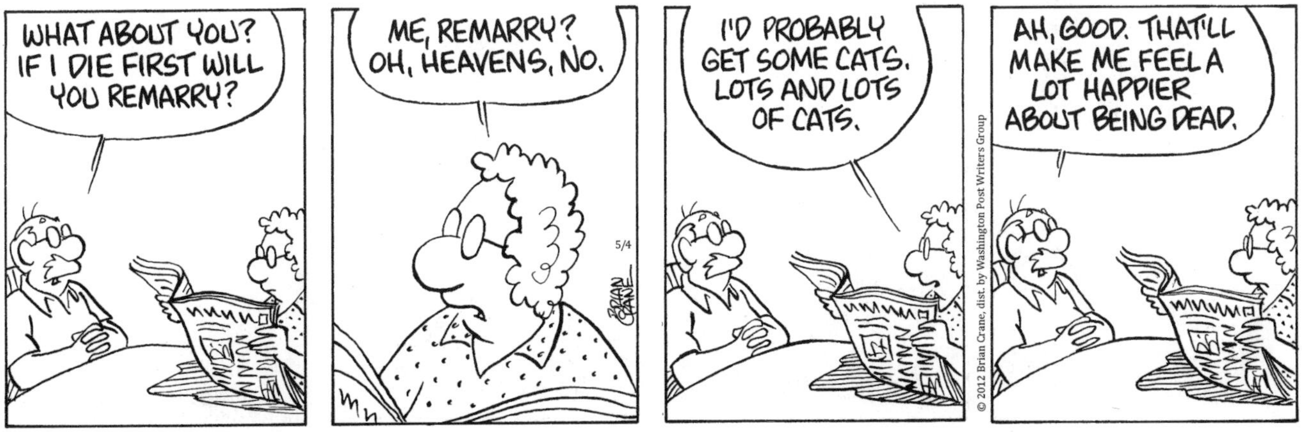
WHAT ABOUT YOU? IF I DIE FIRST WILL YOU REMARRY?
ME, REMARRY? OH, HEAVENS, NO.
5/4
I'D PROBABLY GET SOME CATS. LOTS AND LOTS OF CATS.
AH, GOOD. THAT'LL MAKE ME FEEL A LOT HAPPIER ABOUT BEING DEAD.
© 2012 Brian Crane, dist. by Washington Post Writers Group

The End

Brian Crane

For over twenty years, Brian Crane's comic strip, PICKLES, has been delighting readers around the world. This sixth collection continues the adventures of Crane's beloved characters--the crotchety but endearing grandparents, Earl and Opal Pickles; their precocious grandson, Nelson; some quirky family members and friends; and the family's dog and cat, who offer their own distinctive views of the goings-on. This is an often ironic but always warm-hearted view of the foibles of family and the challenges of aging.

Twice nominated, Brian Crane is the recipient of the prestigious 2013 Reuben "Cartoonist of the Year" Award. PICKLES appears in over 800 newspapers worldwide and has been nominated twice for "Best Comic Strip". PICKLES received the honor in 2001. Crane lives in Sparks, Nevada with his wife and they are the proud parents of seven children and eight grandchildren.